CAMPING EUROPE

BY CAROL MICKELSEN

CARTOGRAPHY
BY DION GOOD

D1738324

TO MY SONS

Gregory and Ashley

Every effort has been made to make this book as accurate as possible, but information for travelers changes quickly. The author, cartographer, and publisher accept no responsibility for any inconvenience, disappointment, or injury sustained from information contained in Camping Europe.

This is an enlarged and updated second edition of Camping Your Way Through Europe copyright 1996 and is published by

Affordable Travel Press
P.O. Box 3296
Half Moon Bay, CA 94019
affordabletravel@coastside.net

Distributed to the book trade by Publishers Group West through

Carousel Press
P.O. Box 6038
Berkely, CA 94706-0038
510-527-5849
info@carousel-press.com
www.carousel-press.com

Copyright 2001 Carol Mickelsen
All rights reserved.

First Printing 2001

Library of Congress Cataloging-in-Publication Data

Mickelsen, Carol
Camping Europe/Carol Mickelsen-enlarged, completely revised, and updated edition
(Camping Your Way Through Europe)
Includes index

1. Travel/Budget/Europe 2. Camping/Europe 3. Driving/Europe

ISBN 0-917120-18-3

Cartographer: Dion Good
Editorial Consultant and Preliminary Copy Editor: Carole Terwilliger Meyers
Interior Design and Production: Hayden Foell
Cover Design: Michael Wong

Manufactured in the United States of America

AUTHOR'S NOTE

Camping guides to the United Kingdom are already available in English, so in this book I'm including only countries where English is not the local language. The countries covered have many established campgrounds, and when you camp at them you'll join middle-class local families relaxing and having fun. The opening and closing dates of the campgrounds are conservative. Call ahead to see if they will be open if you are traveling early or late in the season. The closed days for museums refer to the summer months. The cost of travel goes up as prices go up. But the cost of renting a car and buying gas and groceries will be close to what it costs you at home. Keep in mind that you would probably spend that amount even if you stayed home. Because of the number of countries covered in this book, full descriptions, detailed maps, accent marks, and exact mileage is impossible for me to provide. So I recommend securing additional guidebooks and maps for the areas you'll be traveling to.

ABOUT THE AUTHOR

Carol Mickelsen is a professional chef. She bought and restored a dilapidated but historic hotel with restaurant and bar in Half Moon Bay California, a small town on the Pacific Coast, south of San Francisco. She named it the San Benito House. The restaurant has received rave reviews from Gourmet and National Geographic Traveler magazines. She sold the business to her oldest son giving her time to travel and write.

The accompanying, video, Camping Your Way Through Europe, she filmed in Switzerland.

She has traveled throughout the world and finds budget travel fascinating, fun, and easy.

ABOUT THE CARTOGRAPHER

Dion was born in Chicago and developed an early interest in maps. He studied geography and cartography at San Diego State University and has been a cartographer for 8 years, helping to produce books on such diverse places as the Rocky Mountains, Los Angeles, Costa Rica, and the Great Lakes. He has traveled widely throughout the US, Mexico, and Turkey. When not making maps, he reads history, takes photographs, rides his bike, and follows baseball. He and his wife Tülin live in Oakland, California. This is his first solo book.

CONTENTS
Author's Note/About the Author/About the Cartographer

COUNTRIES OF WESTERN EUROPE

WHY NOT CAMP?

Have you dreamed of taking a trip to Europe but thought you couldn't afford it? Then please read on, this book is for you! I will show you that by car-camping with a tent and sharing expenses with a companion, you will be able to travel to Northern and Central Europe for about $60 a day, and to Turkey, Greece and Eastern Europe for about $50 a day. This figure includes a car, if rented and arranged ahead from home on a lease basis for 21 days or more, gas, insurance, groceries, campground fees, museum/historic sites admissions, and a daily treat. In other words, everything but the airfare.

I have car-camped in Europe for over 25 years and wouldn't think of traveling any other way. I travel because I want to see and feel the soul of the country and its people. I love the magnificent historic areas that make history come alive. I love the breathtaking beauty of the natural areas. And I love sharing everyday experiences with the local people. In a campground's common area, it's easy to start a conversations with fellow campers by commenting on the beauty of the area or asking for information about taking public transportation or seeing the local sights. Your cooking aromas mingle, extra food is passed around, and smiles and giggles are exchanged. Soon you are going over maps with your neighbors, telling funny travel stories, and sharing hints about the best places to camp. Upon parting, addresses and sometimes hugs are shared. Letters or postcards are sent and received. This camaraderie develops between campers because they share a love of being a part of a place and its people. And doing this doesn't take expertise in a foreign language. In fact, often only a few words are understood, and the rest is conveyed with hand gestures and smiles.

I prefer to camp in summer, especially in July and August, when the festivals and weather are at their best. I enjoy camping when the campground is active with campers. It's easier to meet people then. I get up early to enjoy the fresh morning air, and I'm at the showers, roads, and museums with the few early birds.

It takes me only minutes to set up my camping place. Everything is well organized in the trunk of my car. European campgrounds might be different from what you are used to at home. Besides being located at the mountains, lakes, and beaches, they are also found close to the historic areas of cities and towns. Generally they are large grassy areas with shade trees, usually in an attractive setting. Almost always there is a covered common area, often a deck or terrace overlooking the view. Fellow campers come here to cook and eat, relax, and meet other campers. Public transportation to historic areas is usually available nearby. Listed campgrounds have a building which houses showers, wash basins, and toilets, and along the outside wall a place for washing dishes and laundry by hand. The water temperature in the showers varies from tepid to hot, and tokens or coins are often required to use them. Usually wash basins have only cold water. In a few countries the toilet is the squatting type. Always carry toilet paper. In less developed countries, because the plumbing is not adequate for paper, a wastebasket is in the toilet area for depositing toilet paper. It is important and polite to use it.

The campgrounds listed are safe. They have gates that are locked at night, and they are small enough for the owners and staff to keep track of everyone. Because people who camp don't usually carry a lot of money, thieves don't hang out in campgrounds. Fellow campers aren't interested their neighbor's equipment. They have their own. I can usually park right next to my campsite, making it easy to lock valuables back in the car when I leave for a day of sightseeing.

My thermal mattress is as comfortable as my bed at home. As I drift off to sleep in my beloved tent, I hear a symphony of cicadas, a gurgling creek, or the crashing surf. In the morning I awaken to melodious birdsong, fresh air, and my own delicious coffee. Then I sit back in my comfortable collapsible chair and meditate on the surrounding beauty. As I make plans for the day, I don't need to worry about an itinerary or reservations. I can go where I please. And you can, too!

EXPENSE EXPECTATIONS

Expense Expectations for two peopletraveling together	Northern and Central Europe	Turkey and Greece	Eastern Europe
Gas/140-300 km a day	$12-25	$10-25	$10-25
Highway tolls	$5-15	$0-5	$0-5
Groceries/dinner Entrée, starch, vegetable bread	$10-12	$6-8	$5-6
Bottle of Local Wine	$7-8	$5-6	$5-6
Groceries/breakfast Cereal, bread, coffe/tea	$4-5	$3-4	$3-4
Groceries/lunch Make your own sanwich, fruit, soda	$4-5	$3-4	$3-4
Treat/Sitting in an inexpensive café and having a glass of wine or beer or an ice cream	$8-10	$6-7	$5-6
Campground (not upscale) for 2 people/car/tent	$18-22	$12-18	$10-18
Museum/Historic site entrance fee	$10-20	$6-15	$4-8
Total for two people	$79-122	$50-88	$42-76
Total for one person	$39-61	$24-44	$20-38

My mid-size car, on a lease basis out of Frankfurt, Germany, in 1998 cost $18 a day; with the $6 CDW insurance it came to $24.   In 1999 my mid-size car cost $23 a day on a lease basis out of Amsterdam; with the $6 CDW insurance it came to $29 a day.   Divide that in half for a per person cost of $12-$16.   My homeowner's policy covers theft.

TAKING YOUR BIKE

I take my bicyle along to Europe wherever possible. Europeans are avid pedalers so cycle paths and locking racks are common. I enjoy pedaling around historic areas, down grand boulevards, into small neighborhoods, and along country roads. The fresh air and exercise are invigorating. Whenever I have a whim for a ride, my bicyle is there.

Most, but not all, major airlines sell cardboard "bike boxes" for just a few dollars. They are bought at the ticket counter and you must be ticketed with that airline to buy one. Because I don't have a place to store the box while I'm traveling I discard it after use and buy a new one when I am departing for my return trip home.

Take your bicycles to the airport on the same bike rack you'll use on the trip. Give yourself plenty of time to pack the bicycles. I bring foam sheeting, extra cardboard, and plastic covered wire to cover the gear and sprocket areas. I pre-measure these and cut them at home, save them for the return, and reuse them on other trips. I also bring two rolls of duct tape and scissors. Find a quiet area, close to the oversize luggage area check-in, to pack your bicycles. Take the pedals off, loosen the handlebars, and deflate the tires. Encase the socket and gear areas with protecting foam and cardboard. Attach helmets, bike locks, the bike rack, a tool kit, and extra small duffles of miscellaneous things to the bicycles. Slide the bicycles into their boxes. Secure the boxes with lots of duct tape, reinforcing the handling holes so the cardboard doesn't rip. If you need to get to another level ask to use the freight elevator if the regular passenger elevator is too small.

When you make your airline reservation, check with the agent about the cost of bicycle transport and the availability of boxes. Check again several days before leaving. Upon arrival in Europe, check with the airline you'll go home with, about availability for your return. When none are available airline personnel can usually get one from another airline. A charge of $60 each way for transporting a bicycle is typical. Most airlines no longer let you claim the bike as part of your allowable luggage. I consider this extra cost a gift to myself.

DRIVING IN EUROPE
NAVIGATING HINTS

Driving in Europe is just like driving at home. At home when you drive in a major city you've never been to before, you would buy a good map. (Free car-rental maps aren't detailed enough.) You would also get written directions at the car rental desk on how to get to your first destination.

That's what you do in Europe. Your most challenging moments will be getting out of the airport and onto the right road to your first destination. Start by having the car rental agent draw a map for you, detailing the directions in writing. Be sure all the exits and the distances between them are shown.

Before you drive out of the airport both the driver and the navigator need to compare the agent's drawn map with the bought map. You will both need to have a concept of the route. Make an easy to read list of the exits. Look at the bigger picture of the map and predict what the signposting will be. Know where you don't want to go. Once you are on the road with heavy traffic you won't have much time to look at the map.

If you see a road sign listing places you don't recognize, pull over and find each name place on the map. Pulling over in front of signs is a good habit. Use the map's index if you don't find the place readily. Before entering a roundabout, read the road sign and note whether you want the first, second, or third exit. Going around again until you are certain where to exit is not a waste of time. Never continue when you are uncertain. Turn around and go back to your last sign. This effort will save you time, money, and frustration.

Stay calm. Don't let angry drivers bother you. Anticipate heavy, fast moving traffic. Drive in the slow lane for the first few days. The navigator should know where you are on the map at all times. Use a highlighter to mark the route. The navigator needs to anticipate the signs ahead and inform the driver. European drivers are alert, make quick decisions, and check their mirrors constantly so they know what is happening around them. You'll need to do the same.

Realize that being either the driver or the navigator is difficult and keep peace between you. Learn from your mistakes. Congratulate each other on their expertise. Celebrate your skills.

ADVANTAGES OF DRIVING

Having your own car gives you the freedom to go where you want, when you want to. It enables you to stop for spur-of-the-moment pleasures. Time isn't spent on getting ticketed and then waiting for buses and trains. You don't have to lug bags or backpacks. You'll organize your things so that you are set up at your campsite in just a few minutes. It will become a quick routine. At the morning market you can purchase wonderful foodstuffs inexpensively and store them in the cool box in your car. (Cool boxes are inexpensive and can be purchased at the same places you'd find them at home.) Lunches and dinners made at the campgrounds or at special stops along the way will be memorable and cost just a fraction of what it would cost to eat even at inexpensive places.

THE CAR AND ITS EXPENSES

As companies compete for business, the cost of renting or leasing a car seems to go down rather than up. When you rent for 21 days or more you qualify for lease terms. This decreases the daily rate considerably. There is a sizable difference in car rental rate from one country to another. Generally it costs less if you return the car where you picked it up. For the best rate, make your reservation at home. Use your credit card so you can dispute the charge if there is a problem. Don't use the rental company for collision damage waiver (CDW) insurance. If you rent a car and purchase insurance from the same company, it is a conflict of interests. You can get this same insurance from less expensive sources. The rental/lease cost generally includes third party insurance (damage to the other party) but be sure this is written in your agreement. It's a good idea to have theft insurance. If you have a home policy, it might cover you on your trip. Be sure to check. See the appendix for rental and insurance companies.

European cars are fuel efficient and distances between sights aren't great. Unleaded fuel is called petrol or benzine. Diesel is gasoil. Tolls can be expensive, but if you want to get somewhere fast, pay them. In countries that have a highway-user tax, you can be pulled over for not having the sticker and must pay on the spot, sometimes with an additional penalty. Inform the car rental agent, when you pick up the car, what countries you might travel in. They will be able to research the roadway taxes that apply and give you information on where to pay them.

GETTING DIRECTIONS

Signage in Europe is very good. Europeans are used to directing foreigners, so they use international graphic signs rather than linguistic ones. Fellow travelers and locals you meet in gas stations can be helpful. Be sure to have your map and a piece of paper and pencil with you when you ask for directions. Use your phrase book to write your questions down in the local language if you don't feel confident about your skill in speaking the language. Always start by saying "Hello, Could you help me?" in their language. Show them your paper with name of the place you want to go printed in large letters. Hand them a paper and say, "Please" in their language then indicate to them you want them to draw a map or write down directions.

On the outskirts, stop at a gas station and buy a good city map. Locate your destination on the map. Ask someone to direct you to your next exit. Keep pulling off to ask for directions as you need them or to reconfirm what the last person said. Keep in mind that every time you ask for directions, you have a small conversation with a local. The smiles and "Thank you", in their language feel good.

PARKING AND TOLLS

Many cities have parking areas adjacent to historic areas. Look for a ticket dispenser in the area. Feed coins into the dispenser for the time you plan to be gone. Display the ticket on your dashboard. Keep change available for this. Always look at how the other cars are parked and follow suit. Parking costs and time limits will be the same as at home. The closer you get to historic areas of large cities, the more expensive and limited in time the parking will be. In large underground parking garages, push the button to receive a ticket upon entering. Before you get back in your car to leave, take the ticket to a central processing machine and insert the amount of local currency indicated on the screen. When you leave with the car, insert the paid ticket into the machine to lift the bar.

Clamping a lock onto a tire of illegally parked car is common. To release the clamp you must go to the police station, pay the fine and wait for them to unlock the clamp. Tickets for illegally parked cars are paid with stamps you buy in a kiosk. Affix the stamp to the ticket and mail it promptly or you will pay for the ticket plus penalties when you settle your car rental bill.

If you bring your bike you can park outside the conjested area and pedal in. It's a great way to get a sense of the city. I enjoy pedaling almost as much as prowling through the monuments and museums. If you haven't brought your bike, you'll find good public transportation close to large parking areas.

When you enter a toll road, a machine issues a ticket. Keep it handy, always putting it in the same place in the car. When you leave the toll road hand your ticket to the agent at the station. Your charge will be shown on the screen. Tolls can be paid with charge cards as well as local currency.

ROAD SIGNS AND RULES

Round signs with red borders indicate prohibitions. Triangular signs with red borders warn of dangers. Blue indicates positive information that you can take advantage of. In all cases graphics inside the sign tell more. Parking areas are signposted with a "P", campgrounds with a tent, and airports with an airplane. The word stop is used for stop signs throughout Europe. A yellow blinking or steady light means that a red light is imminent. Street signs are usually posted on buildings and have an unnerving way of changing names on the same route. To leave a city, follow the signs that say "all directions". See the appendix for more details.

Be cautious around trams and never overpass them when they are stopped. Pedestrians have the right of way in crosswalks, as do cyclists in bike lanes. A fixed green arrow on a red traffic light indicates you can turn in that direction after coming to a full stop. In a roundabout you must yield to traffic that is already on it. If two lanes enter a roundabout you need to stay in the lane you are in and use your blinker to change lanes. Public buses have the right of way and you must obey any signal they give. Headlights are required to be on in many countries whenever driving.

CAMPING AND COOKING EQUIPMENT

- Tent with rain fly
- Tarp for outside the tent
- Inflatable sleeping mattresses
- Bedding for summer travel: Except for Scandinavia or mountainous regions, I find a sleeping bag too warm for summer camping. I prefer to make a pillowcase for each thermal mattress from twin bed sheets. I fold the sheet in half lengthwise and sew the bottom and the open side. The mattress slips into this easily each time I set up a campsite. I take an additional twin bed sheet for the top sheet and a thermal blanket for each person. This bedding makes sleeping more home-like.
- Inflatable pillows and pillow cases
- Collapsible ground chairs
- Battery operated mini light
- Plastic showerbag for handy warm water (Store on back shelf of car to warm while driving.)
- Inner tube or inflatable mattress and bike pump for river floats. Optional
- Stove: I prefer Mountain Safety Research's Dragonfly Multi-Fuel stove. When white gas or gas cylinders are not available it can operate on unleaded gas. It has easy maintenance features that other stoves don't.
- *Small duffel that becomes the "kitchen bag" for storing and transporting cooking equipment to the cooking area
- Stove Board: I make this at home. It keeps the stove level if I'm not cooking on a table. To make one, measure the bottom of your "kitchen bag"*. Use this measurement to cut a 1/4-inch piece of plywood the same size. Cover it with contact paper.
- One 8" sauté pan: ideally heavy aluminum or calphlon with sloping sides and lid
- Two 1 1/2-quart lightweight pots with lids: one for coffee or tea water and one for food.
- Thermos with filter for making coffee or tea
- One 8-inch and two 4-inch metal bowls
- Metal tongs
- One slotted and one unslotted cooking spoon
- One rubber and one metal spatula
- Can opener
- One 8-inch and one 4-inch good quality knives
- Small jar with lid for salad dressings
- One quart-size storage container
- Plastic cups, bowls, plates and silverware
- Sponge, scrubber, two dish drying cloths
- Plastic bowl for washing dishes
- Tablecloth

All of the above fits easily into three duffels. This gives two persons an extra duffel for personal items without going over the allowable luggage limit for air travel.

PREPARING FOR YOUR TRIP
BUYING YOUR AIRLINE TICKET

Start by calling agencies specializing in budget travel. Consider their reputation for reliability and restrictions before you book. Here's a list.

- STA Travel (student/young travelers) 800-777-0112; www.sta-travel.com
Specializing in world-wide travel, this agency's tickets are very flexible. Making a change in plans or arranging for "open jaw" (flying in and out of different airports) travel is easy and penalty free.
- Council Travel (budget travel for the general public) 800-2-Council; www.counciltravel.com
Founded in 1947, this non-profit agency is dedicated to international exchange. Popular with students, they work with the general public as well.
- Consolidator/Bucket Shop Tickets
Consolidators, or "bucket shops", are wholesalers. They buy a large number of tickets that regularly scheduled airlines aren't able to sell and then sell them at a lower price than the airline. If you decide to take a trip close to your departure time this could work well for you. Ask if your ticket can be exchanged for a ticket on another airline, because if there is a problem with the flight you might need to take another carrier. Usually these tickets have unusual schedules with multiple stops, which is why the airline has made them available to the consolidator. The seat selection won't be as good as at full fare, but all other amenities are the same. To find a consolidator, check the travel section of your Sunday newspaper.
- Charter Flights
Charters flights follow the high-season traffic. They usually fly full, often with tighter seating and fewer amenities than on a commercial carrier. Their ticket has no value with another airline or even with the airline it has contracted with. It has value only with the charter company. If seats are still available close to departure, the company might discount the ticket even further to assure that the flight goes out full. Stand-by tickets are also available. To find charter flights check the travel section of your Sunday newspaper.
- Apex Tickets (Advanced Purchase Excursion Fare)
Offered by regularly scheduled airlines, these are considerably cheaper than the full economy fare. You can reserve and select your seat in advance and then pay just 21 days in advance of departure. You must travel as ticketed to avoid extra charges. The advantage of these tickets is that they will be honored by another airline if your airline has unforeseen problems, and you can travel in the high season without the inconveniences of a charter or consolidator ticket. Seating choices and amenities are the same as if you paid full fare. Departure and arrival times are good, and flights are often nonstop. If you call the airline directly, let them know you are interested in traveling as cheaply as possible and that you are flexible on the departure and return dates. It is cheaper to fly midweek or on the weekend. Highest prices occur at the beginning and end of the week, when business travel is at its peak. After you are quoted a price, call a budget travel agent and see how the price compares. They will know about current consolidator and charter flight offers.
- Open Jaw Tickets
These tickets allow you to start your trip in one place and return from another. They cost more but can be worth the cost if you don't want to make a loop in your route to return to where you started. Note that your car rental will also usually incur additional costs if you don't return it where you picked it up, particularly if you want to return it in a different country.
- Other Important Details
Always use your charge card for payment. This protects you if there is a dispute. Never pay with cash or check. Ask how many stops your flight makes before it reaches your destination. Each time it stops, there is a chance for delay. The most desirable flight goes nonstop to your destination. Request your seat assignment for both legs of your journey when you are making the reservation. Reconfirm the reservation and seat number by asking for a faxed or e-mailed confirmation. Carefully examine this immediately. Mistakes are made. Unless you catch the mistake immediately, you might be charged a re-ticketing fee. It is your responsibility to make this final check. Mark your calendar and reconfirm the flight at least 72 hours before departure.

GETTING YOUR DOCUMENTS

Apply for the documents you will need: passport; visa; senior citizen card; international driver's license; international camping card; international student; teacher or youth identification cards. Check the expiration date on your driver's license. If the magnetic strips on your ATM and charge cards are worn, get new ones. See appendix.

GETTING VEHICLE RENTAL/LEASE INFORMATION

Renting or leasing your car from home is much cheaper than making arrangements when you are at your destination. For safety, it's best to have a separate and lockable trunk, not a hatch-back or 3-door. However, I've traveled with a 3-door without a problem.

Make a list of questions to ask each company and keep track of the answers. If you are booking a vehicle for 3 weeks or more, you'll probably qualify for a cheaper lease program. They will need to know where you are picking up and dropping off the vehicle. If you do this at the same airport, the rate is usually less. Make sure the VAT (value added tax) is included in their quote. Inform them you'll be getting CDW insurance from another company.

Ask: Does the country where you are picking up the car have a highway tax? Is it included in the cost? Is unlimited mileage included? Is third-party (damage to the other car and persons) insurance included? What is the minimum and maximum age limit for drivers? What is the cost for an additional driver?

If you want a particular car, be clear that you don't want a substitute and have it noted on the agreement. When the transaction is completed, ask for a fax of the agreement and check it carefully. You'll want any mistakes corrected so the right car is waiting for you

If you plan to rent a RV, check to see if bike racks and a table with chairs can be rented. Some RV companies carry these, but you need to reserve ahead. Ask them to fax or e-mail a confirmation, along with a map to their pick-up area, which is usually in a suburb. See appendix.

ARRANGING INSURANCE

CDW (collision damage waver) insurance is compulsory in most countries. This covers you for loss of or damage to the car you rent. Purchasing the car rental company's CDW insurance is not advisable. If you rent a car and purchase insurance from the same company making a claim becomes a conflict of interest. Other sources are cheaper. Keep your car rental voucher and CDW insurance verification together with your hand-held luggage so they are easily accessible when you pick up your car. Have the rental company mark your vehicle papers to show that you have "green card" insurance for border crossings. Theft insurance for your personal belongings is a good idea. Your home insurance policy might cover this. See appendix.

PURCHASING MAPS

It's fun to look at maps before a trip. Visit your local travel bookstore or map source. Maps and atlases with a scale of 1/400 000-1 cm: 4 km will show the detail you need to find camping places. Check to see if the major cities you'll be driving into are expanded on the maps you have. If they are not detailed enough, you should buy an additional map. Check the publication date to confirm the map is current. High quality detailed maps are a good investment. They make it easy to plan routes and find campgrounds and they save time, gas money, and frustration.

CHOOSING A GUIDE BOOKS

A good guidebook is essential. To select one suited to your interests, read about the same city and a particular sight in several guidebooks, then determine which approach you like best.

LEARNING ABOUT THE COUNTRY

Use your library. Your trip will be more rewarding if you spend time getting to know the important historical events and artistic characteristics of the countries you will be visiting.

Learning at least some words of the local language will help you have more fun. There is a remarkable difference in the response from locals when I approach them using their language, even if it is just a few words. They appreciate my effort and exert more energy in helping me. Several months ahead of a trip, I purchase language tapes that include a phrase book. I play them in the car and use a headset to listen while I do housework, cook, and garden. At first, I just listen and repeat back, even if I don't know what I am saying. Then I start attaching meaning to the words. Finally, I write down little quizzes for myself. Even though learning another language can be difficult. I keep reminding myself that I will have more fun if I learn some basic phrases. And I do want to have fun!

SCHEDULE FOR PREPARATION AND PACKING

I like to get ready for a trip in a relaxed manner. Here's how I do it.

4 MONTHS BEFORE DEPARTURE:

I purchase airline tickets and arrange for seat assignment. I examine the tickets carefully to make sure they are correct. Mistakes are made. I mark my calendar with departure time, return times, and flight numbers. I check the expiration date on my passport because it needs to be valid for 6 months while I travel even for a shorter vacation. I make sure the magnetic strip on my the credit cards isn't overused and order new cards if they are. I check to see if that my driver's license will be valid during my trip. I obtain an international camping carnet card for the reasons and from the source listed in the appendix. I arrange the rental car and insurance.

3 MONTHS BEFORE DEPARTURE:

I purchase maps and guide books. Using the suggested reading sections of the guidebooks, I check out books from the library and start reading so that what I am seeing and experiencing while I am traveling means more. I start studying the local language.

2 MONTHS BEFORE DEPARTURE:

I check my camping equipment, duffels, camera, and carry-on bag so I can leisurely purchase or borrow things I will need. I decide what clothing and personal items I will take. I make the foam padding for the parts of the bicycle that will need protection during transport. I photocopy all tickets, car rental confirmations, insurance confirmations, passports, addresses and phone numbers for family, friends, and service for credit cards, cash cards, and insurance. I keep one set for myself and give one set to someone I can call in an emergency. I add to their copy only credit card and pin numbers.

1 MONTH BEFORE DEPARTURE:

I pack. I leave notes on the duffels, carry-on, purse, and money-belt to remind me to include things I am still using or need to purchase. I reconfirm my rides to the airport and pickup on return.

2 WEEKS AHEAD:

Everything I am going to take is packed and placed in one location. Reminders about including drivers license, credit cards, cash cards, airline tickets, passports, and money are attached to carry-ons. I am ready to go. My mind is free to concentrate on arrangements for work and home while I am gone.

TRAVELING SMART AND SAFE

Although most places are very safe it's important not to be naive. The following tips will keep you safe while traveling in areas notorious for petty theft. Most important, be aware that distraction is the con artist's tool and that thieves often are friendly and don't look unusual.

Always remove your car keys from the ignition or trunk. Keep them with you even if you are getting out of the driver's seat for just a moment. Check your guide book and if car theft is a problem it's not a bad idea to bring a steering wheel lock from home. In these same areas one adult passenger should always stay with the car. Keep the car locked even when passengers are inside. Thieves want the car vacant. They will try to get you out of the car. An old trick is to put plastic bottles in between the tire and fender in hopes that when you start driving the noise will get you out of the car to see what is wrong. Making tires look damaged is another standard trick. If someone tries to distract you, don't get out of the car. Keep the doors locked and the windows rolled up. Act as if they aren't there, and drive away.

Make your car look local. Buy a local paper and keep it visible. Add a local sports club sticker to the fender. Never leave anything visible that announces you speak English or that you are a tourist. Look inside local cars to get an idea of what is left visible and copy what you see. Park where there is pedestrian traffic. In an attended parking area, choose a spot that is easily visible by the attendant. Don't rent or lease an expensive car. Keep the car a bit dirty.

You probably won't have a collision, but in case you do, lock the car when you get out. Never sign anything that hasn't been translated to English. Sign only if the information is acceptable. Make sure the other party prints information legibly. Report the accident immediately to your rental or lease company. Emergency road phones are common on major highways throughout Europe.

Wear a money-belt that you tuck into your clothes or wear around your neck. Your passport, credit cards, cash card, currency, traveler's checks, car vehicle numbers, and the essential part of your airline ticket should be kept here. Your companion should have a different cash card and charge card so that you still have something to work with if one is lost. Put your money in your money-belt before you leave the cash machine or bank. Keep enough currency handy so that you don't have to get into your money-belt in public.

When you are in an area known for petty thief, you want to be inconspicuous. Walk with purpose. Don't look like a tourist sightseeing. Carry an inexpensive backpack for your guidebook, camera, lunch, and jacket. Don't reveal your native language by talking to your companion. Use eye contact and hand gestures instead of language. Sit rather than stand in the bus or metro if possible. Leave expensive rings, watches, and jewelry at home. Stand against a wall when you look at a map. You are less vulnerable. Talk quietly. If someone approaches you, don't speak or respond in anyway except to move on. Step into a store if you feel unsafe. Congestion and confusion are a thief's friend and a thief can be well dressed and approach in a friendly manner.

Though campgrounds are very safe, and filled with families and couples relaxing and having fun, for ease of mind, lock valuable camping equipment in the car before leaving for the day.

USING PUBLIC TRANSPORTATION

Know how to board and validate your ticket. Board buses where the validation box is located, usually at the rear of the bus. Metro and train validation boxes will be obvious. If you don't see locals validating their ticket, it will probably because they have a monthly or weekly ticket. Inspectors, in plainclothes, check tickets for validation. They get part of the violation fee and consider tourists easy prey. You must pay for a violation on the spot.

Have a fellow camper give you the details about the bus or metro stop. Have them write down the name of the place you want to get off and the name of the stop for returning to the campgrounds. Be sure this is in large, bold letters so it is easily read by a fellow passenger who might not have their glasses. Show the name of the stop you want to a fellow passenger. They will help you. For safety reasons, bus drivers don't want to be distracted by reading.

If you aren't used to taking a metro or subway there are a few things you need to know. Metro "lines" or routes are named, numbered, or color-coded. A train doesn't deviate from this route. The direction the train is going is its last station. A large map of the entire metro system is posted in the station. Plan your route. Transfer stations have good directional signs to the other lines. Inside the train, the train's route is posted over a door. When you are on the train watch for the names of the stations as you pass them; checking these with the posted route. If you're going in the wrong direction just get out at the next station and follow directional signs to trains going in the right direction.

CAMP COOKING HINTS

Start by gathering all food ingredients, spices, packaged mixes, utensils, pots and pans, and eating utensils that you will need for the meal. Wash all the produce you have bought that day. Store what you won't be using for this meal. Start your vegetable and fruit preparation placing what will be cooked together in one bowl.

Braising is an excellent way to use a less expensive and less tender, yet flavorful piece of meat. Trim off excess fat and membrane. Cut the meat into 1 1/2-inch pieces. Put a small amount of oil in the sauté pan. Over high heat, let the oil get smoking hot. Place the meat in the pan at little a time, allowing enough room around each piece so it will brown well. This seals in the juices. If you put in too much meat at one time the juices will run from the meat and the color will be gray instead of brown. If you are including vegetables with the meat, brown them after you have finished the meat. The particles of meat left in the pan will add flavor so don't throw them away. When the meat and vegetables are braised, turn down the heat to medium-low. Add spices, bouillon cubes, or packaged mix. Add enough water, wine, or chicken stock to make one inch of cooking liquid in your pan. Cover with a tight-fitting lid and continue cooking over low heat. Always taste as you cook and adjust spices accordingly. It's fun and helps to develop your palate.

Marinating meat and fish enhances the end result. Meat benefits from 3-4 hours of marinating. Fish needs only a few minutes. Curing pork is easy to do and makes a world of difference in taste.

Some vegetables such as green beans, broccoli, or potatoes need blanching before you sauté them. Bring a pot of boiling salted water to a boil. Add the vegetables and cook until they are softened but still have a bit of firmness. Remove them with a slotted spoon. Save the hot water for cooking pasta, rice, polenta, or for cleaning up.

To sauté vegetables, place a small amount of oil in a frying pan over moderately hot heat. When it is almost smoking hot add the vegetables turning them as they brown. To sauté meat or fish proceed as above but allow space between pieces so the juices are sealed by browning.

To cook pasta place about four times as much water in the pot as the amount of pasta you are going to cook. Add enough salt so the water tastes salty. Cover the pot and bring the water to a boil. Add the pasta stirring occasionally to keep the pasta separated. When it is almost cooked, take it off the heat. Cover and set aside. Cover with a towel. While it rests and stays warm, it will finish cooking. When you are ready to serve, drain the pasta. Add sautéed vegetables, meat, or packaged mix.

Polenta is a wonderful, flavorful, and filling starch. Serve it like you would potatoes. You'll probably find it in the same section in the store where rice is shelved. It swells in cooking to the amount of liquid it is cooked in. It requires 4 times liquid to the dry polenta. One cup of dry polenta makes four cups of cooked polenta. Bring water to a boil. Pour in the polenta stirring constantly. Turn down the heat and let it bubble slowly. Stir frequently to avoid lumps. When it is thick and smooth, remove from the heat and cover with a towel until you are ready to serve.

Clean up as you cook. Have a plastic bag in your cooking area for throw-away stuff. Keep a basin of warm water close to where you are cooking and wash and dry equipment as you cook. I try to have everything washed or soaking before I start to eat so that the after-meal clean up is minimal.

MARINATING OIL FOR MEAT AND FISH

Stir ingredients together. Rub flavored oil into meat and let it rest for 30 minutes. Less tender cuts of meat profit from longer marination.

1/2 cup olive oil
2 teaspoons lemon juice
salt and pepper
Optional additions: garlic, fresh or dried herbs, teriyaki sauce, sugar, lemon zest, or mustard.

CURING LIQUID FOR PORK

Simmer ingredients together for five minutes. Let cool. Place pork into a storage container and pour cooled curing liquid over it just to cover. Keep in cool box with ice for 24 hours. Remove the pork from the curing liquid. Dry with paper towel. Discard the used liquid.

3 cups water
1/2 cup lemon juice
2/3 cup sugar or 1/2 cup maple syrup
1/4 teaspoon cinnamon
1 tablespoon salt

USING THE PHONE AND E-MAIL

Phone cards and multilingual instructions in phone booths make using the phone in Europe easier than ever. Phone cards are available wherever newspapers and magazines are sold. You just slide the card into the slot in the phone and press in the phone number. An electronic readout will tell you how much value is left on the card. Buy a phone card at home and practice using it before the trip if you have never used one before. To make an international call, press the international access number of the country you are calling from, it's usually 00, the country code of the country you are calling, the area code, and number. For calls within the country do like you do at home, press the area code and the number. If you want to use a direct phone service, use a phone card to call the toll-free access number listed on the back of your calling-card and an English speaking operator will assist you. Within Europe using the phone card is cheaper than using a direct service. If you have trouble ask a local to help.

At a calling call center you can place your call from a quiet phone booth, get assistance from staff if you're having problems, and pay when you're finished without using a phone card.

Cyber cafes can be fun if you want to stay in touch via e-mail. Tourist offices, computer stores, and major hotels can direct you to the nearest one.

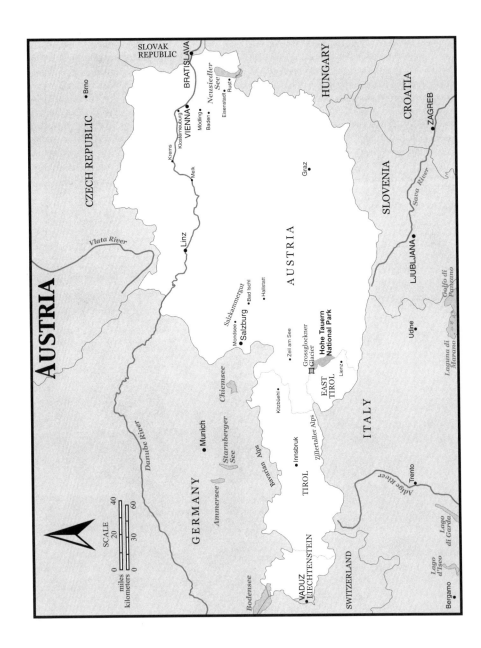

AUSTRIA

Austria is dramatic, theatrical, and loves a good time. Well-marked walking trails lace magnificent mountainsides cradling flower-filled meadows. Close by are sophisticated cities in love with the best of the European music and Baroque architecture.

Adoring the outdoors, the Austrians are avid campers. From among the country's hundreds of campgrounds, I've selected those that are scenic and not resort-like.   Well maintained campgrounds with warm showers are de rigeur. Most have covered common areas and children's playgrounds that are great places to chat with the locals on vacation and to share stories and information with fellow international travelers. Austrians love their country and will happily help you enjoy it, too. Start a conversation by simply saying "hello" in their language. Then apologize for not knowing their language, if possible in their language. This will soften them up a bit. Then ask for information. They will probably be able to speak at least a few words in English or find someone who does. Campgrounds are moderately priced considering their excellent maintenance and scenic locations. Camping for two persons, a car, and a tent is around $20 USA per night in the campgrounds I've listed. Plan to arrive by 11 a.m. or after 2 p.m. During lunch and rest time, the office is closed. Stores in small towns and villages also observe these hours. Cycling is a popular sport. Pedaling along backroads through the magnificent scenery and through charming historic villages and towns is delightful. Bringing your own bike and a bike rack is recommended.

Driving is a pleasure. With such fabulous scenery, good signposting, and excellent roadways, it's no wonder Austria has a highway tax for all motorists. Car-rental companies within the country automatically include the tax payment. If you arrive in Austria from another country, pay the tax on arrival at the border crossings and post your stamp immediately on the windshield. The tax is based on the length of your stay and is under $20 USA for a week. Expect additional tolls or "mauts" for long tunnels or special Alpine roadways. Blue parking zones indicate limited-time parking. Look carefully for the ticket dispenser. If the parking is free but timed, use the rental car's clock disc in your glove compartment to show the time you left. Buses have priority on mountain roads, as do cars coming downhill. Circular blue signs with a cross and red border mean no stopping. A diagonal slash means a stop is permitted for the length indicated. Parking and road tax stamps are closely regulated and the stiff fines are added to your car rental bill if you don't pay on the spot. Austrian police accept credit cards for payment.

VIENNA

Vienna is Europe's historic heart of music. With rich endowments and patronage from both the imperial court and wealthy patrons, Vienna attracted the likes of Haydn, Mozart, Beethoven, and Mahler. The showy elegance of the waltz, with it's curving and evasive movements, made a perfect match for Vienna's Golden Age populace who longed for a carefree life. The music of the era pulls on the heart, filling the mind with romantic imaginings and longings; it has gemutlichkeit the Austrians say, or "sweetness".

With a flair for harmony and design, its architecture is like a melody from a heritage of diverse cultures and races. Tiny streets, some almost alleyways, are lined with red, steeply pitched roofs where charming wrought-iron signs announce sidewalk cafes. Roses wind around street lamps, pigeons swoop down for food, the sound of music drifts out through upper-story windows, and the air is laden with the sweet smells of pastries. To stand in a narrow street and whisper reverently, "That's where Mozart lived when he wrote the "Marriage of Figaro," or "That's where Beethoven wrote "Fidelio," is magical. But Vienna's streets are not just a quaint setting for tourists or a walk through time. They are the setting for a way of life.

The Ringstrasse, Vienna's circular grand boulevard shaded by leafy chestnut trees, is a hallmark of Viennese culture. Start your exploration at the Stephansdom. This cathedral, with its vast multi-

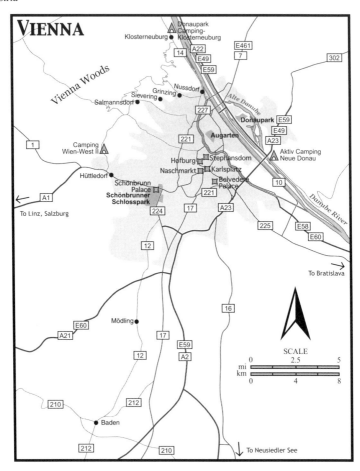

colored roof and ornate towers, is the heart of the city. Elaborately carved pillars guard the impressive net and star-ribbed vaulting of the nave. Begin your exploration with a climb or elevator ride to the tower's observation areas for panoramic views of the Danube canal, the Belvedere, the Vienna Woods, and the Imperial Palace; open daily. Directions: U-bahn 1 or 3 to Stephansplatz.

Purchase "Vienna A to Z" at the campgrounds and, using it as a guide, walk over to the Figaro House, just east of Stephansplatz at Domgasse 5, and climb the stairs as Mozart did when this was his residence for over two years. To stand in the room where he lived with his lively family and composed the opera "The Marriage of Figaro" and the "Hayden Quartets" is exhilarating and eerie at the same time.

Living long in close contact with the imperial family, the Viennese developed a love of ceremony and intrigue. Every emperor tinkered with the imperial palace-the Hofburg-making it a city within a city. After viewing the staggering treasures of gold, silver, and jewels in the Schatzkammer, or treasury, you will understand the power of it's royal occupants; closed Tuesday. Then wander over to the Royal Stables, or Stallburg. This lovely Renaissance building was converted to stable the royal stud during the hey day of haute ecole horsemanship. The parentage of the famous snow-white Lipizzaner horses stems from the Moorish occupation of Spain and their beauty is a blend of unusual physical strength and graceful lightness. Saved from war, sickness, and fire, the Lippizzaner horses have a special place in the Austrian heart. The Lipizzaner Museum in the Stallburg is open daily. Directions: U-bahn 3 to Herrengasse, then walk south on Herrengasse to Michaelerplatz.

The Neue Hofburg houses four very impressive museums: the National Library, the Collections of Musical Instruments, the Collection of Weapons, and the Ethnographical; all closed Tuesday. Consider splurging on rented headsets in the Collections of Musical Instrument. Directions: U-bahn 2 to Museumplatz, or take trams 1 or 2 to Heldenplatz and walk 100 meters to the southwest. Your "Vienna A-Z" will guide you through the inner city of the Hofburg.

In keeping with its historic role as apex for European music, Vienna's new museum, the House of Music, invites visitors to personally interact with music. Housed in the historic Archduke Charles' Palace, your musical journey through the musuem includes an exciting tribute to historic composers and conductors, an experience with the tones and sounds that create music, a chance to pick up the baton and direct an orchestra, and finally a chance to create new music yourself. Don't miss it; open daily, including evenings. Directions: U-bahn 1 to Oper, then trams 1 or 2 to Schwarzenbergplatz.   Then walk or take trams D or 71 north 3 blocks to the end of Schwarzenberstrasse.

The Albertina is one of the greatest graphic art collections in the world. Its permenent home is in the 18th century wing of a palace off Albertinaplatz. While the palace undergoes extensive restoration a significant portion of the collection is being housed at the Akademiehof, at Marktgasse 3. Directions: Trams 1 or 2 or U-bahn 1 or 3 to Oper.

Revolting against the Baroque splendors of Imperial Vienna, the new age thinkers of the early 1900s shocked Vienna. Stop in front of the Michaeler Platz entrance to the Hofburg, and turn to look across at the Loos House. Nicknamed the building without eyebrows, the four huge slabs of marble stand like modern versions of Greek columns. Unwilling to compromise, the young thinkers caused a great stir in the city. Coffeehouses, the fulcrum from which the Viennese operated, buzzed with heated arguments

The Habsburgs were avid supporters of the arts, and their collection from the lands under their control is outstanding. In the Kunsthistorisches Museum, the visitor is treated to an excellent collection of Rubens, Brueghel, Bosch, and Rembrandt; closed Monday.   Directions: U-2 to Mariahilfer Str. The Museu fur Angewandte Kunst (MAK), or applied arts, has some terrific exhibits in glass and furniture and a stunning freize by Klimt; closed Monday. Directions: Trams 1 or 2 or U-bahn 3 to Stubentor.

Many consider the Opera House Vienna's most important building. During July and August, it is closed for performances but a tour of the building is available. You'll be able to conjure up the strains of fine music and a picture of the wonderful finery that brightened the staircase: elegant women in sparkling tiaras and brilliant jewels, and proud men bearing brightly polished medals on their immaculate uniforms-all glittering in the light from the great candelabras; open for tours daily. Directions; U-bahn 1 to Oper,

At Karlsplatz, take time to admire the old station buildings designed by Otto Wangner. Their curving lines and rosette patterns on the iron railings, the green copper roofing, and the gold trim all represent the elegance of the turn-of-the-century Jugendstil art movement. Turn to view the twin marble columns and green copper dome to Karlskirche, a monument of imperial greatness. A Henry Moore sculpture graces a small pond in front. Directions: U-bahn 1, 2 or 4 to Karlsptatz

Devoid of unnecessary frills both inside and out, the turn-of-the-century Secessionist Building and the art that it houses was an affront to the Viennese sensibilities at the turn of the century. An open filigree bronze ball of laurel leaves and berries graces the top of this geometric building. A famous freize by Klimt, honoring Beethoven's "Ninth Symphony", is downstairs; closed Monday. Directions:

On the west side of Karlsplatz. Vienna and its environs are filled with delightful art nouveau treats. Buffs can get a special brochure from the tourist office and seek out its finest addresses. Reminiscent of the old Halles Market in Paris, the huge out door Naschmarkt, is feisty and humorous. Perfuming the air, the wurst and pastry stalls are plentiful and not indulging would be sinful; closed Saturday afternoons and all day Sunday. The adjoining Flohmarkt, or fleamarket, is a memorabilia bridge from past to present. Here a new generation finds meaning and continuity with the older generations; best is on Saturday. Directions: U-bahn 4 to Kettenbruckengasse.

Austrian Baroque is triumphant in the magnificent stairway, grandiose halls, and gilded and painted ceilings of the Hildebrandt designed Belvedere Palace. Built on a slope in the southeast corner of the city in the early 1700s, it was the summer palace for Prince Eugene, the military hero in the wars with the Turks. Graceful gardens flow down the slope joining the former residence with the reception hall. The stunning gilded masterpiece, "The Kiss", by Klimt is housed in the Oberes Belvdere along with other exciting works by Schiele, Kokoschka and Makart; closed Monday. Directions: U-bahn to Karlsplatz, then Tram D to Schloss Belvedere. The lower palace houses an extensive collection of sculptural works; closed Monday.

Not to be outdone by the glamour of Louis IVX's Versailles, the Habsburgs built Schonbrunn Palace. The views of Vienna from the colonnaded pavilion, Gloriette, are superb. It is an exuberance of Baroque art, with the theatrical effects of elaborate fountains, symmetrical gardens, and statuary. The opulent gilded interior includes the Millionenzimmer decorated in priceless Indian and Persian miniatures, a grand ballroom, the piano and room where six-year-old Mozart played, and a dining table mechanically drawn up through the floor. This is a popular tourist destination. Purchase tickets for the interior, then enjoy the gardens until your tour time; open daily. Directions: U-4 to Schloss Schonbrunn. It's on the southwest edge of the city and well signposted off A1.

Beethoven, Mahler, and Kafka all loved the Vienna Woods that tuck the city in like an amphitheatre. You can tread along their favorite footpaths. Directions: Southwest of the city center, the scenic winding road is bordered by the towns of Baden and Modling and easily accessed from A2 or A21. Vineyards embroider the hillsides of northwestern Vienna, and it's a Viennese custom to enjoy time off in their congenial heurigen, or wine gardens. A pine tuft hung from the end of a pole jutting out from one indicates that the new wine is being served. The wine gardens also offer tasty picnic fare. The villages of Nussdorf, Sievering, and Stammersdorf are better choices than touristy Grinzing. Directions: Northwest of the city and south of Klosterneuburg, scenic little roads wind through the woods and villages.

Throughout the summer, Vienna is lively with a wide range of concerts, exhibitions, and theater. The Vienna Festival Weeks of mid-May through mid-June are particularly extravagant. Use the web for information on advance ticket purchases for the most notable performances. However in this musical city, tickets for lesser-known performances are readily available and attending one doesn't have to be costly.

Laced with cycle paths, pedaling is encouraged and is a very enjoyable way to see the city. You can join the locals cycling along the banks of the Danube. Bicycles can be carried on the U-bahns for half fare. The campgrounds have information on rentals and routes.

****Camping: *Northwest of the city, close to the Danube, in Klosterneuburg off 14. Drive east of Klosterneuburg toward the train station, then continue toward the river following signposting north. Donaupark-Camping Klosterneuburg (022-432-5877); large, in a recreational area with large swimming pool and tennis; doable by bike along the Danube to the historic area; camp shuttle bus and close by public transport to the historic center; all the amenities; open all year; $$$. *Closest to the city. On the east side of the Danube, close to the intersection of A22 and A23 exit Olhafen Lobau. Aktiv-Camping Neue Donau (01-202-4010); large; traffic noise; public transport close by; all amenities; open mid-May-September; $$$. *West of the city in the suburb of Hutteldorf. On A1 follow signs to centrum and then Hilleldorf. Turn left on Huttelburg Str., and continue to the campgrounds. Camping Wien-West II (01-914-2314); large, bungalows; all amenities; public transport close by; open all year; $$$. Ten kilometers southwest of the city, exit A2 for Rodaun. Camping Rodaun (01-888-4154); smaller; traffic noise; open April-October; $$$$.

VALLEY OF THE DANUBE

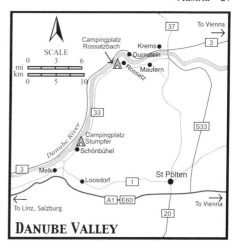

DANUBE VALLEY

For as far as you can see, vineyards blanket the steep and rocky terraced hillsides in Austria's most famous wine-producing region. The fruity aromas of grapes, peaches, and apricots produce a heavy elixir in the air. The region's ancient towns date to Roman times following the Danube with castles, monasteries, and fortresses crowning their hillsides. A terrific cycle route along the valley's length makes it very popular with cyclists. The attractive squares, narrow cobblestone streets, and 15th century buildings are charming. The route travels along the Danube between Krems and Melk. One of the most romantic towns on the route is Durnstein. The ruins of a castle in which Richard the Lionheart was imprisoned crowns her terraced hillside and are in remarkable condition. Friendly cafes are filled with flowers and wine tasters. At the south end of the route, the vast and famous Benedictine abbey of Melk sweeps majestically up from the Danube. Its sandy colored walls, red-tile roof, and twin church towers punctuate the skyline. Heavily Baroque, the monastery has a rich and colorful history. Although you can wander around on your own, the tour is fascinating. Directions: Krems is 83km west of Vienna on highway 3. There are picturesque small roads from Krems to Melk on both sides of the Danube. ****Camping: *In Rossatz, close to Durnstein, at the north end of the route. Campingplatz Rossatzbach (02-714-6317). *In Schonbuhel, at the south end of the route. Camping Stumpfer (02-752-8510). Both are: small; on the river; popular with cyclists; open April-October; $$.

NEUSIEDLER SEE

Salt marshes and reed beds characterize the spring-fed lake of Neusiedler See, making it an important bird-watching area. Searching for frogs, tadpoles, and fish, great white herons and egrets quietly forage alone, occasionally taking flight on long, broad, slowly flapping wings. Tranquil ducks dabble and dive, then explode suddenly in the air with a burst of flapping cacophony. Swans float regally followed by a line of their charming youngsters and storks nest on rooftops in the village of Rust. Colorful sails of wind surfers dot the lake when the wind picks up. When just a soft wind blows it's a good place for beginners since the lake is so

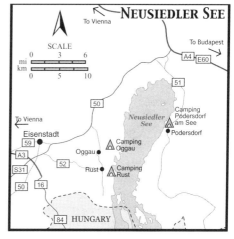

SALZBURG

To Linz

156   E55   1

155

Camping
Nord-Sam ⚠   ⚠   ● Nord-Sam
Camping
Stadblick-
Rauchenbichl

E55
A1

To
München

158

Salzach River

⊡ Mirabellgarten

Dom ⊡

⊡ Hohensalzburg

1   ✈
Salzburg
Maxglan
Airport

● Aigen

Camping
Schloss-Aigen ⚠

SCALE
0   0.5   1
mi
km
0   1   2

150

A10
E55

To A10,E55,
Villach   Glasenbach ●

shallow and rentals are readily available. Cyclists enjoy the cycle path that winds through the reed beds along the lake. Once this region was Hungarian, but now only the southern edge is. Still a Magyar, or Hungarian, air hangs prettily in the village squares. The warm water and swimming beaches are perfect places for sunbathing and children's play. Only 50km from Vienna, the Viennese come here to relax. ****Camping: *On the westside of the lake in Rust. Off A3 or A4 exit for Eisenstadt, then exit east onto 52 and drive 15km to Rust. Camping Rust (026-85-595); nice setting on the lake; popular with families; open May-September; $$$. *In Oggau, four kilometers north of Rust. Camping Oggau (026-85-7271); large; popular with families; open May-September; $$.

*On the east side of the lake in Podersdorf. Exit A4 or 50 onto 51 at the north end of the lake, and drive 20km south to Podersdorf. Signposted north of town. Camping Podersdorf am See (021-77-2279); nice location on the lake; resort-like; thermal swimming pool; open May-September; $$$$.

SALZBURG

Playful Mozart, whose flowing melodic music is a tapestry of both radiance and drama, is a perfect idiom for this beautiful city that was his birthplace. Soaring upward, like his music, is one of the greatest castle-fortresses in Central Europe, the Hohensalzburg. Its looming presence is in harmony with the grandeur of the surrounding Alpine landscape. Dramatic, massive, and sober on the outside, it is lavish with ornamentation and pleasing color inside. Start your city exploration from the ramparts of Hohensalzburg with its spectacular views of Alpine peaks, the winding Salzach River, and the lantern-topped cupolas of the Dom. Aristocratic life during the Middle Ages comes alive on the castle tour, which winds through princely state rooms, a lookout tower, and torture chambers; open daily. Directions: Behind Kapitelplatz, walk up tiny Festungsgasse to the cable-car or continue walking up the steep hill on your own. Return is by an elevator built in solid rock, or you can take a more leisurely walk down.

The massive Dom stands majestically between the city's three main squares. Bright sunlight floods through its monumental barrel-vaulted nave and heavy stucco ornamentation graces its ceiling frescoes, making it a very elegant setting for the opening of the famous Salzburg Festival. Mozart was christened here and later filled it with the passionate tenderness of his music as he played on its great organ; open daily. As you wander through the ancient UNESCO listed old town, you'll be serenaded by a myriad of street musicians and the clip-clop of horses' hooves. Stroll across the bridge to have a picnic in the rose-scented gardens of Mirabellgarten. This lovely rosy-hued palace is the setting for many musical performances. Plan to spend some time in the leafy beer gardens, where beer is dispensed into large mugs and served with delectable wurst.

****Camping: *Close to the city, on the north side of Salzburg in the suburb of Nord-Sam. Exit A1/E55 for Salzburg-Nord and centrum. Follow campground signposting on the right just off the exit, and drive up the hill on a small road. There are two in the area, and both have: nice locations; doable by bike to the historic area; public transportation close by; popular; reserve ahead; open May-September; $$$. Camping Nord-Sam (0662-6604) and Camping Stadblick-Rauchenbichl (0662-45-0652). *South of Salzburg in the suburb of Aigen. Exit off A10/E55 at Anif und

Glasenbach and follow signposting. Camping Schloss-Aigen (0662-2079); lovely location on a small hill with views of the Alps; popular reserve ahead; public transport close by; small; open May-September; $$$.

SALZKAMMERGUT

Looking like gigantic castles with turrets and battlements, the mighty Alps of Salzkammergut cradle gleaming deep-blue lakes that mirror their peaks. Valleys smile openly with lush green meadows joyfully abloom with larkspur and daisies, while shadowy forests are tranquil and secretive. Southeast of Salzburg, the winding roads of the region lead rich pastoral countryside punctuated with picturesque little towns and villages, sophisticated spa towns, and lakeside villages that cling to ledges below towering rocks. Chairlifts and well-trodden walking paths make hiking easier and provide breathtaking views and little mountain cafes provide delectable Austrian treats.

HALLSTATT

Clinging prettily from sheer rocky cliffs, Hallstatt has almost a Mediterranean feeling. One of the oldest towns in Austria, salt has been mined in this area since 1000 B.C. Excavations of amber beads, ivory-inset sword sheaths, and leather shoes proved that a flourishing salt trade took place with the Baltic region. Filled with flowers, this picturesque village is tightly packed with cafes and inns and is a popular daytrip for vacationers. Make your way along the tiny narrow streets and up the ancient steep steps to the church, or Pfarrkirche, overlooking the lake. Its miniscule cemetery is filled with wrought iron crosses and colorful flowers. Because there is no room for cemetery plots, the skulls of loved ones are exhumed and carefully decorated; open daily. Walk farther up the steep steps to reach the ancient salt mine; open daily. (A tram ride is available from the village.) A lake-side walking path running along the east bank, from the Steeg Gosau train station to the resort village of Obertraun, provides some spectacular views of the lake. Above Obertraun, the famous Dachstein Ice Caves' gargantuan curtains of ice are truly impressive; open daily. Arrive by noon to join an English tour and remember "ice" means "cold", bring a jacket. Ferries cross the lake, stopping at various villages. Splendid walking paths pass through gorges, beside thundering waterfalls, and on up to wildflower-splashed hillsides. Purchase a map from the campground. The region is UNESCO listed. Directions: Drive east of Salzburg on 158 for 55km. Exit south at Bad Ischl onto 145, and drive 11km, going just beyond Bad Goisern. Then exit south onto a small road in the direction Hallstatt and drive nine kilometers. ****Camping: South of the Hallstatt-Tunnels, follow signposting. Camping Klausner-Holl ((06-134-8322 fax 061-34-8322); small and popular; reserve ahead; open May-September; $$$. *In Obertraun am See. Continue on the small road, passing Hallstatt, following directions to Obertraun. Strandbad Camping (06-219-6442 fax 06-219-8282); small and popular; reserve ahead; open May-September; $$$.

BAD ISCHL

Once the destination for vacationing Emperor Franz Joseph, who interrupted his relaxation by signing the declaration of war with Serbia in 1914, today Bad Ischl is a sophisticated mountain resort. Vacationeers enjoy the Biedermeier-style facades, Franz Lehar's home, and Franz Joseph's hunting lodge, Kaiservilla. Good cycle paths follow the Traun River, and the summer calendar is filled with various musical events. Directions: Drive east from Salzburg on 158 for 55km. ****Camping: *17km west of Bad Ischl exit off 158 at km 32 for Abersee-Gschwand, and drive to the lake. Camping Primusbauer (062-27-7228); lovely location on the lake; open May-September; $$$. Camping Lindenstrand (062-27-7205); in the same area but more road noise; open May-September; $$$.

MONDSEE

The warm lake waters make lessons at the sailing and wind surfing schools in Mondsee enticing. Attersee, the lake just east of Mondsee, enchanted the Secessionist painter Klimt, and Mahler composed some of his greatest symphonic works in the richly evocative countryside. Directions: *30km east of Salzburg exit south off A1 onto 154 for Mondsee. ****Camping: *Exit 154 at km 21.4 and drive to the lake. Austria Camp (062-32-2927); nice location on the lake; open May-September; $$$. *On the west end of Attersee, 24km from Mondsee. On 151 exit at km 24.5, and drive to the lake. Inselcamping (076-65-8311); nice location on the lake; open June-August; $$$.

THE TIROL

With a backdrop of the dramatic Alps, wood fronted houses drip with bright, well-tended, geranium-filled window boxes. Charming chapels sit prettily in flower-flecked meadows, and a network of walking paths allow you to enjoy the bird songs and the pure Alpine air.

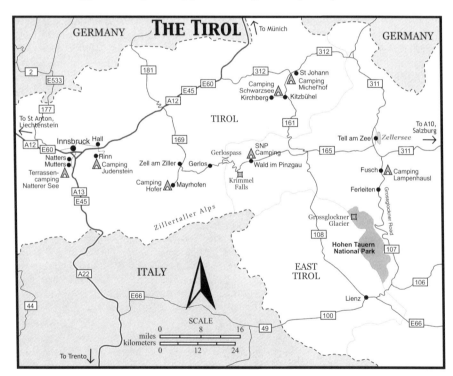

ZILLERTAL ALPS

Cradling lush green valleys, these towering mountain ranges host a wide range of well-known walking trails over wonderful Alpine pastures blanketed in brilliant summer bloom. Lifts to higher elevations via cable cars and chairlifts make the walking easier. In Mayrhofen, pick up the free "Mayrhofen A-Z" for details on paragliding, river rafting, glacier walking, summer skiing, and folk-singing festivals, as well as walking-trail maps. Directions: 40km east of Innsbruck, exit A12 south onto 169 and drive for 23km. At the fork of 169 and 165 continue on 169, the smaller road, for another nine kilometers. ****Camping: *In Zell am Ziller. Cross the river at the fork of 169 and 165, and follow signposting. Camping Hofer (052-82-2248); pleasant meadow setting; open all year; $$$. The resorts of Kitzbuhel, Kirchberg, and St. Johann at the eastern end of the Tirol are beautifully manicured and very photogenic. Directions: 58km east of Innsbruck, exit A12 onto 312, and drive east 34km in the direction of St. Johann. For Kitsbuhel, exit south at St Johann onto 161, and drive ten kilometers farther. ****Camping: In St. Johann, just over a kilometer south of town on 161 towards Kitzbuhel. Camping Michel'hof (053-52-62584); beautiful view of the Alps; open all year; $$$$. In Kitzbuhel. Drive two kilometers west of town on 170 in the direction of Kirchberg. Camping Schwarzsee (053-56-628-06); lovely views; swimming pool; open all year; $$$$.

INNSBRUCK

Once a mountain mining town and later the home of archdukes, including Maximilian I, Innsbruck is now a very likable and fashionable city. Start by climbing up the Stadtturn to look down on the Baroque facades along the main street, Herzog Friedrich Strasse, and across to the Goldenes Dachl, a gilded, copper-tile roof; open daily. Directions: Follow signs for Altstadt and parking. For a change of scene, visit Alpenzoo; open daily. Directions: At the north end of town, on the north side of the Inn River follow signposting on Weiherburgasse. The Renaissance castle Schloss Ambras is worth a visit and the beautiful grounds are a good place for a picnic. Directions: Drive east of the city on A12/E60. It's well signposted just outside the city center. ****Camping: 12km east of the city, exit A12/E60 at Hal, and drive south on the small road toward Tulfes, passing through the village and following the road to Rinn. Camping Judenstein (052-23-8620); nice location in a village setting; open May-September; $$. *South of town in the direction of Brenner, exit A13 at exit 3 Mutters/Natters, and follow signposting. Terrassencamping Natterer See (0512-54-6732); beautiful setting on a tiny lake; large and resort-like with all the amenities; open all year; $$$$$.

HOHE TAUERN NATIONAL PARK

Dazzling capes of ice drape from the rugged shoulders of the enormous Hohe Tauern Mountains even in summer. Thundering falls cascade wildly down through boulder-choked gorges, and crystal-blue waters are clasped in bowls of rock carved out by giant rivers of ice. The famous Grossglockner Road traverses valleys where tranquil cows graze in lush green meadows, then climbs up steeply, affording eye-popping views of the Grossglockner Glacier. Large viewing/parking areas are often coupled with cafes. The road is broad, the turns are wide, and driving in low gear is necessary. The toll road is expensive. You might prefer to sit back and relax in the Bundesbus leaving from Zell am See at the north end or Lienz in the south. At the north end of the road, stop at Wildpark Ferleiten for a closer look at the Alpine animals that inhabit the mountains. Directions: Follow highway 107 between Lienz and Zell am See. ****Camping: In Fusch on the north side of the Glocknerstrasse, 15km south of Zell am See. Camping Lampenhausl ((064-58-8472); lovely location; small; open May-September; $$$.

Equally famous are the Krimmel Falls, a series of giant falls and cascades dropping 380 meters. Hike up the exciting Wasserfallweg, a twisting four kilometer trail with magnificent vistas.

Arrange your hike so you are at the top at midday, when the sun is behind the falls, making them extra brilliant and iridescent. Bring a waterproof jacket for the veils of water. Tickets must be purchased for both the trail and parking. Directions: 55km west of Zell am Zee on 165 south of the Gerlos Pass. There is parking by the trailhead. ****Camping: Just before you drive up 165 to the falls, on the east side of the Krimmel in Wald im Pinzgau. SNP Camping (06565-8446-0); small; nice setting; open all year; $$.

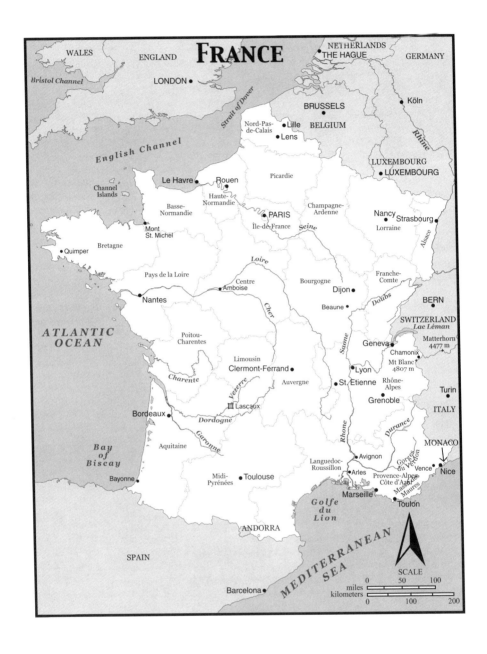

FRANCE

The moment you set foot in France, you know it's appealingly unique. Like its fabulous cuisine, France is a country of great individuality, spontaneity, color, aroma, and taste. Whether elegant or simple, the French always have style. Quality of life is top on their list.

Shopping is an authentic thread in the fabric of the French. Merchants are an intensely proud group of people with a fine set of aesthetics. Their goods are painstakingly arranged, with special attention paid to shape, color, and texture, making a vibrant and lovely mosaic. Lively street markets are moveable feasts with a symphony of aromas and sounds. The marketeers include songsters, comedians, tutors, and culinary advisors. Prices are chalked on a board, and haggling isn't appreciated. Formal, politeness is central to all transactions in France. It is considered rude if you don't say hello, goodbye and thank-you in *their* language.

The French like to get from here to there quickly. Ultra-modern toll roadways satisfy. Drive with assertion. Being overly cautious or timid can cause a collision. Speed limits are similar to those at home. Fines are heavy for speeding and are paid immediately, credit cards accepted. Blue signs with a white "P" indicate a parking area. After parking, look for a ticket dispenser. If you notice that all the cars are parked on one side of the street but not the other, follow suit. If you get a parking violation, buy a fee stamp at a magazine stand, affix it to the ticket, then stamp and mail it.

France is one of the most popular countryside in Europe to cycle. Rolling hillsides, aromatic with lavender, thyme, and grapes, are embroidered with small roads leading to farms and quiet villages. Major highways leave these small roads relatively free of traffic.

Camping in France is a joy. Long ago municipal authorities appreciated the need for an inexpensive way for citizens to enjoy their beautiful country. Campgrounds were built. Some places are rustic and old fashioned, others are resort-like. There are many more than the listed ones. Opening and closing times listed are conservative. Camping for 2 persons, a car, and tent will cost about $20 USA, resort-like places will be cost just over $25 USA.

PARIS

Paris is a theatrer where actors and actresses, instead of being on stage, are in the audience. Watch the show from a park bench, cafe chair, and museum bench. Stroll through food markets, peek into tiny gardens, and press your nose against the glass of patisseries, charcuteries, boulangeries, boutiques, and antique shops. Like its complex wines, Paris needs slow and thoughtful sipping.

Intoxicating with hundreds of museums, don't miss seeing the most famous, but see smaller ones too. Museums are expensive to staff and maintain, so admissions are pricey. Select carefully, then savor your choice like exquisite cuisine. Most museums are closed on Monday or Tuesdays. Substantial discounts are given to children, students, teachers, and seniors.

Parisian love of innovation enables artists, musicians, and writers to work in a stimulating environment. Today you can visit the neighborhoods where famous residents lived and the cafes where they hungout. You can stand before their original works in museums and visit cemeteries where they are buried.

Before you enter the city, purchase Michelin's Paris Plan 10/12. You'll need it to get to your first camping place. This excellent road map includes metro stations, parking areas, major sights, and gas stations. The free maps aren't detailed enough.

Paris's public transportation system is one of the most advanced in the world. Use the route finder system found by the ticket booth in the Metro to show the route for your desired destination. Press where you want to go, and your route will be displayed. Jot down transfer stations. When you get off the train, look at the wall displayed map by the tracks which helps you to decide what exit to use. Bus stops display routes and corresponding bus numbers. Taking the bus is a nice way to see the local scene inexpensively. Each stop is clearly marked. Always validate your ticket in the machine, or show your Carte-Orange or Formula-One card to the driver.

Many visitors buy a Paris-Visite or Formula-One ticket for traveling on public transport. The ticket is valid for 2 to 3 days, beginning when you start using it. It is good for discounts at some tourist attractions and can be used on metro, bus and, RER (train). It can be purchased at the airport and large Metro/RER stations. But the Carte-Orange ticket is more economical if you arrive at the beginning of the week and plan to spend more than three days. It is also valid on the metro, bus, and RER. Meant to be used by the locals, it is valid Monday through Sunday of the week of purchase, and requires a photo. Bring a passport size photo from home, or have one taken in a photo booth in one of the larger stations, so you can purchase your Carte-Orange on arrival. Speak French when you buy it. At the metro ticket booth, ask for a free Carte-Orange, the "weekly" coupon called *hebdomadair*, and the zone- probably one or two. Fill out the coupon. Your photo will be attached. Each time you come to a turnstile you insert the magnetic ticket in the ticket slot. When you enter a bus with either the Carte-Orange or Formula-One, show it to the driver. Don't put the magnetic ticket into the bus validator. You can also buy tickets in a groups of ten. A regular ticket doesn't allow for transfers from metro to bus or viceversa. The metro stop for Camping du Bois de Boulogne is Pont Maillot Metro/RER station within a zone 1-2 ticket.

Street markets aren't usually listed in guidebooks, so here are my favorites. Rue Montorgueil, beginning at Rue Ramuteau, is authentic and a bit grubby; Metro: Les Halles. Rue Mouffetard, beginning at Rue de L'Epee-de-Bois, is popular with tourists because of the lively hawking and jostling. If you walk a little farther, off Rue de l'Arbalete, you can enjoy the intrigue of the African market; Metro:Monge. Rue du Poteau, begins at Place Jules-Joffrin, above Sacre-Coeur, and is one of the prettiest and most elegant; Metro: Jules-Joffrin. Shopping in the food markets is an intensely important to Parisians. It's here, perhaps more vividly than anywhere else in the city, that you're able to see the authentic soul of the city; closed Mondays.

****Camping: * On the northwest edge of the city at the west end of the large park, Bois de Boulogne. Off the Blvd. Peripherique, ring road, exit Porte Maillot. Start driving through the park, at Restaurant l'Oree du Bois on Av. Mahatma Gandhi, in a westerly direction. Stay on this road as it winds through the park, to the Seine River. Then turn south and take the river road, Allee du Bord de L'Eau, to the camping place. It's on the eastside of the Seine River, just north of the Pont Suresnes. Camping Caravaning du Bois de Boulogne, Allee du Bord de l'Eau (01-4524-3000); convenient and very popular; shuttle bus to the metro station; bungalows; well maintained; open yearround; $$$$. *15km southeast of the city, in the suburb of Champigny-sur-Marne. East of the Blvd. Peripherique, ringroad, and Bois de Vincennes, exit A4 (the Paris-Metz road) at exit 5, Nogent Marne/Champigny. Drive south on Bd. De Stalingrad, D/45, to Av. General de Galle (N303) then turn west. At the second stoplight, turn north onto Bd. De Polangis and follow signposting under A4. Camping du Tremblay, (01-4397-4397); traffic noise; bungalows; fair maintenance; open all year; $$$. *18km northwest of Paris in the suburb Maisons-Laffitte, between A14 and A15. Off A13, exit Poissy and go in the direction of Maison-Lafffitte; good signposting. Camping Caravaning International, Rue Johnson (01-3912-2191); bungalows; well maintained; cycle trail along the Seine; close to public transport to city; open all year; $$$$$.

JUST OUTSIDE OF PARIS

VERSAILLES

Passionate to surpass artistic Italy, the Sun King, Louis XIV, transformed his father's hunting lodge into a dazzling, gilded palace. Vast waterways, fountains and sculpture center on Apollo, the Greek sun god. Be in line for tickets by 8 a.m. Hameau de la Reine, Marie Antoinette's play village and Temple of Love, and the smaller palaces Grand and Petit Trianon are at the north end of the vast gardens. You can drive and re-park there, or get in a royal mood by sailing down the grand canal. Directions: Southwest of Paris, exit the Peripherique onto N12 for Versailles. Signposting to the palace and parking is excellent; closed Mondays.

MALMAISON

Home of Napoleon's wife, Empress Josephine, this mansion is small and intimate with a lovely rose garden. The original furnishings and personal possessions of Josephine bring warmth to the famous couple's memory; closed Tuesday. Directions: West of Paris, exit off Peripherique onto E5 and drive seven kilometers in the direction of St. Germain-en-Laye, exiting north at Reuil-Malmaison. The park and residence are on the southwest side of the village close to the river Seine.

CHARTRES

Auguste Rodin wrote that cathedrals "offer man a spectacle of magnificence, both comforting and inspiring; the spectacle of ourselves, the image of our soul, elevated to eternity." Chartres, a queen of cathedrals, exemplifies this spirit. After a devastating fire in 1194, she was reconstructed using the original Gothic plans but benefiting from the new knowledge of flying buttresses. Of her original 186 pictorial stained-glass windows, 152 remain, filling the cathedral on sunny days or at sunset with unearthly light. Bring binoculars; open daily. Directions: About 80km southwest of Paris, exit A11 or N10 for Chartres. Cross over the river Eure, and the massive cathedral will be majestically before you.

PARIS AREA

FONTAINEBLEAU

With a passion to out-do, cause envy, and exude power, Fontainebleau was built and embellished into a lavish spectacle. A visit here bears witness to those desires. Nearby Foret de Fontainebleau makes an appealing, restful setting for walks and cycling; open daily. Directions: Exit south off the Peripherique onto E15. Avoiding the forks for Orly Airport, stay on E15/Autoroute du Soleil. The park/palace complex is well signposted. ****Camping in the area: *50 km southwest of Paris in the Foret Rambouillet, between N12 and N10. On N10 drive in the direction of Rambouillet. Exit for the town and follow signposting. Municipal Camping de l'Etang d'Or (01-3041-0734); lovely setting; well maintained; open all year; $$. *26 km from Paris, close to Versailles, in the suburb of St Quentin-en-Yvelines, at the fork of A12 and N10. Camping Parc Etang (01-3058-5620); near a sportspark and railtracks, good maintenance; open year round; $$$.

NORMANDY

This is off-the-beaten-track countryside with luscious green pastures, aromatic apple orchards, and brown-and-white Norman cows. Roads meander peacefully through tiny villages passing isolated farms selling fruit, cheese, cider, and Calvados at their gates.

MUSEE CLAUDE MONET/GIVERNY

Monet's gardens burst with the exciting colors and textures seen in his paintings. His home, water lilies, dripping wisteria, and Japanese bridge are as they were when he lived here; closed Mondays. Directions: 76km northwest of Paris, half-way to Rouen, exit A/13/E5 for Vernon. Pass

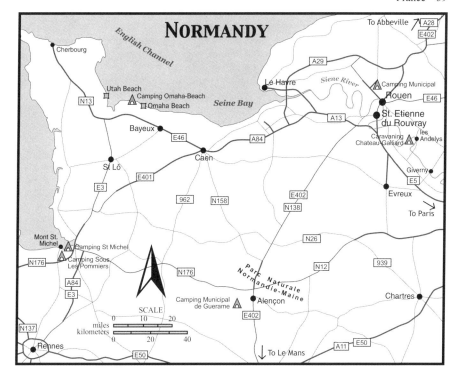

through the little town following signage for seven kilometers to the Musee. ****Camping: *Drive north on the east side of the Seine on 313 for 22km to les Andelys. Then go west, crossing over the Seine to the village of Bernieres-sur-Seine. Caravaning Chateau-Gaillard (02-3254-1820); beautiful setting; well maintained; popular; open April-October; $$$$.

ROUEN

Flamboyant pointed gables, pinnacles, clock towers, and cupolas embellish France's most famous Gothic cathedral. Bells chime throughout the day, filling the air with sweet melodies. Joan of Arc, heroine of France, was martyred in Rouen. Today an immense cross and impressive modern church marks the infamous spot. ****Camping: *Three kilometers northwest of the city in the suburb of Deville-les-Rouen. Follow the signs for A150 out of town, and exit for the suburb. Camping Municipal (3574-0759); traffic noise; well maintained; open all year; $$.

PARC NATUREL REGIONAL NORMANDIE-MAINE

Forests of beech and oak crown the hills and meadows lush with pastureland attract Parisans who want to relax in the timeless beauty here. Canoeing and cycling are popular and rentals are available. Ask at the tourist office in Alecon, pl La Magdelaine. ****Camping: *54km north of Le Mans and A11/E50, off N138 southwest of Alencon on the river Sarthon. Camping Municipal de Guerame (02-3326-3495); nice location; fair maintenance; open May-September; $$.

BAIE DE MONT ST. MICHEL

It's the picturesque setting of the abbey, rising dream-like from tidalflats that is impressive. When the tide rushes in, great masses of birds take to the air. A very photogenic spot, indeed. ****Camping: *Nine kilometers east of Mont St. Michel on D43. Camping St. Michel (02-3370-9690); bungalows; well maintained; open April-September; $$. *Four kilometers south of the abbey on D976, in Beavoir. Camping Sous Les Pommiers (02-3360-1136); bungalows; well maintained; open May-September; $$.

BAYEUX AND THE D-DAY LANDING BEACHES

Wars are never humorous, but finding comedy in them years later is refreshing. A cartoon story of the Norman Invasion was painstaking embroidered nine centuries ago. You can almost hear the giggling embroiders as they stitched their homey, action-filled story. Viewing this at the Musee de la Tapisserie de Bayeux is a lighthearted way to bone up on medieval life. Directions: Follow signs for Centrum off the ring road. The museum is on Rue Nesmond, on the southern edge of the historic area; open daily. Coastal towns in the area have museums with touching memorials for individual troopers. For an overview, drive to Caen and visit Musee Memorial. Then drive or cycle the circuit linking the battle sites. ****Camping: *On the beach in the village of Vierville-sur-Mer. Exit off E46, 15km northwest of Bayeux, for the village and beach. Camping Omaha Beach (02-3122-4173); now a pleasant location; well maintained; open May-August; $$.

BRITTANY

Wildly craggy cliffs, cloud-filled skies, and a tortuous sea give the Bretons a fierce and independent spirit. In tiny villages here ancient stone houses line cobblestone streets and fish markets burst with catch. Along the cliffs, birds soar, screech, and plunge into the spectacu-

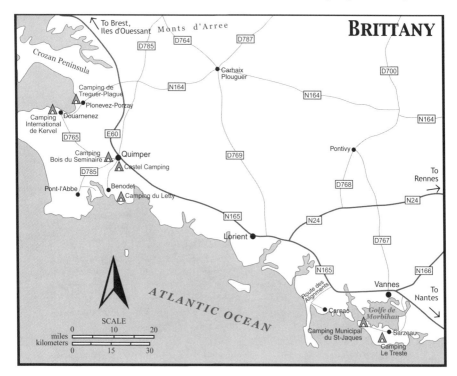

lar sea, while inland, ancient stone megaliths testify to vigorous settlers. The flat terrain makes cycling popular.

QUIMPER

At the Festival de Cornouaille, held the last week in July, Bretons regaled in traditional costumes, celebrate with folk music, dance, and food. On summer Thursday nights, traditional dance and music can be enjoyed behind the cathedral. ****Camping: *West of the historic area, close to the Odet River. Follow signage out of the town for Pont l'Abbe. It's signposted on Rue de Pont l'Abbe. Camping Municipal Bois du Seminaire (9855-6109); popular; fair maintenance; open all year; $$. *South of the city, exit off the ring road. Castel Camping and Caravaning L'Orangerie de Lanniron (02-9890-6202); nice location; excellent maintenance; all the amenities including pool; open June-August; $$$$. *In the town of Benodet, on the Atlantic Ocean in a dune area. Camping du Letty (02-9857-0469); resort-like setting; excellent maintenance; open July and August; $$$$.

PARC REGIONAL D'AMORIQUE

Though relatively small in area, d'Amorique encompasses a wide variety of terrain and natural life. Monts d'Arree is quiet with forests and ancient legends, ferries go to Iles d'Ouessant for bird watching, and the Crozan Penninsula is known for its immense sand dunes. ****Camping: *North of Quimper 24km, in the village of Plonevez-Porzay. Camping de Treguer-Plague (02-9892-5352); nice location by the water; bungalows; all the amenities; fair maintenance; open May-September; $$. *In the same area, Camping International de Kervel (02-9892-5154); resort-like setting; excellent maintenance; open May-September; $$$$.

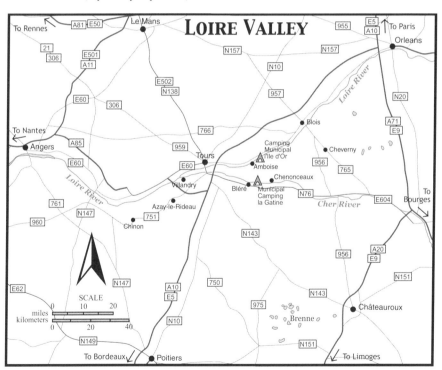

GOLFE DE MORBIHAN

Arms of land embrace the sea here, creating a huge bay where prehistoric man settled. Musee de Prehistoire in Carnac Ville, the Routes des Alignements northeast of Carnac Ville, and the swirl and spiral decorated megalithic stones on the Gavrinis Islands testify to 4500 through 2000 BC settlements. Under starlit skies, a sound and light show adds to the mystique. ****Camping: *On the southwestern tip of the bay, in the village of Sarzeau. Eight kilometers south of Vannes exit west onto 780, the bay road. Drive for about 19km to Sarzeau, then drive out to Pointe St. Jacque. Camping Municipal de St. Jacques (02-97417929); nice location; fair maintenance; open May-September; $$. *In the same area, Camping Le Treste (02-9741-7960); resort-like setting; open May-September; $$$$.

LOIRE VALLEY

Royal France, in the16th century, was filled with gleaming satin, curled wigs, and intrigue. Enjoying books and films set in this era before you leave will make the architecture, furnishings and gardens come alive. This valley has a flat terrain, excellent for cycling. The south side of the Loire

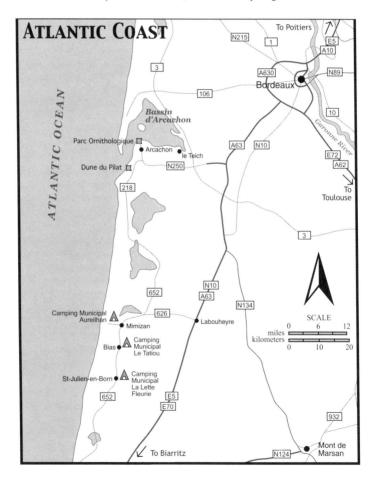

River is most picturesque. The most romantic of the chateau are Chenonceau and Azay-le-Rideau. Gardeners will want to see Villandry. And historians won't want to miss Chateau de Bois. Antique buffs should not bypass Chateau de Cheverny. Entrance fees are high, so be selective. Gardens and exteriors are often the best part. For medieval fanfare, crafts, and food, arrange to be in Chinon either on the first or third weekend in August. For diversion from castles, take a look at the exciting collections of racing cars in Le Mans. ****Camping: *In Amboise, by the bridge over the river east of town. Camping Municipal l'Ile d'Or (03-4757-2337); nice location with view of the castle; popular with families; open May-August; $$. *Southeast of Tours 26km on N76, in Blere by the Cher bridge. Municipal Camping la Gatine (02-4757-9260); nice location; popular with families; swimming pool; open May-September; $$.

ATLANTIC COAST

ARCAHON

Dunes, beaches, and sun attract locals here like bees to honey. Surfers love the area where the waves and scene are the best in France. Dune du Pilat found eight kilometers south of Arcahon, is the highest dune in Europe and fun to climb. Take a canoe trip into the wetlands of Bassin d'Arcachon and Parc Ornithologique, where little streams twist and turn jungle-like amidst lush swamp-loving plants and water birds. Boats leave from Le Teich. ****Camping: Less expensive camping is at the south end. Drive 60km to Labouheyre on A63/N10. *Exit towards beach on 626 in the direction of Mimizan. Camping Municipal Aureilhan (05-5809-1088). *South from Mimizan for seven kilometers to Bias. Camping Municipal Le Tatiou (05-5809-0476) *Ten kilometers farther south on 652, in St. Julien-en-Born. Camping Municipal La Lette Fleurie (05-5842-7409). All of these have good maintenance and are open June-September; $$.

FRENCH BASQUE COUNTRY

BAYONNE

Devishly hansome men, attired only in white except for red scarves around their necks, daringly chase cattle through town during the Fete de Bayonne. The five-day festival begins on the first Wednesday in August. Music, floats, and bullfights add up to a very lively scene.

ST. JEAN PIED DE PORT

Wide overhanging roofs line the narrow street climbing up to the ancient citadel here, an important stop on the pilgrimage route to Santiago de Compostela. From the citadel, absorb the view of backyard gardens, the valley, and Pyrenees. Enjoy warm evenings with locals at the sports field, where beret-topped heads of elders watch stony-faced, every nuance of the younger men as they play pelota. Observe the subtleties between the farmers and buyers selling goats, pigs and sheep at the Marche Couvert on Monday mornings. ****Camping: *On the river Nive by the sports field. Municipal Camping Plaza Berri (05-5937-1119); nicely located on the river; fair maintenance; open May-September $$. *One kilometer west of the village. Europ Camping (05-5937-1278); resort-like; nice location; well maintained, open May -September; $$$$.

GORGES DE KAKOUETTA

Sculpted during the ice age, the gorge now has riverside trail. This is an easy 2-3 hour walk with dramatic cliffs lining the ever-narrowing passage into a fairyland of mosses, ferns, delicate orchids, rushing river, and waterfalls; admission fee; open daily Easter-October. A spider-web of backroads wind through the scenic countryside where handpainted signs on farmyard gates advertise homemade cheese. Purchase supplies, gas and have local currency before you start.

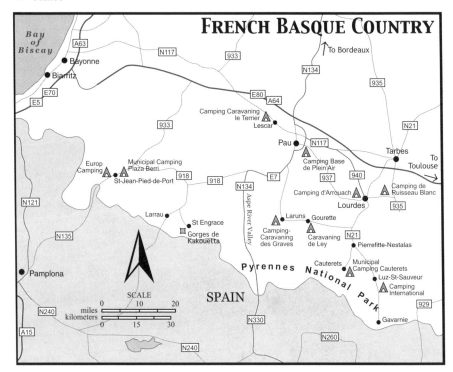

Directions: Exit N134 two kilometers south of Asasp onto 1918 in the direction of Aramits and drive 12km.   Continue three kilometers to Lanne and then eight kilometers to Tardets.   Follow signposting for Larrau for five kilometers to a fork. Take D113 for Larrau and St Engrace. The entrance to the gorge is just west out of the village of St. Engrace, very close to the Spanish border.   Plan to spend the day because after your gorge walk you can walk along a stone walled road into little almost forgotten villages that cling to softly sculpted mountainsides.   Your hike will be enhanced by the jangle of cow bells, meticulous vegetable gardens, a Roman church, and waves to the villagers. *****Camping: Five kilometers past Tardets in the direction of the gorge in Lico. Calamity Jane Camping; wonderful location on the river; popular with cyclists; swimming grotto with deep pools and warm boulders; small cafe; simple; casual maintenance; open May-September; $.   In the same area, farther up the road to the gorge.   Camping Ibarra (05-59-28-7359) better for RVs, scenic setting on the river; fair maintenance; open April-October; $$.

PYRENNES NATIONAL PARK

Near the park, rolling foothills are sweet-smelling with rolled hay. Whitewashed farmhouses, hunched under heavy stone roofs, and diminutive village churches with three-pointed belfries sparkle in the sunlight. The rushing rivers, grassy meadows, and tinkling streams tumbling from turbulent peaks and crevasses refresh hikers on the park's trails. Directions: Drive southwest from Pau on E7, then south on N134 to the Aspe River and Valley and the Pyrennes National Park. From Lourdes drive 50km south on N21, continuing out of Cauterets on 920 up to the park entrance. South of town chairlifts go up to Pont d'Espagne and Lac de Gaube. Donkey rides up to the mountain amphitheatre, Cirque de Garvarnie, leave out of village of Gavarnie. To get there, take the smaller road off N21 at the village of Pierrefitte-Nestalas and go 40km to Gavarnie. ****Camping :*In Laruns, at the east end of the Route des Pyrenees on 934. Thermale Camping-Caravaning des Graves (05-5905-3237); nice location; well maintained; open all year; $$$. *For mountain camping, drive east out of Laruns up the mountain to the tiny hamlet of Gourette. Caravaning de Ley (05-5905-1147); well maintained; open July-August; $$. *In Catuterets, drive north of D312. Municipal Camping Catuterets, Av. De Mamelon Vert; lovely location; fair maintenance; open June-August $$. *North of Gavarnie, 20km in the village of Luz St. Sauveur. Camping International (05-6292-8202); beautiful location; well cared for; open June-August; $$$.

PAU
Beloved by the English, this city gleams with elegant parks and apartments. In early morning, drive up the Blvd. Des Pyrenees to be dazzled by the light and shadow of the writhing peaks of the Pyrenees. ****Camping: *Two kilometers south of the city on 937, in the direction of Nay Bourdettes. Camping Base de Plein Air (05-5906-5737); convenient; well maintained; open May-September; $$. *Northwest of the city nine kilometers, on the south side of A64/E80 in the suburb of Lescar, close to the bridge. Camping Caravaning le Terrier (05-5981-0182); convenient; well maintained; open all year; $$$.

LOURDES
After seeing the famous Bascilica and Grotto, join the nightly torch-lit procession of singing pilgrims. It starts at 8:30 p.m. at the Esplanade du Rosaire. If you are going into the Pyrenees, stop at the Musee Pyreneen. It's housed in a chateau perched high on the rocky bluff on the east side of the river and sanctuaires on Rue Bourg and has a fascinating collection of maps, equipment and photos from the pioneer hikers; open daily. ****Camping: *Two kilometers east of the city on 937 in the direction of Bagneres-de-Bigorre. Camping de Ruisseau Blanc (05-6242-9483); nice location; fair maintenance; open April-October; $. *one kilometer northwest of the city on 940 in the direction of Pau. Camping d'Arrouach (05-6294-2575); nice location; simple; fair maintenance; open all year; $$.

DORDOGNE VALLEY/LANGUEDOC
About 20,000 years ago, people lived here with amazing elegance and simplicity. Evidence of their ice age existence was found in the now world-famous Les Eyzies-de-Tayac caves. Today, the most famous of the cave drawings from Lascaux are protected for scientific study. Musee National de Prehistoire is an invaluable source of information; closed Mondays. At Font de Gaume the exciting10,000-year-old drawings are displayed; book ahead (53-0697-48); closed Tuesday. Painstaking care was given to the reconstruction of Lascaux II, a replica of the original cave; open daily in July and August otherwise closed Monday. Book head for tickets at the tourist office in Montignac. Floating down the Dordogne or Vezere Rivers in a canoe or kayak or your innertube brought from home is a kick. Sarlet-la-Caneda is a beautiful medieval town with a large Saturday market bustling with activity. Wild truffles are a speciality. ****Camping: It's expensive but there are plenty of places. *North of Sarlet-la-Caneda on D47. Camping les Terrasses du Perigord (05-5359-0225); beautiful location; well cared for; open May-September; $$$$.

PARC NATUREL REGIONAL DU HAUT-LANGUEDOC
The mesmerizing drone of the cicadas, the fragrance of wild thyme, the outcrops of rocks too steep for vegetation, and the red tile-roofed houses in tiny forgotten villages make a Greek-like melange. Spelunkers flock to the park, because many of the caves were first explored in modern times by their hero Edouard-Alfred Martel. ****Camping: *Exit N112 at St Pons-de-Thomieres,

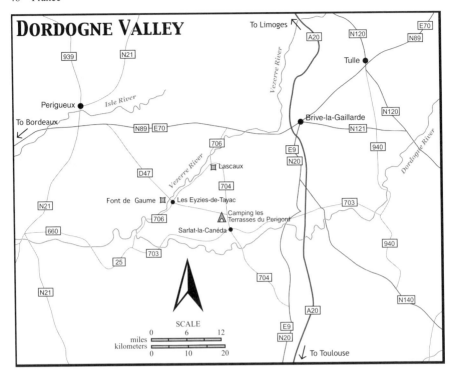

DORDOGNE VALLEY

To Limoges
E70
A20
N120
N89
939
N21
Tulle
Isle River
Perigueux
N120
To Bordeaux
N89 E70
Brive-la-Gaillarde
N121
706
E9
940
N20
D47
Vezerre River
Lascaux
704
N21
Font de Gaume   Les Eyzies-de-Tayac
703
706
Camping les
Terrasses du Perigord
660
Sarlat-la-Canéda
940
703
25
704
N21
N140
A20
SCALE
E9
miles   0   6   12
N20
kilometers
0   10   20
To Toulouse

and drive north up the mountain on D907 to St. Pons and the park headquarters. Then leave D907 and drive west on a small road to Angles. Hotel Camping le Manoir de Boutaric (05-6370-9606); lovely remote location; swimming pool; open May-September; $$$$.

CARCASSONNE

It's easy to conjure up images of Robin Hood and his gang while walking across the drawbridge and into this ancient walled city. Come late in the day and then stay for the evening lighting of the ramparts. ****Camping: *Exit for Cite off A61/E80. There is signposting close to the river. Campeole La Cite (04-6825-1177); convenient; well maintained; open April-September; $$. *Drive north out of the city on D118 to the suburb of Villemoutaussou. Camping Das Pinhiers (04-6847-8190); good for kids; swimming pool; nice location; open May-September; $$.

GORGE DU TARN

To float down the Tarn River through this majestic gorge is a delight. From the put-in at St. Enimie, it's 14km to the take-out at La Malene. Rent a kayak or canoe or use your innertube brought from home. The gorge starts seven kilometers north of Millau. Exit east at Aguessac onto D907. The road follows the river so you can check out the water as you drive. There are seasonal camping places in the area.

ALBI

Toulouse-Lautre's home and a large collection of his works are here at the Palais de la Berbie next to the Cathedrale St. Cecile. His favorite subject was the Moulin Rouge and its neighborhood.

Many of his works are humorous, making this pilgrimage amusing. ****Camping: *East of town in the direction of the suburb St. Jury. Camping Caravaning du Languedoc (05-6360-3706); convenient; well maintained; open May-October; $$.

BURGUNDY

Blazing yellow fields of mustard spread across rolling hills of carefully manicured, centuries-old vineyards. Here and there small villages hug the scarred and crumbling ruins of an empire whose abbeys are testimonies to power and wealth.

BEAUNE

Like a precious jewel in a lovely pin, Beaune sits still rich and charming, in the center of Burgandy. Hotel-Dieu, a 15th-century hospital with a deeply pitched, multicolored tile-roof is justifiably the town's prize attraction; open daily. The Musee du Vin tells the whole story of wine making, from planting the grapevines to uncorking the bottle; open daily. Wander through the dusty cellars sampling wine from upturned barrels at Marche aux Vins; open daily.

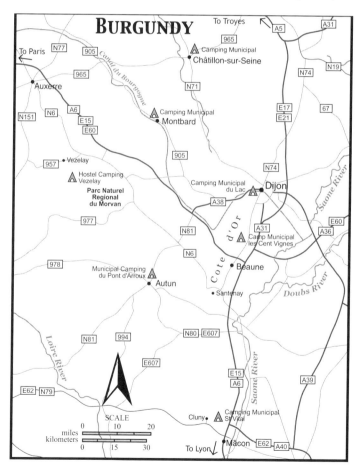

COTE D'OR

To see the vines and visit the wineries of some of France's most famous wines, drive from Dijon to Beaune on N74. This route winds through the Cote d'Or.

DIJON

Palais des Ducs, once the home of the powerful, now houses an outstanding collection of art. Don't miss the room where designer Sambin's work is exhibited; closed Tuesdays. The International Fetes de la Vigne celebrates the grape harvest in early fall.

****Camping in the Area: *Drive north out of Beaune through Porte Saint Nicolas on N74 towards Dijon. Camp Municipal les Cent Vignes, close to Eglise St. Nicolas (03-8022-0391); convenient; well maintained; open May-September; $$. *On the Canal de Bourgogne, off 905 in Montbard at the northwest end of town. Camping Municipal Montard (8092-2160); convenient; well maintained; open March-September; $$. *In Chatillon-sur-Seine at the junction of N71 and 965. Close to the town's swimming pool and park. Camping Municipal Chatillon-sur-Seine (8091-0305); convenient; good maintenance; open May-September; $$. *On the west side of Dijon, signposted off A38, about one kilometer west of the train station. Camping Municipal du Lac, 3 Bld. Chanoine Kir (8043-5472); convenient; well maintained; open May-September; $$.

ABBEY OF CLUNY

Quiet and majestic, this abbey was once an immensely powerful force in France. Today it is an evocative place. ****Camping: *East of town off E15. Camping Municipal St. Vital (03-8559-0834); nice location; well cared for; open June-September; $$.

PARC NATUREL REGIONAL DU MORVAN

Hawks, buzzards and falcons flap slowly in the cool morning air. In the afternoon they circle on outstretched wings making great arcs high in the sky above this wooded countryside clothed in a cloak of green meadows and yellow vetch. Vezelay, a medieval village, sits at the top of a hill, gem-like. ****Camping: *Down the hill from Vezelay, drive south on a small road in the direction of L'Etang. Hostel Camping Vezelay (03-86-332-418); simple; open Jun-August; $$. *In Autun on the Ternin River just north of the Pont d'Arroux. Municipal Camping du Pont d'Arroux (03-8552-1082); nice location; fair maintenance; open May-September; $$.

WESTERN PROVENCE

Aromatic with lavender, graceful with silver-green olive trees, and brilliant under blue skies this countryside was too splendid for the conquering Romans to leave. Instead they graced the towns with art, architectural and technical achievements, and culture.

ORANGE

Orange still hosts grand music festivals in its magnificent Roman theatre. Known for it lively and fun loving spirit, this town is easy to have a good time in. ****Camping: *Ten kilometers north of the city in the town of Mornas. Camping Club Beauregard (04-9037-0208); bungalows; swimming pool; tennis; well maintained; open all year; $$$.

AVIGNON

One of the liveliest summer French festivals, Festival d'Avignon, is held here in July and August. The main festival features mostly theatre productions, while Festival Off has an avant-garde pro-

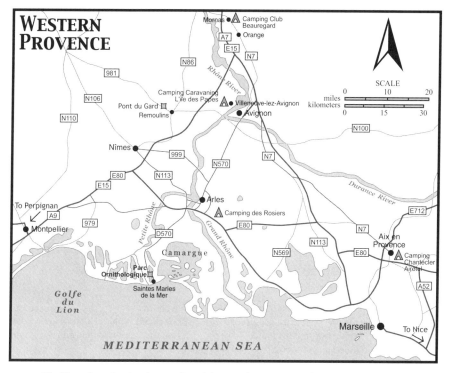

gram. You'll need to plan in advance, buy tickets, and reserve camping. Avignon is a walled city and is dominated by the huge edifice of the Palais des Popes. ****Camping: *Just north of the historic area, across the Pont Daladier exit onto Chemin de la Barthelasse. Camping Municipal Pont-Saint-Benezet (04-9082-6350); beautiful location with great views of the Palais des Popes; well cared for; open April-September; $$$$. *Closer to bridge, Camping and Hotel Bagatelle (04-9086-3039); convenient; good maintenance; open all year; $$$. *Five kilometers northwest of Avignon in the town of Villeneuve-lez-Avignon, exit off D980. TCS Camping Caravaning L'ile des Papes (04-9015-1590); resort-like; bungalows; swimming pool; open May-September; $$$$.

PONT DU GARD

To enjoy the breathtaking achievement of this world-famous Roman aqueduct, rent a canoe and paddle up the river. Directions: 27km north of Nimes, exit A9 for Remoulins and drive northwest for four kilometers.

AIX-EN-PROVENCE

Bursting with rosy-hued peaches, vibrant tomatoes, aromatic basil, and farm-fresh cheese, the morning market in Aixe-en-Provence still takes place in its centuries-old location, the Place Richelme. Drive to the center of the old town, find parking, and follow the ladies with shopping bags. Cezanne loved this countryside and its people. His last studio, Atelier Paul Cezanne, can be visited; closed Monday and Tuesday. Directions: Go north out the market area, up the hill on Avenue Pasteur to 9 Ave Paul Cezanne. ****Camping:*Exit A8 at Aix Est/Les 3 Sautets. Camping Chantecler Airotel(04-4226-1298); nice location; well maintained; bungalows; swimming pool; open all year; $$$$.

THE CAMARGUE

As the Rhone passes into the Mediterranean, it is snuggled in the open arms of the Camargue. In this estuary songs of birds fill the air as they feed on this great abundance of farmlands. Flamingoes, herons, and egrets quietly nibble in the salt flats. The light is different here. Van Gogh loved it, and so did the Romans who settled here.

ARLES

Arles was Rome's first settlement in France. Loving the warm, star-filled summer nights, the Romans built a beautiful stone arena here. It is still well preserved. For a memorable evening, sit under the canopy of stars and enjoy open-air dance and musical performances at the Theatre Antique, just south of the Roman Arena. During the day explore the vine-covered slopes amid sunflowers facing the sun. Then wander down the narrow alleyways in town and you'll understand why Van Gogh fell in love with Arles. At Parc Ornithologique flocks of flamingoes, their bills held up-side-down, swing from side to side feasting in the algae rich waters. In the morning or evening light, bird song, and the smell of marshland create an especially dramatic environment; open daily. Directions: Drive south 38km on D570 in the direction of Saintes-Maries-de-la-Mer. ****Camping: *Drive east from the city on N453 in the direction of Pont-de-Crau. It is close to EUROPA-Hotel. Camping des Rosiers (9096-0212); convenient; fair maintenance; open April-September; $$.

THE PROVENCE

Steeped in sun and all that it brings, the Provence can be lovely. Seductive with color and aroma, street markets overflow with abundance, just like the beautiful people who stroll along the beach. Bougainvillaea and mimosa drip off the decks of fine villas, cafes line the beach, and if you go inland you'll find little villages where you can relax quietly in the sun.

GORGES DU VERDON

This is a small Grand Canyon-like gorge. Steep hiking trails lead off the narrow roadway from sheer drops. But the refreshing river at the bottom rewards you. The hub of the area centers in the village of Castellane. White water rafting is arranged with Aqua Verdon, bungee jumping with Latitude Challenge, and expert cyclists ride the whole route. To find it on the map, look between Aix-en-Provence and Grasse and then a bit north. Several routes lead to the Gorge. N85 is the most popular route. From the west, exit A51 at exit 21 Aubignosc and drive east in the direction of Digne-les-Bains on route de la Lavande. From the south drive north out of Grasse on N85 taking the Route Napoleon. ****Camping: These all have small swimming pools. * Just south of Cassellane on D952. Camp des Gorges du Verdon (04-9283-6364); beautiful location with view of the river; fair maintenance; open June-August; $$$. * South of town on N85. Sites-et-Paysages-Camping (04-9283-6896); nice location; popular with families; excellent maintenance; open June-August; $$$$. *North of town on N85. Camping International (04-9283-6667); nice location; popular with families; good for RV's; well maintained, open June-August; $$$$.

PARC NATIONAL MERCANTOUR

Resting on your back here, under a sweet-smelling pine, you might spot the living metaphor of wild country, the golden eagle. Watch for it soaring high in the air or launching from a rocky ledge with a flapping of wings that can span over two meters. Spotting prey they plummet at high speeds grabbing the prize in their powerful talons. The park is the largest eagle nesting area in France. Sunny and arid, the narrow reserve stretches to the Italian Alps. Archeology enthusiasts come to explore the Vallee des Merveilles and the Cirque de Fontanable. Over 100,000 prehistoric open-air engravings

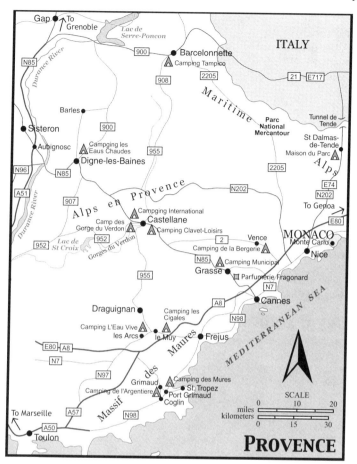

have been found dating from 1800 to 1500 BC. They are not obvious. Consider hiring a guide in St. Dalmas-de-Tende for best viewing. Directions: South end of the park, close to the town of Tende on E74/N204. ****Camping: In Barcelonnette. *Southwest of town on D902. Camping Tampico (04-9281-0255); bungalows; well maintained; open all year; $$. *Eight kilometers west of town on D900; popular with hang gliders; near the river; excellent maintenance; open all year; $$$. *In Dalmas-de-Tende go to the park office to get information for camping in the park. Mercantour Park Camping.

MASSIF DES MAURES

Enchanting hilltop towns, vineyards, chestnut trees, and pines wrap around the Massif which stretches inland and east from Toulon. In the ancient village of Collobrieres, cork and chestnuts are prepared for market. In Grimaud, freshly baked bread from the La Chartreuse de la Verne Monastery's ovens is aromatic and delicious. Medieval La Garde-Freinet hosts street markets on Wednesday and Sunday. Cogolin has artisan studios that can be visited. ****Camping: *Off A8 at exit 36, drive west on N7 along the river to Les Arcs. Camping L'Eau Vive (04-9447-4066); popular with kayakers and families; fair maintenance; open April-September; $$$$. *Off the same exit drive south to Le Muys. Sites-et-Paysages-Camping Les Cigales (04-9445-1208); traffic noise; well maintained, open May-September; $$$$. *In Cogolin off D48 in the direction of St-Maur. Camping de l"Argentiere (04-9454-5786); nice location; swimming pool; tennis; fair maintenance; open May-September; $$$. *At Port-Grimaud, just north of town off N98. Camping des Mures (04-9456-1697); close to the beach; nice location; well maintained; open April-September; $$$$.

GRASSE

Sniffing expensive perfume then breathing in fresh air at the ancient and colorful square, Place des Aires, makes a sensuous fusion. Go to where the real essence is produced, the Parfumerie Fragonard. Directions: Drive three kilometers outside of town toward Cannnes to Les Quatre Chemins. ****Camping: Camping Municipal Grasse, on D111 towards Digne (04-9336-2869); convenient; fair maintenance; open May-September; $$.

VENCE

The light, color, and sensuality of the Cote d'Azur were an irresistible allure to impressionist artists. At Fondation Maeght there is a grand display of their art; open daily. Directions: From Vence take the small road south to St. Paul de Vence. Matisse's final masterpiece is at the Chapelle du Rosaire; open Tuesday and Thursday. Directions: North out of town on Route St. Jeannet, 466 Av. Henri-Matisse. ****Camping: *Southwest of town in the direction of St. Paul. Camping Domaine de la Bergerie (04-9358-0936); popular; fair maintenance; open April-September; $$.

****Camping along the Cote d'Azur: *Expensive resort-like campgrounds dot the coastline.

THE ALPS AND JURA

Massive peaks tower dramatically here above grassy meadows that are cheerful with a host of wild flowers. From the top of a mountain, accessible by cablecar, the light is remarkable and the distant peaks seem close. Alpine villages nestle in the luscious grass. From woods of larch, beech, and pine it is easy to spot a marmot, if alarmed they utter a loud shrill whistle. The famous Grande Randonnee Trail stretches the full length of the Alps, from the Jura to the Mediterranean.

ALPES DE PROVENCE

Hidden in the limestone of Digne-les-Bains is the largest geological reserve in Europe. The Centre de Geologie's exhibits and videos make a good first stop; open daily. Directions: Leave Grenoble on N85 in the direction of Gap/Sisteron. Continue to the north end of Digne-les-Bains. Alexandra David-Neel's incognito and solo (except for her guide), travels to Tibet in 1924 made her famous. Her home, visited twice by the Dalai Lama, is open to the public. Directions: Drive one kilometer out of town on the road to Nice. Watch for signage for Samten Dzong. ****Camping: *Off N85 close to town. Camping les Eaus Chaudes (04-9232-3104); thermal baths close by; good maintenance; open May-September; $$.

PARC NATUREL REGIONAL DU VERCORS

Mount Aiguille or Needle Mountain, stands majestically over a sea of the finger-like protrusions of Vercors. Its natural labyrinthine of limestone tunnels protected resistance fighters during World War II. Spectacular scenery surrounds the drive through the park. Directions: Located between Valence and Grenoble, exit off A49/E713 at St. Nazaire-en-Royans onto D532. Drive east on D531. Gorge de la Bourne and Gorges du Meaudret are part of the loop drive. ****Camping: *At the south end of the park, at the intersection of D518 and D93 in the town of Die. Camping La Pinede (04-7522-1777); popular with families; well maintained; open June-August; $$$. *In the same area, exit off D93 at the village of Verchany. Camping Les Acacias (04-7521-7251); on the river; popular with kayakers; well maintained,;

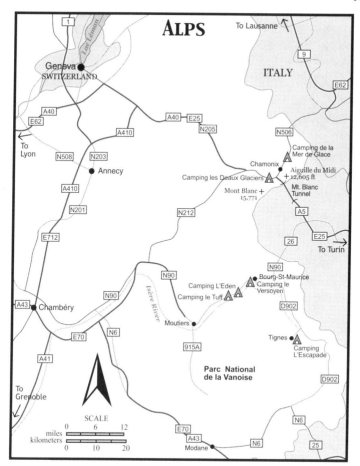

open May-September; $$$. *At the north end of the park on N532, in St. Paul-les-Romans. Camping Municipal de Romans (04-7572-3527); convenient; fair maintenance; open May-September; $$$.

LYON

Many of France's best chefs have apprenticed in Lyon. It's a place of pilgrimage for people involved with food and wine. In the late afternoon, wandering around the old town, you'll sniff enticing aromas drifting out of the kitchens' back doors. ****Camping: *North of the city, exit off A6 for Anse. It's close to the junction of A6 and A46. Camping Les Portes du Beaujolais (04-7467-1287); nice location on the Rhone River; well cared for; open all year; $$$. *South of the city, exit A6 for Vienne-Nord in the suburb of Vernioz. Camping du Bontemps (04-7457-8352); nice location in a park; swimming pool; tennis; well cared for; open May-September; $$$.

PARC NATIONAL DE LA VANOISE

Now a refuge of the Alpine ibex, Vanoise was France's first national park. Its peaks are the biggest in the Alp range. The protected meadows glow with an overwhelming profusion of flow-

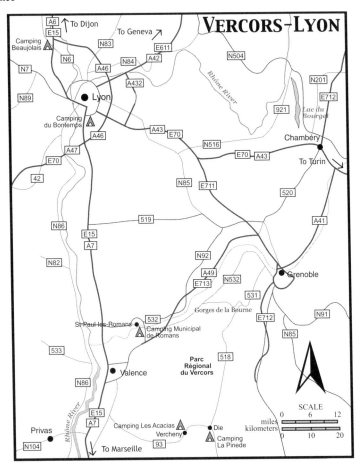

ers. ****Camping: *Off the Routes des Grandes Alpes N90, northeast of Moutiers in the village of Centron. Camping le Tuff (04-7955-6732); beautiful location on the river; well maintained; open June-August; $$$. *In the same area, Camping-Caravaneige L'Eden (04-7907-6181); close to chairlifts and river; swimming pool; excellent maintenance; open June-August; $$$$. *At the north end of the park at the intersection of D902 and N90, in Bourg-St. Maurice. Camping le Versoyen (04-7907-0345); nice location; well maintained; open June-September; $$. *On the east side off D902, in Tignes-les-Brevieres. Camping Europeen L'Escapade (04-7906-4127); beautiful location; close to a chairlift; small swimming pool; open June-August; $$.

MONT BLANC/CHAMONIX

The cable car ride to Aiguille du Midi from Chamonix is exciting. Because the mountains often cloud over by noon, arrange to be at the top by 9 or 10 a.m. Book tickets ahead, or arrive at the ticket booth by 7 a.m. To view the Mer de Glace and Grotto, a huge glacier and cave, buy additional tickets for the cog railway from Gare du Montenvers and for the cable car to the Grotto. Directions: The station for the cable car to Aiguille is on the south side of the river off Route des

Pelerins. In the village of Col. Des Montes, the Reserve des Aiguilles Rouges provides a pleasant botanical walk. Directions: Route des Nantes north out of town. ****Camping: *Three kilometers south of Chamonix, signposted off N205. Camping les Deux Glaciers (04-5053-1584); beautiful location; well maintained; open all year; $$. *North of Chamonix in the village of Les Praz. Camping de la Mer de Glace (04-5053-0863); beautiful location; well maintained; open May-August; $$$$.

THE JURA

Tinkling cow bells, torrential waterfalls, and cool caves where the famous comte cheeses age all await the visitor in the Jura. The word for forest, in the language of the Gauls is Jura and today timber and skillfully worked wood are still important sources of income. Because the limestone soil has revealed outstanding fish and dinosaur fossils, scientists named the Jurassic period after this region. For a scenic drive or cycling, follow the Doubs River on D437. A good place to start is at Pontarlier. On the route, stop at the Langoulette Gorge, the Defile d'Entre-Roche, Villers le Lac, and the waterfall Saut du Doubs. ****Camping: *South of Pontarlier on the lake. Camping Caravaning Municipal de St. Point-Lac (03-8169-6164); nice location; popular with families; well maintained; open June-August; $$.

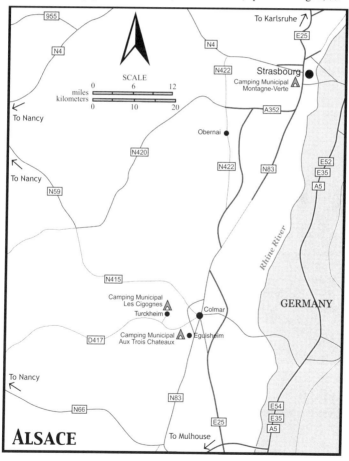

ALSACE

Half-timbered houses bursting with geranium-filled window boxes and a rolling countryside neatly planted with grapes make Alsace ideal for relaxing and cycling. Strasbourg is refined and graceful, with interesting museums and cathedrals. Colmar's cobblestone streets and sweet bridges are perfect for photographs. And winding through it all is the wine route where there are plenty of places to sample the product. All through the summer, wine festivals and street markets enliven the friendly ambiance. ****Camping: *West of Colmar off D417, along the Rhine River in the village of Turckheim. Camping Municipal Les Cigognes (03-8927-0200); beautiful location; well cared for; open April-September; $$. *South of Colmar in town of Eguisheim, off N83. Camping Municipal Aux Trois Chateaux (03-8923-1939); nice location; well cared for; open May-August; $$. *South of Strasbourg in the suburb of Montagne-Verte, exit #4 off A35. Camping Montagne-Verte (03-8830-2546); traffic noise; convenient; open all year; $$.

LORRAINE

Lorraine's wide plains echo with the memories of war and the troops of Julius Caesar, Charlemagne, Napoleon, and Hitler. Spend some time in the Musee Memorial de Fleury where the basement holds a reconstruction of the once shell-torn village. Afterwards, go see to the battle-fields at Verdun. ****Camping: *South of Verdun near D34. Camping les Breuils (03-2986-1531); convenient; well maintained; open May-September; $$.

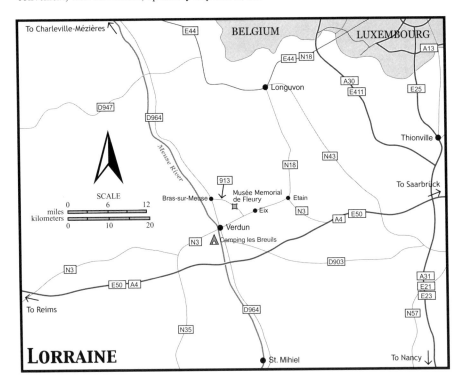

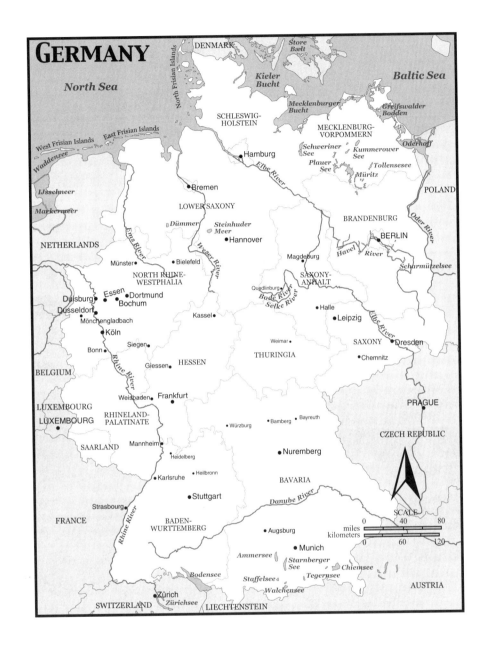

GERMANY

Passionate to learn, create, and excel Germans strive to be a model of modern society. Their passion for the arts has filled their museums with fabulous, artistically presented collections. Lovers of music and frivolity, their summer festivals, symphony halls, churches, cathedrals, and beer halls are all delightful. Their cities burst with a multicultural mix of exotic flavors and colors created by the job opportunities from their profitable industries. Proud of the best of their legacy, the country spends immense sums on restoration and exhibitions. Avid for the outdoors, the country is laced with walking/hiking/cycling trails, and recreational equipment is readily available for rental.

The Germans are trail-blazing campers. Campgrounds are easy to find, well maintained, beautifully located, and popular. Locals set up large tent vacation homes on sites they lease in the campgrounds, spending time in them on holidays and weekends. The owners of the campgrounds like the extra income from those of us who stay only a short time, but it's easy to feel like an intruder at a private club. I've found that if I compliment their gardens, children, and pets in German they smile and we can have a little conversation. Campground rules include being quiet in the morning and during the afternoon nap time. Being neat and tidy also brings a star of approval. I make an extra effort to keep the shower-toilet area clean after use, and I check my camping place thoroughly before leaving to make sure it's clean, too. Thursday through Saturday, it's wise to check in by 2 or 3 p.m. On Fridays, if you're close to the cities or popular recreation areas, check in by 11 a.m. Reception areas in smaller campgrounds may be closed for a long lunch. About $20 USA will cover the cost for two persons, a car, and tent in most places. Resort-like campgrounds and those located in popular areas will cost just over $25 USA.

Because the Germans are leaders in the building of vast, efficient roadways, you won't find getting around hard. Use the fast lanes with caution and only for passing. A car that seems a long way back is suddenly right behind you. Good navigating skills will make your life on the road easier. Even though signage is excellent, traffic moves quickly, leaving little time for indecision. Be particularly cautious around trams, where the pedestrian has the right of way. Pedestrians also have the right of way at crosswalks, as do cyclists in cycle lanes. A fixed green arrow on a red traffic light allows you to turn in that direction after coming to a full stop. Germans are serious about their rules. On spot ticketing and fine paying keeps it this way. Autobahn signs are blue, and the number is preceded by A. International roadway signs are green with a preceding E. Secondary roads have a preceding B. Gas stations abound; most open early and close late. Adjoining mini-markets and cafes provide modern conveniences. Emergency phones are placed along roadways with pictorial instructions. Your roadway insurance from home is respected. Roadway attendants probably won't speak English, but gestures and a phrase book or dictionary will probably suffice.

Parking is handled efficiently. At tourist and market areas, parking payment is often made at a centrally located ticket dispenser. Keep change handy for them. The cost of parking is about the same as it is at home. Large car parks are found just outside the conjested areas and public transportation close by. Bringing your bike from home to pedal through the historic areas and countryside is rewarding. You'll join the locals.

BERLIN

Because of the long-held German passion for art and archeology, Berlin is home to some of the world's most outstanding collections. Artistically displayed in their grand museums, the collections can be overwhelming if you aren't selective. Tree-lined boulevards and brilliantly colored flowerbeds soften the gargantuan monuments and buildings. Whimiscal Tiergarten Park, sitting right in the middle of it all, is filled with raffish youngsters on skateboards, Turkish women in colorful scarves enjoying barbecues, sunbathers stretched lazily on grassy meadows, mothers chatting as they push baby strollers, and kids trying to perfect their skill on bicycles. Locals go out of their way

To Hamburg
E55 E26 10
96 ↑ To Baltic
E251 ↑ Coast
109
To Finowurt, Oberuckersee
E55
10
E26
111
E55
E28
10
2
11
SCALE
0   2.5   5
miles
kilometers
0   4   8
273
5
Tegeler See
Spree
Schloss
Charlottenburg
100
Tiergarten
Central Berlin
2
Trebelsee
DDC Campingplatz
Berlin-Kladow
Kladow
100
Flughafen
Berlin-Tempelhof
Spree
1   5
E55
10
Schlänitzsee
Havel
BRANDENBURG
BERLIN
Grosse Muggelsee
Grosse Zernsee
BERLIN
BRANDENBURG
Teltowkanal
E55
10
Pottsdam
Havel River
Dreilinden
Campingplatz
Hettler under Lange
DDC Camping
am Krossinsee
Schmockwitz
Langer See
Camping
Sanssouci-Gaisberg
B1
Templiner See
Caputh
Campingplatz
Himmelreich
Flughafen
Berlin-Schönefeld
Zeuthener See
Wernsdorf
Glindow See
Camping
Riegelspitze
E51
115
Schwielowsee
E55
E30
10
B2
113
Zernsdorf
To Slubice
E51
To Leipzig
E30 E55 10
BERLIN-POTSDAM
13
E36 ↓ To Dresden
Krupelsee

to help you find your way and it's easy to chat with them in a museum or cafe. Beautiful and stimulating, it's a hard city to leave. Bring a good guidebook and visit the excellent tourist information offices, particularly the one at Europa Center. Only a few museums will be open on Mondays, and most are reasonably priced. It's an easy city to enter and park, and bicycles are a terrific way to get around. Directions: From 100, exit onto 1/96-Potsdamer Str.; follow signposting to Kulturforum, where there are parking areas. Or exit 100 onto 2/5 Ost-Bismark Str./17 Juni, and drive to Tiergarten Park, where there's parking at the northeast end on the edge of the Spree River.

Highest priority should be given to the Pergamonmuseum. I suggest going straight for the antiquities on the first floor in order to view the enormous Pergamon Altar, excavated in Bergama, Turkey. The energy exuding from the freize, depicting a battle between gods and giants, is masterful. On the second floor, the collection from the Middle East stars the Ishtar Gate and Processional Way, a huge Babylon piece from the 6th century BC. Reconstructed around original pieces, it's very impressive. Its original size and importance can be appreciated when you look at the intricate model. This immense museum is fascinating. Take it in steps, with rests in between. Recorded sound tracks and texts in English are available. In this same area you'll find the Alte Nationalgalerie, housing Germany's most important collection of art from the 18th and 19th centuries. Peeking in to see the lovely Roman Rotunda is free. The Bodemuseum, also in this area, is undergoing large-scale renovation; it should be terrific when finished. Directions: Go east from Brandenburg Gate, passing over the River Spree on the Schlossbrucke, and turn north along the river on Am Kupefergraben.

Crossing back across the Schlossbrucke, wander down the famous Unter der Linden, Berlin's Champs de l'Elysees. The Deutsche Historisches Museum is free and friendly, with photos and objects dating from 900 A.D. to the present. Directions: On Unter der Linden towards the Tiergarten at Unter der Linden 2. You'll want to stop and gaze up at Frederick the Great on his magnificent horse and the Brandenburg Gate. Use your guidebook to recall all the immensely important historic events that have taken place here.

On the south side of the Tiergarten, between the park and the canal, beautifully landscaped streets wind around the Kulturforum. At the Philharmonie you can listen to the Berlin Philharmonic, one of the world's best symphonic orchestras. Tickets are sold between 3:30 P.M. and 6:00 P.M. weekdays, and from 11 a.m to 2 P.M. on weekends. The Museum of musical instruments is next door. The striking architectural design of the Neue Nationalgalerie makes it hard to miss. It houses a stimulating collection of German art from the 19th and 20th centuries; closed Monday. The Bauhaus-Archiv is a pilgrimage site for modern applied art enthusiasts; closed Tuesdays instead of Mondays.

Save some energy for the Egyptian Museum because the breathtakingly beautiful, 3000-year-old Bust of Nefertiti is a glorious treasure for the city. Throughout the rest of the museum the amazing finds uncovered by skillful German archeologists working in Egypt are artistically exhibited; closed Monday. Directions: North of the city at Schloss Charlottenburg. Take exit 6 off 100. The museum is across from the entrance to the Schloss Charlottenburg.

The ethnographic sections of the Museen Dahlem are outstanding. If you have children with you, don't miss it. Kid's eyes bug out when they see the enormous ancient boats from Oceana, but the whole museum is exciting. Directions: Southwest of the city in the suburb of Dahlem. Exit 100 onto 1 south in the direction of Dahlem, then follow signposting for the museum.

****Camping: None are close to the city. *West of the city, off 5, exit south onto 2 for 18 km, then drive southeast in the direction of Kladow for two kilometers. DDC Campingplatz Berlin-Kladow, Krampnitzer Weg 111-117 (030-365-2797); lots of vacation home campers; open all year; $$$$. *Southeast of the city, east of the Flughafen Berlin-Schonefeld, between E55 and 113. Exit E30/10 at exit 9, and drive north along the waterway to Wernsdorf. Then go west towards Schmockwitz. DDC Camping am Krossinsee (030-675-8687); nice location on the Krossinsee; bungalows; recreational area; open all year; $$$$. *South of the city, off E51 at exit 5A next to the autostrata at Dreilinden. Campingplatz Hettler under Lange (033-203-796-84); better for RV's; open all year; $$$.

POTSDAM/SANSSOUCI

Sumptuous palaces surrounded by lavish gardens that impress even the most jaded horticulturist make Sanssouci a must-see destination. Delightfully small for a palace, extravagent Schloss Sanssouci is well worth the effort it takes to get a ticket. You can almost feel the presence of its former royal residents, guests, and pets as you wander through on the guided tour. Get to the ticket booth by 8 a.m so you can be close to the front of the line, which is very long by 9 a.m when the palace opens; closed Monday. While waiting for your tour time, explore the rest of the gardens and palaces. The Neues Palais, built grandiose and showy to exemplify the wealth and power of the Prussians is closed Tuesdays instead of Mondays. Wind your way around to Chinesisches Teehaus, a Rococo pagoda, built to the whims of Frederick. You'll probably never see anything like it again; closed on Friday, but the extravagant outside can be viewed daily. Directions: Signposting in Potsdam for Sanssouci is excellent.

****Camping: *Drive southwest on B1 for five kilometers. Camping Sanssouci-Gaisberg, An der Pirschheide (033-275-5680); lovely location on the Templiner See; all the amenities; open May-September; $$$$. *Six kilometers farther west on B1 on Glindower See. Camping Riegelspitze, 14542 Werder-Petzow (033-274-2397); nice location; bungalows; all the amenities; open May-September; $$$$. *On the southeast side of the Templiner See. Exit north off E55, and drive north on B2 for two kilometers. Exit west for Caputh. Campingplatz Himmelreich, 14542 Geltow-Caputh (033-097-0475); nice location; open all year; $$$.

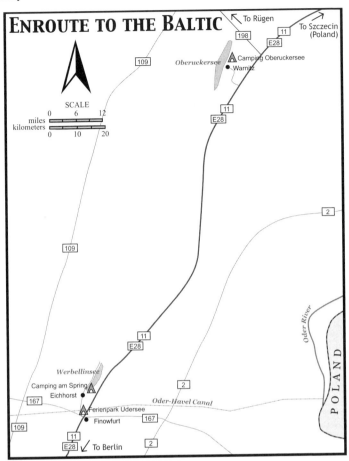

ENROUTE TO THE BALTIC

****Camping: Exit E28 west at exit 12, and then go north on B198 to the village of Eichhorst. Drive north on a smaller road for three kilometers to Werbellinsee. All of the following have nice locations on the water, are popular with families, and are well maintained. *Camping am Spring (033-363-4232); open all year; $$. *Close to E28, take exit 12 to Finowfurt, then drive west to the water. Ferienpark Udersee (033-35-218); open May-September; $$$. *Exit E28 west at exit 7, then go for six kilometers to the village of Warnitz and the Oberuckerseee. Camping Oberuckersee, south of the village on the water (039-963-459); open May-September; $$.

DRESDEN

A Grand Dame, dignified Dresden stands quietly surveying the beautiful River Elbe from her magnificent balcony, the Bruhlsche Terrasse. Her fabulous treasures are safely stored in the Albertinum Museum's Green Vault, where they still dazzle onlookers; closed Thursday. The important collection of old master paintings housed in the Gemaldegalerie, hint at Dresden's former glory as the Florence of the North; closed Monday. Stroll or bike across the Elbe via Augustusbrucke to the charming park and plaza of Neustader Markt. Turn west to Japanisches Palais. The exquisite, carefully selected treasures here make a nice change from over-abundant collections. Stroll through the courtyard, and you'll smile at the 18th century's passion for everything chinoiserie; closed Friday. Pleasurable excursions down the Elbe, with wonderful views of Schloss Pillnitz and locals relaxing at their river, start on Terrassenufer. There's a cycle/walking path along the river, too. Directons: Dresden is 220km south of Berlin. ****Camping: *South of the city in the suburb of Modkritz, signposted off B172. Camping Mockritz, Boderitzer Str. 30 (035-471-8226); quiet, surburban atmosphere; open most of the year; $$$. *West of the city, exit E40 south at exit 77 and drive four kilometers, then drive east on B173 for three kilometers to

Altkranken. Camping Altfranken, Otto-Harzer-Str 2 (035-1410-4200); nice location with a view of Dresden; open May-September; $$$. *Northeast of the city, close to Gross-Rohrdorf. Exit E40 at exit 85, and drive south just over two kilometers then east for two kilometers to the small lake at Kleinrohrsdorf. Camping Lux-Oase (035-9525-6666); popular with families; open all year; $$$.

NEARBY SIGHTS

Impressively restored Schloss Moritzburg, a Baroque hunting lodge, makes a nice place for a picnic lunch and photographs. Directions: 14km north of Dresden exit E40 west at exit 81B, and drive about 12km farther. Dresden porcelain fans wouldn't think of missing Meissen, the site of Europe's first, and one its finest, porcelain factories. Staatliche Porzellan-Manufaktur Meissen is southwest of town two kilometers in the direction of Triebisch. Schauhalle is another porcelain factory in the vicinity and makes a good alternative if lines at the former are too long. Both have interesting tours of porcelain production and showrooms; open daily. Directions: Drive 30km north of Dresden on E40. ****Camping: *On the south side of the Elbe River, about six kilometers south of Meissen in the village of Scharfenberg. Camping Rehbocktal (035-21-452-680); small; bungalows; open May-September; $$. *Between Meissen and Moritzburg. Drive northeast out of Meissen for four kilometers to Niederau. Pass through the town going southeast for just over two kilometers, then follow signs for Oberau. Campingplatz Waldbad (0352-433-6012); lovely location; popular with families; open May-September; $$$.

WEIMAR

Wandering through this quiet, park-like town, where artistic geniuses Goethe, Schiller, and Lizt mediated and created, is like going on a pilgrimage. By threading

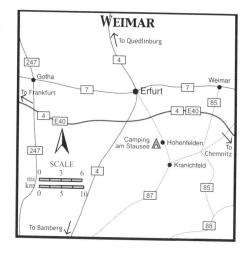

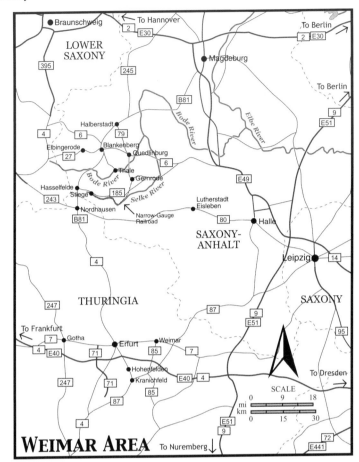

through the former homes of these illustrious greats, you get a feel for what they were really like. Chosen as a European City of Culture in 1999; Weimar is not pompous but instead amiable and softly beautiful. Beauty, the philosophers felt, was a political concept that should be part of the established order, and the town exudes this. As you enter town, Liszthaus is at the north end of the park. Goethe's and Schiller's homes are a few blocks farther toward the center. All are closed on Mondays. The original Bauhaus, founded by Walter Gropius, is still functioning happily as a school of design. Take time to wander about in the Park an der Ilm, where you'll see Goethe's summer retreat amidst the beautiful trees; closed Tuesdays. Directions: Weimar is 260km northeast of Frankfurt, close to Erfurt. ****Camping: *20km west of Weimar. exit E40 south at exit 47 in the direction of Kranichfeld and drive to Hohenfeldern. Camping am Stausee (0364-504-2081); peaceful location on a tiny lake; open all year; $$$.

QUEDLINBURG AREA

The quintessentially 14th century German town, Quedlinburg is a joy to wander around. Filled with over 1,000 half-timbered houses and boasting a castle, a beautiful river, and meticulous gar-

QUEDLINBURG-BODE VALLEY

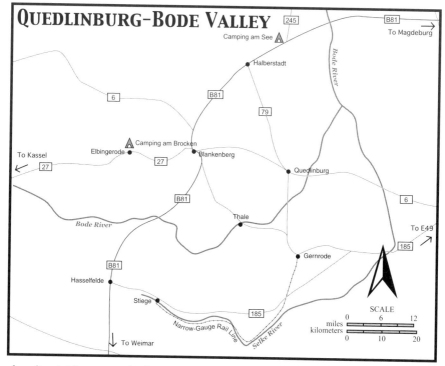

dens, it maintains an everyday life that isn't centered around tourism. Directions: Quedlinburg is between E30 and E51, southwest of Magdeburg. ****Camping: *Out of Halberstadt, drive east on B81 for three kilometers, then exit north to Halberstadter See. Camping am See (039-41-60-9308); nice location; separate nude bathing area; open all year; $$$.

Selke Valley/Narrow-gauge rail line

For a rest from driving, take this scenic train trip through a countryside of secluded lakes and peaceful meadows. It begins and ends in Gernrode and passes through the lovely Selke Valley to Stiege.

BODE VALLEY

Goethe loved this beautiful area. There are over 150km of marked walking trails in the area. Wildflower and bird enthusiasts particularly enjoy the three kilometer walk to Devil's Bridge. It begins southwest of Thale, ten kilometers south of Quedlinburg. From the bridge the trail rises steeper, climbing above the river with panoramic views of the Bode Valley and dramatic gorge, Bodekessel. There is a cable car to Hexentanzplatz and a chairlift to Rosstrappe, both beautiful and popular viewing areas. You can also drive to Hexentanzplatz if time is short. The tourist office in Thale, across from the railroad station, has maps of the walking trails. ****Camping: *West of Thale in Elbingerode, northwest of town. Camping am Brocken, (0394-544-2589); nice location; open all year; $$$.

MURITZ NATIONAL PARK AREA

If you have a yen for wilderness and water sports, this area has hundreds of lakes with connecting waterways. All kinds of boating equipment can be rented. Bird enthusiasts will enjoy the bogs and marshes. ****Camping: All of these places are beautifully situated; well maintained; popular with families; open May-September. *Two

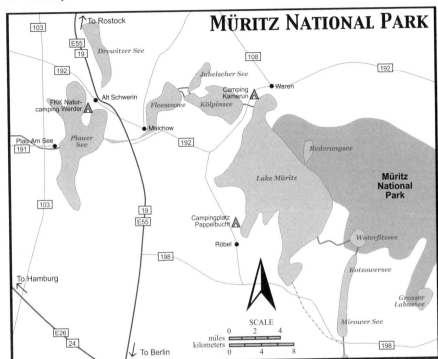

kilometers west of Waren at the north end of Lake Muritz. Camping Kamerun (039-112-2406); $$$$. *Southwest edge of Lake Muritz, three kilometers north of Robel. Campingplatz Pappelbucht (039-9315-9113); tent camping ; $$$. *North end of the Plauer See, off 192 at Alt Schwerin. FKK-Naturcamping Werder (039-9324-2074); nudist camp; $$$. There are many more camping places to choose from.

THE BALTIC COAST

The magnificent rugged coastline here has a wild and natural appeal. ****Camping: *Over the bridge, east of Stralsund, on the Rugen Ostee exit E22 at the village of Altefahr. Campingplatz Am Strelasund (038-3067-5483); tent camping; $$. *Four kilometers west of Barth on the Bodden See in the village of Bodstedt. Camping am Schaproder Bodden (038-309-1234); $$. There are many more places.

MUNICH

Besides beer gardens and an all-round party atmosphere, Munich boasts fine museums, lovely gardens, and a well-run zoo. Munich's museum collections vary extensively. Top museums include: the Residenzmuseum, an immense museum/palace; the Schatzkammer, with dazzling jewels; Altes Residenztheatre, Europe's finest Rococo theater which literally drips with gold and intricate carvings. All are closed Mondays. Other highlights of the city's museums include the Alte Pinakthek, housing one of Europe's finest collections of 14th through 18th century paintings and sculpture, and the Neue Pinakothek, which is justifiably proud of its 18th and 19th century collections. Both are closed Mondays. The hallmark Deutsches Museum is famous for its replicas and models, interactive displays, and demonstrations covering a wide range of scientific and technological fields. It is gargantuan so rest in between by watching an IMAX movie at the northeast corner of Museumsinsel, in the Technical Forum; open daily. Don't miss it. Signage to the Marianplatz, the central historic area, is good.

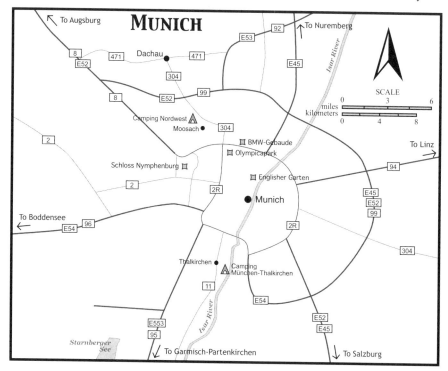

Use the towering Mariensaule column to guide you. Parking garages make parking easy. Pick up the city's free map at a hotel to orient yourself then when you're on Marianplatz, go to the tourist office in the Rathaus to refine your sightseeing selections. Have a picnic lunch in the magnificent Englisher Garten. Excellent cycle paths make cycling a very enjoyable way to get about.

For a side trips from historic Munich, castle-lovers will enjoy Schloss Nymphenburg located northwest of the city. The complex includes a porcelain museum, royal coaches, lovely gardens, and intriguing pavilions; closed Mondays. Oympicapark, built for the 1972 Olympic events, is so large a little train takes visitors on tours. A gargantuan swimming pool is a good place to frolic with the locals. All sorts of sporting events and other celebrations take place in the park. If you are fond of cars, walk over to the west side of the park to see the stately towers of the BMW-Gebaude, and view their display of elegant models; open daily. Dachau was Hitler's first concentration camp. Today it is only slightly softened by the grass. An explicit exhibit of photographs documents the horror. See the film; you don't need wait for the English version to understand. Small religious chapels of various religions are in the complex. Locals like to float down the Isar River on warm summer days. You can join them if you've brought an inner tube or inflatable mattress from home. Most people start their float from Wolfratshausen or Bad Tolz, south of Munich. ****Camping: *Four kilometers south of the city, along the western bank of the Isar River in the suburb Thalkirchen. Follow the signs for the Zoo/Tierpark, then go farther south. From E33 take exit 2, and drive east towards the river. Camping Munchen-Thalkirchen, Zentallandstr 49 (089-723-1707); best location for the city and very popular; fair maintenance; open April-October; $$$$. *Northwest of the city in the suburb of Moosach; close to the intersection of E52/99, the ring road, and 304/Dachauer Str.; not far from Olympiapark. Exit south off E52/99 onto 304, and drive in the direction of Munchen centrum, then exit south for Moosach. Camping Nordwest, Auf den Schrederwiesen 3 (089-150-6936); noisy with trains and traffic; fair maintenance; $$.

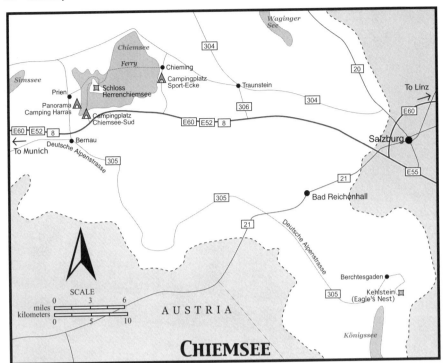

CHIEMSEE

The most fascinating part of the Schloss Herrenchiemee, a Ludwig II extravaganza, is the fascinating exhibit of his memorabilia in the museum. Boats to Herreninsel, where the palace museum is, depart from Prien. The sparkling lake has many tourist-oriented activities. Directions: 90km southeast of Munich on E52, in the direction of Salzburg. Exit north at exit 106 for Prien and Lake Chiemsee. ****Camping: All camping places mentioned are close to the lake, popular with families, well-maintained, and open May-September. *Two kilometers south of Prien on the lake-side road. Panorma-Camping Harras (080-519-0460); $$$. *In the same area, but take exit 107. Campingplatz Chiemsee-Sud (080-517-540); $$$. *On the east side of the lake, exit E52 north at exit 109, and drive 13km to Chieming, then one kilometer south of town on the lake road. Campingplatz Sport-Ecke (086-64-500); nudist camp; $$$$.

BAVARIAN ALPS

Towering mountains, exciting cable cars, frescoed houses, more of Ludwig's castles, scenic drives, and well-marked hiking trails draw hosts of holiday visitors to this area. In the 1930s the Deutsches Alpenstrasse was built to facilitate scenic drives through the German Alps. The road meanders through pretty villages, along pleasant rivers, and up to meadows sweet with summer vetch. There is also a gorgeous route from Oberammergau, over the Ammer-sattel, and down to the Plansee to Reutte. It is long and winding but breathtakingly beautiful. Little trails lead out for pleasant walks. Check with the tourist office to verify whether the whole route is open before setting out. The area is riddled with expensive but exciting cable cars and narrow-gauge railways. Check with

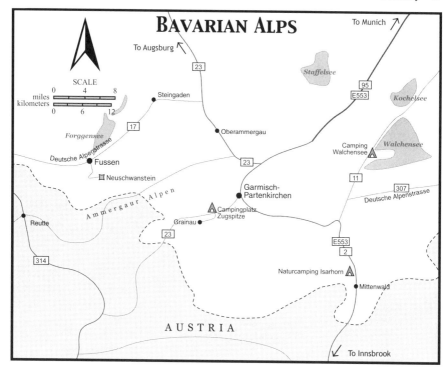

the tourist office in Garmisch-Partenkirchen for full descriptions. The Berchtesgarden National Park has a fjord-like setting with cable cars and excursion boats. High up in the mountains at the eastern end of the park, Hitler established his famous Eagle's Nest. The final ascent is a torturously steep with hairpin curves so most people board an excursion buse or cable car. Directions: Eagle's Nest is reached through the village of Obersalzberg about 50km south of Salzburg. From E55 south of Salzburg contine south on 160, then 305, then 319. ****Camping: *In Graineau, three kilometers west of Garmisch. Campingplatz Zugspitze (088-21-3180); close to the road; $$$. *In Mittenwald, off E533/2. Naturcamping Isarhorn (088-235-216); beautiful location; $$$$. Both are open all year. *On the southwest end of the Walchensee. Camping Walchensee (088-58-237); lovely location; fair maintenance; open May-September; $$$.

NATURPARK ALTMUHLTAL

Canoe and kayak enthusiasts should take time to quietly paddle down the lovely Altmuhltal River. Rentals and shuttle services are readily available. All the camping places are nicely located and cared for. ****Camping: On the river close to the town of Beilngries. *Exit off E/45 at exit 58, and drive east along the river to town, then go south to the river. Camping An der Altmuhl (084-61-8406); $$$. *Off the same exit on E/45 but drive farther south, passing under the roadway to Kipfenberg. AZUR Camping Altmuhtal (084-6590-5167); $$$$. *Farther west along the river, west of Eichstatt in the town of Dollnstein. Campingplatz Dollnstein (084-228-46); $$. *In the same area but farther west along the river to the town of Pappenheim, just east of B2. Camping Pappenheim (091-43-1275); $$$.

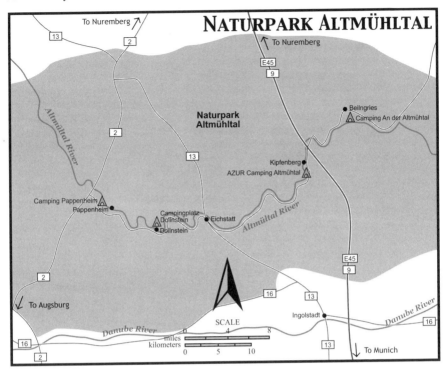

NUREMBERG

Alive with street music, artists, and remnants of a rich 16th century merchant town past, Nuremberg is an easy place to enjoy. A museum documenting the events of the city during the Third Reich and the trials at the conclusion of World War II is scheduled to open soon. ****Camping: *Four kilometers southeast of the historic area, exit off E45/E51 at exit 52, and drive about six kilometers to the centrum. Follow signposting for camping. Campingplatz im Volkspark, Dutzendteich Hans-Kalb-Strab 56 (091-181-1122); by the famous stadium; well maintained; open May-September; $$$$.

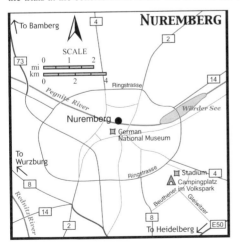

BAYREUTH

The most famous artists, composers, and writers of the 17th century were invited by a lively princess to spend time here, creating one of the most elegant and sophisticated courts of the times. A large opera house was built for Richard Wagner's huge productions, considered today to be some of the best opera in the world. But because the tickets are sold

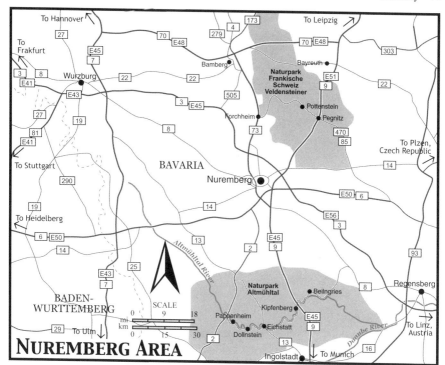

NUREMBERG AREA

out a year in advance, most Wagner fans will have to be satisfied with seeing the museum filled with his memorabilia and with just a tour of the glorious opera house. ****Camping: *In Frankische Schweiz nature reserve, between Beyreuth and Nuremberg. Exit E51 west at exit 44/Pegnitz onto 470, and drive about ten kilometers to Pottenstein. Camping Barenschlucht, Weidmannsgesees 12 (092-43-206); lovely location; well maintained; open all year; $$. *Three kilometers farther on 470. Campingplatz Jurahohe (092-439-173); better for RV's; lovely location $$.

BAMBERG

Strolling through Bamberg is like walking through the pages of beautiful photographs in an art or architecture book. The elaborately carved stucco, colorful frescoes, entrancing sculptures, and soothing waterways remain untouched by war. The city impresses even the most jaded traveler. Try to get tickets to the town's renowned Bamberger Symphoniker. Held outdoors under a canopy to stars, the setting and music make for a very memorable evening. The tourist office sells tickets; reserve ahead (0951-871-154). Leafy beer gardens are sprinkled throughout the city and hills. Beer-makers, lured by the beautiful surroundings, produce 200 varieties of the brew. ****Camping: *Five kilometers south of town in the suburb of Bug, on the west side of the Regnitz River just south of B22. Campingplatz Insel (0951-563-21); lovely location; well cared for; open all year; $$$.

WURZBURG

When Tiepolo, the Italian fresco master, and Neuman, the master German builder, joined forces, the grandiose Wurzburg Residenz became one of the finest palaces in Germany. Heavily influenced by the

French, it's reminiscent of Versailles. ****Camping: *Close to the palace, at the intersection of 19 and E43 in the suburb of Heidingsfeld. Camping Kalte Quelle (093-165-598); nice location; open April-October; $$.

STUTTGART

Hi-tech, prosperous, and surrounded by vineyards, Stuttgart is home to both the Mercedes Benz and Porsche automobile plants and museums. Stuttgart has beautiful parks, an outstanding zoo, a botanical garden, an excellent modern art museum, and Roman ruins. Join the locals cycling along the banks of the Neckar. During August the town is even more vibrant with street music, wine, beer, and food booths while locals take a break from work and celebrate Sommerfest and Weindorf. ****Camping: East of the city center, in the suburb of Bad Cannstatt on the east side of the Neckar River, sandwiched between B14 and B29. Campingplatz Cannstatter Wasen, Mercedesstrasse 40 (071-155-6696); convenient; open all year; $$$$.

HEIDELBERG

Mark Twain's hilarious descriptions, visions of magically lit landscapes painted by Turner, and sweet nostalgia for military life in the army while being based here, make Heidelberg a popular destination for vacationing Americans. Historic pageants, open-air concerts, and opera performances make the town jump with visitors throughout the summer. Check their web page. The centerpiece for all of this is the Schloss. Start your city exploration by boarding the funicular at the lower Kornmarkt Station, which takes you to the ramparts of the castle. Or relive medieval times vividly by walking up the steep cobblestone lane.

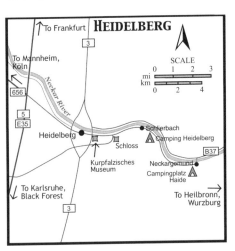

Spend some time in the touristy but fun student taverns, filled with a jumble of faded artifacts. In the Kurpfalzisches Museum, housed in the Palace Morass on Hauptstrasse, the bones from the 500,000-year-old-Heildelberg Man are safely tucked away, but you can see a copy of his jawbone and an amazing lime-wood Altar of the Twelve Disciples; closed Monday. Well-marked underground parking garages make parking fairly easy in Heidelberg. Pick up a free city map from a hotel as you proceed into town. ****Camping. *Five kilometers southeast of the city on B37, on the Neckar River in the suburb of Heidelberg-Schlierbach. Camping Heidelberg (062-2180-2506); $$$. *In the suburb of Neckargemund. Campingplatz Haide (062-232-2111); better for RV's; $$$. Both are well maintained and open May-September.

SCHWARTSWALD/
THE BLACK FOREST

Just the name, Black Forest, gives this area a certain mystique. Once the forest was so densely packed with trees it was dark, even during the day. Today light filters down on well-marked gravel paths. It is a popular tourist destination. Favorite destinations are: the old-fashioned open-air museum in Gutach northeast of Freiburg off 531; the Hermann Hesse museum in the Nagold Valley at Calw (west of Stuttgart off 295); the clock museum in Furtwangen (northeast of Freiburg off 500). For indulging in spa bathing in Baden-Baden, the Friedrichsbad or Caracalla-Therme spas are good choices. Directions: ****Camping: *East of Lahr exit E35 at exit 56, and drive east for 12km to the village of Seelbach, then south to the river. Camping Ferienparadies Schwarzwalder Hof 078-23-2777; beautiful location; open all year; $$$$.

BODENSEE/LAKE CONSTANCE

Water-loving vacationers fill these shorelines. It's not hard to find a camping place.

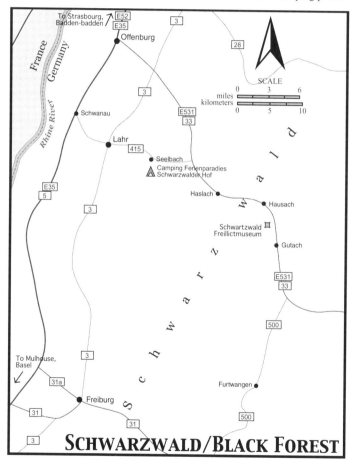

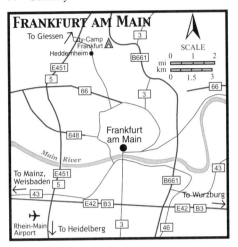

FRANKFURT AM MAIN

Besides having one of the busiest airports in the world, Frankfurt has some very good museums, an excellent zoo, and a beautifully restored old town. Museum highlights are the Historisches and Judisches Museums in the Altsadt area and all the museums along the other side of the river called the Museumsurfer. All are closed Mondays. The light-hearted Deutsches Filmmuseum is delightful, and to gaze upon Goethe's original writing desk in his birthplace home is a thrill. ****Camping: *North of the city, in the suburb of Heddernheim. Exit B661 at exit 7, Eschersheim/Heddernheim. Drive north staying right, following signposting. City-Camp Frankfurt, An der Sandelmuhle 35 (069-57-0332); convenient; popular; reserve ahead; open all-year; $$$$.

KOLN/COLOGNE

Cologne's enormous cathedral, built on the site of a Roman temple, is breathtaking. Mysterious light from the magnificent stained-glass windows and finely etched spires give a weightless look to the elaborate stone edifice. The Cross of Oak carved in 976 and the bigger-than-life-size figure of Jesus were masterpieces of art in their time. Use a guidebook for more details. Right next to the Cathedral, in striking ultra-modern buildings, are two of Germany's most important museums. The Wallraf-Richartz houses an enormous and important collection of 15th to 19th century art. In stark contrast, the Ludwig displays 20th century art including many famous surrealist pieces. In the Romisch-Germanisches Museum, Bacchus/Dionysos stars in a huge excavated Roman floor mosaic. Created with over a million pieces of tile and glass, its state of preservation is amazing. This muse-um's collection of glass is said to be the best in the world. Medieval Cologne was an imperial city, and today it is home to a masterful group of Romanesque churches. ****Camping: *South of the historic area about six kilometers, along the west side of the Rhine in the suburb of Rodernkirchen. Exit

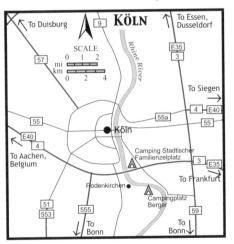

E40 at the intersection of E/40 and B555, and drive east towards the river and park. Campingplatz Berger, Uferstrasse 71 (040-392-211); open all year; $$$. *On the other side of the river, cross the Rodenkirchener Brucke, take the first exit, 13. Drive back to the river. Camping Stadtischer Familienzelplatz, Weidenweg (040-831-966); open May-September; $$.

HAMBURG

The best way to start enjoying and under-standing this grand city of commerce and finance is on a harbor cruise. Choose a small ferry rather than a large one. Relaxing on this harbor cruise you'll see quays with ware-houses and docks, and ancient restored ships

HAMBURG

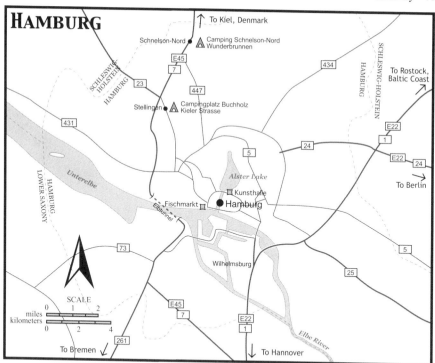

↑ To Kiel, Denmark

Schnelson-Nord ● ▲ Camping Schnelson-Nord
                     Wunderbrunnen

E45
7

23

447

Stellingen ● ▲ Campingplatz Buchholz
                  Kieler Strasse

431

434

434

HAMBURG

SCHLESWIG-HOLSTEIN

To Rostock,
Baltic Coast

E22
1

E22   24

→
To Berlin

Unterelbe

5

24

Alster Lake

Kunsthalle
● Hamburg

Fischmarkt

Elbtunnel

HAMBURG
LOWER SAXONY

73

Wilhelmsburg

25

5

SCALE

0   1   2
miles
kilometers
0   2   4

E45
7

261

E22
1

Elbe River

To Bremen ↙

↓ To Hannover

moored alongside the gargantuan hulls of the container ships. Then the small ferry turns into the canals to Speicherstadt for wonderful old town views. Directions: Purchase tickets and board at Pier 2. One of the wealthiest cities in Germany, Hamburg's art galleries are filled with fine collections. Vibrant markets offer goods from around the world, and the exceptional zoo was the first in world to display animals in their natural environment. As in all seaports, the bars and brothels make their colorful contribution, but the city has a low crime rate. Today the St. Pauli area is monitored by the police. You can safely wander about enjoying the eclectic environment, made even more famous by the Beatles' presence in 1960. Directions: S-bahn to Reepebahn. Hamburg is justifiably proud of the Kunsthalle and its important collections. The large display of Friedrich paintings, with their haunting landscapes of mountains and the Baltic coast, is outstanding. By wandering around in the Museum fur Kunst und Gewerbe, an applied arts museum, you can transport yourself through the centuries; the Art Nouveau section, or Jugendsil, is extraordinary. Directions: Both are north of the Hauptbahnhof. If you are in town on Sunday, get up early and be at the Fischmarkt by Landungsbrucken by 8 a.m It's wildly noisy with the excitement of hawkers selling their wide range of wares. It opens at 5 a.m and starts slowing down by 10 a.m Directions: U or S-bahn to St. Pauli Landungsbrucken. For relaxation, locals head to the parks and colorful gardens framing Alster Lake. Line skaters gracefully glide along the lake-side path accompanied by cyclists and walkers, while sailboats joyfully scoot across the beautiful water. ****Camping: *Eight kilometers north of the city in the suburb of Stellingen. On E45, exit at 26 for Stellingen. It's on the east side of the highway and convenient to the zoo and volkspark. Campingplatz Buchholz Kieler Str. 374 (540-4532); open all year; $$$$. *16 km north of the city, exit off E45 at exit 24 Schnelsen-Nord, then drive west towards the IKEA market.   Camping Schnelsn-Nord Wunderbrunnen 2 (559-4225); better for RV's; $$$$.

ITALY

Like its food, Italy is a full-bodied and generous country. Some areas are simple, with rich flavors and aromas, others are more graceful and elegant. It is a country where love, food, art, and business are joined in near perfection.

With hundreds of campgrounds, Italy is an extremely popular camping destination. The level of cleanliness, newness of plumbing, and all-around neatness is not on par with Germany or Switzerland, but campgrounds here are less expensive. An easy-going ambiance pervades. If you play tennis, bring your racket, as many of the campgrounds have tennis courts. The registration office and gate are often closed for a long lunch and rest. Ask about the cost of showers when you register, and get change or tokens. The opening and closing dates listed are conservative but reliable. Depending on the weather, you might find them opening earlier or closing later. Most campgrounds charge about $20 USA per night for two persons, a car, and a small tent. Simple campgrounds cost less. Resort-like campgrounds cost over $24 USA.

If you are used to driving on fast freeways and in big cities, you'll be fine driving in Italy. Keep commute times in mind when you are coming in or out of a big city. The lightest traffic occurs early on Sunday morning. Expect tolls, and carry change. Major toll roads take charge cards. Renting or leasing a car in Italy is more expensive than in most other countries, so consider renting in a neighboring country.

Admission to major museums and historic sites is expensive. Be selective and then thoroughly enjoy the ones you chose. Use a guidebook to enjoy them more completely. If you study Italian history and art before your trip, your visit will be more meaningful. You can now book ahead at the tourist office for some of the major museums. Some museums open only for a long morning, and most are closed on Mondays. Check the current opening hours with the tourist office. Italians put eating and relaxing high on their priority list. Long midday closing periods are common. This might be where the saying "When in Rome do as the Romans do" originated. Join the locals and do your sightseeing in the morning and your shopping later in the afternoon.

Italy is a festive place in summer. Some events feature well-known performers. Contact the Italian Government Tourist Office and visit web sights in your home country for calendar and ticketing information. You'll need to purchase tickets in advance for the most popular ones, but do go as they are exciting and memorable. Book the campground ahead, and arrive early if there is a special event in town

ROME

Historically one of the most important places in the world, Rome's history crowds in and over every corner of its twisting cobblestone streets, grand piazzas, cathedrals, and ancient ruins. It's a city that is best savored when you've immersed yourself in its history before the trip. Some say there is more to see here than any other place in the world.

Start early each day. Most of the major museums close at 2 P.M.. Afternoons can be spent leisurely absorbing its incredible atmosphere. Some ticketing for museums can be done ahead at the tourist office. A good city map is essential, and a compass

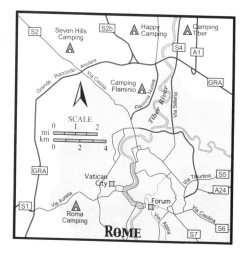

can help. I find riding around on my bicycle most enjoyable and getting a little lost is part of the fun. Enjoy the simple pleasures of everyday life in Rome. Pick a few major sites that are important to you, and savor them slowly, as you would a delicious meal.

Line up for the Vatican Museums early in the morning at the entrance on the north side of the Vatican City wall. Purchase a Guide to the Vatican Museum and City here, and read it while you wait in line. The line moves fairly quickly, so don't be disheartened if it is lengthy. The self-guided tours are color-coded. Choose the one that suits your interest, and follow the color. The richness of the treasures you'll see is almost beyond belief. Be sure to allow time and energy to fully enjoy the Raphael's Stanze; the harmony, colors and sensitivity of the artist's work are breathtaking. The Sistene Chapel and Michelangelo's overwhelming ceiling frescoes of the Creation and the Last Judgement will probably be the most fabulous large-scale painting you'll ever see. But these two sights are just the cream on the top of a very rich cauldron. Saint Peter's Piazza and the Basilica, with Michelangelo's Pieta, the glories of the dome, and the views from the roof won't disappoint.

Try to make history come alive as you wander. In your mind, recreate the sounds, smells, and life of the Romans as you view the Colosseum, Palatine Hill, the Roman Forum, Piazza del Campidoglio, Piazza Venezia, the Pantheon, and Campo de' Flori.

For touristy fun explore the Piazza Navona, the Piazza di Spagna, and the Fontane di Trevi. Take a break in the restful gardens of the Villa Borghese or at one of the cafes in the tiny squares in Trastevere. Use your guidebook to select from the multitude of other fascinating sights. Pick up a free This Week in Rome for the current happenings in concerts and exhibitions.

For a break from city life, pack a picnic and drive out to Tivoli, about 40km east of the city, and immerse yourself in the old elegance of the gardens at the Villa d'Este or Villa Adriana.

****Camping: *Closest to the historic area. Westside of the GRA. Close to S1 take exit 1 in the direction of San Pietro/Centrum. Drive east on Via Aurelia for just over one kilometer. Watch for large Silo Market sign on the north side of the road and the smaller camping sign on the south side. The campground is on the south side. Roma Camping, Via Aurelia 831 (06-662-3018); minutes from the Vatican by bus; doable bicycle ride to the historic area; good place to meet fellow international travelers; close to a wonderful covered open market; bungalows; good maintenance; open all year; $$. *On the north side of town, close to S2 and S3, take exit 6 off the GRA. Drive south onto Via Flaminia Nuova, staying left. Camping Flaminio, Via Flaminia 821 (06-336-26401); close to public transport; close to Tiber River walking/cycling trail; good maintenance; open all year; $$. *In the same area but a bit north. Exit off the GRA at exit 5, and drive north on S2 bis and Via Cassia Veientana. It's close to the intersection of Via Cassia Veientana and Via Prato della Corte. Happy Camping, Via Prato della Corte 1915 (06-336-26401); swimming pool; camp shuttle bus to metro; well maintained; open April-October; $$. *In the same area just west of A1 exit off the GRA, at exit 6. Drive north just over one kilometer on to S3/Via Flaminia. Drive east onto Via Tiberina. Camping Tiber, Via Tiberina km. 1400 (06-336-12314); next to the Tiber River; camp shuttle bus to metro; bungalows; swimming pool; fair maintenance; open April-October; $$. *In the same area. Exit the GRA at exit 3 onto S2/Via Cassia. Seven Hills Camping, Via Cassita 1216 (06-303-10826); swimming pool; bungalows; disco; shuttle bus to metro; well maintained; open year-round; $$.

LAZIO AND UMBRIA

Vibrant fields of sunflowers turn their faces in unison to the sun, giving your eyes a feast as you travel on tree-lined back roads. In summer, the fields are decorated with the lavender and pink of wild sweetpea. Here and there, perched high on a hill seemingly in the middle of nowhere, medieval walled villages sculpt the skyline. Farmlands roll out like colored quilts. The air is fresh, driving is a pleasure, and summer festivities abound. Ask the Italian Tourist Office in your country to send you a current calendar and ticketing information. Book ahead for the most famous. This is a good area for a camping experience in an agriturist-a small farm that has a few rooms and camp sites. You'll share food and homemade wine with the family owners. These places are harder to find, so get directions from the local tourist office before setting out

LAZIO

ORVIETO

Located halfway between Florence and Rome, Orvieto is an ideal stopping place. Masterfully perched on top of a volcanic plug, the ancient town looks down peacefully on the farms below. The drive to the top ends at Piazza Popolo, where parking is easy. Walk or bike through the narrow streets to the Duomo. Then sit in the shade with the locals and just gaze on this fantasy of stunning mosaics, sculpture and spires. The colossal bronze doors are breathtaking. ****Camping: *In Rossa Ripasena, a small hill of tiny farms just west of historic Orvieto. After descending the hilltop from Piazza Popolo, cross the bridge over the river, and staying left on the small road. *Agricampeggio Sossogna, Rocca Ripasena 61 90 (07-63-343141); lovingly restored farmhouse; extremely peaceful and comfortable; tents only; excellent maintenance; $$$. *On Lago di Corbara. Follow S448 south of Orvieto. Continue east nine kilometers to the lake. Camping Orvieto (07-64-950-240); close to the lake; swimming pool; fair maintenance; open June- September; $$.

SPOLETO

This graceful and sophisticated town is a beautiful setting for the world-famous musical, cinema, and cultural events that fill its summer's calendar. You'll need to book ahead for the well

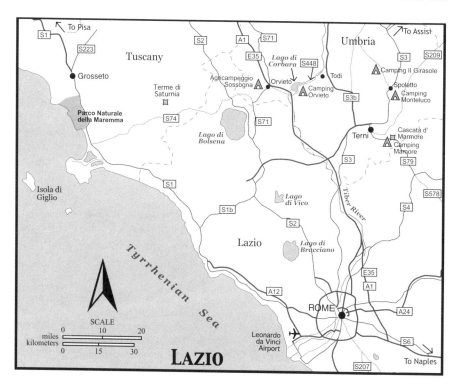

known ones. ****Camping: *Before climbing the hill and just after you've crossed the bridge, exit S3/Terni-Rome road east, passing the Chiesa di San Pietro. Turn south on Monteluco. Camping Monteluco (07-43-22-03-58); tiny and crowded but very close to the events. *Exit off S3 in the direction of Montefalco. Take the small road north ten kilometers. It's outside the village of Petrognano. Camping II Girasole (07-435-1335); swimming pool; tennis courts; bungalows; well maintained; open year-round; $$.

CASCATE DELLE MARMORE

In the pleasant warmth of the summer evening people come to enjoy the sound and light show at one of the largest waterfalls in Europe, Cascate delle Marmore-initially created by the Romans to protect the area from flooding. The show starts in the early evening, usually between 5:30 and 6 p.m. Check at a tourist office for the current time schedule. If you're in the area during the day when the water flow is turned down, it's fun to soak in the swimming pools at the bottom of the cascade. Look for parked cars, and follow the path. Directions: Southeast of Terne, between S209 and S79 in the village of Marmore. ****Camping: *In the village of Marmore. Camping Mamore (07-446-7198); basic; fair maintenance; open June-August; $.

TODI

Located on a craggy hilltop Todi is away from the tourist trail. It was an important Etruscan settlement, but its history goes back to the Iron Age. It's easy to imagine yourself in medieval Europe when you sit in the perfectly preserved Piazza del Popolo where you can enjoy summer art and music festivals while taking in an eagle's view of the surrounding countryside.

UMBRIA

ASSISI

The spirit of St. Francis, a monk who renounced wealth and lived a life of charity and poverty, still hovers in the tranquil air of the beautiful Basilica, Duomo, and Santa Chiara tucked up into Mount Subasio. Eremo delle Carceri, the caves where he lived and prayed, however, are more in keeping with the monk himself. There's good parking outside the walls of the cathedral area at both the north and south ends. The Basilica has an upper and lower church. Plan to see both. Bring small change so you can light up the walls to see Giotto's famous frescoes of St. Francis's life. A guidebook makes this a more meaningful experience. Shorts and sleeveless shirts aren't allowed. The hiking trail and road up to the Eremo are just outside the gate of Rocca Maggiore, the Porta Cappiccini. It's an uphill climb of four kilometers, but not terribly steep, and the views are magnificent. ****Camping: *On the Eremo Delle Carceri road about one and a half kilometers up from Porta Cappiccini. Camping Fontemaggio, Strada Eremo delle Carceri (07-581-3636); fabulous views; tranquil; basic amenities; open May-September; $. *Three kilometers west of Assisi, on S147. Camping International Assisi, (07-581-3710); easier for RVs; full amenities; open all year; $$. *In between Assis and Spoleto, close to Foligno, exit S75 west onto S316 in the direction of Bevagna. Camping Pian di Boccio, in Bevagna (07-423-60391); bungalows; disco; swimming pool; open May-September; $$.

PERGUGIA

A university city and the regional capitol, this city exudes style and energy. To get a real sense of the place, join the locals in their evening stroll on Corso Vannucci. Well-known musicians fill the air with exciting sounds throughout the summer. Buy tickets ahead for the most important ones. A large car park is on the main road, Via Lorenzo, at the bottom of the hill and escalators take you up the hill. The tourist office at Piazza IV November will fill you in on events and provide a map. ****Camping: *West of the city on S75, at km 13 exit north onto a small road. Climb the hill for four kilometers to

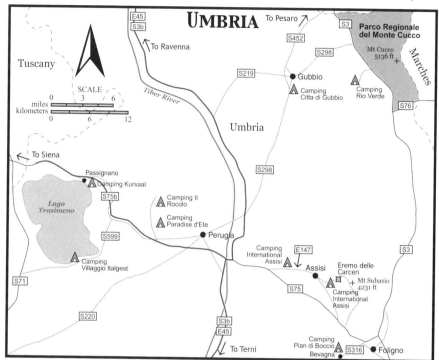

the village of Colle della Trinita. Camping Paradise d'Ete (07-579-517); nice location; small; bunga-lows; fair maintenance; open June-August; $. *On the same road. Camping II Rocolo (07-517-8550); better for RVs; fair maintenance; open June-August; $$.

LAGO DI TRASIMENO

This is a popular vacation destination for locals who come to relax and have fun. Wind surfing, waterslides, paddle boats, and horseback riding keep kids and the young at heart entertained. ****Camping: *On the north side of the lake in Passignano, on the lake road Val di Chiana. Camping Kursaal (07-582-8085); all the amenities; bungalows; well maintained; open April-September; $$$. *On the south side of the lake, exit S599 at Sant'Arcangelo. Campin Villaggio Italgest (07-584-8238); large pool with waterslides; tennis; bungalows; children's program; all the amenities; well maintained; open May-September; $$$. The lake is dotted with campgrounds. It's easy to drive around the lake and choose one that suits you.

GUBBIO

Besides being a lovely hilltop town, Gubbio's Museo Civico houses the Eugubian Tables-bronze tablets dating from 200 to100 BC. They are the earliest record of Umbrian language. The forest-ed Apennines mountains and cascading waterfalls can be seen right in town and like Siena, the buildings and narrow cobblestone streets have a rosy hue. ****Camping: *Exit town on S298 in the direction of Perugia, and drive just over one kilometer. Camping Citta di Gubbio, in Ortoguidone (07-592-72037); nice location; swimming pool; bike paths; well maintained; open May-September; $$.

PARCO REGIONALE DEL MONTE CUCCO

This park is a haven for cave lovers from all over Europe. Centro Nationale di Speleologia, in Costacciaro at Corso Mazzini 9, books cave exploration. Hang gliding is also popular in the area. Directions: East of Gubbio "as the crow flies". Exit S3 for Costacciaro. ****Camping: *Drive east up the mountain road to the village of Fornace. Camping Rio Verde (07-591-70307); lovely location; basic amenities; fair maintenance; open May-September; $.

TUSCANY

Quintessentially Italian, Tuscany boasts fabulous art, mouth-watering food, and rolling fertile hillsides that are meticulously lined with ancient grapevines, silver-leafed olive trees, and sunflowers. Entering this area is like facing an enormous buffet of delicious food knowing unfortunately, that you can only eat so much before you are full.

FLORENCE

Florence, like Rome, is best savored if you have read about the main characters in its history before you arrive. The major museums are expensive. Choose just a few, and spend your time leisurely enjoying them. Use a guidebook and don't feel guilty for skipping some things. Main sights are closed on Monday. You can confirm museum hours, purchase advance tickets for major museums, and peruse the city's current offerings at the main tourist office north of the Duomo at Via Cavour 1. Everything slows down or closes during midday in Florence.

Piazza Duomo is a good place to begin an exploration. Brunelleschi's brilliant Duomo will mean more if you read its fascinating and touching story. Giotto's work on the Campanile, Ghiberti's on the Baptistery doors, and the sculptural works of Michelangelo, Donatello, and della Robbia in the Museo dell'Opera del Duomo will take a long morning to see.

Leave time to walk over to Market Centrale, one of the most fabulous fruit and vegetable markets in the world. You'll get a sense of the prideful Tuscan personality here from both the merchant and the customer. It's not far from the Piazza Duomo, but Florence is a maze of little streets in this area. Ask for directions. Market Centrale is housed in an old two-story warehouse and closes at 1

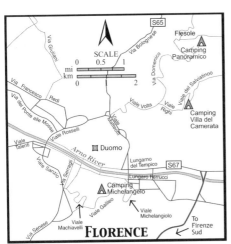

p.m. A flea market operates outside the entrance. Charming, inexpensive trattorias are tucked in and about the area.

The Bargello and the Uffizi Museums are similar in scale to the Louvre in Paris. If time is short, choose one. Once inside, plan a route to see your favorites while your senses are still fresh. The Bargello houses the best sculptural works of the Italian Renaissance. The Uffizi's extraordinary art collection will leave you breathless. Michelango's David, is housed in the Galleria dell'Accademia. Arrange your ticketing ahead for all three to avoid waiting in line. All are closed Monday.

Save time for watching children feed the pigeons in Piazza della Signoria, for checking out the goods being sold on the Ponte

Vecchio, and for draping yourself over the Arno River wall to watch canoeists. It is easy to cycle in historic Florence.

****Camping: The best for the city. *South of Florence, exit A1 at Galluzzo. Drive north toward the center of Florence on the Siena/Florence road/S2. Go up through the park on Viale Galileo, following signs to Piazzale Michelangelo. Camping is just past the monument and viewing area. Camping Michelangelo, Viale Michelangelo 80 (05-5681-1977); very popular; good place to meet fellow international travelers; book ahead or arrive early; fabulous views of the Duomo and Arno River; easy bike ride to the historic area; close-by bus; stairway down to the Arno River; covered common terrace area overlooking the city; well maintained; open all year; $$. *South of the city, exit A1 at Firenze Sud. Drive north three kilometers to the Arno Bridge. Turn west onto S67 and drive about two kilometers. Follow signposting north in the direction of Fiesole. Camping Villa di Camerata, Viale Righi 2 (05-5601-451); on the grounds of a hostel; close to a large supermarket and public transport; casual maintenance; open year-round; $. *In the same area. Follow the same directions, but continue farther up the hill to the historic village of Fiesole. It's just north of the historic town on a steep narrow road. Camping Panoramico, Via Peramonda 1(05-5590-069); wonderful views; shady with trees; bungalows; bus service from the piazza in Fiesole to Florence; well maintained; open all year; $$$. *Near A1 and S2, south of Florence. Camping International Firenze, Bottai, (05-5237-4704); swimming pool; convenient to the autostrata; bungalows; well maintained; open May-September; $$$.

WESTERN TUSCANY
SIENA

Siena hosts the most famous festival in Italy, the Palio. It is a thrilling spectacle of bareback horse-racing in the historic square, the Campo. On non-festival days the Campo is a great place to rest. You can picnic and snooze a bit right in the square. As you rest, study the Duomo. It's a perfect example of Gothic architecture. Park outside the walls, being careful to note which of the many gates of the walled city you enter. ****Camping: *Northeast of town, exit S2, at Siena Nord. Drive south, back toward Siena to climb the hill. Follow signposting. Camping Colleverde, Via Scacciapensieri (05-77-280-044); panoramic views; swimming pool; well maintained; open April-September; $$$. *Eight kilometers north of Siena off S2. Exit north for Castellina Scalo, and drive three kilometers. Camping Luxor Quies (05-7774-3047); convenient to the autostrata; good maintenance; open June-August; $$.

TERME DI SATURNIA

This is definitely an off-the-beaten-track kind of adventure. Cascading down the hillside, the sulphur springs of Terme di Saturnia form natural rock pools that are a kick to soak in. Directions: The springs are west of Lago di Bolsena. From S74 at Manciano turn north on S322, and drive two kilometers. Follow signage for Saturnia. Before entering the town, exit for Terme di Saturnia. Look beyond the spa hotel for a small road with parked cars. Park, and follow the path to the cascade.

PARCO NATURALE DELLA MAREMMA

On the coast south of Grosseta, in a protected coastal reserve, umbrella pines, birds, and long stretches of unspoiled coastline make for a tranquil outing. Directions: Park in the main square at Alberese. Visit the park headquarters to enhance your knowledge of the area and pick up a trail map. Entrance is by park bus only.

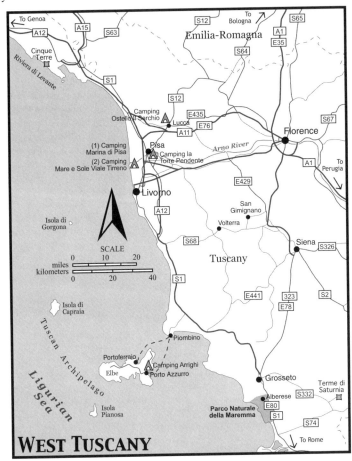

PISA

Pisa is easy to visit. Quiet and green, Campo dei Miracoli boasts a quartet of masterpieces. The Leaning Tower never fails to impress, and the Baptistry, the Duomo, and Camposanto are all delights. Musee dell'Opera de Duomo is excellent. Use your guidebook to help you choose what you want to see, and purchase a combo ticket for those sights. This university town hosts many summer festivals. Plenty of parking is available outside the Campo walls. ****Camping: *Off A1, drive into Pisa on S1. North of the Arno Bridge, take Viale delle Cascine east for half a kilometer. Camping la Torre Pendente Viale delle Cascine 86 (05-0561-704); convenient, bungalows; good maintenance; open May-September; $$. *On the beach at Marina di Pisa. Camping Marina di Pisa, Via Litoranea (050-365-53) or Camping Mare e Sole Viale Tirreno (050-327-57); both are popular with locals; well maintained; open May-September; $$.

ISLAND OF ELBE

The clear water and sandy beaches of Elbe are warm and inviting. Camping is resort-style and expensive. Board the car ferry from the mainland at Plombino. ****Camping: Lots! *A less

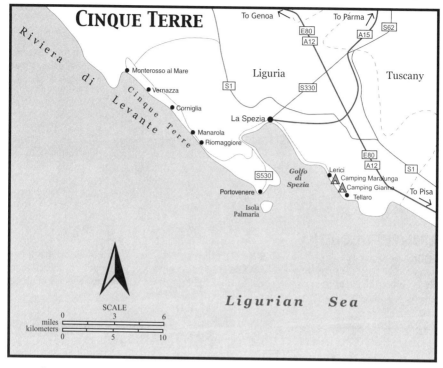

expensive area is Porto Azzurro. Camping Arrighi, km 12 (05-6595-7822); on the beach; good maintenance; open May-September; $$$.

LUCCA

A classy city that seems to do things right, Lucca is the capitol and heart of Tuscany's rich agricultural region. Visit the bustling morning market on Wednesdays and Saturdays at Piazza Anfiteatro where the aroma of basil, vine-ripened tomatoes, and sweet peaches perfumes the air. The array of mouthwatering foodstuffs will be tempt you to buy too much. ****Camping: *On the north side of the walled historic area, at the Piazzale Martiri della Liberta. Drive northeast on Via Batoni, then turn right at Viale Civitali and right on Via del Brennero. Camping Ostello Il Serchio, Via del Brennero 673 (05-8334-1811); a hostel and campground; basic amenities; fair maintenance; open May-September; $.

RIVIERA DI LEVANTE AND CINQUE TERRE

Woven through these tiny mountainside villages is a marvelous walking trail that connects all five. The panoramic view of the spectacular coastline can't be beat. Framed by terraced vineyards, lemon and olive trees, the tiny fishing villages cascade down into narrow ravines. Pack a picnic lunch and a swimsuit. Don't try to drive into the villages; take public transportation. ****Camping: * South of the villages on the Bay of Lerici. Camping Maralunga (0187-966-589); tents only; terraced; close to the water; good maintenance; open June-August; $$$. *Farther south in Tellaro. Camping Gianna, on the Lerici-Tellaro road (0187-653-49); good for RVs; nice location; well maintained; open June-August; $$$$.

EASTERN TUSCANY
SAN GIMIGNANO

Be in this tiny and perfectly preserved town late in the day to join the locals in their evening walk to watch the sun set. Good parking is provided just outside the walls. ****Camping: *Two kilometers south of the town on the road to Volterra, in the village of Santa Lucia. Camping Boschetto (05-77-940-352); good maintenance; open May-September; $.

VOLTERRA

Italy's best collection of artifacts from Etruscan settlers is housed in Volterra's Museo Guarnacci. After viewing, take a walk into the eerie Balze ravine, where bits of the ruins of Etruscan Volterra are exposed. A Crossbow Contest is one of the town's more colorful summer events. ****Camping: *Northwest of the historic area, follow signage to Borgo San Giusto and Balze. Continue northwest to Via Mandringa. Camping Le Balze Via Mandringa (05-8887-880); tennis courts; swimming pool; well maintained; open May-September; $$.

MONTEPULCIANO

Highest of Italy's hilltop towns, Montepulciano invites travelers to imbibe their delicious chianti wines in tiny atmospheric wine cellars. Look in a gift shop for a driving itinerary of the Tuscan wine region then thread your way through the stunningly scenic countryside. A Thursday morning market is held outside the Porta al Prato.

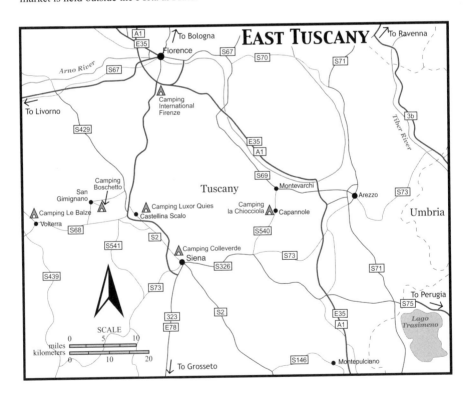

AREZZO

On the first weekend of the month, antique collectors gather at the Piazza Grande in Arezzo to sell and buy. It's a mind-boggling spectacle of goods. While here, don't miss the sensitive masterpiece frescoes of della Francesca. They are in the Chiesa di San Francesco. ****Camping: *About 30km southwest of the city. On the west side of A1. Go south of Montevarchi on S69. then farther south on the small road in the direction of Capannole. Camping la Chiocciola, in Capannole (05-5995-776); on the river; tennis; swimming pool; well maintained; open May-September; $$.

THE MARCHES

Located between the Apennines and the Adriatic, this region is popular with sun-seeking locals and tourists boarding the ferries at Ancona. Well-versed travelers know there is more. The region boasts Urbino, a classy university hill town with beautiful art and architecture, medieval Ascoli Piceno, and Monti Sibillin's Gorge of Hell.

URBINO

Urbino was a prestigious city during the 15th century. Montelfeltro, a ruling figure of outstanding intelligence built a city incorporating a fine fusion of aesthetics and practicality. Today the Palazzo Ducale still sculpts the skyline. Fortress-like on the outside, it sparkles inside with the splendid architectural touches of Bramante and the elegant masterpeice of della Francesca. The Studiolo, a grand triumph in illusory perspective, is open daily. Urbino is lively with summer events. Be sure to stop at the tourist office to find out what's happening. ****Camping: *East of Urbino on S73b, drive 5km in the direction of St. Bernardino. Camping Pineta, San Donato (07-224-710); small, nice location; good maintenance; open May-September; $$.

PESARO

Pesaro was famous during the Renaissance for its ceramics, and a good collection of these early works can be seen in the town's Museo Civico. Opera buffs enjoy visiting the home of Rossini at Via Rossini 34. A morning market is held off the main square, Piazza dei Popolo. ****Camping: * Seven kilometers north of the city on strata Panoramica to Gabbice Monte. Camping Panorama Gabbice Monte (0721-208-145); beautiful views of the sea; steps down to a secluded beach; good maintenance; open May-September; $$. *South of the city five kilometers. Exit off S16 for the village of Fossoseiore. Camping Camp Norina, Fossoseiore (07-2155-792); on the beach; bungalows; good maintenance; open May-September; $$.

GROTTO DI FRASSASSI AND THE ESINO VALLEY

Driving through the Esino Valley into the dramatic narrow gorge, Gola di Rossa, and then walking through Grotto di Frassassi, one of the largest caverns in Europe makes a nice half day diversion. Directions: Exit A14 at Ancona. Drive north, then west on S76 for about 50km. The caves are well signposted.

RECANTI

If you stop in Recanti for a few hours you can examine the costumes and memorabilia of the famous tenor Gigli which are housed in the Palazzo Communale. After walk over to Palazzo Leopardi, home of one of the 19th century's finest poets, where you can ponder over some of his original work; it's just down from the main square. Directions: Exit the coast highway A14 at Porto Recanti. Drive west on S77 for 11km.

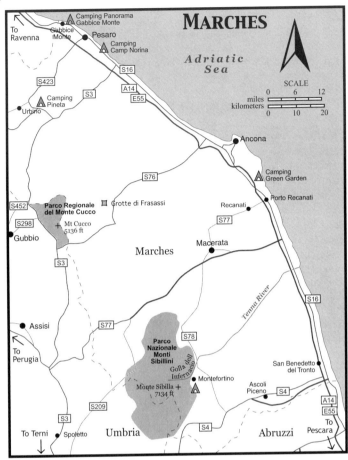

ABRUZZI

ANCONA

This is the largest port for ferries, with routes to Greece, Turkey, and Croatia. The port is well signposted. Tickets are sold at the Stazione Marittima at the waterfront. Follow signs for mercato pubblico if you want to stock up on food. It's a short walk from the waterfront to Corso Mazzini 130, where outside tables at inexpensive cafes make nice places to rest and soak up the atmosphere. ****Camping: *18km south of the city on the beach road to Sirolo, or exit A14 for Numana or Sirolo and drive east seven kilometers. Camping Green Garden, Sirolo (07-1933-1317); close to the beach; good maintenance; open May-September; $$.

MONTI SIBILLINI AND THE GOLA DELL'INFERNACCIO

Mount Sibillini, in the southwestern region of the Marches, bordering Umbria, is popular with

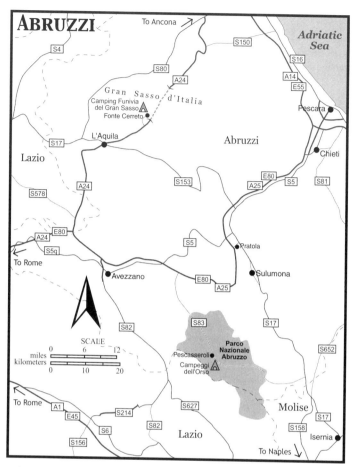

outdoor enthusiasts. Walking trails, hang gliding, and horseback riding enhance a stay. To take the dramatic walk through the Gorge of Hell, look for the trailhead just before you start the climb to the village of Montemonaco. Directions: Monte Sibillini is between Ancona and Pescara, northwest of the medieval village of Ascoli Piceno. From A14 exit onto S4, and drive west in the direction of Ascoli Piceno. Pass the town, driving seven kilometers farther to S78. Drive north 35km on S78, a beautiful small, and winding road to Montefortino. ****Camping: *Close to the trailhead at Isola S. Biago, between Montefortino and Montemonaco. Camping Gola dell'Infernaccio, Isola S. Biago; beautiful location; basic; open June-August; $.

GRAN SASSO

This massif is the highest of the Apennines peaks. If you take the cable car in Fonte Cerreto outside of L'Aquila, you'll ascend 2117 meters to Campo Imperatore, where there are panoramic views and trails down the mountainside. Directions: Northeast ten kilometers of L'Aquila on A24 to the village of Fonte Cerreto. ****Camping: *In Fonte Cerreto. Camping Funivia del Gran Sasso (60-606-163); scenic; good maintenance; open June-August; $.

ABRUZZO NATIONAL PARK

The mountain setting, old-fashioned villages, and walking/cycling trails make Abruzzo a popular family vacation spot. The visitor center in Pascasseroli has a museum, small zoo, and trail maps. ****Camping: *In Pascasseroli, on the river road to Opi. Campeggi dell'Orso (41-919-55); nice location; well maintained; open June-August; $$.

EMILIA-ROMAGNA

The rich farmland of Emilia-Romagna has fostered a cuisine that is one of the best in Italy. It's markets bulge with mouthwatering foodstuffs. Great composers and operatic virtuosos gave it a sophisticated musical palate and racing cars, the toys of the rich, have a home here.

RAVENNA

After the Goths sacked Rome, Ravenna became the capitol of the Western Roman Empire. The Byzantine rulers, anxious to outdo their rival cities in magnificence, developed a crowning level of mosaic art. By placing glass at diffferent angles, the artists achieved an unusual intensity that is almost beyond belief. The Basilica di San Vitale holds the most breathtaking and oldest array of mosaics. Have change so you can illuminate them. Maxamillian's exquisitely carved ivory throne is on view at the Duomo. Dante's tomb is next to the Chiesa di Francesco. Dante wrote much of the Divine Comedy in Ravenna. Musical events fill the city's calendar. You'll find a good morning market in the Piazza Andrea, north of the Piazza Popolo. There's a large carpark area near the Basilica.
    ****Camping: *Just north of the city center at Marina di Ravenna. International Camping Piomboni, Viale della Pace 42 (0544-530-230); close to the beach; trees; disco; tennis; well maintained; open May-September; $$. *In a dune area just southeast of the city center, Lido de Dante. Exit S16 at km 157 onto Fiumi Uniti, and drive to the beach. Camping Ramazzotti, Lido di Dante (0544-772-768); olive trees; close to the beach and dunes; well maintained; open May-September; $$.

BOLOGNA

Bologna's famous university gives this city a dynamic atmosphere easily felt in the central squares of Piazza Maggiore and Piazza del Nettuno, where street theater and music are on-going. Large parking garages are located off the ring road at Piazza 10 Septtembre, near the bus station. Park, and take a bus or ride your bicycle south down the Via dell'Indipendenza to the squares. The enormous Gothic Basilica di San Petronio has impressive door carvings by della Quercia. Across from the Basilica, ask about the local events at the tourist office; many are free. To see the Leaning Towers, walk or bike along Via Zamboni east into the university area. The Pinacoteca Nazionale has a terrific collection of works by Giotto, Raphael, El Greco, and Titian; look for it beyond the Palzzo Poggi. Bologna is proud of its cuisine. Shopping is a mouth-watering experience at both the huge indoor Mercato Ugo Bassi at Via Ugo Bassi 27 and at the outdoor morning market close to Piazza Maggiore on Via Pescherie Vecchie. ****Camping: *North of the city, take exit 8/Fiera di Bologna, off the ring road. Then take the next main road north to Via Romita. Camping Citta di Bologna, Via Romita 12/4a (05-132-5016); convenient location; bungalows; well maintained; open year-round; $$.

FERRARA

Castello Estense, this town's main monument, was once the glittering home of the eccentric Este dynasty. Now its fascination lies in knowing the family story so you can conjure up images of how it once was. Stock up on foodstuffs at Mercato Communale on Via Mercato, next to the Duomo on

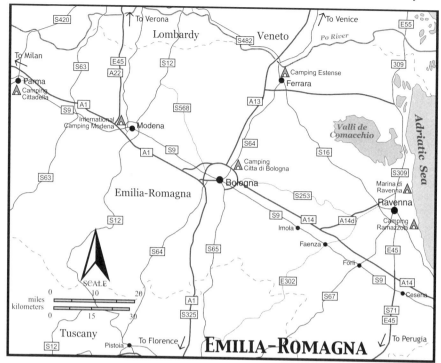

Via Garibaldi. ****Camping: *On the northern edge of the city, take exit 4 off the ring road. Camping Estense, Via Gramicia (05-3275-2396); convenient location; well maintained; open all year; $$.

MODENA

Not only is Modena the home town of the famous contemporary operatic tenor Pavarotti, it is also the birthplace of the exciting Ferrari and Maserati cars. To drool over the cars, go to Galleria Ferrari for a fascinating display of antique, modern, and Formula One Racing automobiles. Directions: Take S12 southwest of town for 23km. Exit for Maranello just south of the intersection of S12 and S467. Signposting leads you to Via Dino Ferrari 43. The gallery is located in a flashy glass-and-steel building; open daily. While you're here, visit the Duomo, one of Italy's best preserved Romanesque cathedrals. ****Camping: *Just west of the city, exit A1 at Modena-Nord. International Camping Modena, Via Cave Ramo 111, in Brucita (059-980-065); convenient to the autostrata; good maintenance; open May-September; $$.

PARMA

Prosciutto, Italy's famous cured ham, is so carefully tended here that the hams are now sought throughout the world. This charming town straddles the Po River. The tranquil air provided a harmonious environment for the famous composers Verdi and Toscanini and inspiration for the 17th century artists Parmigianino and his student Correggio, whose masterpieces are housed in the Duomo. Opera buffs come on pilgrimage here to visit Verdi's birthplace, the museum, Teatro Verdi, and Villa Sant'Agata in Roncole. Directions: Drive west from Parma on S9 for 23km to Fidenza.

Turn north onto the small road S588, cross under A1, and follow signage for 13km to Roncole Verdi. ****Camping: *Inside the old fortress, on the youth hostel grounds. On the eastside of the Po River, south of the main historic area. Camping Cittadella, Parco Cittadella 5 (0521-961-434); good location for the Po River and historic area; well maintained; open May-September; $$.

VENETO AND VENICE

Aristocratic, proud, and shamelessly self-satisfied, Venice is brilliant in her dress of gilded treasures. The whole scene shimmers with dreams of moonlight ecstasies. But it can also feel like a very large, crowded museum so it must be approached and discovered like a cat seeking prey. Museums are closed on Mondays.

When you've caught your breath after arriving at Piazza San Marco, visit the tourist office to purchase a good detailed map of the historic area and to check the events happening while you're here. Don't depend on discovering Venice's treasures with a free map; they won't have the detail you need. To get to the tourist office, walk from the Piazza to the waterfront, and then head west. The tourist office is by the vaporetti (boat-buses) boarding and ticketing area. Wander through Venice's maze of waterways, over its ancient bridges, and into its tiny squares, enjoying the labyrinth.

Take the vaporetti to the Accademia. Before entering the big museum wander over to Palazzo Venier and the Peggy Guggenheim Collection, which houses an eclectic display of excellent modern work and a whimiscal garden. Reboard the vaporetti back at the Accademia, from the side you departed, and ride up the Grand Canal to the Rialto Bridge. Cross over the bridge and, using your map, wander over to the Campo San Polo, where you can rest with the locals and watch children

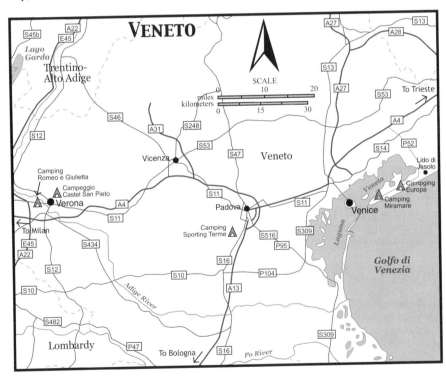

play. Then visit Frai, a massive Gothic cathedral holding masterpieces by Titian and Bellini. Behind the cathedral is the Scuola Grande di San Rocco with its unrivaled collection of Tintorettos. You'll find cafes and trattorias nearby at prices the locals can afford.

Wait to enjoy Piazza San Marco in the evening when the crowds have left. Then dance for free under the stars, while orchestras play from the sidelines. Take the ferry back to your campgrounds, enjoying warm breezes as you ponder the starlit sky and the fading silhouette of this most magical place.

On your second day, get a very early start, and take the ferry back to Venice. Wander over to the open market at the Rialto, where you'll see gondolas unloading their fruits and vegetables. Joke with the fish merchants while you examine their vast selection, noting the cuttlefish, Venice's specialty. Have a picnic lunch on the steps of the Accademia while you watch the gondolas slide by. With your guidebook in hand, you are ready to tackle the bigger stuff. The Accademia's fabulous collection documents the history of Venetian painting from the 14th to 18th century. The treasures in the Palazzo Ducale vividly portray the self-aggrandizement of the founding statesmen and Basilica di San Marco is a rich and exotic jewel case.

****Camping: Exit A4 north of the lagoon area, following signs to Lido di Jesolo. Drive south on the main road in the direction of Cavallino and Punta Sabbioni. There are plenty of campgrounds and markets. Many are full-scale resorts. These two are smaller. *In Punta Sabbioni, Camping Miramare, Lungomare D. (04-1966-150) or *In Cavallino, Camping Europa, (04-1968-069); both are close to the ferry and beach; bungalows; well maintained; open May-September; $$. There's parking at the ferry landing or take the bus.

PADOVA

Giotto's masterpiece of 36, incredibly well-preserved fresco panels, illustrating the life of Jesus and Mary, are cherished in this charming town. A beautiful park surrounds the Cappella degli Scovegni where they are housed. Shopping at the morning market at Piazza della Fruita amongst the coming and going of baskets and old-world commerce is a delight. Directions: Exit A4 north of town for Centrum/Train Station/Cappella. Park in the public lot across from the train station, and cycle, bus, or walk south on Corso del Popolo. The grounds of the Cappella degli Scovegni are just south of the train tracks. ****Camping: *South of the city, exit the ring road onto S10. Drive south for eleven kilometers to Montegrotto Terme. Camping Sporting Termale (04-9793-400); tennis; swimming pool; casual maintenance; open May-August; $$$.

VERONA

Romantic, with rosy-hued historic buildings, lovely bridges across the Adige River, and world-famous opera and theater, this un-touristy walled town is beautifully restored. It's easy to walk or cycle into the historic area. To enjoy the famous opera performances at the Arena, book ahead with Ente Lirico Arena di Verona; 045-800-5151, Piazza Bra 28. For theatre performances at the ancient Teatro Romano, inquire at the tourist office; 045-592-828 close to Arena and Piazza Bra at Via Leoncino 61. Get calendar and ticketing information from the Italian tourist office before your trip. ****Camping: *Exit A4 south of Verona onto S12 in the direction of Centrum. Stay just outside the ancient walls, and drive east on Via Franco. Cross the Ponte Francesco, driving north on the east side of the Adige River on Via Lungadige. Just past the Ponte Peitra, the pedestrian bridge, take the main road Via Nievo east, and wind your way up the hill. Campeggio Castel San Pieto, Via Castel San Pietro 2 (04-5592-037); tents only; charming; fabulous location on a hillside within walking distance of the historic area; can be crowded, but it's a fun and easy place to meet fellow travelers; open May-September; $$. *West of town exit A22 at Verona-Nord, driving north on S12 then east on S11 towards Verona to km 295. Camping Romeo e Giulietta, via Bresciana 54, (04-5851-0243); good for RVs; bus to historic area; swimming pool; well maintained; open May-September; $$.

LOMBARDY AND THE LAKES

Once ruled by the French and the Austrians this crossroads of Western Europe is the richest and most developed region of Italy. Lucky local workers take holiday breaks at the nearby lakes.

MILAN

The fashion and corporate capital of Italy, this city is energized by work, money, and style. Shopping is a passion, and people show off their most recently purchased goods at the cinema, theatre, and musical performances. Bargains can be found in second-hand shops and warehouses selling last-year's fashions.

The heart of the city centers around the Duomo, which has been embellished for five centuries and is now the largest Gothic cathedral in the world. On the northern corner of the Piazza del Duomo is the almost as famous Galleria Vittorio Emanuele, with an opulent glass-dome, expensive shops, and cafes. Passing through it leads you to Piazza della Scala and the world's most famous opera house, La Scala. A small but fascinating museum is open daily; Metro 1: Duomo. The tourist office is at Via Marconi 1 on the southeast corner of Piazza Duomo. Their bilingual yellow-page-like directory is very useful. Museums are closed on Mondays.

Milan holds some of da Vinci's most famous works. His "Last Supper," housed in Chiesa di Santa Maria delle Grazie, sensitively captures Jesus' words, "One of you will betray me." Its sad deterioration adds to its impact; Metro 1: Conciliazone, or Metro 2: Cadorna. Da Vinci's scientific work is displayed in one of the world's largest technology museums, Museo Nazionale della Scienza e della Tecnica; Metro 2: Sant' Ambrogio.

Avoid Milan in August. It's hot, and many businesses close for vacation. During the first 10 days of June, you can enjoy the lively parades, street food, music, and theatre of Festa del Naviglio. Use the metro into and around the city. Get metro directions from the campgrounds. ****Camping: *West of the city, exit the ring road west at San Siro-Via Novara. Campeggio Citta di Milano Via G. Airaghi 61 (02-4820-0134); near the autostrata and metro to the city; bungalows; fair maintenance; open year round; $$$. *In the town of Monza, northeast of Milan. Exit Viale Brianza von Monza, about four kilometers north of town, for the Autodromo. Campeggio Autodromo, Parco di Monza (02-039-387-771); popular with Formula One fans; many permanent residents; fair maintenance; open May-September; $$$.

CREMONA

The delicate Stradivarius violin was created in Cremona. Fascinating musical displays are seen in the tiny Museo Stadivatiano at Via Palestro 17. Around the corner in the Museo Civico, an entire room is dedicated to violins; closed Mondays. Parking is easy close to the train station on Via Mantova. From here it is an easy walk or bike ride into the historic area and the museums. ****Camping: *Southwest of the city, cross the river on Via del Sale, driving south in the direction of Piacenza. Camping Parco al Po, Via Lungo Po Europa, (03-7227-137); nice location; fair maintenance; open May-September; $$.

THE LAKE AREA

Popular and tourist-oriented, this beautiful lake area is a good place to rest and watch the world go by or take part in an active sport. Excursion boat trips ply the lakes, cable car take you up to the Alps, wind surfing, paddling and cycling are all popular pursuits and rentals are available. The local tourist office bursts with glossy brochures. Many of the camping places are full service resorts. I've listed some smaller ones.

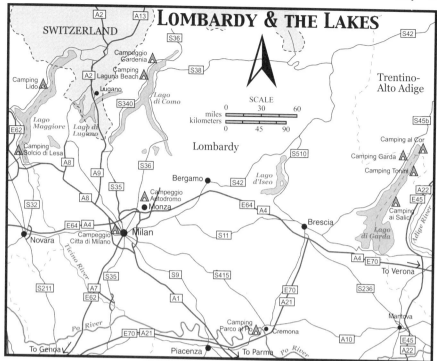

LAGO DI GARDA

Sirmione, on the southern end, is a popular tourist stop off. Walk across the surrounding moat and up through the almost Disneyland-like village to the northern end of town for a tranquil view of the lake. Gardone Riviera, on the western side, is worth a stopover to view the villa of bizarre nationalist d'Annunzio, il Vittoriale; closed Monday. Riva del Garda, the most elegant area, is at the northern edge of the lake. Wind surfing, rock climbing, and mountain biking are all popular activities, and rental equipment is readily available. ****Camping: *In Torbole, at the northeastern tip of the lake. Camping al Cor (04-6450-5222); bungalows; well maintained; open May-September; $$. *In Limone, on the northwestern end of the lake. Camping Garda, off S45 at km 101.5 (03-6595-4550); close to a boat launch; good maintenance; open May-September; $$. *On the eastern side of the lake, in Malcesine, halfway up the lake. Camping Tonini, on S249 at km 72 (04-5740-1341); close to boat launch; fair maintenance; open May-September; $$. *Southeastern end of the lake in Pai, north of Torri del Benaco where there are excursion boats. Camping ai Salici, off S249 at km 55.5 (04-5726-0196); nice location; fair maintenance; open May-September; $$.

LAKE COMO

For a view from the lake of the gardens and elegance of Villa d'Este, Cernobbio and Villa Carlotta, near Termezzo, take an excursion boat ride. For an eagle's view of the lake, take the 750-meter cable car ride to Brunate. It's a gentle walk back down the mountainside. Directions: Both are boarded at the waterfront in Como. ****Camping: *On the northwestern side, in Domaso. Camping Gardenia, off S340 at km 20 (03-4496-262); bungalows; good location; well maintained;

open May-September; $$. *In Pianello del Lario, Camping Laguna Beach (03-4486-315); nice location; good maintenance; open May-September; $$.

LAGO MAGGIORE

At the base of the Swiss Alps, in Stresa, drive or take the cable car up to Monte Mottarone for views and hikes. The garden and zoo at Villa Pallavicino are restful picnic spots or take a ferry out to one of the islands. ****Camping: *On the northwestern end of the lake in the town of Cannero. Camping Lido (0323-788-176); on the lake; well maintained; open May-September; $$. *On the southwestern side of the lake in the town of Solcio di Lesa. Camping Solcio di Lesa, Via Campeggio (03-2274-97); on the lake; bungalows; well maintained; open May-September; $$.

VAL D'AOSTA

Dramatically beautiful and crisscrossed with hiking trails, this area has been carefully protected by locals and tourism is well organized and low key. Val di Cogne, a narrow gorge sculpted by the wildly beautiful Eyvia River, is a highlight. The lush green meadowlands in Cogne are sweet with colorful wildflowers, and there are magnificent views of the mountains. In Valnontey, a breathtakingly beautiful trail follows the river. For an on-the-water experience, book a raft trip in Villeneuve or Courmayeur. ****Camping: *Six kilometers west of Aosta, take S26 in the direction of Sarre. Exit onto S507, and drive south in the direction of Cogne. Camping Lo Stambecco, in Valnontey (01-6574-152); gorgeous views; close to an Alpine botanical garden; well maintained; open June-September; $$. *In the same area but better for RVs. Camping Les Salasses, in the village of Lillaz close to Cogne (01-657-4252); beautiful location; close to a chairlift for hiking; well maintained; open June-August; $$.

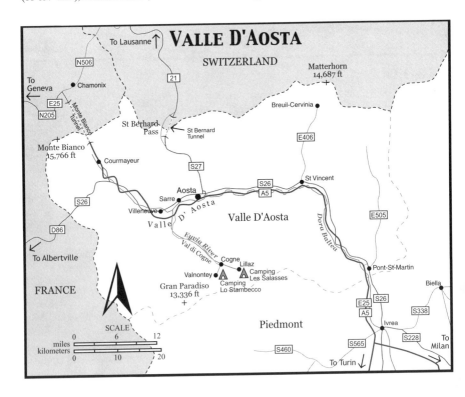

THE NAPLES AREA
HERCULANEUM AND POMPEII

Mount Vesuvius' sudden eruption buried the wealthy Roman cities of Herculaneum, Erolano, and Pompeii, all founded in the 7th century B.C. The destruction eerily froze in time their way of life. Fascinating mosaics, frescoes, ovens, and baths remain as they were, with the best artifacts safely displayed in the Museo Archeologico in Naples. The still-active Mount Vesuvius dominates the area. Drive up to the top and walk around the edge of the crater. Peer into the cauldron and get a good whiff of the sulphurous aroma. Directions: South of Naples on A3, exit Pompeii. Follow signposting for Pompeii Scavi. ****Camping: *In Old Pompeii, outside the main entrance. Camping Zeus (081-861-5320); bungalows; good maintenance; open year-round; $$.

SORRENTO AND THE AMALFI COAST

A narrow road winds for 50km along this breathtaking coastline. Large tour buses coming from the opposite direction can cause your knuckles to whiten as you anxiously grip the steering wheel. Get an early start on this drive, so you can watch the sun rise and enjoy the view. ****Camping: *On the Capo di Sorrento. Villaggio Turistico, Santa Fortunata Campogaio (081-807-3579); fabulous views; bungalows; well maintained; open May-September; $$$$. *Off the same road but better for RVs. International Camping, Nube d'Argento, Via Capo 21 (081-8781344); bungalows; nice location; well maintained; open all year; $$$$

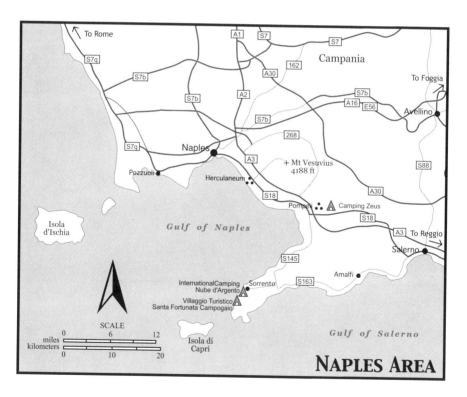

SICILY

Famous for its beautiful beaches and infamous for its Mafia, Sicily also has a sensuously appealing countryside, Greek ruins, and mild weather in the winter. Spend time in the countryside and at the beach first, then come back to Palermo. The scenery is varied and spectacular. Inland, Enna is an engaging mountain town that is close to Piazza Armerina and its Roman mosaics. The rugged Tyrrhenian coast is exciting and photogenic. Syracuse's historic area, out on the island of Ortigia, is connected by bridge to the mainland. Taormina is a stylish resort. Beneath Monte Pellegrino, Palermo boasts Museo Archaeologico's magnificent collection. Always use an attended parking area.****Camping: There are good campgrounds all around the island. Here are just a few. *North of Taormina and the village of Letojanni. Paradise Camping (09-42-363-06); at the beach; good maintenance; open May-September; $$. *On the Tyrrhenian coast, on the bei Castellammare del Golfo, off S187 west of Castellammare del Golfe. Camping Baia di Guidaloca (09-24-541-262); beautiful views; beach close by; good maintenance; open May-September; $$. *In Cefalu. Exit S1113 at km190. Camping Sanfilippo (0921-420-184); close to the beach; shade; good maintenance; open April-October; $$.

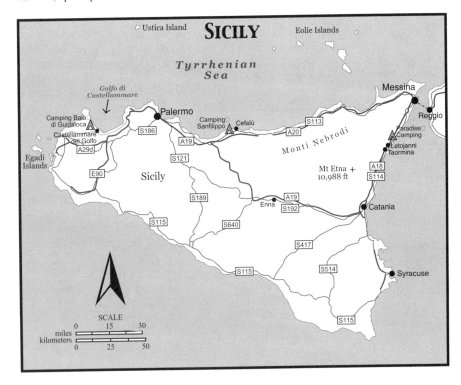

PORTUGAL

Viana do Castelo •

Braga •

Guimaraes •

Vila Real •

Parque Nacional
da Peneda-Gêres

Parque Natural
de Montesinho

Douro River

Porto •

Arouca •

Serra da Arada

Viseu •

ATLANTIC
OCEAN

Buçaco
National
Forest

Coimbra •

Guarda •

Parque Natural
de Serra da Estrela

• Covilha

Zêzere River

Leiria •

Batalha • Fatima •

Barragem
do Cabril

Alcobáça •

• Tornar

Ilha Berlenga •

Tagus River

Obidos •

To Madeira (1000km)
and the Azores (1300km)
←

PORTUGAL

SPAIN

Sintra •

Merida •

• **LISBOA**

Setubal •

Sesimbra •

Evora •

Badajoz •

Sines •

Porto Covo •

Guadiana River

SCALE

0   30   60

miles

kilometers

0   50   100

Seville •

Tavira •

Sagres •   • Lagos

Faro •

Parque Natural
da Ria Formosa

PORTUGAL

When the exploration of outer space was launched scientists knew that the moon was there and that they could invent the technology to reach it. In the 15th century, without knowledge and instruments the Portuguese navigators launched discoveries that were more speculative than trips to outer space. They sailed into an unknown, where, in their time, they were taught that they would fall off the edge of the earth. All great achievements need inspiration and leadership, and Prince Henry, though not a navigator in the narrow sense, played this role for Portugal. With a passion to know what lay beyond, he organized and financed the building of ships, the schooling of navigators, and the cost of many exploratory voyages. The Portuguese navigators were the first to measure and find a relationship between the world's oceans and land. They tied this knowledge together with maps, and produced instruments that gave the Old World a New World. It was a geographical revolution.

The Portuguese today regard their navigational history with pride but don't care to do it again. They never intended to rule the world. They just wanted to enjoy the riches of buying low and selling high. Cathedrals and museums throughout Portugal are today a silent requiem to this remarkable age.

Loving to be with family and friends, the Portuguese often take time out from their usual routine of hard work to participate in grand processions where exquisitely embroidered capes, elaborate dresses, meticulous suits, flower-bedecked floats, and marching bands are all part of the colorful affair. Fond of sharing food, the fiestas include a huge communal meal where traditional food of the region is proudly prepared by locals and generously served to family, neighbors, and visitors. It's worth planning your itinerary to indulge in one.

Roadways have been vastly improved in the last few years. Scenic six-lane divided roads connect major cities. Secondary roads connecting small towns and villages are well surfaced, and traffic is generally light. Drivers are courteous and no longer fit into a reckless stereotype. Locals will go out of their way to help you. Driving regulations and speed limits are what you are used to at home. Standardized international pictorial signs are used. As in the rest of Europe, your membership in a nationally approved roadside emergency club will be honored. Gas costs are similar to the rest of Europe. Be sure the map you use is current, because many new roadways have replaced older ones.

Portuguese love to barbecue and so campgrounds have plenty of grills. You can expect covered cooking and dish washing areas. Showers have warm water and are spacious. Information about the local sights, public transport, and tourist cards are usually available at the campground office. Municipal campgrounds are well maintained and often a better choice than private campgrounds, which cater to families renting large tents. Two persons, a car, and a tent will rarely cost over $20.

Food costs are less than in most European countries. In small towns, trucks loaded with fruits and vegetables provide good quality food stuffs at a reasonable price. Join the locals and shop from them, too. Twenty-four-hour cash machines are popular and easy to find outside banks. Before leaving a larger town, get local currency, fill up with gas, and purchase supplies. Museum entry fees are reasonable, and most are closed on Mondays.

Travelers are surprised to find northern Portugal so mountainous, the Azores so beautiful and untouched by tourism, and a culture happy with the way they are.

LISBON/LISBOA

Built in tiers on seven hills this beautiful city has a grand setting on the Tagus River. Though large, it feels like a town partly because the locals accommodate visitors so well. One of the most severe earthquakes ever caused almost complete destruction of the city in 1755. But the Portuguese, no strangers to seemingly insurmountable problems, faced the devastation with

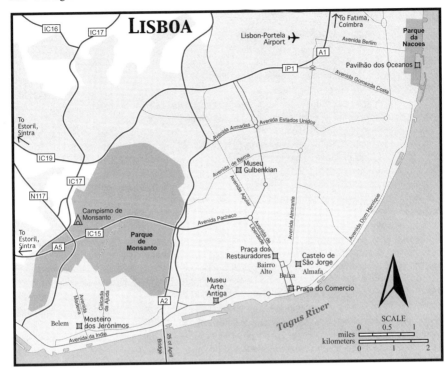

focused practicality, emerging years later with a new city featuring lovely tree-lined boulevards, cobblestone streets, and mosaic sidewalks that are essentially 18th century.

With her back to the rest of Europe, Portugal has always looked out to the sea and been lured, almost as if by mermaids, to explore it. Very daring and courageous sailors left the comfort of their 16th century homes to set sail into this unknown. It is this courage that is commemorated in Belem, a good place to start your exploration of the city.

Begin with the magnificent Mosteiro dos Jeronimos, built soon after Vasco de Gama returned from his historic voyage with monies from the lucrative spice trade. Its decorations exalt both the secular and sacred with joyful exuberance. Note the delicate tracery of the cloister, where slender octagonal pillars rise like palm trees in exotic lands to a spectacular vaulted ceiling. Throughout, sea motifs of shells, rope, and anchors give testimony to the glories of this Golden Age. Pay tribute to Vasco de Gama at his tomb, located just inside the entrance and marked with a caravel. Then turn to admire the monument to Portugal's most revered poet, Luis Camoes, marked with a lyre and quill; closed Monday.

The Museu da Marinha, in the west wing of the monastery, houses a fascinating collection of small boat replicas showing the transition from bark-built boats to the faster square-rigged caravels. Also on display are navigational instruments and maps from the 16th century and artifacts from trading in India and China. Real boats, including an 18th century royal galley, a rabelo from the Duoro, and fishing boats from the Algarve, are on view in the museum's extension; closed Monday.

Emerging from the museum, cross over towards the waterfront to the Monument to the Discoveries fronted by Prince Henry the Navigator. It is a tribute to explorers famous and not so famous, the poet Camoes, and the painter Goncalves. On the north side of the monument is a huge paving mosaic compass decorated with galleons and mermaids and a map showing the sailing route of the 15th and 16th century explorers. Just beyond, an elevator tower provides views of Belem and the Tagus River. Once sitting in the middle of the Tagus River to welcome homesick sailors while at the same time guarding the city, the Torre de Belem looks like a gigantic Moorish-inspired chess piece. If you climb to its roof, you'll enjoy a fine view; closed Monday. Stop by the Centro Cultural de Belem, the stark modern building west of the monument, to see the current exhibition and calendar of performing arts; open daily. Directions to Belem: From the waterfront, tram 15; from the campgrounds, bus 50.

Fascinated with fine art and treasures from around the world, and grateful to the Portuguese people for giving him refuge during World War II, the Armenian oil magnate Calouste Gulbenkian, founded Museu Gulbenkian. Set in a lovely park, the light and airy galleries display the remarkable work of worldwide artists and craftsmen. It's one of Lisbon's highlights; don't miss it; closed Monday. Directions: Northeast of the city: Metro Palhava or Sao Sebastiao. The Centro de Arte Moderna is just across its garden; closed Monday.

The Pavilhao dos Oceanos' enormous and diverse collection imaginatively recreates all the ecosystems of the world's oceans. With an emphasis on the relationship of one ocean to another, this innovative oceanarium is the second largest in the world and is designed for foreign visitors with informative text and videos in several languages. It's another don't miss; open daily. Directions: On the Tagus River at the eastern end of the city at Parque da Nacoes. Metro Gare do Oriente or drive and park.

In the Museu de Arte Antiga, Portugal's national gallery, you can examine a fascinating collection of Chinese porcelain and Portugese faience, the country's most important paintings, and treasures that link the country's relationship with Brazil, Africa, China, and the Indies; closed Monday. Directions: Southwest corner of Barrio Alto; buses 27, 40, 49, or 70.

In the late afternoon go up to Castelo de Sao Jorge, a former Moorish castle. From its ramparts you'll have a panoramic view of Lisboa; open daily. After, walk downhill to the Miradouro de Santa Luzia, a tiny park-like terrace where you can watch the broad expanse of the Tagus River turn golden in the sun. Then continue down through the Alfama's narrow streets where life is still authentic old Portugal. Directions: Take tram 28 ot bus 37 to the top. After walking down, take a waterfront tram to Praca do Comericio and then bus 43 back to the campground.

A traveler doesn't experience all that Portugal has to offer without hearing fado, the emotionally powered, poignant music nurtured on the earthy back streets. Unique to the music is the guitarra, a mandolin-shaped instrument whose echoing sound enhances the singer's voice. Fado houses, run by the artists themselves, are popular with the locals as well as the tourists. Brazilian and African ties have brought some of the most exciting music and food you'll find in Europe. The music will make you want to cry, laugh, and dance almost simultaneously. Ask the English-speaking staff at the tourist office to help you make a musical selection or use your guidebook.

These are only highlights. Lisboa offers much more for the traveler. Stop by the main tourist office at Praca dos Restauradores, a beautiful tree-lined square at the northwest end of the Baixa; open daily. Directions: Metro to Restauradores.

****Camping: *On the western edge of Monsanto Park. From 1C19 or A5 drive west in the direction of Estoril and follow signposting. Campismo de Monsanto (01-760-2061); extra nice; in a pine forest setting; pool; bungalows; close-by public transport; office sells public transport tickets and tourist cards, cafe has live music and is a good place to meet fellow international travelers; open all year; $$.

LISBON REGION
SINTRA

Lovely wooded hills and natural springs lured the Moors to this enchanting setting. Since then the royal, rich, and eccentric have planted exotic gardens and built elaborate palaces. Today this UNESCO-listed town is still very popular. The Royal Palace in the main square, is built on Moorish foundations and is an amalgamation of many styles of the royals who have occupied it. Colorful stories about the inhabitants add to its intrigue; closed Wednesday. Romance must have been foremost in King Ferdinand's mind when he built his elaborate palace on Sintra's highest peak. Called Palacio da Pena, it exudes kitsch charm with an arabesque entryway, life-size torchbearers holding giant candelabras, and eclectic furnishings from all over the world. Trails through a wild garden lead to secret ravines, gazebos, fountains, and a romantic chalet; open daily. Directions: From the Lisbon road, follow signposting at the bottom of the hill by Sao Pedro church. Similar garden intrigues can be enjoyed at UNESCO-listed Quinta da Regaleira; obligatory guided 90-minute tour in Portuguese only; open daily. Directions: Walk half a kilometer beyond the tourist office following signs for Monserrate. The exotic Monserrate gardens spilling down the steep hillside are only partially kept up, but it's still easy to imagine the romance and fantasy the setting provided. Directions: Follow the signposting four kilometers up the hill behind the tourist office. Desiring to be remote from the world, 14th century monks carved retreats in the rocky hillside. Hidden among the pines and oaks the hermitage of dwarf-like cells, called the Convento dos Capuchos, provided simple seclusion for 300 years. Directions: Follow signposting up the hill for Palacio de Pena, at the fork continue on EN247-3 in the direction of Capuchos and Peninha. ****Camping: *In Praia Grande. Follow signposting from Sintra for eleven kilometer to Colares then one kilometers to Praia Grande. Campismo Praia Grande (01-929-0581); older; pool; popular with families; fair maintenance; open all year; $$.

ILHA BERLENGA

Thousands of gulls, puffins, and cormorants find the calm summer waters and rocky shores of this preserve perfect for nesting and raising their young. Comical and sweet, the young birds are fun to watch. As soon as you get off the ferry arrange for the exciting and popular boat trip into the 75-meter tunnel, Furado Grande, to the beautiful Covo do Sonho. Ferry tickets must be bought at least a day ahead in July and August from offices on the jetty below

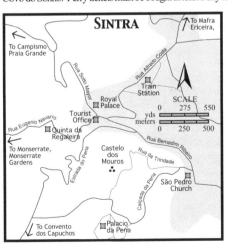

the fort in Peniche. Snorkeling, diving, and fishing trips can be arranged ahead with Turpesca; 262-789-960 or Berlenga Praia; 262-782-636. Take a walk out on the narrow causeway beyond the lighthouse to the Forte de Sao Joao Baptista, now a hostel. If you want to spend the night, both the hostel and campgrounds need advance booking at the turismo in Peniche. ****Camping: *Two kilometers north east of Peniche in Baleal. Campismo Baleal (262-769-333); beautiful setting; small; $$. *On Ilha Berlenga. Campismo Natural Preserve Ilha Berlinga basic; $. To camp on the Ilha arrangements must be made ahead with the Turismo on the river at the east end of Peniche. *In Peniche. Drive north of town on the beach road. Campismo Peniche Praia (262-783-460; beautiful location; pool; open May-September; $$$.

OBIDOS

If you climb up the steep stairway to this charming town's rampart walls, you can look down on red-tiled roofs, white-washed houses, and a pleasantly simple Renaissance church. Shades of deep color from lemon trees, bougainvillea, and pelagoniums brighten the narrow cobbled streets lined with little shops selling hand-icrafts and art. For a thrill, continue walk-ing the ramparts, being careful because at times the walkway is very narrow and there are no handrails. Directions: From Praca de Santa Maria follow sigposting for Ingreja de Sao Tiago and the street that leads to the wall. ****Camping: *At the beach in Sao Martinho do Porto. Drive

north of Obidos for 20km on IC1 then on N366 in the direction of Nazare. Exit for Sao Martinho do Porto and drive four kilometers to the beach. Turn north and drive one kilometer. Campismo Colina do Sol (262-989-588); very popu-lar with families because of its location at a wind protected beach; little shade; open all year; $$$.

ALCOBACA

The monastery at Alcobaca commemorates and gives thanks for the Portuguese victory over the Moors in 1147-the event that founded their nation. The magnificent Cistercian monastery is one of Portugal's most impressive monuments. Enormous soaring columns lift a vaulted roof of great sim-plicity in the central nave. In an adjoining nave attentive angels sweetly guard the tombs of Pedro I and Ines de Castro, whose romance ended in disaster; open daily. ****Camping: *Follow signs from the main square for the sports field and camping. Muncipal Campismo (262-422-265); pleas-ant terraced setting next to a playground and tennis courts; well maintained; open June-September; $$. *At the beach in Nazara. From Alcobaca drive north on N8 for ten kilometers to Nazara. Stay east of the centrum following signage for N242 and Marinha Grande driving two more kilometers. Campismo Vale Paraiso (062-56-1546); lovely dune area with pines; large and popular; pool; parking separate from tent site; open all year; $$$.

BATALHA

Undaunted by hopeless odds against the Spanish and with a genius for strategic planning, Nuno Alvares Pereira led his men with such great courage he has been com-pared to Alexander the Great. Spanish Juan I was married to Portugal's legitimate heir and was so confident of his success on the battlefield that he brought his falcons along in order to enjoy a hunting expedition after what he thought would be a brief foray.

Some Portuguese supported the Spanish king, making the Battle of Aljubarrota a civil war with brothers fighting brothers. Today the Dominican Abbey at Batalha celebrates and gives thanks for the glorious Portuguese victory and independence from Spain in a profusion of rampant joy. Embellished with an orgy of Manueline flourishes, the abbey is one of Portugal's most significant monuments and is the burial place of Prince Henry the Navigator; open daily.

FATIMA

Prayerful devotees approach the devotional shrine of Fatima with intense emotion. Completed in 1953 the enormous Basilica has stained-glass windows that tell the story of the miracle of the sun and the appearances of the Virgin; open daily.

TOMAR

Guarded by the stone walls of a massive Knights of Templars' castle, Tomar's interesting history, pleasant river park, and sidewalk cafes make it good place to take a break in your journey. Every two or three years a famous week-long fiesta draws Portuguese from all over the country to this usually quiet little town. The Fiesta dos Tabuleiros is celebrated with a bullfight, fireworks, barbecues, dancing, and a culminating procession of white-clad women balancing four-to-five-feet-high trays of bread and flowers. ****Camping: *South east of town on the reservoir lake. Drive seven kilometers south of town on N110 exit east and drive six kilometers to Castelo do Bode. Campismo Castelo do Bode (249-849-262); nice lakeside location under the pines; well maintained; open May-September; $$. *Seven kilometers north of town on N110. Campismo Rural (249-301-814); peaceful countryside setting; popular with cyclists; bike rental; well maintained; open May-September; $$.

CENTRAL PORTUGAL

COIMBRA

Perched on a hillside with views grand enough to broaden the perspective of its students, Coimbra University also enhances the town with Portugal's grass roots fado music. Don't miss stopping in one of the darkened taverns to hear black-shawled women wail mournful tales of love and abandonment. Start your exploration of the city by walking up through the old quarter. Then climb the steps up to the massive university gate and patio. Directions: Walk up the stairs from Rua San Pedro on the southeast end of the old quarter. The Mondego River plunges from Portugal's highest peak before reaching Coimbra, where it passes gracefully through the town. Along the river's banks, people gather for a bus shuttle up to Penacova to kayak. For kayaking on weekdays, call one day ahead, in the evening, to the English speaking staff at O Pioneiro Mondego; 239-478-385. For weekends,

COIMBRA AREA

reserve one week ahead. Shuttling is best from Coimbra, not Penacova. ****Camping: *On the east side of the municipal stadium and pool. Drive into the stadium entrance and make a sharp right turn just before the gate into the grand stands. Municipal Campismo Coimbra (039-71-2937); popular with international tourists; shady and pleasant; well maintained; traffic noise; open all year; $$.

PENACOVA

This is one my favorite areas of mainland Portugal. The Rio Mondego's glistening waters inspire musings from poets and artists and whoops of joy from cyclists, paddlers, and fishermen. It's an easy scenic 20km paddle to the first take-out or 25km to Coimbra. Along the way you can jump into the river from large boulders. You'll see morning glories shrouding stone walls, scarecrows trying to ward off hungry birds from tiny terraced vineyards, and spectacular black and white plumed hoopoe birds swooping down for fish and then riding the current. Cycling along the river roads into villages that tumble down hillsides, with stops for a dip in the river, make for a very enjoyable day. In town, park in the main square and shop in the small but excellent bakery, butcher shop, and produce market. Directions: Drive south of Coimbra on the east side of the river. Turn east on N110 and drive 18km to Penacova. ****Camping: *Cross over the bridge just south of Penacova and turn north. Campismo Penacova (039-477-946); wonderful location on the river; bike rental; peaceful; well maintained; church bells ring throughout the night; open all year; $$.

BUCACO NATIONAL FOREST

Moss-covered stone walls, giant ferns, and steep steps up to a cascade of spring water are among the magical sights in this arboretum-like woodland which is particularly pleasant mid-week. In the 6th century, Benedictine monks sought sanctuary here under the hermitage of trees. In the 15th century monies from the overseas expansion built a Carmelite monastery on the site of the present Palace Hotel and provided for the planting of a wide variety of exotic trees and plants. The Palace Hotel was built as a royal hunting lodge and is a bizarre pastiche of the Manueline style. In its arcades are tiled scenes from the great epic The Lusiads by Camoes. Marked paths lead through the woods passing cork-lined hermitages used by the monks. Don't miss the path to Cold Fountain, whose waters rise in a cave within the mountain and then cascade down 144 steps into a lively pool lined with magnolias and hydrangeas. Nearby is delightful Fern Valley Lake. Either drive or hike up to Cruz Alta for a panoramic view that includes Mondego valley and the Serra da Estrela. Directions: North east of Coimbra on N235 follow signposting for ticket gates into the walled forest.

VISEU

Vasco Fernandes, known as the Great Vasco, was born in Viseu and helped found a school of painting that thrived here in the 16th century. Inspired by the Flemish painters, particularly van Eyck, Vasco's paintings exude the intricacy and richness of his mentor's work. The Museu de Grao Vasco's collection includes one of his best pieces, St. Peter On His Throne; closed Monday. Directions: On the north side of the Se, or cathedral. Viseu's fine 12th century cathedral square is graced by the elegant baroque façade of the beautifully proportioned Church of Misericordia, but the highlight of interiors is the Renaissance cloister of the twin-towered Romanesque Se. Directions: Follow signposting from major roadways for Se. ****Camping: *East of town exit I5/E80 for Parque do Fontelo. Campismo do Fontelo (032-261-46); some shade; fair maintenance; open May-September; $$.

PARQUE NATURAL DA SERRA DA ESTRELA

In glacier-formed valleys likable little villages with narrow schist-paved alleyways sit quietly beneath the peaks of Estrela. Here a centuries-old way of life is still undisturbed. At the praca, or square, you can savor a treat at an outside table of a tasca, or cafe, and look out across the valley. In these mountain villages the economy is based on sheep and goats, and they produce fine smoked sausages and exceptional hand-made cheese. With generations of acquired knowledge and discipline, the people live close to the land and learn early not to waste anything. Around the houses, which appear almost to have grown out of the rocky hillsides, hens cluck, and pigs grunt, and on the hour you'll be treated to a concert of church bells bonging, cocks crowing, and dogs barking. On the slopes, where modern machinery is unsuitable, heavy burdens are still carried on harvesters' heads. Narrow, steep roads cut into forests of pine and eucalyptus and are scented with golden broom, rosemary, and lavender. As you drive or walk along them, you'll notice fountains fed by mountain streams built especially for the burden-carrying villagers. Stop here and raise your cup of water in a toast of gratitude, as they do. As you watch the herds of sheep or goats pass by, note the extraordinary sheepdogs. They look like athletic saint bernards. Left with the responsibility of the flock, they are authoritative, with a powerful stride and sharp bark, and you can't help but admire their skill in keeping the herd in tow.

The park preserves antiquities and along walking paths connecting the villages you'll see ancient stone huts and enclosures built painstakingly from piled brown-orange slate. Alongside rushing streams, vintage water mills still stand under leafy chestnut and oak trees. In cultivated green valleys, rivers flow beneath scree-covered slopes where pink and white forget-me-nots peek from the clinks in rocks.

The trailhead for Poco do Inferno and Valle de Rio Zezere begins in the spa village of Manteigas. The trails have wonderful views of the serras, streams are sweet-smelling with anise, and old granite bridges remind you how ancient the path is. You'll hear flocks of goats crying like children as they follow the music from the nannies' brass and steel bells. It's fun to watch them trotting down the hillside's invisible trails, hopping from rock to rock, only occasionally stopping for a rub of the head or a nibble of grass. Midway between Manteigas and Gouveia you'll see strangely shaped rocks on a hillside rugged with gorse and bracken. This region is a landscape of sharp contrasts. Stop at the national park office on the main street in Manteigas to talk to English-speaking staff, to examine the topographical map, and purchase a guidebook. Don't pass up buying some of the famous serra cheese, a hunk of tasty regional sausage, and crusty bread for a picnic.

Penhas da Saude is not a village but a starting point for serious hiking. Desolate looking in the summer, it is the heart of the serra and close to the highest peaks. The park office in Seia on Praca de Republica is a good source for maps and guide books. Linahares, 20km southwest of Celorico da Beira, is a miniscule living-museum-style-village. In the ancient church, you'll see paintings by Grao Vasco. Then follow the little road near the schoolhouse in the direction of Figueiro da Serra, where you'll walk on heavy slabs of rock that were once a Roman road. ****Camping: *Five kilometers northwest of Covilha on the road to Penhas de Saude   Piao Camping (075-314-312); simple; nice mountain setting; open May-September; $. *In Gouveia follow signposting from the center of town.   Campismo Curral do Negro (0238-491-008); convenient; fair maintenance; open May-September; $$.

SERRA DA ARADA

In this charming area of Portugal, small towns ripple down off steep hillsides covered with oak, pine, and chestnut trees into their river ravines.   Goat trails lead to the bottom of gorges where bubbling streams still carve bedrock.   Narrow roads worm their way along hillsides connecting villages populated with modest, frugal people.   As you walk through villages, you'll

breath in the fragrant aroma of grasses, nod to the occasional resident who will usually nod back, and peek into walled gardens where kids play two-man soccer and women tend vegetable gardens. In the evening blackbirds sing out with pleasure to the setting sun in a melody that ripples across the valley.

Arouca is the hub of the area.   Get information on early summer white water rafting, hiking, and interesting drives at the tourist office on the main square.   Take your map and confirm your routes there.   Directions: Between Aveiro and Porto exit IC2 at Oliveira and drive east on N224 for 12km in the direction of Vale de Cambra.   Drive through town following signposting for Arouca continuing for another 20km on N224. ****Camping: *In the Serra da Ferita at Merjal, 18km southeast of Arouca, close to the Seven Crosses.   Exit Arouca at the roundabout on N326, west of the main square, and drive south up the mountain following signposting for Firiz and Figueiredo.   The narrow road winds up the mountain passing the villages.   At the fork to Granja stay west following signposting for Vale da Raiz.   Take a rest and enjoy the fabulous views at the top of the mountain. Then descend the mountain in the direction of Merujal, passing the Seven Crosses.   Muncipal Campismo Serra da Freita (256-947-723); nice setting under the pines; covered cooking area; fair maintenance; open May-September; $.

NORTHERN PORTUGAL
PORTO

A famous wine, the country's language, and the country's name all stem from this important Portuguese city.   Located on the estuary of the Duoro River, it has long been attractive to merchants.   The Romans settled here in the 3rd century, but the Phoenicians were here even before them.   Prince Henry the Navigator built the ships here that lead to the discoveries of new lands and their profits.

Take a rattling tram ride along the riverside and up through the narrow streets where stacked houses are decorated with the morning wash, bird cages, and bicyles.   Directions: Tram 18 from Hospital Santa Antonio on Rua do Carmo.   From hillside Calcada de Vandoma walk down into the alleyways that plunge into the Porto's atmospheric medieval quay-side; UNESCO-listed.   Directions: Take a bus to Sao Benito train station and walk down Avenida Afonso Henriques. After, walk over the Ponte Luis

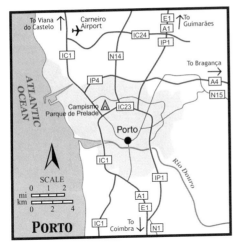

bridge from Cais de Ribeira for beautiful views of the tiered Porto's old town, then tour the port lodges. The smaller ones have an intimate feel; Sandman's has a museum. Visit Cais da Ribeira waterfront market stalls and examine the handsome port-carrying rabelo boats. It's particularly magical to stroll along here at night, when the cafes light up and the views across the river of the city's wine treasures can be savored. Don't miss the ultramodern Fundacao de Serralves and its excellent collection of highly contemporary modern art; closed Monday. Summer musical events are held in the museum's lovely garden; check with the tourist office. Directions: Take tram 18 to the top of Avenida Gomes da Costa and walk 500 meters. For Islamic art stop by the Casa-Museu Guerra Junqueiro, former home of the poet. It displays his lifetime collections of art but the Islamic collection is particularly intriguing; closed Monday. Directions: Down from the southeast corner of the Archbishop's Palace and the Cathedral or Se. ****Camping: *North of the city exit all major roadways onto IC23 then exit for Parque de Prelade. Campismo Parque de Prelade (02-812-616); older; shady; public transport close-by; fair maintenance; open all year; $$.

GUIMARAES

Grand and with a sense of history, Guimaras was Portugal's first capital and is one of the most attractive places in the country. Gold and silver work as well as linen crafts are still high prized, and you'll find artisans working in shops down tiny alleyways. From the main square, Largo da Oliveira, walk up the Rua de Santa Maria to the heart of the old town, where iron grill work and granite arches decorate the superbly restored old buildings. Continue up to the massive battlements of Castelo de Sao Miguel. Climb the ancient narrow stairway winding up to the tiny tower and then stroll along the ramparts for the views. You'll look down on feudal-size plots of land where the famous vinho verde vines climb like snakes onto wooden frameworks. Making a living is hard here, and success isn't from grand and daring ideas but rather from modest, relentless work. There are no long siestas, and lunches and evening meals are eaten early and simply rather than later and elaborately.

At the impressive archeological site Citania de Briteiro a network of paths leads visitors past paved streets, subterranean cisterns, and aqueducts built by the Celts in the Iron Age. Two replicas of the ancient circular dwellings have been recreated on original stone foundations. The museum displays a large collection of excavated artifacts; open daily. Directions: Exit N101 five kilometers north of Guimares and follow signposting east for eight kilometers. ****Camping: *Exit town northeast following signposting for Caldas das Taipas. Campismo Caldas das Taipas (053-576-274); pleasant riverside location; pool; well maintained; open June-September; $$. *Up the mountain south of town in Parque da Penha. Municipal Campismo da Penha (053-515-912); lovely location; pool; popular with families; open June-September; $.

BRAGA

Catholicism is part of being Portuguese. The nation's history can't be separated from it. Believing that good fortune is a gift not a triumph, the Portuguese give thanks for their blessings by hosting some unique and colorful religious processions. In the sumptuous church interiors, priests

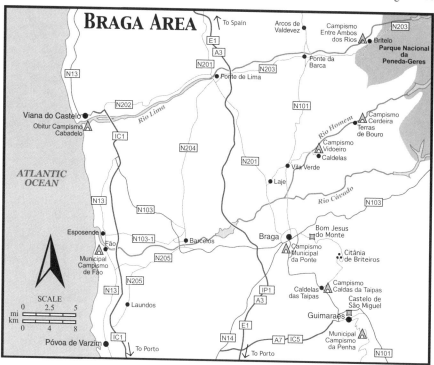

lead the congregation in prayers of thanks, tearful woman and stoic men kneel and pray, and there is a heavy scent of incense. After, a solemn procession leaves the church to the death march-beat of drums and the funeral music of brass bands. The Virgin, dressed in her finest raiments, is carried high for all to see. Black-cloaked penitents march slowly together followed by solemn faced dignitaries. Afterwards everyone relaxes and has fun at a lively communal meal where buxom women vigorously rub chickens with a mixture of finely chopped red peppers and garlic-oil before slapping them over red-hot coals. The mouth-watering aroma will entice you to join a smiling group of locals who will welcome you at a long table overflowing with platters of chicken, baskets of chewy bread, bowls of salad sprinkled generously with radishes, and pitchers of local wine. All of this will be relished along with much laughter and toasts to neighbors and family.

Climbing for spiritual solace is one of the world's most widespread traditions. At Bom Jesus do Monte the climb is up a glorious and fanciful ornamental stairway that cascades down a lush green hillside. Here Jesus' last journey to Golgotha is symbolized in fountains built into the walls of the staircase and tiny chapels with tableaus of life-size terra cotta figures. Ultimately your reach the summit, the church, and the three crosses on the rocky crest of Golgotha. If you don't feel like climbing, you can ride a funicular. Directions: Just outside of Braga drive east out of town on N103 and follow signposting. ****Camping: *South of town next to the municipal park with swimming pool and tennis courts. Campismo Municipal da Ponte (053-733-55); nice terraced location; some shade; good maintenance; open May-September; $.

VIANA DO CASTELO

Baroque facades flecked pleasingly with moss decorate this popular beach town settled in the

18th century by merchants made wealthy by Brazilian gold and diamonds. It is the capital of the Minho folk culture and there are rich examples of azulejo tile work. If you are anywhere near the area in mid-August, plan to stop for their romaria in which every village in the surrounding area is represented with a float. The fiesta includes a blessing of the fishing boats, and the streets close to the wharf are "painted" in religious themes with colored sawdust. The whole three-day festival is an old-fashioned good time with barbecues, fireworks, and dancing. Feudal-size strips of land stretching inland from the sea have encouraged mini-size cooperative farming. You'll see iodine-rich seaweed drying on frames and fences waiting to be incorporated into the soil as fertilizer. Behind high granite walls, farm equipment and vegetable gardens surround square monolith homes with red-tiled roofs. ****Camping: *At the mouth of the Lima River at Praia de Cabedelo. Obitur Campismo Cabedelo (058-322-167); popular with families; close to the beach; shady with pines; fair maintenance; open May-September; $$$.

MARKETS

For a heady dose of old Portugal, join the bustle of people from the countryside heading for the weekly open market. You'll breathe in an earthy fragrance from huge mounds of potatoes, kale, apples, and fava beans. When merchants return your greeting it will be in an almost shy and reticent manner. You'll be gently pushed aside by ample-figured women in black, squeezing past looking for bargains. Tables are piled with Portuguese sweet bread golden with egg. Racks drip with hand-stuffed linguica carefully smoked over chestnut wood and bowls of olives glisten with flecks of garlic and chilis. Sharp-eyed shoppers carefully watch the scales and penciled calculations.

Business is brisk at the following markets: Barcelos; every Thursday; the largest, it is a real extravaganza from dawn until late afternoon, taking place at the main square, the Campo da Republica, in the center of town. Ponte de Lima; bi-monthly on Mondays, takes place along the river. Ponte da Braca; every other week on Wednesday evenings, at the15th century bridge. Arcos de Valdevez; alternates with Ponte da Barca every other Wednesday night, at the main square. Directions: Barcelos is 20km west of Braca on N103. Ponte da Lima is 35km north of Braca on A3/E1. Ponte da Braca is 18km east of Ponte de Lima on N203.

At the end of summer the usually taciturn Portuguese let down their hair at festivals that become going-away parties for family and friends who are returning to their homes and work abroad. The celebrants parade in carnival-like huge costumes called gigantones, brass bands march, and fireworks explode. Special markets are held for linens and other folk arts. The longest and liveliest festival is Ponte da Braca's Feira de Sao Bartolomeu during the third week of August. In Ponte de Lima the celebration is on the second and fourth weekends in September and in Arcos de Valdevaz the second weekend in August. ****Camping: *On the beach three kilometers south of Esposende in Fao. Municipal Camping de Fao (053-981-777); pleasant location; good maintenance; open all year; $$. *See Braga.

PARQUE NATIONAL DA PENEDA-GERES

Walks in this beautiful national park are scented with the fragrance of years gone by. You'll pass columns of hay drying on ropes hung from the limbs of chestnut trees, tiny walled patches of corn, and ancient cross-decorated stone espiqueriros, or graneries. Stop in one of the villages huddled next to a stream, and pass through the beaded curtain of a tiny grocery store to buy some local mountain cheese and smoked linguica. Choose a bottle of vino verde from a shelf of dusty bottles. The narrow roads here twist through lush fertile valleys up to wild ridges where the rest of the world is left behind.

The best interpretative center is at the park office in Ponte da Barca. Here you can talk to English-speaking staff, examine a large-scale map, and view photographs of the unusual flora, fauna, and agriculture. The trails threading through the mountains to ancient villages are the same that generations of herders and villagers used, and marking is poor. Consider hiring a guide if you want to take a long hike; you'll be contributing to the local eco-tourism and will gain a trouble-free, interesting experience; call a day ahead to the park office in Ponte da Barca; 258-452-450. Directions: Exit A3/E1 35km north of Braga at Ponte de Lima. Drive east 18km on N203 in the direction of Ponte de Barca. Stop at the interpretative center. Directions: From the old bridge follow Rua Conselheiro Rocha Peixoto east to Largo da Misericordia. ****Camping: *Ten kilometers east of Ponte da Barca on N103 on the river just outside the entrance to the park in the village of Britelo. Campismo Entre Ambos os Rios (258-683-61); close to the villages; simple; open June-Spetember; $. *In the spa town Caldas do Geres. Exit A3/E11 nine kilometers north of Braga at the village of Laje and drive five kilometers east in the direction of Vila Verde passing through town and continuing east for another eight kilometers to Caldas do Geres. Campismo Vidoeiro (253-391-289); nice setting on the river; popular with families; well maintained; open May-September; $$. *Eleven kilometers farther into the park from Caldas do Geres north of the village of Terras de Bouro. Campismo de Cerdeira (053-351-005); part of the park system; simple; well maintained; open May-September; $.

****Enroute Camping: 22km south of the Spanish autostrata A52 in Chaves. Exit N103 at Chaves and follow signposting to the river and bridge. Campismo Municipal Sao Roque (076-227-33); simple; convenient; well maintained; open May-September; $.

PARQUE NATURAL DE MONTESINHO

Softly rolling plains, painted ochre in summer, stretch out lazily in the sun enticing travelers with a quietness that is broken only by the twittering of birds, the humming of insects, and the rustling of leaves. Here and there the carcases of fortress walls still stand in this wild country touched little by tourism. In remote villages hidden in the hillsides, villagers have learned to share equipment, labor, and ideas in order to survive. Decisions affecting the community are made at chamados, or town meetings, rather than in the region's capital building. There is no pressing need here to be anything other than what you are. It's the calm beauty of this isolated region that's so enticing to walkers and cyclists. ****Camping: *Eight kilometers west of Braganca on N103. Campismo Cepo Verde (273-999-371); pleasant location; pool; fair maintenance; open June-September; $$.

SOUTHERN PORTUGAL
EVORA

The production of grain has long been important in this region. During the Roman era, Pliny the Elder described Evora in his Natural History as Ebora Cerealis. Later, when the Moors from Africa arrived, their geographer described it as having a strong castle with stone walls and a surrounding area of pasture lands. Today the plains of Alentejo stretch out like oceans of cork trees with only the occasional sprinkling of towns. Evora rises from the plains, almost surreal-like, with parts of her walls still intact. Throughout the Middle Ages Evora grew steadily in importance and was the headquarters of the Knights of Avis, who ruled the region. Luckily, its elegant 16th century mansions were tapped by UNESCO, making restoration possible.

In the heart of the old walled city, fourteen Corinthian columns stand elegantly reminiscent of the city's 2nd century Roman rule. Across from the Temple Romano, guests pay well to sleep in the cells and dine in the cloisters of the ancient Convento dos Loios. Walk from here down the hill to the severe, fortress-like Se, or cathedral, where soldiers fought and residents took refuge against

Spanish and French intruders. After passing through its Gothic interior, climb the stairway to the coro alto, or terrace, for a photogenic view of the two unusual towers. Don't leave before viewing the highlight of the museum's treasures-an exquisite ivory statute of the Madonna whose midriff opens to a tiny triptych of scenes from her life. Directions: Follow signposting for parking on Estrada da Circunvalacao then walk up the hill to the main square, Praca do Giraldo, to the tourist office on the southwest corner. For exercise, take a bicycle tour of the megalithic sights; the mysterious stones date from 4000 BC. With a picnic lunch, the bicycle trip along the quiet roads can be a pleasant day in the Portuguese countryside. Directions: Get a map and information about rentals in the tourist office. ****Camping: *Two kilometers southwest of town on N380. Campismo de Evora (069-251-90); pool; well maintained; open all year; $$.

THE ALGARVE

On a finger of the Atlantic that leads through the Strait of Gibraltar to the Mediterranean Sea, beautiful sandy beaches have long attracted sun seekers from northern Europe. Mediterranean-style resorts now vie for space between white-washed villages tucked into harbors. Dramatic bluffs and sea-water lagoons are interspersed between stretches of fine sand that seems to go on forever.

TAVIRA

Filigreed balconies grace the houses along this town's Rio Gilao, and a Roman bridge still crosses it. The Moors occupied the Algarve longer than anywhere in the country. Climb up to the Moorish castle at the top of the hill for a view of the peaked red-tiled roofs, the lagoon, and the sea that separates Portugal from Morocco. At the harbor-side morning market you can purchase some of the luscious oranges and densely sweet figs that were exported by ancients fleets traveling to far way places. After, wander down to the port to breathe in the aroma of the sea and the morning's catch as you wander through the piles of fishing nets and salt-encrusted boxes. Tuna is the star on the menu, and it's difficult to pass up a tasty snack or a fresh piece for cooking later. Beautiful sand dunes and beach stretch for miles on the island. ****Camping: *On the island. Take the ferry two kilometers south of town at Quatro Aguas. Campismo Municipal da Ilha de Tavira (081-235-05); beautiful location; small store; good maintenance; open May-September; $$.

PARQUE NATURAL DA RIA FORMOSA

In a labyrinth of lagoons, channels, and wetlands birds stop enroute between Africa and Europe to breed and raise their young. The rare purple gallinule resides here all year. Resembling a chick-

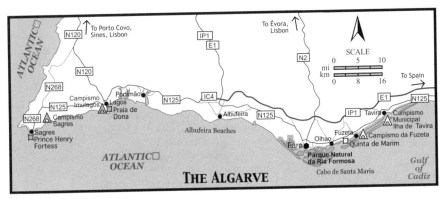

en, except for a brilliant red beak and feet, they are fast runners but poor fliers. Originally from Eastern Europe, the red-crested pochard ducks can be seen swimming side by side then suddenly rising straight up to literally run across the water. Fiddler crabs scuttle in between tides searching for tasty morsels. Take your binoculars in the early morning and evening to watch the vast numbers of bird and crustaceans feeding on these sand islands that are only recently protected. Directions: Three kilometers east of Olhao exit off N125 for Quinta de Marim, the interpretative center for cultural history of the region as well as the fauna and flora of the lagoon. ****Camping: *16km east of Faro in Fuseta. Exit off IP1/E1 for Olhao. Drive south three kilometers on N398. Exit east onto a small road following signposting for nine kilometers to Fuzeta. Campismo da Fuseta (089-793-459); open all year; $$

LAGOS

Swimming at sunset or in the morning through the tunnels and caves at Praia de Dona may be one of your most memorable times in the Algarve. Between swims you can rest in tiny coves sheltered by towering cliffs of purplish-tinted rock. Directions: West of town on waterfront road over the hill to the promontory. This town was Prince Henry's base for the deplorable slave market. It is marked today only by a plaque on the arcades where trading took place next to the Customs House on Rua da Senhora da Graca off Praca da Republica. Directions: East of the hospital off the waterfront road Avenida dos Descobrimentos. Although the 1775 earthquake and subsequent mountainous waves caused extensive damage to the town, some Moorish archways of the old walls survived. Directions: Walk from Praca Republica west on Rua do Castelo dos Governadores. ****Camping: *West of town on the waterfront front road. Campismo Imulagos (082-760-031); nice shady setting at the beach; large; bungalows; pool; tennis; fair maintenance; open all year; $$$.

SAGRES

One of the best places to get a sense of what the early navigators must have felt is within the fortress that Prince Henry used as a school of navigation. Out on this windswept promontory his students looked down on the enormous rock-made rose compass, studying the strengths and directions of the prevailing winds, and then sailed out to Brazil, Angola, the Cape of Good Hope, Goa, and Macao. ****Camping: *Two kilometers north of Sagres on N268 close to Praia do Martinhal. Campismo Sagres (282-624-351); popular with surfers; basic; fair maintenance; open May-September; $$.

SOUTHWEST COAST
SESIMBRA

Located in a sheltered south-facing bay, protected from the cold north winds by the Serra da Arrabida, Sesimbra's fishing-village character has been replaced by sidewalk cafes, beach resorts, and second homes. Climb up to the Moorish castle for wonderful panoramas of sea and countryside. ****Camping: *In Sesimbra close to the waterfront old fort. Campismo Municipal

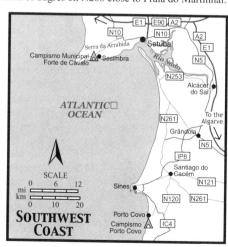

Forte do Cavalo (01-223-3694); nice location; well maintained; open April-October; $$.

PORTO COVO

White-washed houses trimmed colorfully in blue and red line the streets of this tiny village situated fourteen kilometers south of Sines. Relics of an old fort sit high on a bluff above its cove beach. Colorful fishing boats transport people to the offshore Ilha do Pessegueiro for beach picnics and swimming. ****Camping: *Exit IC4 eight kilometers south of Sines and follow signposting south in the direction of Porto Covo for six kilometers. Campismo de Porto Covo (069-951-36); beautiful location on the beach; well maintained; open all year; $$.

THE AZORE ISLANDS

Carpets of lush green pastures, serenely embroidered with the blue and pinks of hydrangeas, spill from mountainsides to the endless blue of the sea in these mid-Atlantic islands located 1300 kilometers west of mainland Portugal. Pristine crater lakes, some warmed by hot springs, reflect the passing clouds. Cows herded by youngsters, horse-drawn carts loaded with milk cans, and walking villagers share with a few cars and pick-ups, winding two-laned roads banked with hydrangas and ginger lilies. Walking paths lead up and into once active volcanic craters, to waterfalls lined lushly with ferns and azaleas, and to isolated rustic stone villages. Throughout the Azores beautiful cove settings have been used to construct natural swimming areas that the whole family can enjoy. Small walls have been built to contain seawater, forming lagoons where snorkeling is possible. In another area the water is allowed to come in as breakers, making bodysurfing great fun. An adjoining swimming pool with diving board and toddlers' wading pool completes the fun for the whole family. Eco-tourism is catching on in the Azores. Check with the

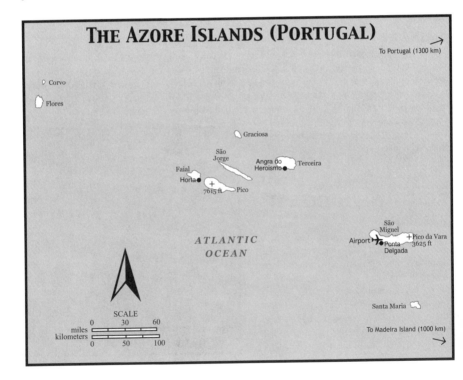

tourist office in the larger towns to book guides and rent equipment for fishing, hiking, scuba diving, and boating. In small towns and villages a carefully tended bandstand is the center of town celebrations. Hilltop churches are affectionately outlined with strings of lights. As you wander down the streets, you'll smile at little homey scenes and your greeting will be returned by people who seem to be at peace with themselves. In today's world it is hard to find a place so naturally beautiful and yet relatively unaffected by tourism.

Trucks loaded with fruit and vegetables pass through the villages, providing quality goods for a reasonable price. Join the locals and shop there, too. Meat in the market is frozen, so buy it in the morning so that it is ready to cook in the evening. Barbecuing is very popular, and parks and campgrounds have grills. Include charcoal on your shopping list. Each island listed has at least one campground. Sometimes toilet and shower facilities will show wear and age but they cost next to nothing and the beauty of the scenery makes up for it. Always wear rubber-soled shoes when hiking. The basalt rock of the volcanic islands can be slippery on some of the cobblestone paths. Sometimes the paths pass through gates; be sure to leave them as you found them.

The Azoreans love festivals and fill their summer with them. Emigrants return from abroad for vacations in the warm welcoming of family and friends. Streets are carpeted by petals in extravagant designs. Processions of proud parents and family follow youths draped in exquisitely embroidered capes. From hay-filled carts, pretty girls in scarves pass out loaves of crusty bread. Afterwards visitors are welcomed to feasts of Sopas do Espirito Santo, a hearty soup, and Alcatra, a tasty type of barbecued beef. Bands play, girls flirt, boys wink, and there is much laughter and dancing.

The two-lane roads that skirt the islands' coastline meander through or by all the villages. Always fill up with gas in the larger towns. Only one or two roads actually cross the island. You won't zip from one place to another on the Azores. It's a leisurely pace in a leisurely place.

SAO MIGUEL

Largest of the nine islands, Sao Miguel is still only 65km long. International flights to the Azores arrive and depart from its capital Ponta Delgada. Three 18th century arches grace the waterfront, where walking paths are elaborate patterns of tiny tiles constructed with exacting thoroughness. Visit the Museu Carlos Machedo to see the large relief model of the island, paintings of Azorean life by Rebelo, and exhibits reflecting life on the islands; closed Monday.

Before you leave the airport stop and talk with the friendly English-speaking staff at the tourist office. They have the driving and hiking maps you'll need for all of the islands. Have them help you make the pre-arrangements necessary for hiking into the forest preserve on Sao Miguel. Confirm the current dates for the various island festivities, and pick up a schedule for the ferries.

Traveling from one island to another on a ferry is fun and not expensive.
Nordeste is one of the loveliest parts of the island. It shelters a campground at the mouth of the river close to a beautiful natural swimming pool. From the campground, you can walk up the hill to a simple village and then farther up the luscious green mountainside. A 19th century seven-arch bridge forms a graceful entrance to the tiny town. Sit in the square and admire the 15th century Igreja de Sao Jorge as you absorb the tranquil simplicity of everyday life. Walk over to the traditional crafts school and watch the women weaving on hand looms. Hike up through Planalto dos Graminhais to Pico da Vara at 1105 meters for a fabulous view of the northeastern side of the island and the sea. Directions: Drive west from Nordeste on R1-1. After passing Feriera Grande, watch for signage for Planalto dos Graminhais. Drive up the hill to Espigao dos Bois, where the trail begins. You'll need to plan ahead for this hike, because it needs special permission from the forestry department in Ponte Delgada. Have the tourist office call for you when you arrive at the airport. If you are athletic and adventurous take the steep hike from Lombadas to Pico da Vela. Directions: East of Riberia Grande turn inland, following signposting for Caldeiras da Ribeira and Lombadas. At the fork continue following signposting for Lombadas. Park at the Lombadas water-bottling factory and walk behind the factory where the trail begins. Follow the stream on the left side. At the crossing sign the trail begins to climb steeply but you are rewarded with magnificent views of the lush valley below. At the top the trail levels out and has fine views of an exquisite turquoise lake, Lagoa do Fogo. The drive south of Nordeste is unbelievably beautiful; leave plenty of time to stop at the miradouros, or view points. Continue south and then west to Furnas, where dramatic terraces of rock steam with hot bubbling springs. Hibiscus, camellias, and azelas are colorful under a stunning collection of century-old trees that shade the stream and ponds in the park behind the Terra Nostra hotel. Take a picnic and spend some lazy time at the remote beach Praia do Fogo. The water is warmed by underwater volcanic activity. Drections: From Furnas, drive south six kilometers to Ribeira Quente. ****Camping: *At the northeastern tip of the island in Nordeste. At the north end of town follow signposting to the bottom of a steep stone road. Campismo do Nordeste (296-488-185); lovely location at the mouth of the Guillerme River; close to the natural swimming pool; parking separate from camping; simple; open May-September; $.

Like two sisters in silk, the emerald green and sapphire blue lakes sit pristine and quiet in their crater bowls of verdant green. Caldeira das Sete Cidades, seen on the cover of many Azorean tourist brochures, is on the northwest end of the island. Start your exploration from the top of the caldeira at Vista do Rei where the rim walking path begins. Directions: From Varzea, follow signposting up the mountain for Sete Cidades, stopping at Vista do Rei before you descend to the lovely lakes and the pretty little village of Sete Cidades. It's a very tranquil place. You'll hear only the song of birds and the whisper of wind in the trees as you walk around its of twelve kilometer circumference. ****Camping: On the lake. This is not an official campground so be discreet and set up the tent in the evening and take it down in the morning.

PICO AND FAIAL

Only the ghosts of the whalers, known as sea wolves, remain in Pico, which was once the center of the Azorean whaling tradition. Today people go out on to the ocean in exciting inflatable eight-to-ten man rafts to see the baleeiros, or whales, and the dolphins give a show. To appreciate the courage of the whalers and to make your own trip more meaningful, examine the fascinating whaling canoe, exquisitely carved whale bones, tackle, and memorbilia at Museu do Baleeiros in Lajes on the south side of the island before going out. Expert guides at Espaco Talassa in Lajes are led by radio messages from staff who scan the sea from the former vigias, or lookouts; 092-67-2010. In the last week of August, join hundreds of Azoreans in a gleeful celebration of the whales. During the rest of summer, you can whoop it up with the locals at the Emigrant Festival in July, when the locals welcome back their family and friends who work abroad, and in the first week of September, when they celebrate the harvest of the grapes that make their fine verdelho wine.

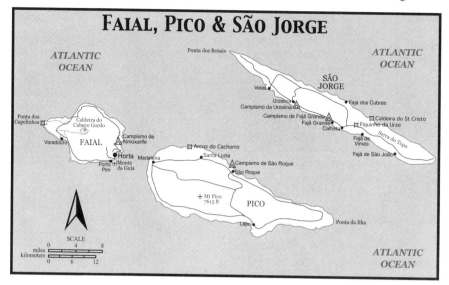

FAIAL, PICO & SÃO JORGE

Mount Pico rises majestically in the center of the island, daring the adventurous to climb its peak. At the top hikers climb into the 30-meter deep crater or walk around its 700-meter circumference. Fumaroles still steam from its base. Hiring a well-informed guide promotes the ecotourist economy and makes the trip trouble-free and interesting; make arrangements at the tourist office in Madalena on the west end. For a less strenuous experience walk through the dramatic Arcos do Cachorro, where the ocean thunders through tunnels and grottos of lava. Directions: Follow signposting on the north side at Santa Lucia, east of Madalena.

Take the daily ferry over the narrow ocean canal to tiny Faial, an island popular with international yachtsmen crossing the Atlantic. Intricate carvings in fig wood are an island craft and are the highlights in the Museu da Horta collection of nautical memorabilia. Don't miss it; closed Monday. Drive up to the Caldeira do Cabeco Gordo to peer down into the mystical, and silent steep-walled crater. A path winds around its rim. Directions: Drive west of Horta on the coast road following signposting to Varadouro. Just before the town, follow signposting up the mountain for Caldeira. At Vulcao dos Capelinhos it's easy to imagine what a holocaust would look like. In 1957 and 1958 the area was devastated when a volcano erupted burying a lighthouse and homes with its molten lava. Directions: Drive west of Horta to the promontory Ponta dos Capelinhos. Drive or hike up to Mount Guia for spectacular views of Faial and Pico then descend to relax on the sandy beach at Porto Paim. Semana do Mar, or Sea Week, in the first week in August, draws a generous sprinkling of international enthusiasts for an all-around good time highlighted by sailing and kayaking regattas. ****Camping: *On Pico in Sao Roque. Campismo de Sao Roque do Pico (292-642-422); wonderful setting; basic; open May-September; $. *On Faial north of Horta at Praia do Almoxarife. Campismo de Almoxarife (292-292-131); beautiful location on the beach; well maintained; open May-September; $$.

SAO JORGE

The dramatic vistas from Sao Jorge's Serra do Topo trail stretch down from steep mountain slopes to tropical fajas, or slopes, where the climate is so tropical passion fruit grows. Hikers tread old cobblestone paths along streams that once turned the tiny water mills now hidden in the lush vegetation. Then they descend into a crater to the remote and beautiful Calderia do St. Cristo lake before hiking down to Faja dos Cubres, a tiny harbor where fishing boats launch. Directions: For a very reasonable fare friendly taxi cab drivers will pick up passengers from the campground, take them to the trail head, and then pick them up at Faja dos Cubres. Contribute to eco-tourism by letting a local show you what he is proud of; he'll fill your day with the best the island has to offer. The trail begins northeast of Calheta at Piquinho da Urze and ends at Faja dos Cubres on the north side of the island. For a steep hike with spectacular views, start at the old road at Faja dos Vimes. The trail crosses the Cavalete river, climbing up steeply at first, then moderately before descending to Faja de Sao Jorge, where there are beautiful views of waterfalls. Then it crosses the Sao Jorge river and continues into the village of Faja de Sao Jorge, where a taxi can be called. Sao Jorge's cheese is savored in fine European markets, so be sure to sample it while you're here. ****Camping: *North of Calheta at the beach in Faja Grande. Campismo da Faja Grande (295-412-214); beautiful location on a seaside bluff; well maintained; open June-September; $$. *South of Velas at the beach in Urzelina. Campismo da Urzelina (295-414-401); beautiful location; terrace above a rocky shoreline; pool; well maintained; $$.

SANTA MARIA

At Santa Maria's Mare do Agosto, or August Tide Festival, it's music that counts. The festival takes place at one of the Azores' longest sandy beaches, Praia Formosa, during the second week in August. You'll mingle with camping guitarists and vocalists and hear music mixed with the crash of the surf under a romantic canopy of stars. At Sao Lourenco Bay, considered to be one of the most beautiful bays in the Azorean archipelago, vineyards are carefully divided by basalt walls that give a lush checkerboard effect to a half-crater hillside before it reaches the sea.

The closest island to mainland Portugal, Santa Maria was the first to be settled. Coming from the Algarve, the pioneers brought their chimney designs with them, and the fine cylindrical forms still rise from pyramidal-bases on white-washed houses. Fine examples can be seen in the village of Malbusca. Grateful to be home, members of Christopher Columbus West Indies crew landed here and gave thanks in the tiny 15th century church in Anjos, probably the oldest church on the islands. With only indigenous materials to work with, the islanders have carefully carved the native basalt into lovely designs to decorate their churches. Particularly impressive is the Baroque façade of Nossa Senhora da Purificacao in the village of Santo Espirito. Santa Maria is a small island, so enjoy some countryside walks between villages. ****Camping: *At Praia Formosa. Campismo da Praia Formosa (296-882-213); wonderful location at the beach; fair maintenance; open May-September; $.

TERCEIRA

Terrorized by an invading force of 16th century Spaniards, the weaponless islanders cleverly gathered what they had-an enormous herd of cattle-and released the mooing creatures on the beach, preventing the Spaniards from landing. Seemingly never tired of being courageous, they have played vital roles in Portugal's civil war and in World War II and today are honored by UNESCO for heroism. Angra do Heroismo's historic area also exemplifies the wealth it once knew when the galleons, heavy with gold from South America, landed for supplies and repairs.

After a devastating earthquake in 1980, the UNESCO listing gave the city the support it needed for restoration. Housed in the lovely Convento de Sao Francisco, the exhibits in the Museu de Angra do Heroismo reflect this past; closed Mondays. After, step inside the church next door and remember Vasco da Gama's sorrow after his return from his first trip to India, when he laid to rest his brother Paulo.

A huge lava flow, now only slightly covered by the sea, makes a fun and popular place for a swim. Called Biscoitos, or biscuits, because of the pools created by the lava, it's on the north side of the island. Wine makers of the fine Biscoitos wine have long felt that foot-pressed grapes produce a finer wine than machine-pressed grapes. In their interesting wine museum you can see the big vats where people danced knee-high in grapes (not an easy task) while the fiddler played. Midway between Angra and Biscoitos, stop at Algar do Carvao and stand inside the 100-meter-deep volcanic blast hole where the origins of Terceira are vivid; open daily. ****Camping: *On the southeast corner of the island at Baia da Salga. Campismo da Salga (295-905-451); beautiful location; well maintained; open May-September; $$.

THE ISLAND OF MADERIA

Closer to Morocco than mainland Portugal, Maderia is a jumble of high mountains, steep ravines, and coastal lowlands created from volcanic action. In a voyage financed by Prince Henry the Navigator, the Portuguese explorer Joao Zarco found a warm island abundant in water and heavy with forest perfect for growing "white gold," or sugar cane. Slaves were brought from close-by Africa to terrace the hillsides and create the irrigation channels that are still keys to Maderia's prosperity.

Though lacking the sandy beaches and peaceful remoteness of the Azores, Maderia has a charm of its own. Often shrouded by rain forest-like foliage Madeira's levadas, or irrigation channels, have trails alongside them that provide exhilarating walks of great beauty. Directions: Drive west from Funchal on 101, passing through the long coastal tunnel, following signposting to Ribeira Brava. If you don't mind driving along a narrow road clinging precipitously above the ocean with dark one-way tunnels, turn north onto 104 and climb up the terraced mountainside where

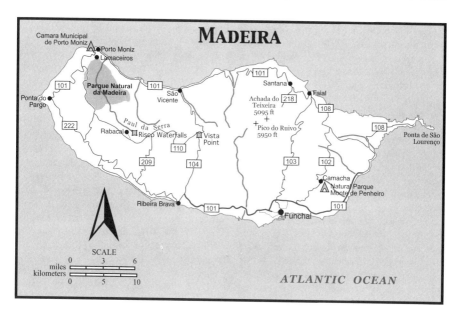

bougainvillea drips prettily from white-washed villas and banana trees grow wild. Stop at the vista point at the top for a terrific panoramic view, and then descend down the winding forested road to Sao Vicente and the sea. Turn west onto 101 where the rock-hewn narrow road clings just above the sea. Be prepared for a little "whitening of the knuckle" driving for 53km out to Porto Moniz, where the island's campground is located and where there are trailheads for levada walks. Otherwise continue west from Riberia Brava on 101 for 12km to 209. Turn north onto 209, and climb up the mountain for eleven kilometers to 110. Turn west and follow the high plateau road for 23km through the Paul da Serra and Parque Natural da Maderia, and then descend down the mountain to 101. Turn north and drive seven kilometers on 101 to Porto Moniz. ****Camping: *In Porto Moniz. Camara Municipal de Porto Moniz (091-85-3447); beautiful location close to natural rock swimming pools; small; popular with international travelers; well maintained; open May-September; $$.

One of the most popular walks is from Rabacal on the Paul da Serra plateau to the waterfalls of Risco and 25 Fontes, a less than 2-hour round-trip hike. From the harsh plateau the trail descends to a rain forest-like habitat of mosses, ferns, and water. Directions: From camping in Porto Moniz, drive south on 101 for seven kilometers to the fork for 110. Turn onto 110 and drive 17km to Rabacal. Park in the lot at the viewing and picnic area. Follow the signposted trail to Levada do Risco and descend 100 meters. Enjoy the cascade originating from the tiny Lagoa do Vento, then return on the same trail. Before you reach the parking lot, follow signposting north for Levada das 25 Fontes. When you come to the levada, walk in the opposite direction of the flow of water to a pond and the cascades of 25 Fontes.

Tunnels add fun to the Fonte do Galhano levada walk, where waterfalls, maiden-hair ferns, and miniature begonias shroud the rocky cliffs and forests whisper with laurel and oak leaves. Most people can stand straight up in the tunnels and don't feel nervous after the first one. Inside the trail isn't overly narrow and the levada wall is knee-high, but you'll need a flashlight or headlamp. Many of the tunnels are short, less than 100 meters; two are 200 meters. At times you'll be in complete darkness except for your flashlight. The tunnels are clean and free of flora and fauna. This is a four-to-six-hour round trip hike. Bring a waterproof jacket for changeable weather, energy food, and water. Directions: From camping in Porto Moniz, drive one kilometer up the hill to the village square, mercado, and bank. Continue up the hill for three more kilometers following signposting for Lamaceiros. At the flower-planted divider strip, turn east following signposting for Lamaceiros. Drive through the village. At the fork and signposting for Porto Moniz, turn away from Porto Moniz and drive to the reservoir station in the forest and park. The trailhead is across the road from the station's office building.

Hiking in central Maderia is highlighted by the ascent to Pico do Ruivo, where the views over the rugged rocky landscape and down into the narrow river gorge are superb. Ethereal clouds and the rising sun make for heavenly scenes at sunrise. Directions: From Funchal, drive north on 103 for 28km to Faial. Turn north on 108 and drive six kilometers to Santana. Turn inland and drive up the mountain on R218 for seven kilometers to Achada do Teixeira. Park at the trailhead. Include a waterproof jacket for changeable weather, water, and energy food in you daypack, and wear rubber-soled shoes. Follow the well-marked trailhead three kilometers to Pico do Ruivo. To extend the hike, continue along the backbone of the mountain, where you'll have a choice of trails descending and then ascending in several directions. ****Camping: *(Important note: To camp here you must have permission procured from the office of parks in Funchal. This can be done by fax from home; fax 00-351-291-203-803 or call 00-351-291-232-014.) South of Camacha at the preserve at Monte de Penheiro. Directions: East of Funchal exit 101 north onto 102 following signposting for Camacha. At the fork for Camacha and Pismo exit onto the Pismo road and following signposting for the preserve at Monte de Penheiro. Natural Parque Monte de Penheiro; lovely setting in the pines; used for outdoor education; well maintained; open all year; $$.

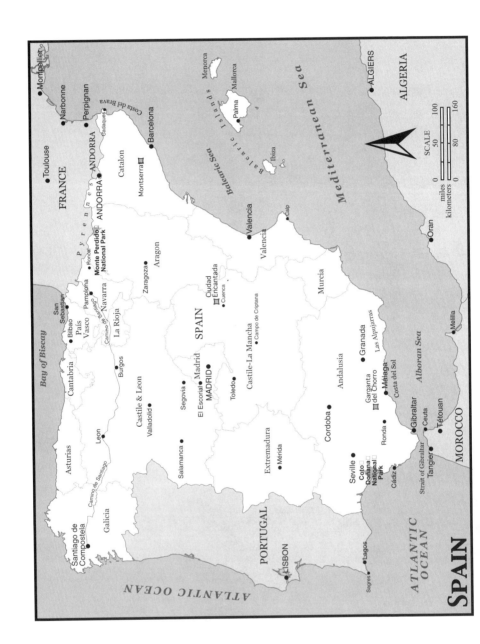

SPAIN

Nothing is more important to a Spaniard than his roots and native region. It is this regionalism that gives Spain its unique character. To experience it, you must get off the beaten track.

Every town is a center of intense social and political life, with the plaza mayor as heart and core. Here the pleasures of eating, drinking, and conversation are foremost. You'll hear church bells strike with purpose rousing and summoning rather then chiming for pleasure and in the country at dusk lambs and goats bleat, dogs bark, and children's voices ring out in play.

Somber Romanesque cathedrals exteriors are offset by altarpieces fanning out in rampant joy and dazzling with an orgy of gold. Here Mudejar or Arab elements are firmly embedded in the architecture with finely carved geometric patterns interlaced with figures of saints and plant motifs.

Spain's a romantic, erotic country where poetry speaking of tragedy, desperation, or betrayal is prized. The subtle rhythm and beat of music is provided by clapping hands and stamping feet while dancers, in a theatrical locking of eyes, move in rhythmical courtship.

With warm weather, beautiful beaches, savage mountain terrain, dramatic architecture, exciting art, and lively street life, it's no wonder that Spain is one of the world's most popular vacation destinations. Europeans, longing for sun, have packed their camping gear and headed south to Spain for many years. Campgrounds abound. Some are resort-like while others are simple grassy areas with a few shade trees. A swimming pool, a simple store, cafe, terrace, and hot showers are almost de-riguer in the well maintained campgrounds listed. A tent, car, and two persons will usually cost just under $20 USA. Resort-like campgrounds or ones that are close to major tourist sights will be closer to $25 USA.

Driving is not difficult. Roads are well signposted, and reasonably priced parking is often provided in underground parking areas. Roadways are in good condition and many are divided, but remote roads are narrow and often winding. A few toll roads are found along the popular coastal areas that bypass the beach towns. In major cities, leave your car at the campground and take public transport to the city. Your best source of information about this will be your fellow campers who know the important details that perhaps campground staff forgets to mention.

Except in remote areas, cash machines are easy to find and use. Gas cost is similar to the rest of Europe, and supplies cost what you are used to paying at home. Some major museums and sights no longer close for the traditional long lunch and rest, but most still do, allowing you to enjoy them in the early evening. Spaniards are friendly, easy to be around, and want to make your stay and visit as pleasurable as possible. They enjoy a good time and want you to have one, too.

MADRID

One could start their visit to Madrid at the Puerto del Sol because it is the city's point of reference as well as a meeting place and the location of Madrid's famous bear fountain. Directions: Metro Sol. Or perhaps begin at Plaza Mayor, a masterpiece of Renaissance architecture built by the Hapsburgs when Spain was at its height of power. Directions: Metro Sol then walk west on Calle Mayor. But I like to start at Retiro Park where I can join the promenade of Madrilenos along its tree-lined walkways, laugh with the kids at the puppet show, and drop some coins in the "living" statue's box so the gold-glazed figure will turn slowly to bow and wink. Directions: Metro Reterio. After absorbing the ambiance here I am ready to tackle the bigger stuff and I stop at the tourist office on the southwest corner of the Plaza Mayor.

At the Prado, Madrid's most famous museum, spend some time scrutinizing Velazquez's powerful portraits of weavers and blacksmiths as well as his complex masterpiece Las Meninas. Goya's witness of the brutality and suffering of war made his powerful and famous black paintings almost terrifying. See them but then look for the evocative ones he painted in France. Don't leave the museum without smiling at the fantastic pleasures seen in Hieronymus Bosch's Garden of

Delights. The museum boasts not only the largest collection of Titians, but important works by Raphael, Correggio, and van der Weyden. Don't try to see the whole museum. Use a guidebook to seek out what interests you most; closed Monday. Directions: Metro Banco de Espana then walk south along the Paseo del Prado. The stunning Museo Thyssen-Bornemisza gracefully takes the viewer through a remarkable collection. Try not to miss it; closed Monday. Directions: Across the plaza from the Prado, on the northwest corner.

In the evening, nibble tapas with Madrilenos at a sidewalk table around the Plaza Ana and it's spiderweb neighborhood. You'll imbibe a Madrid distillation watching the apartment dwellers walk their dogs, university students intense in excited debates, and old and young walking slowly hand in hand. Directions: Metro Sol then walk south on Calle Carretas then east on Calle de la Bolsa.

Spanish art is closely connected to its history. Picasso's huge mural size Guernica depicting the destruction and terror during the Spanish Civil War is almost stupefying. It hangs in the Centro de Arte Rein-a museum-cultural center whose collection concentrates on 20th century art; closed Tuesday. Directions: Metro Atocha.

****Camping: *Close to the airport. Eight kilometers east of the city exit off N-11 at km. 8.3 in the direction of Barajas and follow signposting west of the railroad tracks. Camping Osuna (91-741-05); older; little grass or shade; casual maintenance; noisy; metro to city center; open all year; $$$. *20km southwest of the city. Exit Madrid's ring road M40 at exit 36 and drive west on 511 in the direction of Boadilla del Monte to km. 7.8. Follow the road south in the direction Villaviciosa de Odon to km. 12. Camping Arco Iris (91-616-0059); pool; tennis; some shade; well maintained; transportation to city by bus and metro; open all year; $$$$.

MADRID REGION
EL ESCORIAL

Built as a place to bury the royal families of Spain, El Escorial is a forbidding lonely monument to royal excesses. The royal mausoleum, monastery, and enormous church were finished after twenty-two years of labor provided by three hundred men working round-the-clock. Phillip II watched the construction from his rock-hewn chair carved out of the mountainside. He filled the great library with priceless manuscripts, paintings, and tapestries designed by Goya. Later, sick and dying, he spent hours watching services from a tiny room off the choir, his diseased leg propped up on a special chair; closed Monday. Directions: Northwest of Madrid 60km follow signposting off either M505 or NVI.

The best part of visiting Valle de los Caidos, Franco's monumental tribute to himself and those that fought for him, is the view; open daily. Directions: Nine kilometers north east of Escorial on M600 just off NVI. ****Camping: *Three kilometers south of town off M600. Camping El Escorial (918-902-412); large; nice location; popular with RVs; some shade; all the amenities; well maintained; open all year; $$$$.

SEGOVIA

Seen in front of the orange and gold explosion of a Spanish sunset, the giant, double-decker, unmortared stone arches of Segovia's Roman acqueduct are breathtakingly dramatic. Towering 30 meters above the Plaza de Azoguejo and reaching an expanse of 800 meters, they are an engineering feat that is almost beyond comprehension for its day. Directions: Southeast corner of the town; follow signposting from major roadways.

The florid construction of both the Alcazar and Cathedral is impressive and photogenic; open daily. Directions: At the northwest end of town; follow signposting inside the ancient walls. ****Camping: *Southeast of the city follow signposting for acqueduct and camping. Camping Acueducto (921-425-000); shade; pool; small; well maintained; open April-September; $$.

SALAMANCA

Graceful and harmonious like San Marco's in Venice, the Plaza Mayor in Salamanca is etched with shady paseos, or arcades, along buildings that glow with great amber beauty in the setting sun. Take

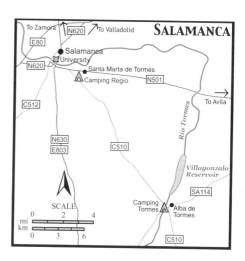

time to study the intricacies of the plaza's accents, balconies, and facades. Along with the universities in Bologna, Paris, and Oxford, the university in Salamanca was one of the finest in the medieval world. When you walk through the library and cloisters, it's easy to imagine scholars discussing new ideas; open daily until 1 P.M. ****Camping: *South east of the city exit C510 for the suburb of Santa Marta de Tormes and following signposting. Camping Regio (923-130-888); shady; pool; well maintained; open all year; $$. *23km south of the city on C150 in the town of Alba de Tormes follow signposting one kilometer south of town. Camping Tormes (923-160-998); pleasant setting close to the river; little shade; open all year; $$.

LEON
From the mammoth stained-glass windows in Leon's Gothic cathedral, a kaleiscope of brillant red and gold hues dance on the somber stone walls. You'll swear there is more glass than stone; open daily. Directions: East end of the historic area; follow signposting from all major roadways. ****Camping: *34km south of Leon on N630 exit east onto 621 and drive eight kilometers towards Valencia de Don Juan. Camping Pico Verde (987-750-525); pleasant setting on a grassy lawn; some shade; well maintained; open June-September; $$.

ENROUTE CAMPING
Between Burgos and Leon *45km southeast of Leon on N120 in Sahagun follow signposting. Camping Pedro Ponce (987-781-112); near the public park with swimming pool and tennis courts; some shade; well maintained; open April-September; $$.
Between Burgos and Madrid *In Aranda de Duero. Follow signposting north of the city off N1 at km. 162. Camping Costajan (947-502-070); natural setting with pool and shade trees; well maintained; open all year; $$.

BURGOS
Burgos provides a nice stopping place between more famous destinations. Its gigantic Gothic cathedral boasts two immense spires richly decorated in a florid fantasy; open daily. The pedestrian plaza in front of the cathedral is a good place to relax in the sun or shade. ****Camping: *Two kilometers southeast of town on the river. At the intersection of N120 and N623 exit southeast for Cardenadijo. Camping Municipal Fuentes Blancas (947-486-016); pleasant setting on the river; pool; large; well maintained; open April-September; $$.

TOLEDO
As you approach Toledo, the town walls, rooftops, imposing Moorish Alcazar, and 100-meter spire of its Gothic Cathedral rise sharply above the bridge over the Tagus River. It is famous as El Greco's home. Born in Crete in the mid-1500s, El Greco traveled to Italy and studied the works of the great Renaissance masters with Titian. In his mid-thirties he came to Toledo in hopes of large commissions from Phillip II that didn't materialize. Having rejected the Renaissance concepts of perspective and proportion, he was unencumbered by patronage and free to develop his own style of loose brushstrokes and sharp contrasts of light and shadows. Today in Santo Tome Church, you can view his masterpiece, Burial of the Count of Orgaz; open daily. A large collection of his work can be viewed at Casa del Greco. However his best works are in the collections of museums throughout Europe and the USA; closed Tuesday. His real home, where he lived with his mistress and mother of his son, was a large apartment in a friend's mansion once located in the Juderia where Paseo del Transito is today. The park is a good place to wait until the museums reopen after lunch.
Across from this park, visit the Synagogoa del Transito, built with the town's Moorish heritage in mind. Hebrew inscriptions decorate the walls, and artifacts of Jewish life in Spain are displayed;

closed Monday. A few steps away in the Santa Maria La Blanc, which was once the city's oldest synagogue and later became a church, you're treated to mosque-like rows of columns in a quiet corridor.

In the Cathedral off the Plaza Mayor, examine the carved choir stalls telling the story of the Christian conquest of Granada from the Moors. Then look at the Cathedral's high altar, which soars in such a great fantasy that you are left dazed by the orgy of gold; closed Sunday morning. The windows of the Alcazar provide fine views of town and photos from the two-month siege in 1936, when the Nationals occupied the Alcazar, are displayed; closed Monday.

In the late afternoon, when the day-tripping tourists have left, locals come out for some conviviality with their neighbors at Plaza de Zocodover, making it a great place to see a little of the real Toledo. The Museum de Santa Cruz, down from the eastern side of the square, houses several El Greco masterpieces, works by Goya and Riberia, and a large collection of rugs and tapestries; open daily. In the early evening, drive up the hill high above the gorge of the Tagus to view tiny Toledo, suspended on a rock above the river and glowing in the fiery orange light of sunset. It could be your most lasting memory of Toledo. ****Camping: *On the west side of Toledo. Drive west of town in the direction of Pueblo de Montalban on 502. Cross the bridge over the Tagus and follow signposting for less than a kilometer. Camping El Greco (925-220-090); lovely setting; pool; bus to historic area, well maintained; small store and café; open all year; $$$.

OLD CUENCA

High up from the plains, on a broad flat plateau perched above two rivers, Old Cuenca still clings to the edge of almost vertical cliffs. The famous Hanging Houses, an intriguing complex of buildings that cantilever precariously out over the river valley, now house the well-known Museum of Abstract Art and its collection of the best of Spanish abstract artists; closed Monday. Narrow streets lead through tunneled passageways to treacherous flights of stairs. Not far from the Hanging Houses, the Archeological Museum displays a fair collection of Roman statuary plus interesting paintings of the people who once lived in old Cuenca. You'll find parking close to the cathedral and square. Directions: 70km southeast of Madrid on E901 exit east onto N400 at Tarancon, and drive 84km. ****Camping: *Exit north of town into the Jucar Gorge and the limestone park Cuidad Encantada on CU921, and drive six kilometers. Camping Cuenca (969-231656); nice location on the river; shady; fair maintenance; open Easter-December; $$.

LA MANCHA AND THE WINDMILLS OF DON QUIXOTE

A few white windmills made famous by Cervantes' romantic hero, the indomitable Don Quixote, still stand like flailing giants in the village of Campo de la Criptana in the La Mancha region southeast of Toledo. Once an area devoid of shade and water, today it is a vast flat land of fields filled with wheat, corn, and vines. Stop in the nondescript little town's park to eat your picnic lunch. As you rest, you'll see a classic Spanish scene: old men intense in a game of boule, women dutifully sweeping the sidewalk, and dogs sleeping in the shade. Directions: 68km southeast of Toledo on 400, at the junction of 400 and E05 at Madridejos, drive east 30km on 400 to Alcazar. Outside of town exit east onto 420 and drive seven kilometers to Campo de Criptana.

CORDOBA

With great Moslem zeal, Emir Abderrahman I began in 785 the construction of what he hoped would be a mosque rivally any in Arabia. Today the Mezquita still stands as one of the greatest Moorish monuments in the world. A crew of skilled craftsmen and 16 tons of small pieces of glass for the mosaics were provided by the Christian Emperor in Constantinole. Columns were brought from the ruins of Roman and Visigothic buildings. Varying in height, some of the columns were buried deeper in the ground and others were raised. Resting on the top of each row of pillars, a tier of horseshoe arches was built and atop this a second tier, forming an intertwining of branches as in a forest. As the population of the city grew, the mosque was expanded, and 200 years later it was double the original size. The many doors of the mosque opened out into a large patio, letting light filter into the vast space. Among the few ornaments in the patio were oranges trees whose blossoms perfumed the air, a slender minaret or prayer tower where devotees were called to prayer, and a lovely fountain where they cleansed themselves before praying. The prayer niche, or mihrab, was octagonally roofed by a dome carved from a huge block of marble and is resplendent with intricate carvings. Once an enormous bejeweled Koran lay on an altar of ivory and precious wood. Perfumed oil was lit in 300 candelabra, some of whose lamps were made from bells stolen form the Santiago shrine in 997. When the Christians conquered Cordoba in 1236 most of the doorways were filled in and in the 16th century, to the protest of the local citizenry, a large choir was built in the center; open daily. Directions: On the westside of Rio Guadalquivir. Follow signposting from E/5 for Central Cuidad. Park on the eastside of the river by the small Arab fortress and walk across the bridge to the Mezquita.

After, walk west into the Juderia, or Jewish quarter, where white-washed houses line quiet back streets. Seek out the small statue of Maimonides, considered by many to be one the foremost Jewish thinkers. Born in Cordoba, he lived close to where the statue is tucked. Peek into tiny courtyards, where patio floors are paved with pebbles in pleasing designs and flower pots drip with the tendrils of sweet-smelling jasmine vines. At 12 Judios Street, stop at the Cordoban House Museum to get a sense of the 12th century charm evident in its tranquil patio, fountain, and furniture. Next to the craft center, or Zoco, you can look at bullfighting memoribilia in Museo Taurino. Outside the Puerta de Almodovar stands a statue of the philosopher Seneca. Born in Cordoba in 4 BC, his philosophy has been an important influence in Spanish thought. Directions: North end of the Juderia. The Museo Arqueologico houses its collection of artifacts from Iberian, Roman, Islamic, and early Christian eras amid the ferns and shady courtyards of a Renaissance mansion; closed Monday. Directions: Walk northeast out of the Mezquita. ****Camping: *In Cordoba. Exit E5 for Mezquita. Cross the river passing the Mezquita and old town on the south side. Drive north on the main boulevard following signposting for Parador. The road changes its name as it threads its way through town. At the Plaza de Colon turn north onto Brillante and drive one kilometer. Camping Municipal El Brillante (957-282-165); popular with international travelers;

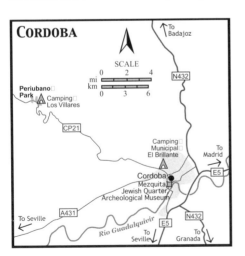

swimming pool, small store; bus to the historic area; open all year; $$. *In Parque Periurbano, a nature center. Follow the directions for El Brillante but continue 500 meters farther. Turn east onto San Jose de Calasanz following signposting for Los Villares. Continue up the hill for eight kilometers. Camping Los Villares (957-453-211); natural setting under the pines; spacious sites; interpretive center; covered terrace; well maintained; open May-September; $$.

SEVILLE

Under starlit skies, warm breezes mingle with the notes of a quavering guitar and a voice deep with the laments of sadness, love, and loss-all poignant reminders of ancient Seville when the region was so fruitful it was beyond the belief of her neighbors. The Moors from Africa constructed palaces, dykes, quays, and towers that were marvels of engineering. They repaired the old Roman acqueduct, built a bridge over the Guadalquivir, walled the river, and constructed towers to guard the city. Ships traveled up the river, and Seville became the emporium of the Mediterranean. The Moors built a fabulous Alcazar, or palace, and their mosque vied in splendor with the Mosque of Cordoba. On the imperial tower Giralda, four great spheres proclaimed greatness. The city's intellectual pursuits gave them unquestioned leadership in the medieval world.

The Mediterranean climate, dry mountain terrain, and groves of olive trees here, reminiscent of Israel, attracted Jews. They flourished under the Moorish rule, holding important positions as emissaries and ambassadors among the various Moorish kingdoms. Many of the caliphs had Jewish physicians, and Jewish scholars refined the courts. Seville was great, noble, and rich, replete with every comfort and luxury and a rendezvous of scholars and artists

This was the city that Ferdinand III, the Saint, surrounded with his immense army in 1247. They burned houses, destroyed orchards, trampled harvests, and tore out vineyards. The siege lasted for 16 months, and in the end, hunger and despair caused the inhabitants to surrender. The great mosque of Seville was torn down, with only the Giralda left standing. Inside, you can walk up the rampway, built to allow mounted passage, to the bell tower for fabulous views; open daily.

On the site of the mosque, an enormous cathedral was built with a special chapel for Ferdinand III. He lies enshrined there in a massive silver casket, near his son, Alfonso X the Learned, one of the great rulers of medieval times. The cathedral is the third largest in Europe; open daily.

Only a small portion of the original alcazar, next to the cathedral, remains. Various rulers have added and changed the palace to suit their taste, but the Mudejar art remains highly colored and imaginative. In the apartments used by the navigators there is a model of the Santa Maria-the ship used by Columbus-and the famous painting Virgin of the Navigators; closed Monday. Grand, well-planned gardens adjoin the palace, and a small passageway leads to the shady miniscule squares and streets of Santa Cruz.

Both an outstanding collection of the sensitive paintings by Zubaran and El Greco's portrait of his son can be viewed at the Museo de Bellas Artes; closed Monday. Directions: North of the historic area, east of the river and the Plaza de Armes bus station.

Community celebrations are at the heart of Spanish culture and, whether they celebrate a saint or a season, they are immersed in ritual.

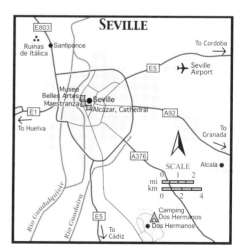

With almost everyone participating, the shared experience binds the community together. Around Easter, Seville celebrates Semana Santa and Feris de Abril with an Andalucian brilliance. Experiencing even a part of either one of them brings memories that last forever.

Because of the extraordinary color of the sand and the proportions of the ring itself, the Maestranza, Seville's bullring, or Plaza de Toros, is probably the most handsome in Spain. Some of the most famous events in bullfighting have taken place here. Arranging for tickets is difficult and expensive, but it's easy to tour the museum; closed Sunday. Directions: West of the Cathedral, along the Guadalquivir.

Italicia, a 3rd century Roman town, was the birthplace of three emperors: Trajan, Hadrian, and Theodosius. At this archeological site, use your imagination to see 40,000 people in the grand amphitheater and then examine the fanciful birds in the mosaics. Directions: Exit the northwest corner of the Seville onto E803 and drive north for eight kilometers through the village of Santiponce following signposting. ****Camping: 12km south of the city in the suburb of Dos Hermanas. Exit A4/E5 at km 554 and drive east several kilometers. It's across from the round-about in the center of town. Camping Dos Hermanas (95-472-0205); best for Seville; large pool; bus to historic area; well maintained; open all year; $$.

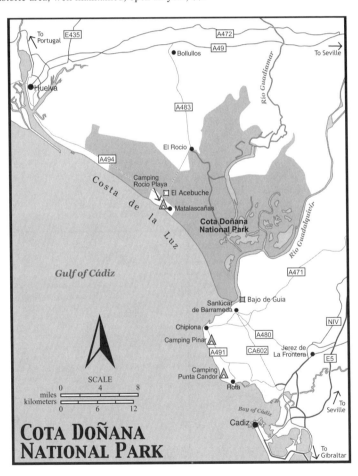

COTO DONANA AND AROUND

COTO DONANA NATIONAL PARK

This mobile sand desert of marshes, dunes, and shallow waterways is one of Europe's most important nesting areas for migrating birds. Warm weather and rich-silted marshlands make a perfect duo for the exotic birds. Fragile flamingoes bow their long necks, relishing the algae-rich soup. Herons and egrets watch silently for a passing fish and launch, as if from a springboard, when disturbed. Long-billed stilts bow and preen in courtship rituals. Visitor centers and obligatory guided tours enhance your study of this UNESCO World Heritage biosphere. A four-hour boat ride up into the park's marshland, with several stops for bird-and-animal watching and a look into the simple fishermen homes constructed from indigenous materials, makes a nice outing. Binoculars can be rented on board. The boat launches from the Bajo de Guia quay in Sanlucar, across from the interpretive center; operates daily in the morning and afternoon. Directions: From Sevilla drive south on A/4 for 85 kilometers. Take exit 4 off A4 and drive west four kilometers to Jerez de la Frontera. Follow signposting through town for Sanlucar/480 continuing for 24km. At the football field at Sanlucar drive north on the main road staying north until you reach the Bajo de Guia. Serious ornithologists can call ahead to arrange for a guided tour from the visitor center El Acebuche, five kilometers north of Matalascanas; 959-448-711. This visitor center also has daily overland tours by Land Rovers. Directions: From Sevilla drive west on A49 for 50km to Bollullos. Take exit 10 onto 493 and drive south 34km in the direction of Matalascanas and the beach. The visitor center is signposted El Acebuche five kilometers north of Matalascanas on 493.

FLAMENCO

The art of flamenco flowered and bloomed best in the towns where there was a large population of gypsies. Eccentric, bohemian, and heartrending, the music in its purest form is elusive to the outsider. Visit the Centro Andaluz de Flamenco, which preserves and promotes the rich literary-musical background of flamenco with archives of recordings, books, videos, and photographs. Staff can recommend penas flamencas where you can experience good cante, or song; open weekdays 9 a.m. to 2 p.m.; free. Directions: In Jerez de la Frontera at Plaza de San Juan in the elegant Palacio Pemartin. Take exit 4 off A4 onto 382 and drive east towards the centrum.

CADIZ

Zurbaran's essays of light, color, and texture are particularly powerful in his paintings of the Carthusian monks. Calling himself the painter of imagination, his textural work is masterful. The Museo de Belle Artes houses an exceptional collection of his work; closed Monday. Directions: Northwest end of the town at Plaza de Mina. Take exit 6 off A4 and drive west following signposting for the port, then continue north passing the Plaza de Espana. Turn south at the waterfront and follow signposting for tourist information. Park and walk to Plaza de Mina. Beautiful parkways line the water at Bahia Cadiz so take a leisurely stroll and indulge in freshly fried fish from one of the stands. ****Camping: *On the beach west of Jerez de la Frontera in Rota at Punta Candor. Drive north of Rota on the coast road 604 for two kilometers to the roundabout. Camping Punta Candor (956-813-303); beautiful location; well maintained; bungalows; open all year; $$$. In Chipiona. Drive south of Chipiona three kilometers on A491 following signposting for Rota. Camping Pinar Chipona (956-372-321); older; shady; pool; fair maintenance; open all year; $$. *In Matalascanas at the beach. Camping Rocio Playa (959-430-238); large; good location; well maintained; open all year; $$$.

RONDA AND AROUND

RONDA

Over several generations, one highly talented family, the Romeros, developed classic bullfighting traditions. Francisco Romero started using the cape in 17th century. His son, Juan, introduced the use of a matador support team. His grandson, Pedro Romero, perfected the classic technique and became one of Spain's all-time greats in bullfighting. To be able to look upon Pedro's original bullfighting attire in the Museo Taurino and to see the historic bullring where they all fought is a thrill for aficionados. Photos of Ernest Hemingway and Orson Wells intently watching the spectacle are also part of the museum's collection; open daily. Directions: The Plaza de Toros is well signposted from all roadways.

Ronda sits atop a narrow gorge whose sheer walls rise up 100 meters. A path from the Plaza Maria Auxiliadora leads down to the Guadalevin river. Take your camera, because the view of the immense 18th century bridge, the Puente Nuevo, is especially impressive from here. Walk to Puente Arabe and then down the hillside to see the newly restored Banos Arabes, or baths; closed Monday. Directions: Ronda is 70km from the Costa del Sol. Exit E/15 14km south of Marbella and drive north on A376 for 70km. ****Camping: Exit town on the southwest side following signposting on A369 for Algeciras for two kilometers. Camping El Sur (287-59-39); nice shady location; pool; popular with international travelers; small store; well maintained; open all year; $$.

GARGANTA DEL CHORRO

Sheer 400 meters walls rise from a placid lake whose waters thread through a narrow gorge. Halfway up, hanging precariously from the cliff wall, are the remnants of a concrete catwalk called the El Camino del Rey. Directions: From the campground walk along the lakeside path leading up the hillside past the old stone bridge. When you are almost at the top, you'll see the treacherous El Camino across from the railroad bridge. For safer walks, continue up the hillside following goat paths that lead farther into the valley. Directions: Drive west out of Malaga for 19km on A357 in the direction of Cartama. Continue driving on the west side of the river for 14km. Cross over the bridge three kilometers beyond Cerralba and drive six kilometers to Alora. Staying on the west side of the river, continue 17km to El Chorro. Cross over the dam to the east side of the lake and follow signposting for camping. ****Camping: At the lake and mouth of the gorge. El Chorro Camping (95-211-26-96); beautiful natural setting; especially nice pool with grassy areas; well maintained; friendly staff; cafe; open May-October; $$.

GARGANTA DEL CHORRO

THE SOUTH COAST BEACHES

Enticing sunny days, warm evenings, sandy beaches, and a beautiful blue sea bring tourists to the Costa del Sol in droves. These are just a few of the many nice campgrounds along this coast. ****Camping: *33km east of Malaga exit N340 for Torre del Mar. Drive south west of the town on the coast road. Camping Laguna Playa (95-254-0631); close to the beach; pool; some shade; open all year; $$. *South west of Estepona. Exit N340 at km 142 for San Luis de Sabinillas. Camping Chullera II & III (95-289-0196); nice location on the beach; open all year; $$. 45km west of Almeria exit N340/E15 at Adra and follow signposting for La Habana. Camping La Habana (950-522-127); natural setting along a reedy beach at the end of the road; well maintained; open all year; $$. In the same area, drive two kilometers west of Adra on N340 and follow signposting. Camping Las Gaviotas (950-400-660); nice terraced setting; close to the beach; open all year; $$. *30km east of Almeria exit N344/E15 in the direction of Campohermosa and drive 21km in the direction of La Negra and the beach. Camping Nautico La Caleta (950-525-237); lovely location on the beach; small; swimming pool; well maintained; open all year; $$.

GRANADA

Granada was the last stronghold of the Moors. It took eleven years for Christian Spanish forces to conquer her. The cultural superiority of the Moors to their Christian adversaries in agriculture, engineering, manufacturing, philosophy, and music is most evident in Granada.

On a low, fertile hillside, within sight of tall mountain peaks, Granada hides her treasure, the Alhambra. The Moors kept in touch with their outposts in the mountains from the Alhambra's somber fortress walls and towers, the Alcazaba. The view over the city and the surrounding countryside is magnificent and it's a good place to start your tour. From the start the path is lined with tall cypress trees, boxwood, and ponds reminding you that this is a very large complex of woodlands, water, gardens, and buildings. Use your guidebook, take a picnic, and plan to spend the day. For detailed study, spend time in the Museo de Arte Hispano-Arabe examining their outstanding collection of artifacts belonging to Islamic culture; open 10 a.m. to 2:30 p.m. and closed Monday. The stalactite traceries, delicate geometric patterns, and inscriptions of Arabic poems that intertwine the artistic motifs, arches, and slender cushioned columns in the palace are almost beyond belief. If you arrange your time so that you are here in the early evening, the lacy chain of rooms become mystical and the sound of water resembles the poetry it was meant to be. Many consider the Alhambra the most impressive Moorish monument in world; open daily. Ticketing must be done at a minimum by noon a day ahead. If you'll be here in August arrange tickets before you leave home by faxing 958-210-584. Tickets aren't available at the Alhambra; they are sold at the Granada bank in town. Luckily the campground is computer-linked to ticketing. Purchase your tickets when you check in. Directions to the Alhambra: For inexpensive, unlimited parking, use the underground parking at Neptune Shopping Center. Exit N323 at exit 132; the shopping center is just off the roadway. Park, then walk up Calle de los Recogidas to Plaza Nueva. Take the Alhambra shuttle bus up the wooded hillside to the entrance.   To enlarge your study of Moorish, Roman, and Visigothic settlements in the area, visit the Archeological Museum housed in the richly decorated Casa de Castil; closed all day Monday and Tuesday morning. Directions: From Plaza Nueva walk north along the river road Carrera del Darro to number 43. Close by at Carrera del Darro 31, three water spigots-one warm, one cold, and one perfumed-filled the baths for the Moors at the Banos Arabes; closed Monday and afternoons. After, wander around the neighborhood, which still exudes a Moorish ambiance.

Once a silk market, the narrow streets of the Alacaiceria are now filled with shops and cafes. The Plaza Bib-Rambia is a good place to rest and absorb the scene. The fanastic marble royal mausoleums of Ferdinand and Isabella in the Capilla Real of the Cathedral were made more elaborate than they wished; open daily. Directions: The Cathedral is in its center of Alacaiceria; follow sign-posting from main street leading up to the Alhambra.

The home of Garcia Lorca, one of Spain's most beloved poets and dramatists, is sweet with memories; closed Monday; guided tours only on the hour 10 a.m. to 1 p.m. and 6 p.m. and 7 p.m. Directions: Northwest of the Granada in Fuente Vaqueras. Exit N323 onto A92 and drive eight kilometers west exiting for Fuente Vaqueras. Follow signposting north on a small road for eleven kilometers passing fields of tobacco and their drying sheds. Drive to the center of the village to the roundabout. Follow signposting north for 500km. Park by the arcade of wisteria. The almost unnoticed house/museum is across from the theater on a small side street at Calle Garcia Lorca 4.

****Camping: Four kilometers north of the city in the suburb of Peligros. Exit A92 at exit 241A onto N323 for Peligros. Drive south one kilometer. Take exit 123 for Peligros. Drive east over the overpass into the village. Follow signposting and drive north up the small paved hillside road for one kilometer. Camping Granada (958-340-548); lovely setting on a hillside with views of Granada and the Alhambra; tranquil, small, well maintained; open all year; $$$.

THE ALPUJARRA

Bound on the north by the Sierras and on the south by the Mediterranean coast, the Alpujarras were once a hide-out for bandits and Moorish rebels. Boabdil, Granada's famous caliphate, sought sanctuary here after he sadly turned over the keys to the Alhambra to Ferdinand and Isabella. Embracing the cul-

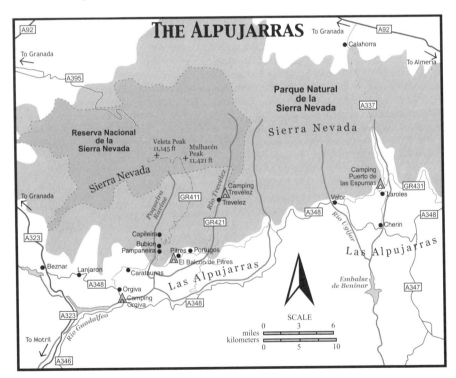

tures of Arab-Andalusia, the tidy white-washed villages are perky with geraniums and bougainvillea dripping from wrought-iron railed balconies. Narrow, twisting streets lead to charming shops where resident weavers, ceramists, and painters work. An international mix of travelers relax in miniscule squares. You can join summer pilgrimages, or romerias, from a village church, and walk with the locals into the mountains, watch reenactments of the battle between the Christians and the Moors, and take hikes on trails with sweeping views of the terraced mountainsides and high peaks. The Alpujarra paths thread down to rushing rivers, alongside levees watering the fertile terraced farmlands where poppies and daisies decorate fields of fava beans, wheat, and potatoes. Some continue into wooded areas that are shady with chestnut, walnut, and oak trees. Distinctive circular chimneys top flat-roofed houses with stone-slab roofs. Donkeys still carry loads of hay and grandmothers dressed in black knit in the sun.

Orgiva, the capital and commercial hub for the area, has a sizable group of international residents. Inside the 16th century Moorish palace on the main street, new-age marketers sell whole-grain bread and other natural food products along with jewelry and incense. Fill up with gas, purchase supplies, and get local currency here. The road heading into the Poqueira Ravine, whose terraced walls rise to Veleta Peak, is just west of Orgiva. On your way up through the villages, stop in the village of Pampaneira and visit the information center for the Sierra Nevada, called Nevadensis. A good topography model of the Alpujarras, a large posted map, hiking maps and booklets, and a friendly English-speaking staff person will assist you in planning walks, hikes, and horseback rides in the area; open daily. Directions: In the northwest corner of the small square. Woven rugs with Alpujarran designs dating from Moorish times are draped over the wrought-iron rails of small weaving shops, inviting admiration. A tiny Tibetan monastery, renowned because its foremost monk is a prominent disciple of the Dalai Lama, offers lectures and retreats. To make arrangements, call or stop by the travel agency Global Spirit on the main street in Bubion; 958-763-054. All day or several day guided horseback rides into the gorge are offered at Dallas Ranch, two kilometers outside of Bubion, call ahead; 958-763-135. From Bubion, there's a pleasant six kilometer walking path to Pitres. Directions: The trailhead is signposted on the main street down the hill from Teide cafe. Capileira is highest of the three villages, and trailheads begin here for the peaks of Mulhacen and Veleta, both about 3400 meters. For an easy walk, take the path by the Pueblo Alpujarra complex leading down to the river. It passes through terraced fields and by farmhouses tidy with vegetable gardens and fruit trees. In the village museum in Capileira, you can examine handicrafts, tools, photographs and traditional clothing of old world Alpujarra. To join in a romeria, or pilgrimage, to Veleta Peak, be in Capileira in the first week in August or in Pitres in the second week of August. In mid-September reenactment of battles between the Christians and the Moors are especially memorable in Valor. Directions: 38km south of Granada on N323/E902 exit east onto A348 close to the town of Beznar in the direction of Lanjaron and drive 15km. Then turn north onto a small road in the direction of Carataunas just before entering the town of Orgiva. Drive 14km up into the mountains towards the village of Pampaneira. Two kilometers east of Pampaneira is a fork; stay left and drive four kilometers more for Capileira. Further east the Trevelez Ravine is stark and savage with villages that are less prettified and touristy than those in the Poqueira Ravine. Trevelez is considered by many to be Spain's highest village at 1476 meters. The trails to the high sierra peaks are marked better from here, so serious hikers climbing the peaks usually start in Trevelez. Directions: At the fork to Bubion/Capileira stay right instead of left and drive four kilometers following signposting for Portugos. From Portugos it's a14km winding and steep drive to Trevelez. ****Camping: *Just west of Pitres. El Balcon de Pitres; nice location on a terraced hillside; swimming pool; fair maintenance; open all year, $$. *In Trevelez. Camping Trevelez; basic; $. *In Orgiva. In town take the road south along the Rio Guadalfeo and drive two kilometers. Camping Orgiva (958-784-307); small; pool; little shade; casual maintenance; open all year; $$. *Further east In Laroles. On A348 exit north at Cherin and drive seven kilometers to Laroles then continue north another kilometer in the direction of Lacalahorra. Camping Puerto de las Espumas (958-760-231); convenient for Valor festivities; beautiful views of the Sierras; well maintained; some shade; open all year; $$$.

THE EASTERN COAST
BARCELONA

Barcelona is by its very nature exhilarating. Its rhythm defies a rational description; you must let it absorb you. Like a younger sibling relishing all that an older one does, Barcelona keeps an eager eye on France. Rather than looking back at her mountains she looks out to sea, getting ideas from her neighbors and gaining a kaleidoscopic sophistication that is never stagnant. Begin experiencing the city by going to Los Rambles-a unique pedestrian boulevard that is a world of its own. It's the heartbeat of Barcelona. Stroll idly, without going to any place in particular, letting its rhythm flow over you. Perfectly still, living statues turn slowly, bow, raise a hat, or wink when an admiring pedestrian contributes to their fund. An old man sings the same song again and again as he mournfully strums his guitar, while close by a vigorous middle-aged woman stamps her feet and clicks her castanets to an accompaniment of rhythmic clapping. A cacophony of birdsong draws you to myriad of colorfully feathered creatures ready for admiration and sale. You can't help but smile. Without noticing you'll pass one of the world's best opera houses, the Liceu and the elegant Rococo Palau de la Virreina where you can purchase tickets to the city's special entertainment. Perhaps your eye will catch the gaping doors to the Mercat de La Boqueria and you'll wander into this vast emporium, overwhelming with piles of foodstuffs, and select a snack from a hundred varieties of olives. At end of Los Rambles, the tall column dominating the harbor area is the monument to Christopher Columbus. Crossover here to breathe in the salty air and admire the sea flecked with sailboats. Directions: Los Rambles begins off the southeast corner of Placa de Catalunya.

Tucked into narrow streets that are shadowy even on a sunny day is the ancient but still vital Barrio Gothic. Walk to the Placa de Sant Jaume, the spacious square where Romans once held forums and where people still gather for music and lively conversation. On the weekend, musicians play and you can watch or join in Catalunya's heartfelt folk dance-the sardana. If you watch carefully, you'll notice that quietly, without anyone giving a signal, a woman will carefully put her purse on the flagstone. Another will join her, then a man will carefully fold his jacket and place it on the pile, too. Soon a large circle forms of people of all ages who dance silently. At first their steps are slow, turning left and right while holding their arms closely to their sides. Then the beat picks up and with faster steps they raise their arms slightly. Finally, with faster steps and hands held high above their heads, their bodies sway beautifully to the tempo of the music mesmerizing the entire placa. Franco forbid the dancing in fear of an uprising.

Challenged by new ideas from their neighbors, Barcelona's architects developed an intense desire to avoid the standard. Casting aside balance and austerity they invented new pillars and capitals that looked like turbans, mushrooms, and spikes. They spread softly tinted cement onto uneven surfaces, then pressed in brilliantly colored tiles. To evoke a tone for a setting, they built florid, gigantic sculptural groups. When you visit these unique sites of early modernistic architecture, allow time for the enchanting harmony of the place to assert itself. You won't want to miss either the Palau and Parc Guell or La Pedrera, but the

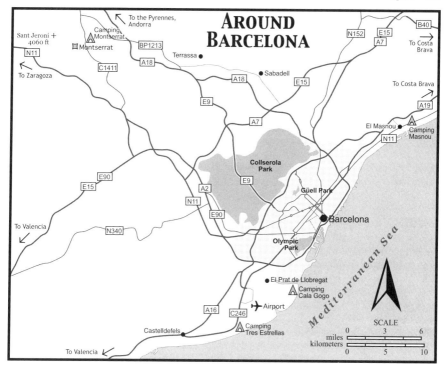

highlight will be the fabulous Sagranda Familia, where Gaudi worked ceaselessly on the plans and construction of this now very famous church. Construction is in full swing, and you can take an exciting elevator ride up to a high balcony, then by climbing stairs to even higher levels you are almost eye-level with some of the spires. Take time to examine the models, sketches and photographs in the museum so what you see makes sense.

Drawings by Picasso when he was young, colorful paintings and tapestries by Miro, and fascinating collages by Tapies are just the highlights in the unique museums devoted to each of these artists. In the new Museu d'Art Contemporani, viewers have exciting encounters with what is happening in the contemporary art world. Escalators take you part way up to the magnificent Palau Nacional, where Velazquez, El Greco, and Zurbaran and a notable collection of photographic work are just part of the Museu de Art Catalunya's huge collection.

These are just highlights of Barcelona's rich and varied offerings. Stop by the tourist office to peruse the fascinating options, inquire about special events, pick up a map, and get information about the easy-to-use metro and buses. The main tourist office is on the main boulevard northeast of the Placa de Cataluya at Orts Calalanes 658. ****Camping: *18km south of the city exit A16 at exit 14 for Castelldefels and C246 and drive to km 13.2. Camping Tres Estrellas (93-633-0637); natural setting in the pines; pool; close to a lovely beach; well maintained; bus to city center; open May-September; $$$$. *Exit off C246 just north of the airport in the suburb of El Prat de Llobregat and follow signposting for beach and camping. Camping Cala Gogo (93-379-4600); large; some shade; bus to city; open May-September; $$. Six kilometers north east of the city exit off A19 at exit 8 for Masnou and drive to km 633 on N11. Camping Masnou (935-551-503); pleasant setting close to the beach; pool; bus to city center; open all year; $$.

MONTSERRAT

One of Cataluna's most important pilgrimage sites, Montserrat is wedged into crevices below rocky spires reminiscent of the great Tibetan monasteries in the Himalayas. It is said that religious hermits who once lived in the caves hid from the Muslims a beautiful wooden statue of the Virgin. When found much later, the Church confirmed it to be the last statue carved by St. Luke. Since then the royal, the famous, and the poor have climbed the steep mountain trail in hope of finding solace; open daily. A web of trails, from easy to strenuous, lead to the ruins of hermitages, past wind sculpted rock outcrops, and onto high peaks. To shorten the hike take the funicular Sant Joan up the first 250 meters; operating daily. Parking is on the hillside on the way up. Payment for parking is made at the toll booth on the way down. Directions: 25km north west of the city follow signposting of E9 or N11. ****Camping: *Below the Sant Joan Funicular. No cars are allowed beyond the parking lot so you'll have to pack in camping gear. Camping Montserrat (835-0251); small; basic; open May- September; $.

VALENCIA

Welcomed by friendly Valencians, who smile readily and are proud of their city and its environs, you'll find enjoying a couple of days here easy. It's the small town atmosphere that's appealing. They love a good time, and their festivals are ongoing. The most famous one, Las Fallas de San Jose, occurs in March. Its highlight is a procession of very elaborate and hilarious papier mache depictions of famous people or events. At the end of the week, the floats go up in flame in an exciting ceremony. The week-long festival is elaborate kids play with adult style and includes fireworks, bonfires, and parades. The best floats and a large collection of photos are displayed in the Museu Faller; closed Monday. Directions: South of the historic area at the north end of the river bed park. Take bus 13 from Plaza del Ayuntamiento. To see how these elaborate floats are made go to the Museo del *Artista* Fallero; closed Sunday. Directions: Take bus 27 from Plaza del Ayuntamiento. Throughout the summer the festival loving-Valencians celebrate. You can dance in the street, watch battles between Moors and Christians, be part of a tomato-throwing free-for-all, or gorge on paella at the national paella contest. For the current dates of these festivals, fax ahead to 34-963-606-430. The tourist office is on the south side of Plaza Ayuntamiento. For fine art, don't miss the outstanding Museo de Bellas Artes. It's considered Spain's third best fine art museum after the Prado and Bilbao; closed Monday. Directions: In the Jardin del Real on the north side of the river bed. Take Bus 11 from the Plaza Ayuntamiento.

In the late afternoon, drive south of the campground and board a small, flat-bottom boat, and drift into one of Europe's largest fresh water lagoons, La Albufera. White herons stand quietly waiting to stab a passing fish or frog, gracefully launching into flight with their long neck tucked in when disturbed. Chattering kingfishers call in flight, but watch for their shaggy, big-headed blue-and-white bodies perched in the waterside reeds. Choose a small family-run boat trip rather then the large one. Directions: Four kilometers south of the campgrounds at El Saler on the coast road.

Drive through the park entrance gate for the best boat trips. It is in La Albufera, surrounded by rice paddies, that hungry fisherman used to cook rice over camp-fires. They added crayfish, sausage, and tomatoes for extra flavor, and paella was born. ****Camping: Seven kilometers south of Valencia in El Saler. Exit A7/E15 at exit 59 and drive east five kilometers to Cullera. Pass through town and take the coast road north in the direction of El Saler and Parque Albufera. It's across from the pedestrian walkway to El Saler Beach. Camping DeVesa Gardens (96-161-1136); shady; pool; well maintained; popular with families; bus to city center; open June-mid –September; $$.

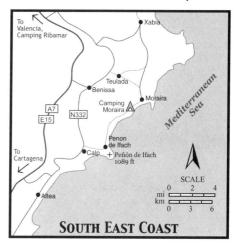

SOUTH EAST COAST

SOUTHEAST COAST

Here and there along the coast, hidden between highly developed coastal resort towns, are some very pleasant places to spend time. Stop in Calp, and climb 332 meters to the top of the monolith-like rocky outcrop Penon de Ifach made more fun by a tunnel trail at the top. The view is magnif-icent all the way up and even more fabulous on the other side of the tunnel. Directions: Exit A7 at exit 64 and drive east in the direction of Altea. Turn north and drive eleven kilometers to Calph con-tinuing out to the spit where there is parking for the hike. The tiny village of Moraira, tucked into a beautiful cove, has made a concerted effort to keep a quiet sedate atmosphere. ****Camping: *In Moraira. Exit A7 at exit 63 for Benissa. Drive north of Benissa four kilometers and follow sign-posting east in the direction of Teulada. Continue east then turn south for Moraira. Drive south of the village. Camping Moraira (96-574-5249); lovely setting on a terraced hillside; extra nice ameni-ties; pool; close to the beach; open all year; $$$. *Between Valencia and Tarragona. Exit off A7 at exit 44 onto N340 for Torreblanca. Turn south and follow signposting for Torrenostra and the beach. Turn north on the coast road and drive eleven kilometers to Alcossebre. Camping Ribamar (96-441-4165); nice location close to the beach; some shade; pool; open April-September; $$.

CADAQUES

Hidden behind hills and accessed only by a small road, beautiful Cadaques was made famous when Salvador Dali built an eccentric home here on the edge of the sea. Strongly influenced by Freud, Dali painted his dreams and paranoia. It's fun to wan-der through his house and studio, imagin-

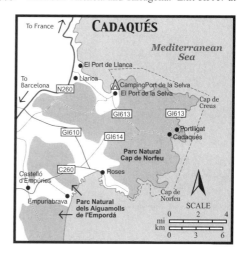

CADAQUÉS

ing it alive with the artist, his adored wife, and their famous artistic and literary friends. Directions: North of Cadaques in the tiny harbor village Port Lligat; open daily. Visiting the art galleries and small art museums can add to interesting walks in the town and harbor area. ****Camping: North west of Cadaques in Port de la Selva. Exit A9/E15 at exit 3 for Llanca and N260. Drive south for two kilometers then north east on N260 for 15km to Llanca. Turn south on the coast road and drive south four kilometers to Port de la Selva. Camping Port de la Selva (97-238-7287); lovely location on the beach; shady; pool; open June-mid September; $$$.

THE PYRENNES

Unlike the lush green French Pyrennes, the Spanish Pyrennes have a savage, rock-strewn beauty. Trails lead from grassy meadows up through chaparral-covered hillsides smelling of rosemary and broom, and on into shadowy gorges where boulder-strewn river-beds lead to refreshing waterfalls. Scattered lightly through the foothills are villages where you'll be welcomed at summer celebrations and small town sports events. Fill up with gas, purchase supplies, and get local currency before driving in.

VALLE DE RONCAL

Extravagant travel posters boasting blue sky and crisp outlines of villages seem overdone but in the Val de Roncal they are real. Lose yourself in the leisurely pace of the villages. You'll find ancient, unassuming churches that have remained pretty much the same as when they were built. In the village square, locals chat, kids play ball, and parents beam as neighbors exclaim over babies. Under shady beech trees, old men watch people passing by, and are happy to help with directions. In the morning follow the delicious aroma of fresh bread along cobbled alleyways to tiny shops. In the evening, watch the sunset bursting into a glorious palate of bronzes and gold. Hiking trails lead over tiny humpback bridges meant for shepherds and bleating herds of sheep and goats, on into gorges deep with shadows, past waterfalls and explosions of wild iris, and up to summits with views of seemingly remote and aloof pyramidal mountains. There's a clear quality to the air and an unusual silence.

VALLE DE RONCAL

Stop at the tourist office in Roncal to examine the large map of the area and find out what summer festivities are on the calendar during your stay. If you are here in May and June, when the water level is high, you can make arrangements to rent a kayak or be part of a white water rafting group. Directions: Exit north onto 137 at the eastern tip of the Yesa reservoir and drive 31km to Roncal. After getting information at the tourist office, continue to the smaller, more picturesque village of Isaba. ****Camping: *North of Isaba at km 6 on 137. Camping Asolaze (948-89-3034); lovely pine scented location; bungalows; popular with hikers and cyclists; sunny meadows; store with a large topographical map and hiking maps.

MONTE PERDIDO NATIONAL PARK AND ENVIRONS

Directions: 13km east of Jaca exit N330 north onto N260 and drive 12km to Biesca. Turn east following signposting for the park.

VALLE DE BROTO

Glacier-formed, this wide valley southwest of the park opens up to grassy meadows edged with nicely forested hills. Country roads wind through pleasant villages where there are trailheads for easy walks and bicycle rides. At summer festivals in Frajen in late July and in Oto in mid-August the locals will welcome you at the town square for music, fireworks, and dancing. ****Camping: *In Viu at km. 484 on N260. Camping Viu (974-486-301); popular with cyclists; hillside setting with beautiful views; open May-September; $$. *In Oto. At the north end of Broto on the westside of the river take the road south one kilometer to Oto. Camping Oto (974-486-075); nice location; close to hiking route GR15; open May-October; $$.

VALLE DE ORDESA

Torla is the tourist center for the national park. Rentals can be arranged at the campground or tourist office for kayaking, mountain biking, rock climbing, and canyoning. In July and August, when the area is heavily impacted, try to arrange a mid-week visit. Private cars are no longer

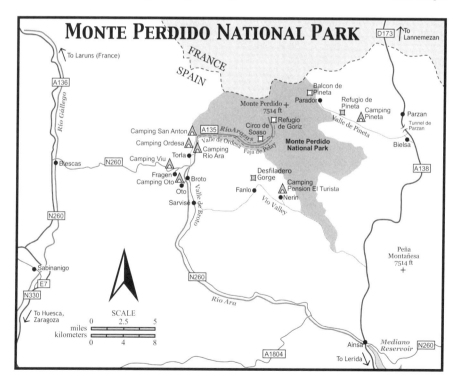

allowed in the park. Park in the large car park just south of Torla's tunnel, and take the shuttle bus. The shuttle operates from early in the morning to early evening. It stops first at the interpretative center, then at the old parking lot and trailheads, and then returns to Torla. Hikes range from easy to difficult. Always carry energy food, water, and a waterproof jacket.

If you want to spend several days inside the park, make advanced reservations for a stay in a refugio so you don't have to pack in a tent and cooking equipment. Just take enough energy food for the time on the trails and enough water for the hike to the first refugio. Once there, your bed and simple food are provided. Refugio Goriz has a good location at the base of Mt. Perdido, two kilometers from the Circo de Soaso at 2200 meters. Call; 974-341-201 or write; Goriz Shelter 22376 Torla (Huesca) Spain.

Traversing the Ordesa Valley by way of the Circo de Soaso is a popular full day hike. The trailhead begins at the Azaras River foot-bridge and climbs to Los Cazadoes, where there are magnificent views, then continues along the Faja de Pelay to the Circo de Soaso. The route passes through a wonderful beech forest, and in May and June the waterfalls along the trail are powerful cascades. For an easy scenic walk from Camping Rio Ara, follow the road north along the eastside of the river for one kilometer to the trailhead. From here the trail continues north for a little more than one kilometer, then turns east into the park. Four kilometers farther brings you to the old car park and the shuttle bus back to Torla. ****Camping: *Half a kilometer north of Torla exit east off A135 onto a small road crossing over the medieval bridge. Camping Rio Ara (974-486-248); grassy lawns and shade trees; close to the river; very popular; cafe; open May-October; $$$. *One kilometer north of Torla. Camping Ordesa (974-486-146); all the amenities; pool; popular with RVs; open May-October; $$$$. *Just over two kilometers north of Torla at km 96. Camping San Anton (974-486-063); nice hillside setting; small; closest to park entrance; open May-October; $$.

VIO VALLEY

Drier and more savage than the Ordesa Valley, the Vio Valley's big attraction is the Desfiladero Gorge. It is popular with international travelers interested in canyoning and is a good place for beginners. Arrange in advance for guides and equipment with the tourist office in Fanlo; 974-486-184. Views of the grand and massive summit of Pena Moutanesa are outstanding in Nerin and if you're here in mid-August you can join the fun at their summer festival. Directions: Exit N260 at Sarvise, three kilometers south of Broto, and drive east for 12km on a small paved winding road in the direction of Fanlo. ****Camping: *In Nerin by the Pension El Turista (974-486-138); basic; open May-October; $.

VAL DE PINETA

Balcon de Pineta, a shelf hanging 1200 meters above the valley floor at the top of Circo de Pineta, attracts expert climbers and hearty hikers. Directions: Exit A138 north of Bielsa just south of the Tunnel de Parzan and drive 15km west on a small paved road in the direction of Parador. ****Camping: *Seven kilometers west of the Tunnel de Parzan on the Parador road. Camping Pineta (974-501-089); comfortable setting; open May-September; $$. *Eleven kilometers west of the Tunnel de Parzan. Refugio de Pineta (974-501-203); new; close to the Parador road; open all year; $$$.

THE CAMINO DE SANTIAGO

It is said that Santiago, or St. James, appeared in a dream promising to lead the Spanish Christian forces in a successful battle with the Moors at Clavigo. Inspired by the dream, the Spanish Christians attacked with such fury that the Moslem forces fled. From that time on Santiago was regarded as the patron saint of the reconquest, and pilgrims began to arrive at the shrine erected in his honor. Later, Alfonso the Great built a much larger church on the site of the original shrine.   When the Moorish General Almanzor assaulted the city, he destroyed the new church and forced Christian prisoners to carry the church bells to the Mosque of Cordoba where they were turned upside down and used as lamps.   When Cordoba was recaptured, the Christians forced their Moslem prisoners to carry the bells back to Santiago.

In the 11th century the shrine was rebuilt, the road improved, and monasteries, convents, hospitals, and hostels were built to accommodate and protect the pilgrims.   The camino, or road, became an international route called the Camino de Santiago.   The full name of the route included the word Compostela, or a field of star, in reference to the star over the grave of St. James.   A scallop shell became the insignia of pilgrims, reminiscent of St. James' use of the shell in baptism.

The route is clearly marked today, and many still walk, cycle, or drive part or all of it as it threads its way through once forbidding landscape now softened by dry farmlands.   As you pass through the old villages, you can admire the workmanship of Roman bridges and the clean lines of simple churches.   The camino leads right through the towns rather then avoiding them as new roads do.   As you pass down the main street you'll take in the ambiance of the town's daily life, and pick up bits of conversation between the local people.   Smile and greet people; they will return your greeting.   Directions: For a map of the route and list of accompanying campgrounds stop by the tourist offices in Pamplona or Estrella.

SANTIAGO DE COMPOSTELA

The grand statute of a zealous St James proclaiming his news as he stands shrouded in a huge cape, greets the traveler to Santiago de Compostela.   His upturned hat is embellished with scalloped shells, his feet are in rough sandals, and his huge hand clutches a massive walking stave. Standing in the immense space formed by the four plazas of the Cathedral at Santiago de Compostela, and looking up at the two tall, flame-like towers and its incredible facade is awe inspiring.   But the real glory is inside at the Great Portico de la Gloria, the 12th century masterpiece of Maestro Mateo.   Mateo worked on the Portico for twenty years, creating a sensitive and harmonious arrangement of hundreds of figures.   Using three arches, the work represents the new Church rising from what they believed to be the false dogmas of Islam, the evils of greed and pride, and the Old Testament.   The natural figures display individual characteristics and moods and were initially rich in color and laced with gold.   Partake of the squares, cathedral, museum, and cloisters slowly, enjoying the details; open daily.   Directions: Follow signposting from all major roadways. ****Camping: *Northeast of the city in the suburb of Lazaro.   Take exit 67 off E01/A9 at follow signposting west back towards the city and camping.   Camping As Canelas (981-580-266); pool; bungalows; some shade; well maintained; open all year; $$.

GALICIA AND AROUND
GALICIAN COAST

The delicious aroma of freshly baked bread, octopus tentacles dripping from salt encrusted boxes, brown hams lightly fringed with mold that hang alongside garlic-scented sausages, and black-shrouded women with sharp dark eyes busily negotiating with merchants is the melange you're treated to in Galicia's morning markets.   On the waterfront, weary fisherman chatter as they laboriously mend nets.   From the coastline bluffs, dramatic ocean vistas offer a lusty beauty.   In estuaries, little villages with miniscule plazas and traditional balcony facades cascade from the hillsides, and in secluded coves nature lovers breathe in the salt air, watch sea gulls feed at the tide's edge, and revel in the surf. ****Camping: These are just a few of the many nice campgrounds. *On the west coast at Cabo Finisterre.   Follow signposting from C550 or C552 to Cocubion then continue southwest to the tip of the pennisula.   Camping Ruta Finisterre (981-746-

302); nice setting with view of the ocean; terraced; pine shaded; open June-mid September; $$$. *17km east of Coruna in the suburb of Bergondo. Exit off N651/A9 at exit 3F for Bergondo and follow signposting. Camping Santa Maria (981-795-826); two kilometers from the beach; well maintained; open May- September; $$. *North of Ferrol in the village of Meiras. Eleven kilometers north of Ferrol exit C464 for Meiras and the beach. Camping Valdovino (981-487-076); pleasant location; small; well maintained; open June- September; $$. *On the north coast 35km west Aviles in Luarca. Drive 12km west of Luarca to the village of Otur. Camping Playa de Otur (98-564-0117); wonderful location close to the beach; parking separate from camping; new; well maintained; open May-September; $$. *40km west of Santander. Exit E70/N634 at Cabezon de la Sal and drive north five kilometers following signposting for Comillas. Camping Comillas (942-720-074); beautiful location on the beach; little shade; well maintained; open June-September; $$.

PAMPLONA *(IRUNEA)*

The capital of Navarra, Pamplona rests at the base of the Pyrennes and except for the frenetic week of the Fiesta de San Fermin, it is a pleasant university town. The running of the bulls is the famous highlight of the Fiesta de San Fermin, but throughout that week it's a round-the-clock celebration with bands, parades, fireworks, fairs, and thousands of tourists and locals out to have an enormously good time. The Fiesta begins July 6 and ends on July 14. Signs in Pamplona are written in Basque and Spanish. ****Camping: *North of town. Stay outside the city center following signposting for Villava/N121A. Pass through the town of Villava following signposting for camping on the west side of N121A in the village of Eusa. Camping Ezcaba (948-330-315); on a shady hillside overlooking the quiet countryside; large pool; bus to city center; well maintained; open all year; $$$$. Note For the Fiesta: Make reservations well in advance. Expect noise throughout the night from partying folks and little space between tents or RVs. Although the campgrounds maintains security from outsiders during the Fiesta lock your valuables in your car when you leave for town.

SAN SEBASTIAN *(DONOSTIA)*

Elegant promenades pass the celebrated beaches of San Sebastian, which are popular with a sun loving international crowd. Signs in San Sebastian are written in Basque and Spanish. ****Camping: These are just a few of the many nice campgrounds. *14km west of San Sebastian in Zarautz. Exit A8/E70 for

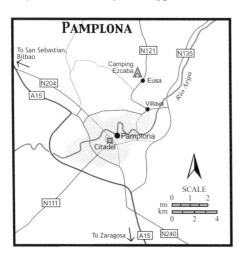

Zarautz. In town drive east following signposting. Gran Camping Zarautz (94-3831-238); wonderful location on the beach; resort-like; bungalows; open all year; $$$. *27km west of San Sebastian on the coast road 638 between the towns of Lekeitio and Ondarroa in the village of Mendexa. Leagi Camping (94-684-2352); beautiful location; little shade; well maintained; open all year; $$. *East of Ondarroa in the village of Mutriku. Camping Aitzeta (94-360-3356); good location close to the beach; well maintained; open all year; $$. *West of San Sebastian in the suburb of Igeldo. Exit A8/E70 for Monte Igueldo. Drive up the hill for five kilometers following signposting for camping. Garoa-Camping Igueldo (94-321-4502); lovely terraced location; shade; open all year; $$$.

BILBAO

Resembling smooth, gleaming sliver swirls of chocolate, the undulating curves of titanium and stone of Guggenheim Museum Bilbao are as exciting as the collection of art that they hold. Works by Picasso, Miro, Tapies, Kandinsky, and DeKooning grace the spacious galleries along with special exhibits that can include sculpture, photography, and applied arts from the very best of the world's modern artists; don't miss it; open 10 a.m. to 8 p.m. closed Monday. Directions: Metro to Moyua then walk north on Alameda de Recalde to the river and the museum. The Museo de Belle Artes holds important works by El Greco, Zurbaran, Goya, and the best of the Basque artists and is considered one of Spain's most important art museums; closed Monday.   Directions: On the river west of the Guggenheim across from the Plaza de Museo. ****Camping: *Close to the beach north of Bilboa in Sopelana. From the major roadways drive north of the city follow signposting for Getxo, then Larrabasterra, and then Sopelana.   Follow signposting towards the beach and camping. Camping Sopelana (94-676-2120); lovely location on a hillside close to the beach; bungalows; pool; cafe; metro to the city close by; open all year; $$$. Between Santander and Bilbao. Exit N634/E70 seven kilometers west of Castro-Urdiales at exit 159 for the village of Islares and drive to the beach. Camping Playa Arenillas (94-286-3152); beautiful location on the beach; some shade; well maintained; open April-September; $$$.

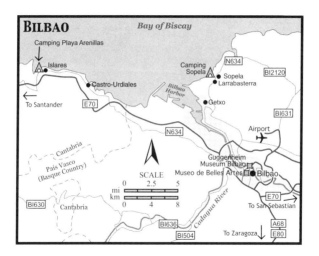

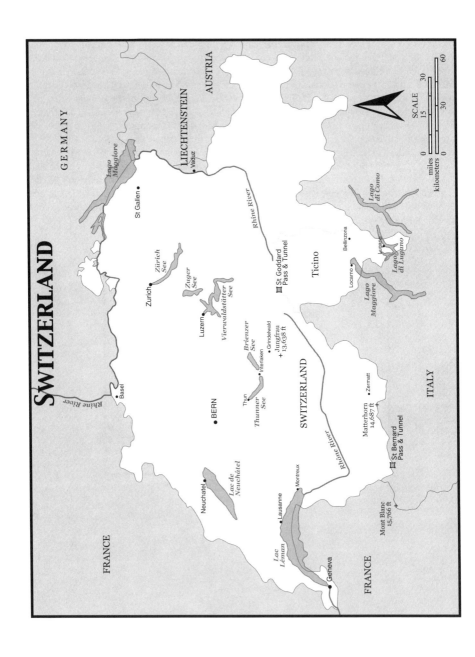

SWITZERLAND

Timeless in beauty, with ancient and deep-rooted bonds to the earth, Switzerland is a paradise for active relaxation in the countryside. Experts at making sports doable for persons at a beginning or advanced skill level, the Swiss provide equipment and clothing rentals, shuttles, guides, and classes. The profusion of Alpine trails are an oases of quiet beauty and adventure. The routes run the gamut of ability levels so that a hiker can appreciate the magnificence of glorious scenery and gain a quiet satisfaction from the experience without being overstrained. Trail markers indicate ability level and approximate time it takes to get from one place to another. Maps give geological and flora information. In meadows, pale lavender foxgloves wave in the breeze and violet-red vetch sweeps across like swabs of paint. Pockets of edelweiss peek like soft stars from steep crags. Sparrow sing gaily, and air-borne hawks display elegance in movement. Cog railways, tramcars, and trains are fun and make getting to the upper meadows easy.

The bold and rugged beauty of sculpted rock massifs lures rock climbers. Guides, schools, equipment, and clothing are available for those who want the thrill of surmounting the pinnacles and crevices. If you'd rather drift bird-like over the spectacular Alpine scenery, try tandem or solo hang gliding or ballooning. To encourage pedaling down the old pass roads or along Alpine trails, the Swiss Rail System rents and transports bikes. Water enthusiasts can paddle down an untamed river, wind surf across a pristine lake, or kayak into fjord-like coves. Steamers ply the mirror-smooth lakes, providing tranquil moments to rest and look at the magnificent mountains.

If you're traveling with kids, or just feel like being one, you can take a bobsled ride that barrels down a winding mountain track, or plunge down immense water chutes at a world-class waterpark, or climb high up into the tree tops on a rope ladder.

To stretch your imagination and knowledge, visit the world-famous Transport Museum in Lucerne, the Kuntsmuseum and its fabulous collection in Zurich, or the Abbey Library in St. Gallen.

Fast superhighways link the major cities. An annual highway stamp, or vignette, costing just over $20 USA must be on the windshield of all vehicles using the superhighways. If you don't rent your car in Switzerland, buy one at a border crossing. They seem excessively expensive to the traveler who is just passing through the country, but they are cost-efficient for the country as a whole. Toll stations are expensive to operate and are gradually being eliminated with stamp-tariffs throughout Europe. Tunnels through the Alps can be very long and should be avoided during commute times. Though they are costly in time and gas the smaller roads are stunningly beautiful, twisting up through pine-scented forests, past medieval villages, and across meadows embroidered with gaily-colored flowers, cascading rivers, and crashing waterfalls. You'll probably want to use a combination of the two. International pictograph signposting is excellent: Triangular signs with red borders warn of dangers; round signs with red borders indicate prohibitions. Public buses have the right of way, and you must obey any signals they give. Switzerland's car rental rates are some of the lowest in Europe.

To encourage bicycling, the Swiss Rail System does not require returning a rented bicycle to the same station you rented it from unless the rental is only for half a day. Pick up the free "Rail-Bike" brochure at a train station, and make reservations for the most popular routes. Cycling routes lead through vineyards, along lakes and rivers, through small towns, and to historic sites. Purchase the excellent "Bicycling Map of Switzerland" at a railway station or airport bookstore. It includes scenic routes for all ability levels, and notes interesting stops along the way. Postal buses pass daily through even the smallest villages, delivering and picking up mail. Check the local schedule and use them as shuttles for walks or cycle rides. The postal bus does not have room for bikes. If you have brought your own bike, park and lock it after your ride. Take the postal bus back to your car, returning with your car to pick up the bike. Steamers allow a limited number of bikes onboard.

Walking or hiking is a national pastime. Paths are clearly marked and pass through dappled green and shadowy mountain gorges, along pristine avocado-green lakes, through tiny old-world villages, and up or down the breathtaking Alps. Beech forests provide a canopy of lacy light-green leaves covering a carpet of ferns. In the early morning mist they are magical. Deep-red alpenrose, a type of rhododendron, can cover acres with a saturation of luscious color. Spikes of purple-hooded monkshood spring from the lush damp meadows. Wild flowers are protected and must not be picked. Although wildlife is scarce, the winsome clank of cow bells or the tinkle of sheep bells are omnipresent, and on trails with rocky crevices the marmots shrill warning cry is heard. Easy-to-read detailed maps and guidebooks are readily available in all of the tourist offices. Many walks begin by parking at the train station and then taking a cable car, cog-rail train, or postal bus to the trailhead. Trails are classified as wandererweg, a low altitude trail marked with yellow signs and berweg, a rough, high-altitude trail marked with red/white/red postings. The trail markers are seen on rocks and trees as well as on regular posted signs. Double signage indicates that the trail has a change of direction. A blue dot indicates a hiking trail, while a red dot indicates a cross-country ski trail. The weather in the Alps can change dramatically, producing a sudden rainstorm in the middle of a sunny day.   Pack energy food, water, a warm waterproof jacket, a sweater, a hiking map, and a compass into your daypack before each hike.

Swiss campgrounds are usually in scenic locations close to a lake or stream. Campers get grassy meadows, covered common areas, warm showers, good maintenance, and fresh bread in the morning. Two persons, a car, and a tent cost about $25 USA. Between noon and 2 p.m. the office will is usually closed for lunch. The Swiss acknowledge the International Camping Card.

Museum hours are typically from 10 a.m. to 5 p.m., smaller ones close for lunch, and all are generally closed on Mondays.   Stores in small towns are often closed on Sundays and Mondays. You'll find good parking close to train stations.

BERNE

From the tower in the Gothic Munster Cathedral, you look down on a huddle of reddish-brown roofs resembling the hats of shoppers in a marketplace. Then your gaze lifts to the peaks, rising up through a sea of mist. With such a panoramic view, this is good place to reflect on the striking achievements of this small country, initially abundant only in stones and water. In their battle for survival in such a hostile environment, the Swiss produced an Alpine character that was suspicious, independent, frugal, and contentious. Having defeated Austrian armies in three battles, even Napoleon realized that their belligerence would never allow them to be turned into French subjects.

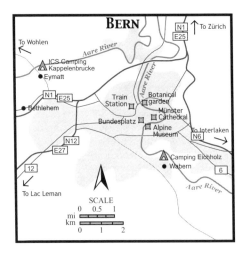

You can only admire the conscientious hard work, frugality, and mechanical genius that have produced an abundance of international patents and a genius for financial management.

Bern is a good place to begin an exploration of Switzerland. It's a Swiss city with a smile. Wandering through the tiny streets of the old town, you'll giggle at the whimsical fountains, delight in the parade of dancing bears and clowns in the clock tower, and laugh at the bears cavorting in the bear pits. Directions: Pick up the colorful walking map for the historic town at the train stations's tourist office. Take a picnic lunch to Bern's outstanding botanical garden. Directions: Cross the Kornhausbrucke from the old town, then continue north along the quay for 200 meters. In Bern's Kuntmuseum, you can enjoy Paul Klee's fantasy and comedy in his distortion of reality as well as a fine collection of work by the 15th century Swiss artist Hodler; closed Monday. Directions: Close to the Lorrainebrucke, on the old town side; Holderstrasse 8-12. Before heading to the Alps, spend some time in the Swiss Alpine Museum. The relief maps and historical photos of early mountaineering feats will make your experience there more meaningful; closed Monday. Directions: Cross the Kirchenfeldbrucke from the old town to Helvetiaplatz, where Bern's major museums are clustered. The Alpine Museum is at Helvetiaplatz 4. If you are here on a Tuesday or Saturday morning, stock up on supplies at the lively open market on Bundesplatz. Directions: On the north side of the Parliament Building. Walk south from the train station to Bundesgasse, then east to the square. It's easy to take public transportation from the campgrounds, and good underground parking is available at the train station.

****Camping: *On the west side of Bern in the suburb of Eymatt. Exit N1/E25 for Bethlehem, and drive north in the direction of Wohlen, where it is by the bridge. ICS Camping-Kappelenbrucke (034-422-7943); large; modern; swimming pool; close to public bus to the city; open all year; $$$. *South of the city in the suburb of Wabern. Exit E27 for Wabern and drive east five kilometers. Camping Eichholz (031-961-2602); closer to the city; bungalows; tram to historic area; open May-September; $$.

EMMENTAL AND JUNGFRAU REGIONS

Just south of Bern, pre-Alpine hills and rolling plateaus are laden with fruit orchards and dairy farms. Clanging cow bells, chiming church bells, and birdsong fill the air with a "Heidi" ambiance. Cheese museums, hikes on ancient trails, and banner waving towns lie beneath the towering mountains.

INTERLAKEN

Interlaken is the main town between, or inter, the two lakes Brienzer See and Thuner See. Paragliding, bungee jumping, rafting, canyoning, and kayaking can all be arranged here. Stop at the tourist office at the train station to pick up colorful brochures and peruse the options. The town hosts a highly spirited stage production of Schiller's beloved story of William Tell and the Swiss fight for independence from the Hapsburgs. Performed in their huge outdoor theatre, it's lively with flower-garlanded cows, galloping horses, and barking dogs; performed Thursday through Sunday nights; 36-22-3722. Directions: Follow the centrum signs from N8 to the railroad station.

The historically accurate open-air museum in Ballenberg recreates country living from every region in Switzerland. Wooden chalets, stone farmhouses, vegetable gardens, and fields where farm animals graze are all tucked into the surrounding woods. Check the schedule at the entrance for demonstrations of life-on-the-farm; open daily. Directions: Located at the northeast end of Brienzer See, three kilometers east of Brienz, it's well signposted; from 6/11 or 4.

For colorful Old World ambiance stop in Thun, where sidewalk cafes and flowers spill from the two-level shopping street of Hauptgasse and up on the hill a turreted castle stands guard. Perched prettily on the edge of the lake at Spietz, Oberhofen Castle is elegant with massive flower gardens and a maze of luxuriously decorated rooms. To see the lakee-side sights, take a sea-gull escorted steamer and enjoy a graceful glide across the lakes of Brienzer See and Thuner See.

Cycle routes in the area include an almost level 23km loop that goes south along the westside of Thuner See, looping to the tiny Amsoldingen and Dittlig lakes. A downhill route of 30km on the south side of Thuner See follows the River Kander through a snowcapped mountain gorge

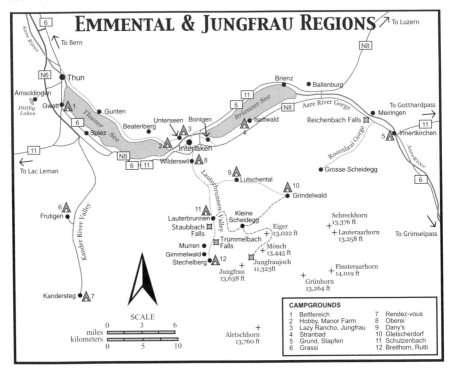

EMMENTAL & JUNGFRAU REGIONS

To Luzern

To Bern

N8

Thun

Brienz

Ballenburg

Amsoldingen

Dittlig Lakes

Gwatt

Gunten

Spiez

Beatenberg

Unterseen

Bonigen

Interlaken

Iseltwald

Aare River Gorge

Reichenbach Falls

To Gotthardpass

Meiringen

Innertkirchen

To Lac Leman

Wilderswil

Lutschental

Grosse Scheidegg

To Grimselpass

Frutigen

Lauterbrunnen

Staubbach Falls

Kleine Scheidegg

Grindelwald

Schreckhorn
+13,376 ft

Murren

Trümmelbach Falls

Eiger
+13,022 ft

Gimmelwald

Stechelberg

Mönch
+13,445 ft

Jungfraujoch
11,323ft

Lauteraarhorn
13,258 ft

Finsteraarhorn
+14,019 ft

Kandersteg

Jungfrau
13,638 ft

Grünhorn
13,264 ft

SCALE

miles
kilometers

0   3   6

0   5   10

Aletschhorn
13,760 ft

CAMPGROUNDS		
1 Bettlereich	7	Rendez-vous
2 Hobby, Manor Farm	8	Oberei
3 Lazy Rancho, Jungfrau	9	Dany's
4 Stranbad	10	Gletscherdorf
5 Grund, Stapfen	11	Schutzenbach
6 Grassi	12	Breithorn, Rutti

bright with flower-filled meadows. Park at the train station in Spietz, and take the train with your bike up to Kanderstag. On the east side of the Brienzersee, from Brienz to Interlaken, an almost level bike route passes good bathing beaches and the picturesque fishing village of Iselwald. At the southeast end, the route turns inland at Boigen and gradually climbs up to the waterfalls in the Lauterbrunnen Valley and the cave-falls at Trummelbach. At the northeast end it is more level, passing through the Aare river gorge to Meiringen. It becomes a challenging route from Meiringen, ascending 1400 meters for a 17km ride up through the magnificent mountain scenery of the Rosenlaui Gorge and to the Reichenbach falls. This could become a downhill ride by taking a train up through the gorge to Grosse Scheidegg. Walkers enjoy this same route. To find the cycle paths, use the "Bicycling Map of Switzerland".

Walking trails lace the entire area, passing the celebrated brown-and-white cows whose jangling bells lend a lighthearted rhythm to your step through the meadows. Routes pass waterfalls that plunge wildly from sheer rocky cliffs where chamois graze. Songbirds twitter sweetly in pine-scented woodlands, and wispy clouds float around the sharp-edged massifs, including the famous Eiger, Monch, and Jungfrau. Trains, buses, and cable cars allow for easy downhill walks. Grindelwald, nestled in a tiny glacier bowl, serves as a picturesque town for cablecar lifts to the mountain meadows, tundra summits, and trailheads for routes into the Lauterbrunnen Valley, Staubbach, and Trummelbach Falls. In July "lul-lul-lahee-o-o-o" echoes joyfully across the stupendous precipices during the town's yodeling festival. Directions: Drive south out of Interlaken for eight kilometers in the direction of Lauterbrunnen and Grindelwald. At the fork, it's 12km to

Grindelwald and four kilometers to Lauterbrunnen. High above the Lauterbrunnen Valley, both Gimmelwald and Murren perch prettily on cliffs with classic vistas of the Jungfrau. Scenic trails wind like lengths of yarn through the entire area. Only if the weather is predicted to be clear should you get up early and take the train to Jungfraujoch, which at 3452 meters is the highest railway station in Europe. The fare is expensive, but early riders get a discount. Dress warmly, bring sunglasses and a picnic lunch, and be ready for lines. The steep ride begins at Kleine Scheidegg, the plateau halfway between Grindelwald and Gimmelwald, picking up passengers from Interlaken, Grimwald, and Lauterbrunnen.

****Camping: Around Interlaken: From Interlaken exit N8 in the direction of Gunten/Beatenberg, and follow good signposting. *On the lake near Underseen. Camping Hobby (033-822-9652); nice location; smaller; cooking facilities; covered common area; open April-September; $$. *In the same area, but larger. Camping Manor Farm (033-822-2264); lovely location; resort-like, very large; open all-year; $$$$. *In Underseen. Camping Lazy Rancho (033-823-2287); nice location; large, cooking facilities, open April-September; $$. *In the same area. Camping Jungfrau (033-822-7107); beautiful views of the Alps; resort-like; open May-September; $$$$.

In the Grindelwald and Lauterbrunnen Area. From Interlaken exit off N8 in the direction of Grindelwald and Lauterbrunnen. *Close to the Brienzer Sea in Matten, on the east side of the tunnel. Camping Jungfrileck (033-822-4414); lovely location; covered common area; swimming pool; close to the highway and rail tracks; open May-September; $$. *Just beyond the exit off 8 in the village of Wilderswil. Camping Oberei (033-822-1335); lovely location; small; close to chairlift; open May-September; $$. * Just beyond the fork to Grindelwald and Lauterbrunnen, in Lutschental. Dany's Camp (033-53-1824); beautiful location; small; covered common area; swimming pool; close to chairlift; open May-September; $$$. *In Grindelwald. Camping Gletscherdorf (033-853-1429); lovely location; swimming pool; tennis; mini-golf; open all year; $$$. *In Lauterbrunnen. Camping Schutzenbach (033-855-1268); lovely location; large; cooking facilities; covered common area; chairlift nearby; $$. *In Stechelberg, six kilometers up the mountain. Camping Breithorn (033-855-1225) or Camping Rutti (033-855-2885); beautiful locations; small; open all year; $$.

South of Spiez, along the Kander River. Exit 6 for Fruitigen and Kanderstag. *In Fruitigen. Camping Grassi (033-671-1149); beautiful location; terraced; covered common area; close to bike path and hang-gliding area; open all year; $$. *In Kanderstag. Camping Rendez-vous (033-675-1534); lovely location; terraced; close to chairlift and hang-gliding area.

On the Thuner See. *Halfway between Spiez and Thun exit 6 for Gwatt. Camping Bettlereiche (033-336-4067); lovely lake-side setting; large; popular with wind surfers; cycle path; open May-September; $$$$. *On the south side of the Brienzer See near Iselwald. Camping Stranbad (033-845-1248); very small; pleasant location on the lake; barbeques; open May-September; $$. *Along the Aare River. Exit 8 at the northeastern end of the Brienzer See onto 6/11, and drive east in the direction of Meringen. Pass through Meiringen, and drive six kilometers farther on a winding road to Innertkirchen. Camping Grund (033-971-1379) and Camping Stapfen (033-971-1348); both are small; quiet; covered common area; open May-September; $$.

LUCERNE

With its heart-center location, Lucerne makes an easy and interesting stopping place on your way to or from the mountains. The Transport Museum alone is worth a detour to the city, particularly with kids. It's a hands-on place filled with trains, airplanes, and boats to inspect or actually climb on. Informative films stimulate the senses while giving rest to your feet; open daily. Directions: On the north side of the lake, close to Camping Lido at Lidostrasse 5. Parking is avail-

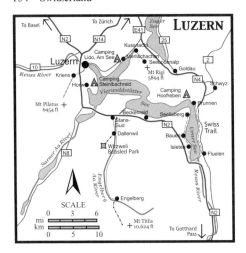

able, or take the bus. Lucerne is an easy town for a stroll. Starting at Kapellplatz, walk across the famous covered bridge, Kapellbruke. Then walk west on Furrengasse to see the brightly painted 15th century facades of the buildings as you wander towards Kornmakt. Stop for a "close-friend peek" of Picasso in his namesake museum on Furrengasse. An immense collection of photos taken by a close family friend, David Douglas, hang on its walls; open daily. Pick up a snack from the quayside stalls along the Reuss River, then drive or take a bus to see Lucerne's famous Lion Monument. Rock-hewn, the melancholy lion gazes sadly over his fountain contemplating the lives of the professional Swiss soldiers who died trying to protect Marie Antoinette from the furies of revolutionary Paris. Directions: At the northwest end of the lake, follow the main street, Alpenstrasse, to Zurichstrasse and Glacier Park. Mark Twain visited Lucene and close by Mt. Rigi. In A Tramp Abroad, he spins a hilarious yarn about how he journeyed to Mt. Rigi to see the sunrise. Directions: Take the train from Kussnacht, on the northern tip of Lake Lucerne, to Seeboldenalp, where there is a nice walking path and a rack-rail train to the summit. Across the lake from Mt. Rigi, a cog-rail train, which advertises itself as the steepest of its kind in the world, whisks riders to the top of Mt. Pilatus.

If you have kids with you, the Goldau Nature Park is a good day's outing. Tame forest animals wander about in the wooded park allowing petting, while others are viewed in natural enclosures. An adjoining adventure playground has a rope ladder leading up into the pine trees. Bring food and charcoal for a barbecue in the picnic area; open daily. Directions: Goldau is off N4, southeast of Lucerne. Drive east of Lucerne towards the Zuger See, then exit onto N4 and drive about 16km. The "Swiss Walking Trail" along the Urner See opened in 1991 to commemorate the 700th anniversary of the Swiss nation. The route's northeast corner is at Brunnen. It follows the lake south to Flugen then over on the west side to Isleten, Bauen, and Seelisberg. Directions: N4 ends at Brunnen at the northeast corner of the Urner See, southeast of Lucerne. To begin on the west side, exit N2 at Beckenried and take the small road as it twists 14km through beautiful scenery out to the promontory and Seelisberg.

For a summer bobsled ride, take the aerial cable ride from Dallenwil up to Wirzweli Bobsled Park; open daily. Directions: From the Stans-Sud exit off N3 it's four kilometers to Dallenwil. Wednesdays river rafting trips on the Engelberg Aa can be booked with the tourist office in Engelberg. If the weather is clear, take a cable car ride up to Mt. Titlis. The Engelberg Aa River recreational area is south of Lucerne, off N2. Directions: Drive nine kilometers south of Lucerne on N2 exiting at Stans-Sud. and proceed south in the direction of Engelberg.

****Camping: *South of Lucerne, on the lake in the suburb of Horw. Camping Steinibachried (041-340-3558); on the lake; large; convenient; close to public transportation to the city; open April-September; $$$. *13km northeast of Lucerne. Take exit 2, the lake-side road, just west of Kussnacht in Merlischachen. Camping Am See (041-850-0055) or Camping Lido (041-370-2146); close to the lake; large; open April-September; $$. *On the eastern end of the lake in Brunnen. Drive north out of Brunnen on the lake-side road. Camping Hoofreben (041-820-1873); on the lake; medium size; open April-September; $$.

ZURICH

Switzerland's inexpensive car rental rates make Zurich a good arrival city. The airport is small and easy to get in and out of for a first-time European traveler and driver. A terrific lake-side campground is relatively easy to find, and its tranquil setting makes a good place to rest from jetlag. The Kuntsthaus houses Switzerland's most impressive collection of fine art, ranging from the 15th century to contemporary. It has a sizable collection of Hodler's oils and Giacometti's sculpture, and a whole room is dedicated to Marc Chagall; closed Monday. Directions: From the closest bridge to the lake crossing the Limmat River, walk east on Ramistrasse to Hirschengraben 1. On a sunny day, the luminous color streaming in through the stained-glass window crafted by Chagall in the Fraumunster Church is breathtaking. From here, walk across the Munster Bridge to examine Giacometti's stained-glass windows in the Grossmunster Cathedral, where Zwingli once preached stern "work and pray" sermons. Directions: The Munster Bridge is the second bridge from the lake. The churches face each other across the river. A zoo is the perfect change of pace, and Zurich has an excellent one. Directions: In the Zurichberg woods, on the east side of the Limmat River, north of the city center. Nice walking paths follow the shoreline of Lake Zurich, which you can enjoy as James Joyce did when he wrote Ulysses. He is buried in Zurich. Stop at the tourist office in the main train station, Hauptbahnhof, and look through the glossy brochures offering a wide range of adventures including kayaking, wind surfing, hang gliding, and ballooning. Kids love Alpamare, an enormous water-park in Pfaffikon; open daily. Directions: Drive south of Zurich on N3 or Seestrasse for 32km along the west side of Lake Lucerne to Pfaffkon.

Radiant in theatrical beauty, St Gallen's Abbey is world renown and should not be missed. Magnificent, intricately illuminated manuscripts can be viewed in the Abbey's library; open daily. It's about 70km from Zurich, close to the Bodensee.

The Gotthard Pass separates Swiss-Italian Ticino from central Switzerland. To take the scenic old Gotthard Road's on the north side, drive up to Goschenen and the north portal of the Gotthard Tunnel, then cycle or walk down to Wassen. Bicycle rental and transport is available at Goschenen; reserve ahead.

****Camping: *Eight kilometers southwest of the city in the suburb of Wollishofen. Drive out of the city on 3 in the direction of Thalwil. At Wollishofen take exit 3, and drive south on the lake side road, Seestrasse. Camping Seebucht (01-482-1612); lovely location on the lake; public transportation close by; covered common area; open all year; $$$. *On the east side of the lake in Stata. Exit 17 northwest of Rapperswil 7km. Camping Kehlhof (01-926-4334); nice location; small; covered common area; $$$. *Near St Gallen. Drive northeast of St Gallen to Wittenbach. Then take the smaller road west to Bernhardzell. Camping Leebrucke (071-298-4969); close to the river; small; open May-September; $$.

THE TICINO

High up in the mountains, not far from the Rhone and Rhine rivers, the Ticino River bursts from its snowbound source to make its way down through granite and gneiss to Lago Maggiore. Linking

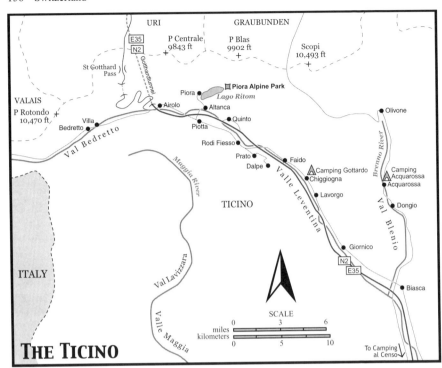

THE TICINO

Italy with Switzerland, the Ticino is more Italian than Swiss in cultural heritage and way of life. Swiss wooden chalets give way to split slab granite roofs covering stone houses in the hillside villages. In this sunny valley and on the terraced hillsides, a Mediterranean ambiance prevails. The lakeshore of Lago Maggiore is heavily indented, separating the towns with tranquil flower-filled lake-side parks. Narrow river gorges, dappled with sunlight from chestnut and pine trees, hide tiny stone-stepped villages, medieval bridges, and friendly wine-grottos.

VALLE LEVENTINA

Those hurrying to Lago Maggiore and Italy often bypass this very scenic area. It begins at the top and south side of the Gotthard Pass. At Airolo, a small road leads west into Val Bedretto, passing the picturesque riverside villages of Villa and Bedretto. On the east side, you can walk or bike along Lake Ritom to Piora Alpine Park. Directions: In Airolo drive south on the old road to Piotta, then take the small road up through Altanca to the power station at Piora and park. Piora Alpine Park is just beyond the north eastern end of the lake. Beyond tranquil Quinto, between the villages of Rodi-Fiesso and Giornico, the old Gotthard Road thunders with tumultuous waterfalls. On the south side of the river at Rodi-Fiesso, a tiny road leads up through the villages of Prato nd Dalpe to high pastures. Post buses can provide shuttles between the little villages for cycle rides or walks. However they don't have room to transport bikes, so if you have your own bike drive up to your starting point and park your car. Take your ride. At the end of your descent, lock your bike to a bike stand and take the post bus back to your car. Return with your car to pick up your bike. It's popular to ride down the old canton road from Airolo to Biasca and bicycle rental is available at the Airolo station. Besides the incredible beauty of the scenery along the way, the little villages make great places for snacks and rest. Rented bikes are returned to the Biasca rail station at the bottom. Use information from the "Bike-Rent" brochure to make reservations ahead. ****Camping: *Exit N2/E35 for Faido, and drive to the village of Chiggiogna. Camping Gottardo (091-866-1562); beautiful location close to the waterfalls; small; open all year; $$$. *South of Biasca 16km in Claro. Camping al Censo (091-863-1753); lovely location; covered common area; open May-September; $$.

VALLE BLENIO

Just east of the Valle Leventina, the Valle Blenio is lush with orchards, vineyards, and wine-grottos. Years ago the grottos became the favorite spot for the men of the village to meet on Sunday. They'd play a game of bocce and talk over a glass of local wine under the leafy shade of trees. Often some-one brought a special snack from home. Over the years the grottos attracted the town residents and later people from the city. In these shady, rustic settings, usually close to a bocce court, people still relax over glasses of local wine and simple food. Without a major railway or highway, Valle Blenio is tranquil and a favorite haunt of the Ticinese. Directions: Exit 2 at Biasca, and drive north to Dongio. The villages between Dongio and Olivone are particularly picturesque. Romanesque stone churches with free-standing bell towers overlook the villages from the hillsides. The dramatic pyramid-shaped Sosto peak looms over the north end of the valley. ****Camping: *Exit N2/E35 at Biansca, and drive 13km north to the village of Acquaross, just south of Dongio. Camping Acquarossa (091-871-1603); restful location; barbeque; covered common area; open May-September; $$.

BELLINZONA

Charming piazzas, shaded arcades, and three castles make this market town a nice stop. Often

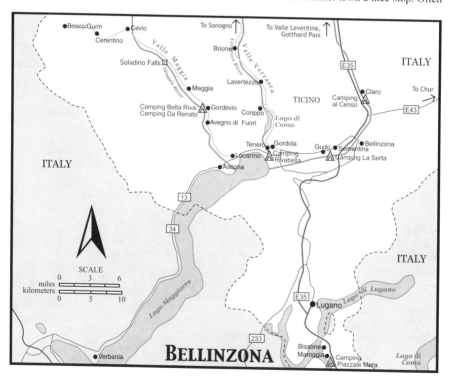

overlooked by vacationeers on their way to the lakes, it retains a small town ambiance. The Saturday morning market in Piazza Nosetto, the town's heart, is superb. The stairs of the narrow alley next to the San Pietro church in Piazza Collegiata lead up to Castello Montebello. From the ancient walls of the Castello, there is a grand panorama of the town, the Ticino valley, and Lago Maggiore. A fine archaeological museum is housed in Castello Grande, noted for its two 13th century towers. ****Camping: *Southwest of Bellinzona, five kilometers west of the town of Sementina in the village of Guido. Camping La Serta (091-859-1155); small and simple; pleasant location on the river; open April-September; $.

VALLE VERZASCA

Secluded and quiet, the road into this shaded valley climbs up past vineyards and through moss-covered tunnels to the tiny cliff-clinging village of Corippo, once noted for its weavers. Built long before cars came along, its streets are for pedestrians only and you must park below. Stone steps lead past a gurgling fountain, eaves drip with bougainvillea, and under shady grape arbors families gather to eat and relax by their miniscule vegetable gardens. The highlight of the valley, however, is the medieval double-arched bridge, Ponte dei Salti at Lavertezzo. In the summer, swimmers dive into the tumbling green waters of the Verzasca River from smooth boulders that line its banks. Directions: Drive west of Bellinzona on 13 for 15km to Gordola. Exit onto the small road heading north into the valley in the direction of Brione and Sonogno. The bridge is ten kilometers from Gordola.

VALLE MAGGIA

A favorite with walkers, the villages of Maggia Valley are set amid meadows and vineyards. Sixteenth-century painted-wood ceilings and frescoes grace the lovely little chapel of St. Maria della Grazia near the bridge in the village of Maggia. Five kilometers farther, the Soladino Falls thunder down from their 90 meter height. At the village of Cevio, another five kilometers, a tiny corkscrew road winds up through the spectacular countryside, through the village of Cerentino, to Ticino's highest village at 1503 meters, Bosco Gurins. Directions: Leave Locarno driving west, then northwest, staying on the east bank of the Maggia River. At the Brolla Bridge continue on the east side of the river, passing the village of Avegno di Fuori. It's nine kilometers from the bridge to the village of Maggia. ****Camping: *In Gordevio, five kilometers south of Maggia. Camping Bella Riva (091-753-1444) or Da Renato (091-753-1364); both are large and popular with families; open May-September; $$$.

THE LAKES AND THEIR TOWNS

Lively Locarno's summer guests enjoy themselves in an al fresco setting. Considered one of the sunniest spots in Switzerland, lake-side beaches and sidewalk cafes are gay with people soaking up the rays. In August, it's jammed for it's International Film Festival. Ascona's narrow streets are beautifully lined with tasteful art galleries, exquisite jewelry stores, and stylish boutiques. But a stroll through Ascona with a stop at the Chiesa St. Pietro e Paollo to admire the interior 16th century frescoes is free. The Museo Comunale d'arte Moderna has a terrific collection; closed Monday. In July, jazz and gospel music fill the warm summer evening air as the town hosts a New Orleans Music Festival. Lugano's beautifully landscaped lake-side parks come alive under starry skies with music festivals and outdoor-movies. While away some time on a boat ride or walk to Gandria, an old fishing village that is now popular with tourists. ****Camping: There are lots of camping places on the lakes. Many are large and resort-like, but these are smaller. *At the northeast end of Lago Maggiore, east of Locarno, in the town of Tenero. Camping Rivabella (091-745-2213); nice location; open May-September; $$$. *At the southeastern end of Lago Lugano. Just south of the bridge at Bissone, exit E/35 at Maroggia. Camping Piazzale Mara (091-649-7245);

nice location on the lake; open May-
September; $$$.

ZERMATT AND THE MATTERHORN

There is something magical about the
Matterhorn. Its colossal overhang, a power-
ful optical illusion, makes you feel that you
are looking up at an enormous, masterly
crafted sculptural piece. Although it is a
magnet for serious mountain climbers from
all over the world, plenty of lower trails
allow for gentle meanders. Take a cable car
or chairlift to trails above the timberline for
the best views. It's often cloudy, so wear
warm clothes. The fascinating stories of
early attempts of climbing the Matterhorn
and the tragedy of the eventual conquest are

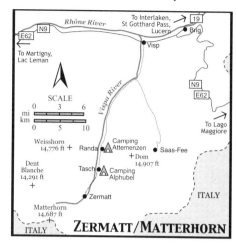

told in the Alpine Museum. A visit here will add mystic to what the locals call the "crooked finger".

Zermatt has no cars. You'll need to leave your car behind and stay at one of the inexpensive
hostelries. Use your guidebook to reserve ahead or check the list in the train station upon arrival.
To reach Zermatt, you must take the train. Drive to Tash, six kilometers from Zermatt, and park
at the railway station. Directions: Zermatt is almost due east from Geneva. 70km east of Martigny
exit N9 at Visp and drive south on the small road following the rail tracks for 30km up to Tash.
****Camping: In Tash. Camping Alphubel (027-966-4667). Just before Tash, outside of Randa.
Camping Attemenzen (027-967-2073).   Both have lovely locations; are large; open May-
September; $$$. There are numerous campgrounds along E62 coming into the area.

GENEVA

When you walk or bike ride along the quay of Lake Geneva, known as Lac Leman in this French-
speaking city, your eyes are drawn to Geneva's symbol-Jet d'Eau, the enormous geyser of water,
that gushes up 140 meters. Gazing farther
out onto the lake, your eyes feast on the
perky sails of sleek yachts, fine old
schooners, and flag-waving steamers. If
you turn from the lake at Jardin Anglais,
you can see the city's other symbol, the
carefully planted flower clock. From here,
amble into the Old Town, Vielle Ville, and
lose yourself down its twisting alleyways.
Stop in one of the neighborhood parks and
join in the contemplation of a game of
chess being played on a giant board.
Meander farther up the hill to the
Cathedrale St. Pierre, where John Calvin
preached his fierce sermons turning
Geneva into the Protestant Rome. The
famous Reformation monument is nearby.
Then take a restful steamer ride, watching

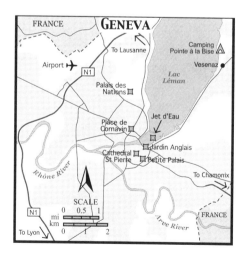

the mountains that nestle the lake pass by. On a clear day, Mont Blanc will be visible, probably swathed in a tulle of cloud. Boats leave from Pont du Mont Blanc. Visit the impressive International Red Cross and Red Crescent Museum, a compelling multi-media experience that is not advised for young children; closed Tuesday. Directions: Take bus 8 from the train station at Place de Cornavin. More than just a grand collection of art, the Petite-Palais's impressive collection, housed in a lovely mansion, is curated to help the viewer understand the various schools of art from 1880 to 1930; open daily. Directions: Take bus 1 or 3 to Blvd. Helvetique. It's in a lovely mansion. ****Camping: *Seven kilometers north of Geneva on the east side of the lake. Exit N5 for Vesenaz, and follow signposting to the lake. Camping Pointe a la Bise (022-752-1296); lovely location; large; all the amenities; cycle path to the city along the lake; public transportation close by; open April-September; $$$$.

ALONG THE LAC LEMAN

In Lausanne, the Musee Olympique dramatically presents the philosophy of the Olympic Games; closed Monday. Directions: On the lake in the center of town, at Quai d'Ouchy. The eccentric collection in the Musee de l'Art Brut, also in Lausanne, is definitely bizarre and a fun change of pace; closed Monday. Directions: North of the lake, just south of the suburb of Prilly follow signage for Palais de Beaulieu. The gallery is at 11 Av. De Bergieres. Montreux's brooding Chateau de Chillon is situated on the lovely swan-dotted shoreline. Its stony pillared dungeon was Bryon's inspiration for The Prisoner of Chillon; open daily. Directions: *Off N9, three kilometers south of town, on the lake. Lively all summer long with music festivals, Montreux's most well known is the Montreux Jazz Festival, a two-week-long festival in mid-July. ****Camping: *On the west side of Lac Leman off E25/N1. On the lake at

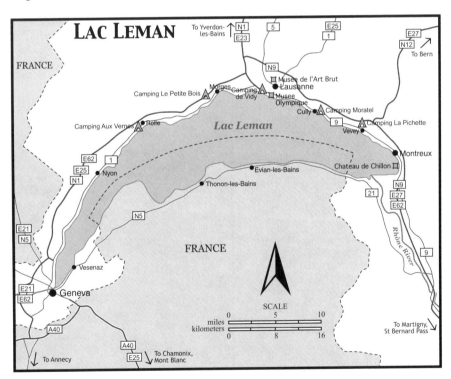

Rolle. Camping Aux Vernes (021-825-1239). *Close to the lake in Morges. Camping Le Petite Bois (021-801-1270). Both have lovely locations; are large; open April-September; $$$$. *Just east of Lausanne, on the lake in the village of Cully. Camping Moratel (021-799-1914); lovely location; small, open April-September; $$$. *In Lausanne. Exit N1 at Lausanne-Sud/La Maladiere, and follow signposting. Camping de Vidy (021-624-2031); very large but convenient lake-side setting; public transportation to the city; open all year; $$$. *Northwest of Montreux in Vevey. Exit off the lake-side road 9, north of town in the suburb of Corseaux. Camping La Pichette (021-921-0997); very simple; open April-September; $$.

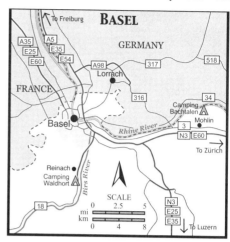

BASEL

Bursting with a wide variety of small but exciting museums, a terrific zoo, and the headquarters of the world's biggest chemical and pharmaceutical firms, Basel makes an enjoyable stop. From the Grossbasel train station, take tram 1 to the tourist office by the Mittlere Brucke. Pick up a city walking map and the English version of their museum booklet to plan your explorations. ****Camping: *On the Rhein River, about 30km east of Basel. Off 3/7 exit at Mohlin following signposting for Rhein for four kilometers. Camping Bachtalen (061-851-5095); small and restful; terraced; pool; tennis and mini-golf; open April-September; $$. *South of the city in the suburb town of Reinach. Exit off N5 south of the city at exit Reinach-Nord, and follow signposting for just over a kilometer. Camping Waldhort (061-711-6429); convenient to the autostrata; public transportation to city center; large; open April-September; $$.

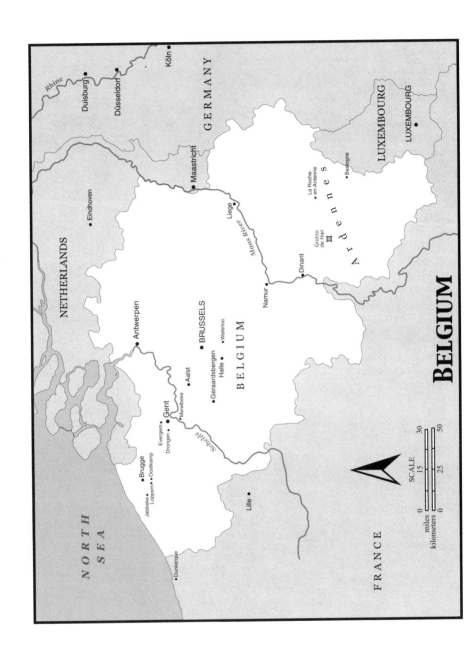

BELGIUM

Peals of laughter, raucous music, and wild stomping bursts Pieter Brueghel's The Wedding Dance. Painted in the 1500s, it still exemplifies the spirit of today's Belgian. In love with carnivals and festivals, their summer calendars are full of color and music

The belle of the ball in the 15th and 16th centuries, Belgium lavished herself with fine silks, jewels, and paintings paid for with monies from her lucrative trade business and with the extraordinarily skill of her craftsmen. Lured by the wealth that could be made from taxation, the Duke of Burgundy, known for his arrogant and flamboyant ways, made her his home. Talented Flemish painters, sculptors, musicians, and architects were encouraged bringing forth a Golden Age of art that rivaled Florence and Venice in splendor. Today the painstaking craftsmanship is on view in the museums and churches. Its care to detail is almost beyond belief in today's art world.

Begium's proud, energetic, and quick-tempered citizens bristled under the weight of heavy taxes and heroically resisted the outside authority. Throughout history, Belgium has continued to face unsolicited outside involvement. Nicknamed "the cockpit of Europe," she has served as a battle zone for Europe, receiving in return enormous architectural, economic, and social devastation.

In an attempt to free herself of this position, she declared neutrality. She rose from the ruins of World War I with heroic determination, and restored the economy with rapid industrialization. But the German invasion in 1940 brought harsh rationing and strict control over everyday living. After World War II, faced again with destruction, the citizenry reevaluated their position and promoted a political alliance system and active foreign policy that lead to the formation of NATO, with Brussels as its administrative headquarters.

Belgium's toll-free highways are in good condition and are well signposted. A detailed current map is essential; purchase one at gas station. Major gas stations have mini-markets. It is important to know that close to Brussels bilingual road signs show the name place in both Flemish and French. So what might seem a name place for two places is often one. Public parking close to historic areas is available with time limits and cost similar to those in urban areas at home. Similiar road rules also apply. It's a friendly country, and the locals are happy to help with directions.

Lovely recreational areas have been built just outside major metropolitan areas, providing scenic and relaxing places for people to enjoy being together. Besides well-run camping areas, these parks have tennis courts, children's playgrounds, cycle paths, and separate fishing and wind surfing lakes. All the camping places listed have good maintenance. Camping for two persons, a car, and a tent will cost just under $20 USA.

BRUGGE

Secluded and unimportant industrially, historic Brugge has scarcely changed since the Middle Ages when it was one of the most important cities in Northern Europe. Merchants were given favorable tax exemptions and flocked here. Russian furs and Spanish fruit were traded for Flemish tapestries and lace. Brugge became an emporium, hosting grand trade fairs in her beloved festive manner. But the relentless silting of the river and England's refusal to sell her wool brought the city's demise. Today's visitor, wandering over miniscule medieval bridges to cross quiet canals, is treated to the venerable spires and the quaintly gabled houses. It and feels as if time has stood still.

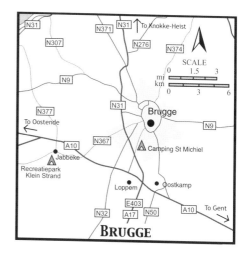

Sparkling with luminous color, harmony, and meticulous detail, the early Flemish paintings of van Eyck, van der Weyden, Memling, and Bosch gleam more life-like than real life. Stately portraits laden with symbolic detail gaze from glittering frames, and sardonic observations of everyday life are spiced with burlesque effects. The best are in the Groeninge Museum; open daily. Amazing in detail, the lace collection in the Arentshuis Museum's Kant collection attests to the love of elaborate dress of both men and women; open daily. A tiny park between the museums is a perfect spot to reflect upon history, eat a picnic lunch, and listen to a concert from the Belfort's carillon. Directions: Walk south of Belfort on Wollestraat. Cross the bridge to Dijver, busy with flea market stalls and turn west to walk along the canal to the complex of museums.

One of the holiest relics of medieval Europe is the phial purported to contain the blood of Jesus that is kept in a magnificent silver tabernacle in the upper chapel of the Heilig Bloed basilica; open daily. Next to the basilica, enjoy the elegant façade and elaborate ceiling work of the Stadius; open daily. Directions: From the northeast corner of the Belfort walk along Breidelstraat to the Burg.

Before the sun sets, climb up the belfry staircase of the Belfort to look out over the rosy-hued town. Then watch the town gently illuminate while you drift down the lazy canal in an excursion boat. Boats are boarded south of the Burg.

In mid-July, Brugge hosts an exciting array of music including blue-grass, blues, reggae, and rock in a three-day open-air festival they called Cactusfestival.

****Camping: *15km west of Brugge. Exit A10 at Exit 6 and follow signposting to camping and Jabbeke. Recreatiepark Klein Strand (050-811-440); lovely location in a large recreational area; bungalows; open all year; $$$. *Southeast of Brugge. Exit A10/E40 at Exit 7 Brugge-Centrum, and drive towards the Ring Road N31. Camping St. Michiel (050-380-819; doable on bicycle to the historic area; traffic noise; open year round; $$$.

GHENT

The ability to quietly discover the inner personality of his subjects was painter Jan van Eyck's gift. Looking with an objective eye, he recorded with infinite detail his findings, revealing secrets that were perhaps otherwise unknown. His most famous masterpiece, the Adoration of the Lamb in St. Bavo's Cathedral, is rich in symbolism and glows with brilliant color. Directions: Follow signage to centrum, St. Bavo's, and parking.

Historic Ghent's medieval gabled guild houses drip with a kaleidoscope of flowers and are delightful examples of the Flemish Golden Age. The Castle of the Counts still looks unfriendly, just as it does in Bosch's paintings. The circular wall curtained the castle, protecting the feudal counts from the unruly citizens. Today visitors pass through these massive walls for a self-guided tour through the castle's labyrinth. Directions: Walk northwest of St. Bavo's, cross the river and following signage for Het Gravensteen.

Bored with the idealized subjects popular during his day, Hieronymus Bosch painted imaginative, and often humorous, pictures of daily life. A good collection of his work is housed along with Bruegel the Younger's wedding pictures in the Museum of Fine Arts; closed Mondays. Around the corner, the Museum of Contemporary Art has an impressive international collection. Directions: South of the historic area, just east of the train station. Follow signs to Citadelpark and parking. The museum is on the northeast corner of the park.

The whole town is very lively during the last week in July during the Gentse Feesten. A wide variety of music, theater, street food, and fireworks go on for nine days. Use public transportation from your campgrounds where you have reserved a place ahead.

****Camping: *West of Ghent in the suburb of Drongen. Exit off A10/E40 at exit 13 for Ghent-West/Drongen. Drive five kilometers in the direction of Ghent following signposting. Camping Blaarmeersen (09-221-5399); on a tiny lake in a recreational area; close to public transportation to the Ghent; $$.

BRUSSELS

To fully savor Brussel's famous flamboyant square, the Grand Place, richly edged with Baroque guild halls, arrive in the evening when all its grandeur is illuminated. Then walk north of the square to experience the fairy-lit quarter of rue des Bouchers, where the elaborate displays of fish restaurants hope to lure customers. Directions: Metro to Central Station then walk west half a kilometer.

Gazing upon pictures that oozed with discreet charm or were secretive or exuberantly witty, but still simple to understand, was a great delight to the wealthy burghers. The powerful works of the notable artists of this Golden Age, particularly Ruben and Bruegel, are still captivating, and a large collections hangs in the Musee d'Art Ancien on blue and brown color-coded routes. Images of dreams both thought provoking and perplexing form the core of the Musee d'Art Moderne surrealist collection, with Delvaux and Magritte being important contributors. In addition to the exciting permenent collection, the museum hosts outstanding temporary exhibits. Both museums are

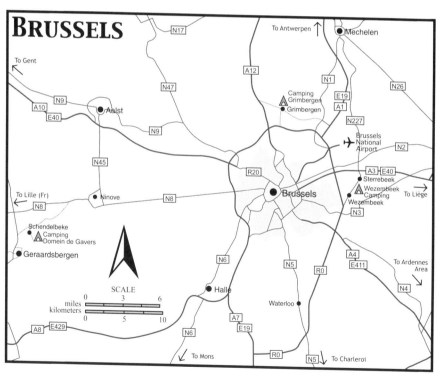

part of Musee Royaux des Beaux Arts. The collections are extensive, so be selective; closed Mondays. Directions: Metro 1 to Parc, then walk south on Rue Royale for half a kilometer to Place Royale and the Museum Complex.

Never using a straight line when he could use a curved one, Victor Horta's art nouveau designs swirl sensously, encompassing magnificent wood, wrought iron, and stone. His light-loving designs allow sunlight to filter through stained glass, skylights, and spacious window glass. His home and studio are now the Musee Victor Horta; open afternoons only, closed Monday. Directions: Metro 1 to Louise, then tram 91 or 94 to the museum.

Haunting and savage sounds of tom-toms, scary masks, and a huge dugout canoe greet visitors to the exotics of Central Africa. In the late 19th and early 20th centuries, Belgium controlled the Republic of Congo. The Museum of Central Africa has a rich collection from those days; closed Monday. Its location at the edge of Foret de Soignes makes it a grand place for a picnic. Directions: Metro 1 to Montgomery, then tram 44 to the tram terminal. It's a short walk on the main road to the museum.

****Camping: *30km west of Brussels and 30 km south of Ghent, in Geraardsbergen. Exit N8 onto N42, and drive south seven kilometers to Geraardsbergen, Follow signposting north in the direction of Schendelbeke. Camping Domein de Gavers (054-416-324); lovely location along a small river in a large scenic recreational area; popular with families; bungalows; open all year; $$$. *Just north of Brussels in the suburb of Grimbergen. Exit the ring road at exit 7, and follow signposting. Camping Grimbergen (02-270-9597); traffic noise, public transportation to city center closeby; open May-September; $$. *East of Brussels in the suburb of Wezembeek. Exit E40 at exit 21. Drive south, passing through Sterrebeek towards Wezembeek. Wezembeek Camping (02782-1009); close to public transportation; open May-September; $$.

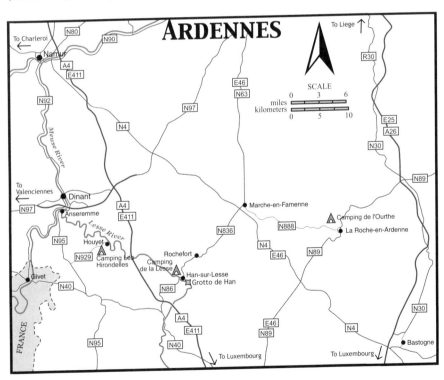

THE ARDENNES

Nestled between France and Luxembourg, the Ardennes make a restful stop. Forests of beech riddled with footpaths hide eerie rock grottos. Rivers wind and twist through gorges providing fun for canoeists. Campers relax along river-side settings next to picturesque villages.

LA ROCHE-EN-ARDENNE

Beloved by the Belgians who come to enjoy the fresh air and tranquility, this friendly little village is a favorite. Canoe and mountain bike rentals are available on the main street, where you can also purchase maps for hiking and biking into the forests and river valley. ****Camping: *South of Liege exit E25 at exit 50. Drive west on N89 for 17km in the direction of La Roche-en-Ardene. From Namur drive 34km southeast on N4, exiting at Marche. Drive east 20km on N888 to La Roche-en-Ardenne. Drive north of the village along the river towards Hotel Liege. Camping de l'Ourthe (056-412-323); beautiful location; popular swimming area; open May-September; $$.

THE LESSE RIVER VALLEY

The Lesse River is a safe and a relatively easy river to paddle a canoe. Call to reserve your canoe with the canoeing company in Anseremme the day before. They will arrange your shuttle. The river is peaceful and scenic, particularly early in the morning; 082-226-186. Directions: Anseremme is south of Dinant off the ring road at exit 3. ****Camping: *In Houyet. Drive south 13km from Anseremme on N95. Exit east onto N929, and drive 13km to the village. Camping Les Hirondelles (082-666-954); nice location; open May-September; $$.

HAN-SUR-LESSE

The Lesse River forced its way through a large dome-shaped mountain, creating huge mystical grottos, then emerged miles later to join the Meuse River. Known as the Grotto de Han, it is one of the largest caves in Northern Europe and a popular excursion. The largest grotto, The Salle de Dome, is immense and very impressive, measuring 430 meters high. Echoing voices adding to the mystique. At the end of the tour, visitors board boats to cross a tiny lake and then float out through a tunnel to the sunlit world. Directions: South of Namur. Exit A4 at exit 23, and drive northeast five kilometers to the Grotto de Han. ****Camping: *In Han-ur-Lesse. Camping de la Lesse (084-377-290); nice location on the river; popular with families; open May-September; $$$.

LUXEMBOURG

SCALE

BELGIUM

GERMANY

Bitburg

Bastogne

Wiltz

Vianden

Bourscheid

Esch-s-Sure

Sure River

Diekirch

Ettlebruck

Echternach

Our River

LUXEMBOURG

Grevenmacher

Bofferdange

Arlon

Walferdange

Saarburg

Wormeldange

Moselle Wine Region

LUXEMBOURG

Hesperange

Remich

Alzingen

Beck-Kleinmacher

Petange

Moselle River

Frisange

Esch-sur-Alzette

Dudelange

FRANCE

LUXEMBOURG

"Once upon a time," she whispered in her best storytelling voice, snuggling the youngsters closer, "a wealthy nobleman built a fortress-like castle high on a hill at the edge of a grand river. He called himself the Count of Luxembourg. Wanting riches and more land the Count waged battles with his neighbors to extend his power. Over the years the ruling families came and went until the very bright Countess Ermesinde spent large amounts of money to make her country better. She founded schools, courts of justice, and theatres. She gave peasants freedom from serfdom. Later the little country had another hero, John the Blind. Being blind did not deter him, he joined his French neighbors and they bravely fought for their freedom against the English who wanted to take their countries. Many years passed with the little country being ruled by mighty rulers from afar. Then, just a little over one hundred years ago, leaders from many countries met and decided that the little country could have its freedom. But the little country was in the path that the powerful passed so battles were still fought and many people died," she recalled sadly. But then smiling brightly she went on, "Nowadays people visit museums and memorials that tell the soldier's and villager's stories. They adventure into the mysterious castles that still cling along the edge of curving rivers or hike up to those that are perched up on craggy hilltops for fine views."

Like a delicious tidbit left over from a grand feast Luxembourg is often over-looked by tourists, which makes it more delectable. Charming, isolated villages are picturesquely set here along swift-moving rivers, and tiny lakes nestle into valleys held by forested hills. Summer festivals add a very enjoyable laid-back ambiance. Luxembourg celebrates its national day on June 23rd with fireworks, parades, and citizens enjoying a day off from work.

Vacationers from the Lowland countries come to Luxembourg to enjoy the peaceful atmosphere of the surrounding mountains and rivers. The tradition of camping is well established. Well-cared for campgrounds, lovely settings, and amenities that appeal to adults and children alike make it a popular family vacation destination.

Special cycle paths make pedaling very enjoyable. One of the most popular routes is along the River Sure. This almost level route twists with the river between Vianden, Reisdorf, Echternach, and Moerdorf, passing through woodlands and by ancient bridges and monuments. It's easy to park in one of the little villages and pedal to the river and cycle path. The tourist office has a colorful brochure describing the cycling paths for the country.

VIANDEN AND ENVIRONS

The tiny medieval village of Vianden is held gently in the hands of the hills that nestle it. Cobblestone streets wind alongside the river leading to the elegant castle that was once home to the wealthy counts who ruled the region. Take the cablecar up 450 meters for panoramic views of the strikingly beautiful countryside, then walk down the path to the castle; open daily. Victor Hugo sought refuge here in 1870. At the house where he lived, you can examine drawings he made of the village and pore over copies of his original writings. Directions: Drive 30km north of Luxembourg City on N7, then three kilometers east to Diekirch, passing through the town. Exit north on N17 and drive 15km farther to the village of Vianden.

Located due west of Vianden, Bourscheid's castle has a spectacular view. During July's medieval days or Schlassfest you can join the locals at barbeques, music events, and jousting contests. The village and castle of Esch-Sur-Sure are famous for their setting on an ox-bow of the river Sure. The little road between Bourscheid and Esch-Sur-Sure follows the river and is particularly scenic for picnics and cycling. Directions: To reach Esch-Sur-Sure drive 30km north of Luxembourg City on N7 to Ettelbruck. Then drive northwest on N15 for 15km. Bourscheid is ten kilometers east, on the Sure River.

In Diekirch's Museum of Military History, life-size dioramas, painstakingly created from pho-

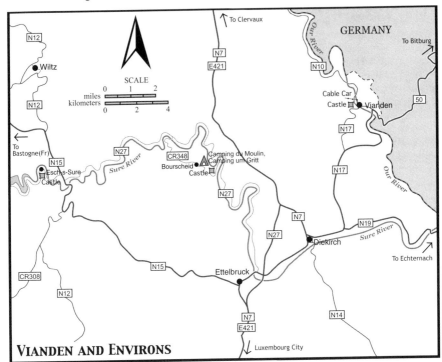

VIANDEN AND ENVIRONS

tographs make a vivid impression of the hardships the soldiers on both sides endured during the freezing cold winter of 1944.   It was here that one of World War II's most bitter confrontations, the Battle of the Bulge, took place. The resistance movement and the internment camp exhibits pay tribute to the local heroes. Directions: To reach to Diekirch drive 30km north of Luxembourg City on N7 to Ettelbruck, then continue five kilometers farther to Diekirch. The Museum of Military History is just off the main square, on Place Guillaume; open daily.

****Camping: *On the Sure River in Bourscheid. Camping du Moulin (99-0331) or Camping um Gritt (99-0449); both have nice river-side settings; popular with families; open May-September; $$$$.

MOSELLE WINE REGION

To see how sparkling wine is produced the old-fashioned way, take the tour at Caves St. Martin in Remich.   Then drive to the adjoining village of Bech-Kleinmacher and wander through a tiny vintner's home, now the Musee A Possen. To extend the your knowledge of wine making take the Promenade Viticole. On it you walk through the actual grapevines peeking up through the leaves to catching a whiff of the heady perfume exuding from the luscious fruit. Directions: Drive 22 kilometers north of Remich along the Moselle River to the village of Wormeldange. Pass through the village to the Caves Cooperative where the self-guided tour through the vines begins. Starting in late August, festivals celebrating the grape harvest are a happy mingling of the farmer-vintner, the hobbyist-vintner, and enthusiastic drinkers. Directions: Off ring road A-1 in Luxembourg City exit east on N2, and drive 18km to Remich. ****Camping: *At the north end of the wine route in Grevenmacher. 20km east of Luxembourg City on E44, take exit 13 and drive two kilometers more to Grevenmacher. Follow signposting to the Moselle River and camping. Camping Route du Vin (75-0234); lovely setting on the river; swimming pool; tennis; popular with families; open April-September; $$$. *At the southern end of the route in Remich. 20km southeast of Luxembourg City on E29, exit for Remich and follow signposting for the Moselle River and camping. Camping Europe (69-8018); nice setting on the river; popular with families; swimming pool; mini-golf; tennis; open April-mid September; $$$.

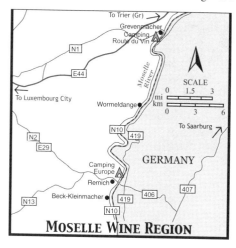

MOSELLE WINE REGION

LUXEMBOURG CITY

The most stunning feature of Luxembourg City is it's setting. To enjoy its full impact, start your tour by gazing over its ancient ramparts, towers, and royal palace from the Kirchberg plateau. Directions: Exit the ring road A1 on the east side of the city at exit 7. Before crossing over the Alzette River on the Charlotte Bridge, exit Avenue Kennedy and wind your way up the hill to the Kirchberg Plateau. You'll pass modern European Union buildings. Park and look out over at the historic area, now UNESCO listed.

To get a sense of the defensive position the city has played through history, wander through the musky tunnels that were carved out of the rock to form the Bock casemates or artillery enclosures; open daily. Directions: On the east side of the river just off the Monte de Clausen bridge. Walk or cycle along the Alzette River and gaze up at the slit-windowed towers of the ramparts. Enjoy the Renaissance façade of the Grand Duke's Palace, then rest in the main square, Place Guillaume. Directions: Walk west of the Palace 100 meters. The Palace is open for tours on weekday afternoons and Saturday morning. Tickets are sold at the tourist office on the square. On Wednesday and Saturdays the square is a lively market place. The interesting high-tech City Museum keeps you abreast with newest inventions; closed Monday. Directions: Walk east of the Palace on Rue Marche aux Herbes. A particularly jolly time to visit the city is during its Schoeberfoer or Market Fair. Opened by royalty the last week in August, the fair continues through the first part of September. One of the largest and oldest of its kind in Europe, this fair is easy to enjoy and definitely worth a detour.

****Camping: *Ten kilometers north of the city on N7 exit four kilometers north of Walferdange for Bofferdange. Camp Dauschkaul 36 rue du Moulin (33-2434); lovely hillside setting with tranquil views; terraced; very small; open May-September; $$$. * Five kilometers south of the city, along the Alzette River in the suburb of

LUXEMBOURG CITY

Alzingen. Ten kilometers south of the city exit A31/E25 onto N13 in the direction of Frisange. At Frisange, exit north on N3 in the direction of Hesperange. Just south of Hesperange follow signposting to Alzingen and the Alzette River. Camping Bon Accueil 2 rue du camping (36-7069); convenient; public transport to the city; close to a recreational park; open April-September; $$$

THE NETHERLANDS

Picture a young woman, her bicycle basket overflowing with a riot of brilliant blooms, steadily pedaling along a leafy canal lined with perfectly symmetrical gabled houses, and you are picturing quintessential Holland. Throughout the country, back roads and cycle paths fringe brilliant patch-works of flowers and apple-green meadows where sky larks sing. They cross canals over wooden bridges, and wind through cheerful towns, bending and curving as if time meant nothing. Bridges lift, holding back traffic while a small boat floats by. Carillon bells ring with favorite hymns, folk songs, and waltzes from tall church steeples. Town halls take the place of palaces with pinnacles, finials, and lace-like arches. Cozy cafes are fragrant with fresh-brewed coffee and apple tarts and hum with music and folks immersed in quiet conversations.

Bicycles are dearly loved and revered. Even the queen mingles with her subjects by riding her bicycle to market. With seeming ease, pets, flowers, groceries, and children are all happily carted on one bike. Public buildings, parking facilities, and public transportation are all designed to accommodate them, and most major roads include a large separate bike lanes.

Roadways are in excellent condition and well signposted. Except for Amsterdam, the cities are easy to drive into. Parking outside the city center is encouraged with large parking garages and public transportation that is efficient, modern, and comfortable.

Masters of innovation and experimentation, the Dutch have applied their knowledge to social issues, agriculture, and industry. Experts in waterways, bridges, and hydraulic dams, they now export their knowledge of water technology. On the globe, the Netherlands is a speck, but in world history the Dutch have played a part way out of proportion to their size. Leaders in banking, shipping, and trade since the 17th century, they established an empire on the other side of the world, set an example of democratic social order at home, and opened a new world of art with an astonishing group of excellent painters.

Camping is a popular recreational pursuit for the Dutch. Campgrounds are modern and well maintained, with small stores and a staff fluent in English. Camping for two persons, a car, and tent will cost about $20 USA. Friendly, kind, polite, and helpful, the Dutch love to talk about their country and will go out of their way to give directions and information.

AMSTERDAM

The great port of the north and the center of banking for Europe, Amsterdam became the first center of bourgeois capitalism in Europe. Its location in the middle of Holland provided a protected harbor and access to both the Baltic and Rhine. Persecuted merchants, driven out of other countries, found refuge here, giving the country the advantage of their centuries-old mercantile expertise.

Today, drifting down Amsterdam's leafy canals lined with dignified and harmonious houses, one can imagine how the markets, where the delectable smell of baking bread and smoking pork mingled with the aroma of fresh leather and exotic spices were swamped in color and carnival. Dressed like birds of paradise, the wealthy members of

the mercantile and craft guilds, highly conscious of their personal dignity and fine attire, strolled like peacocks.

Stop at the main tourist office, VVV, outside Central Station, on arrival. It overflows with glossy brochures and information about current events, museums, and galleries in Amsterdam and all of the Netherlands. During summer, there is an impressive array of events. Many are free. Fit some into your visit. Amsterdam and the whole of the Netherlands have a staggering number of outstanding museums. Buying a museum card at the VVV when you arrive saves considerable money if you plan to see more than just a couple.

The Metro and trams are efficient, convenient, and easy to use. Employees speak fluent English. Buy a strippenkaart, voucher for ten rides, from the campground, metro station, magazine shop, or Central Station. Ask for the free transport map and English guide of the transport system. Each time you travel, validate the ticket for the number of persons using it and the number of zones you are traveling. Take the circle tram first. In summer, one departs and returns to Central Station every few minutes, making a wide loop that passes close to most of the major sights.

The grassy wedge of parkland edged by Amsterdam's most famous museums is called Museumplein. Here you'll find the Rijksmuseum, the Van Gogh, and the Stedelijk. Fascinating books have been written about the most famous Dutch painters; reading some before your trip will make visits to these museums more meaningful. The Rijksmuseum houses the Golden Age works. The collection is huge. Get a museum map and go directly to the galleries that interest you most. With a keen interest in human psychology, the best of the pictures are thoughtful introspection of character with a powerful handling of light and shade. Rembrandts are mingled with Hals, Steens, and Vermeers, and there's a lovely garden at the back; open daily. The new Theo Van Gogh Museum houses not only the riveting pictures by his brother Vincent, but a chronological collection the Post-Impressionists-Gauguin, Monet, Bernard, Pissarro, Signac, and Seurat-curated to help you understand the artistic influences they had on one another. You're treated to the vibrant, radiant, and emotional colors they loved. Theo's son, V.W. Van Gogh, agreed to sell his enormous private collection if the new museum was built. The Kroller-Muller Museum also added many of their important works to the new museum. The sensational Post-Impressionist collection that resulted is the most important in the world; open daily. Afterwards, climb the former skateboard ramp in the adjoining park and enjoy a rest with other locals as you look down at the Concertgebouw, the colorful trams, and the gable work and facades of the neighborhood buildings. The Stedelijk Museum of Modern Art houses permanent and temporary art exhibits extending into photography, ceramics, glass, and sculpture. It is world renowned and an exciting place to visit; open daily. The Concertgebouw, known throughout the world for its wonderful acoustics and world class-performances, sells reasonably priced tickets for its performances from 10 a.m. to 5 p.m. daily and after 7 p.m. for that evening's performance.

Vondel Park, just a few minutes walk west of Museumsplein, has leafy thickets, winding paths, and an extravagant rose garden. Here, children feed the ducks that waddle around the ponds, workers and tired tourists take quick naps on its lawns, mothers admire babies in prams, and joggers keep in shape. A large collection of film memorabilia and screenings from its outstanding achive can be viewed in the old Vondelpark Pavilion, now the Filmmuseum. The park also has an open-air theatre that presents free concerts. Don't miss this delightful way to enjoy the Dutch.

You'll need to consult your guidebook to make selections from the over-flowing and imaginative cup of Amsterdam's offerings.

****Camping: *Southeast of the city, off A9 exit Gaasperplas and follow signposting. Gaasper Camping, Loosdrechtdreef 7 (020-696-7326); close to the metro; best for the city; open May-December; $$$. In Aalsmeer, east of the airport. Off A9 exit #6 for Aalsmeer. Continue south on N231, crossing the canal. Camping het Amsterdamse Bos, Kl. Noorddijk 1(020-641-6868); airport noise; bus to city; open April-October; $$$.

WEST HOLLAND

HAARLEM

Robust painter Frans Hals, admired by both Van Gogh and Manet for his frank, full-bodied colors, and bold-moving strokes is remembered in the 17th century almshouse where he lived out his final years. The collection illustrates his evolution as a painter. The gargantuan picture, *Banquet of the Officers of St. George* bursts with colorful figures wearing immense sashes and established his reputation; open daily. Directions: Off A9 or A208, follow signs for centrum. Use the dome of St. Bravo's to guide you. The museum is just south of it at Groot Heiligand 62.

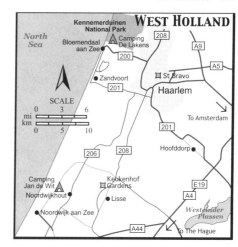

At the Grote Markt, step into St. Bravo and examine the famous Baroque organ boasting 5,000 pipes. Just outside the church, look up at the elaborate and caprious stepped gables of the Meat Market. Behind the church it's a short walk to the canal and the Teylers Museum, the oldest museum in the country, housing a fascinating collection of drawings and artifacts.

Just west of town, an elegant residential area gives way to Kennemerduinen National Park, an appealing dune and beach area. The route is popular for cycling. Directions: Off A208 exit onto 200 for Bloemendaal Aan-Zee.

If you are here in April or May when the tulips are blooming, don't miss seeing the Keukenhof Gardens, perhaps the most fabulous flower garden in the world; open daily. Directions: South of Haarlem on 208 in Lisse.

****Camping: *In the dune area by the park. Off A9 exit onto 200 for Bloemendaal Aan Zee, and drive to the beach. Camping De Lakens, Zeeweg 60 (023-251-902); close to the beach and parklands; open April-September; $$$. *Due west of the Keukenhof gardens in Noordwijk, take the road north along the dune to Noordwijkerhout. Camping Jan de Wit, Kapelleboslaan 10 (0252-372-485); large; popular with families; open April through September; $$$.

LE HAGUE

The Mauritshuis, Le Hague's brightest jewel, houses a renowned collection of the Dutch master painters whose works exemplify a high degree of technical competence. Galleries are filled with evocative landscapes, where light makes the muted colors glow, as well as with scenes depicting lively music and raucous drinking. Directions: From A12/E30 drive west, exiting for Binnenhof and Den Haag CS train station. The museum is in the magnificent mansion on the east side of the Binnenhof; closed Mondays. For a complete change of pace, walk across the Binnenhof to the Gevengenpoort and take a tour of the

prison and its Chamber of Horrors.   Then board either tram 7 or 8 to the Peace Palace and Court of International Justice.   Tours include viewing the valuable gifts given by countries around the globe.   From here it's a short walk to Panorama Mesdag to see the gigantic picture of the fishing port in the late 1880's. ****Camping: *Drive southwest of the city center to Kijkduin and the beach. Vakantiecentr. Kijkduinpark (3170-448-2100); close to the beach; large; popular with families; open all year; $$$$.

DELFT

A pleasant but touristy, leafy canal town, Delft's fame comes from the blue-and-white tiles she produced in the 17th century. Originally copied from the Ming dynasty in China, the tile workers became so skillful that they were able to sell them back to the Chinese! (The best collection is found in the Rijksmueum in Amsterdam.) ****Camping: *On the eastern edge of town, in the city recreational parkland Delfse Hout. Exit A13 for Pijnacker, and drive east following signposting. Delftse Hout Camping, Korftlaan 5 (3115-213-0040); pleasant location; convenient; open all year; $$.

ROTTERDAM

When many European ports became too small to accommodate the huge ships built after World War II, the Dutch, ever determined and optimistic, dredged and built a deep-water port and called Europoort. Today it is one of Europe's largest ports. The best way to appreciate it is to take a waterway excursion trip. To gaze up at the immense container ships and oil tankers from the water is humbling. Directions: Use the Spacetower at Euromast as a guide for parking. Then walk northeast towards Williamsplein and Spido Cruises.

For the best collections of Dutch windmills, go to Kinderdijk. Built in the mid-18th century, a string of 18 windmills lines the main channel leading into polders, or reclaimed land. Inspecting them from inside and visiting the exhibition center rounds out the excursion. But enthusiasts come hear the eerie creaking made as the blades make their majestic turns. They are put into operation on Saturday afternoons in July and August. Directions: Kinderdijk is at Albasserdam, southeast of Rotterdam and signposted off A16 just over the waterway. ****Camping: *On the Oude Maas river in Barendrecht, just south of Rotterdam. From A15 or A29, exit east to Barendrecht and follow signposting to Ijsselmonde, a recreational parkland and campground. Camping de Oude Maas (3178-677-2445); pleasant setting; convenient; open all year; $$.

THE DELTA PROJECT AND EXPO

In response to the 1953 devastation caused by high tides and flooding in Zeeland-a cluster of islands and peninsulas south of Rotterdam- the Dutch embarked on a project that spanned 30 years and resulted in the most complex engineering project the world has ever seen. True to their heritage of group decisions, the Storm Surge Barrier was a compromise between environmentalists, fishermen, and farmers. The Expo, a hands-on experience with water, cleverly appeals to both young and old and should not be missed; open daily. Directions: For the coastal route, use 57; otherwise take A58 to Middleburg, and then go north on 57.

The Wacheren peninsula, located southwest of the Storm Surge Barrier, is a low-key and popular vacation area for the Dutch. Stunningly fields of brilliantly colored flowers, picturesque villages with inviting sidewalk cafes, softly shaped sand dunes, and sunny beaches make it hard not to want to stay awhile. There's a terrific paved cycling/walking path on the sand dunes and also one that fringes the flower fields and then goes through the villages. ****Camping: On the north side of the Storm Surge Barrier in Burgh-Haamstede. Camping Groenewoudt (3111-165-1410); pool; open April-September; $$$. On the south side of the Barrier in Vrouwenpolder. Camping Ornjezon (3111-859-1549); large; pool; small cafe; close to the dunes and

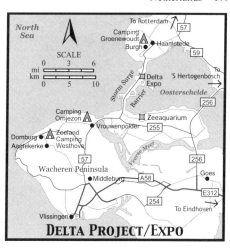

DELTA PROJECT/EXPO

beach; open May-October; $$$$. Close to Domburg on the Walcheren pennisula. Drive south off the Barrier on 57 for nine kilometers in the direction of Middleburg. Exit for Domburg and drive another nine kilometers, following signposting for Aagtekerke. Zeeland Camping Westhove (0118-58-1809); close to the flower fields; villages; and beach; open April-October; $$$.

HOGE VELUWE NATIONAL PARK

Only an hour from Amsterdam, this park is a precious spot of pine-scented tranquilly and beauty, providing a perfect setting for the Kroller-Muller Museum's famous collection of 19th and 20th century art. Noted for it's large Van Gogh collection, it also boasts works by Seurat, Picasso, and Modrian. A large sculpture garden includes pieces by Rodin, Moore, and Hepworth, along with many others; closed Mondays.   Hundreds of bicycles are available free to visitors for use on the lacework of cycle/walking paths. The highlight at the Visitor Centre is the Museonder Museum, the first underground museum in the world. Its mystical and fascinating exhibits are geared to both young and old; open daily. To see the impressive art-deco hunting lodge, St. Hubertus, you must stop at the visitor center on the day of your visit to the lodge, because reservations are only made here; open daily. Directions: From Amsterdam drive east on A1 for about 60km. Pass the exit for A30 and Ede, and drive 15km further on A1, exiting for N310 and Stroe. Drive south on N310, following signposting for eleven kilometers farther for Otterlo and Hoge Veluwe. ****Camping: *Close to the Otterlo entrance to the park. Follow the directions to the park and Otterlo. Continue south through the village on N310. It's signposted. Camping Beek en Hei (0318-591-483); lovely location; close to the main park sights; open all year; $$$. At the Arnhem park entrance in Schaarsbergen. North of Arnhem exit A12/A50 onto N310. Then drive east on N311 to the park entrance.   Camping de Hooge Veluwe (0312-6443-2272); large; convenient; open April-September; $$$.

WATERLAND

Gabled houses here are decorated like wedding cakes with arched doorways rich in fanciful designs. Tiny gardens overflow with marigolds and hollyhocks, and narrow cobblestone streets wind like pieces of a medieval jigsaw puzzle through the little towns of Waterland. In the Rococo interiors of the Town Halls it's easy to picture the Burgomaster in his enormous wig staring intently at the prisoner, humiliated in baggy pants and clumsy shoes, as the "bigwigs," extravagant in ruffs of rich

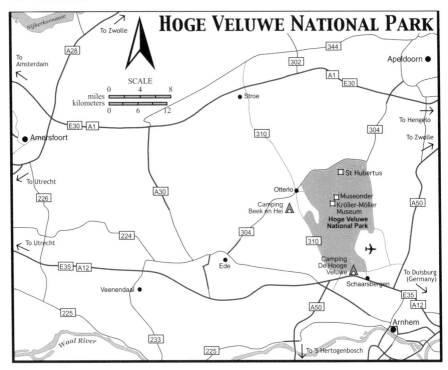

starched lace and plumed high black hats, look on. Canoeing, biking, and wind surfing are popular sports and rentals are available in Monnickendam and at the Het Twiske nature reserve in Landsmeer. Directions: Cross over the waterway on the north side of Amsterdam on A10, and drive north on scenic 247. ****Camping: *In Edam. Exit 247 on the north side of town, and drive towards the harbor. Camping Strandbad (0299-371-994); on the water; popular with wind surfers; small; reserve ahead; open April-September; $$$.

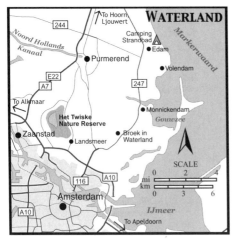

GRONINGEN

In a dramatic decision to cut down traffic congestion, Groningen voted to remove a large downtown roadway and allocated a considerable amount of money for cycling paths. It's a joy to pedal here along with the friendly locals who fill the streets. Carillon bells ring out sweet melodies, flower stalls spill out glorious color, and you wish your hometown had voted likewise. Whimiscal and colorful, the Groninger Museum hangs over the canal inviting you to smile and enter. Start upstairs with the Dutch silver masters and entrancing Chinese ceramic collection. The museum is noted for avant-garde acquisitions and temporary shows; closed Mondays.

Directions: Follow the canal south; the museum is across from the train station. The train station has been restored to some of its 1890 art nouveau grandeur and it's definitely worth the short walk from the art museum. Much of Holland's wealth has, and still does, come from shipping. Imaginatively presented exhibits in the Noordelijk Scheepvaart Museum make it easy to understand the lure the sea; closed Mondays. Directions: North of the train station along the canal. ****Camping: 13km east of Groningen on A7/E22 in the direction of Winschoten exit for Foxhol, and drive south to Kropswolde. Then follow signposting through the Zuidlaardermeer parkland. Camping Meerwijck (3159-832-3659); beautiful lakeside setting in a large parkland; children's indoor pool; open April-October; $$$.

FRIESLAND AND THE ISLAND OF AMELAND

The emerald-green dairy fields of Friesland, carefully reclaimed from the sea by hard-working peasants and farmers, stretch out like a prairie. Flocks of geese waddle around the great farmsteads

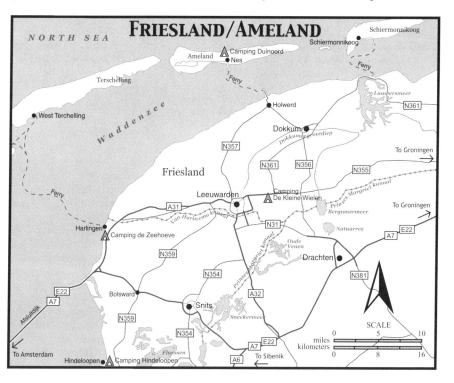

where house and farm buildings are under one roof. Well-fed black-and-white cows contentedly chew and magnificent black horses swish their manes and tails. This pastoral country of cream and butter was a land apart until the causeway over the great dyke was built. Dreams of exotic faraway lands inspired the extraordinary development of fantastic designs in headdress, fabric, furniture, silver, and tile work. An extensive collection is displayed in the Fries Museum in Leeuwarden; closed Monday. Directions: Follow signs to centre and large carpark. Using the steeple of the Grote Kerk as a guide, continue east. The museum is east of Grote Kerk, on the east side of a narrow canal on Turfmarkt.

The island of Ameland is popular with cyclists, bird watchers, and mud-flat walkers. It's a tranquil place even in season. Plenty of bicycles stand ready to be rented at the island's ferry landing. Mud-flat walking is a very strenuous and very unique activity that requires a guide and needs prebooking with the tourist office in Leeuwarden or Dokkum. Fishing and whaling were prosperous industries in these islands, and the sailors and ship pilots that learned to navigate the perilously shallow waters were sought after by the shipping industry throughout Europe. Ferries leave twice each morning and afternoon. Directions: Drive 13km west of Dokkum or 26km northeast of Leeuwarden to Holwerd, and then four kilometers farther to the ferry dock and large parking area. Once an important port supplying Londoners with huge quanities of butter and cheese, Harlingen is a pleasant place to enjoy some fresh fish and small town ambiance. Hindeloopen, a tiny village tied to the sea rather than farming, devised elaborate fanciful designs for their clothing and furniture during the 17th century. Today it makes a colorful village stop. On the weekends, the Ijsselmeer looks like a swarm of butterflies as sails from hundreds of boats and wind surfers color its surface. Directions: Off A7/E22 exit 21km from the north side of the great dyke at Bolsward onto N359. Drive 14km south. Exit for Hindeloopen.

*****Camping: *In Leeuwarden. Exit N355, five kilometers east of the city for the parkland Kleine Wielen and follow signposting. Camping De Kleine Wielen (0511-431-660); large family camp with separate lake-side setting for tents and RV's; convenient; open April-September; $$. *On Ameland. North of the village of Nes follow signposting for Strand Duinoord. Camping Duinoord (0519-542-070); can be windy; open April-September; $$. *In Harlingen. South of town, on N31 follow signposting. Camping de Zeehoeve (0517-413-465); nice location on the water; open April-September; $$. *In Hindeloopen. Camping Hindeloopen (0514-521-452); close to the water; tennis; wind-surfing school; open April-September; $$.

SOUTHEASTERN HOLLAND

Tucked in between Belgium and Germany, the rolling hills, river valleys, and pleasant villages east of Maastricht are popular with cyclists and walkers. The American War Memorial in Margarten is a peaceful resting place for over 8,000 soldiers who died here during World War II. Directions: Drive 13km east of Maastricht on N278 to Margraten. Maastricht, a leafy, low-key city, hosted the European treaty signing in 1992. Every Wednesday and Friday, an excellent morning market is held at the Stadhuis. Directions: Off N278 follow signs for centre and parking. Use the steeple of St. Servaaskerk to guide you. Stadhuis is on the west side of the river, north of the cathedral and main square. For a vivid impression of war and its machinery, stop at the National War and Resistance Museum in Overloon; open daily. Directions: Exit A67/S34 four kilometers west of Venlo and the German-Netherland border, for Venray. Drive north 18km to Venray on A73. Pass through the village, and drive seven kilometers north of town to the village of Overloon. ****Camping: East of Maastricht. Off N278 exit 20km west of Aachen for Viljlen. Drive southwest following signposting. Camping Cottesserhoeve (043-455-1352); lovely location in the hills; open April-September; $$. North of Maastricht 30km. Exit A2/E25 three kilometers south of Echt, at the village of Dieteren, and follow signposting to Susteren. Camping Hommelheide (046-449-2900); nice location on the river; open all year; $$$.

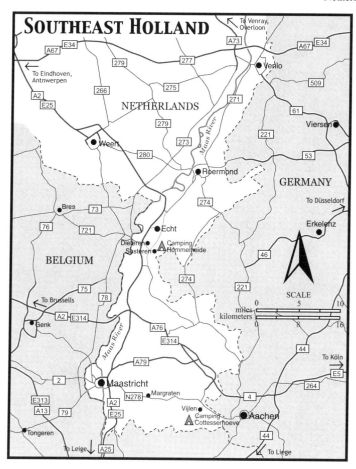

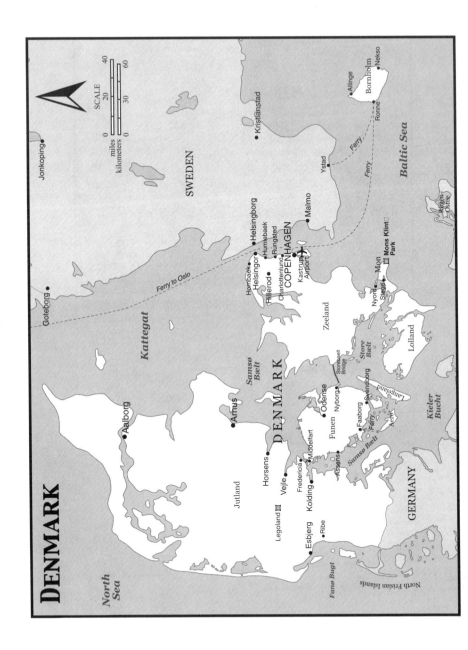

DENMARK

Denmark is an impressive harmony of landscape and people where a rural tranquility pervades. Fine horses and premium cattle luxuriate in verdant green pastures. An endless sky plays with colors and light over golden fields of wheat. White church steeples peek out through tree-shaded towns where secluded courtyards and quiet gardens exude a love of privacy and peace. Miles and miles of beaches, fragrant with heather, dune grasses, and sea-air offer tranquility.

Camping places are well established, well cared for, and convenient to public transportation, historic areas, and beaches. A common area housing toilets, token-showers, laundry room, and a covered cooking/eating area is centrally located and close to a large children's playground. Camping for two persons, a tent, and a car will cost about $25 USA per night. Most have bungalows. A simple one costs about three times the price of tent camping and will include a cook-top, table and chairs, two sets of bunk-beds, plus a small porch. You provide your own bedding and cooking equipment, use the common toilet-shower area, and clean the bungalow on leaving. A small store on the premise stocks some produce, fresh bread, snacks, and basics. The office staff speaks fluent English, has loads of glossy brochures and maps, and often sells the local tourist card. They are knowledgeable about the local sights and transportation and are happy to help. Denmark is popular with international travelers, and it's easy to meet them at the common cooking and eating area.

Roads are excellent, well signposted, and often named for where they go. E45 runs north and south on Jutland, connecting to E20 for east-west transport across Funen and the new suspension bridge to Zeeland and Copenhagen. Islands are usually connected to the mainland by bridges. Gas is not overly expensive. Modern gas stations take charge cards, have small stores, and free toilets. One to two hour ticket-dispensed or free parking is common. Cycling in Denmark's relatively flat countryside is popular.

Cash machines are hassle-free ways of dealing obtaining the local currency. They are found in shopping areas, town squares, and outside banks. They are user-friendly for people from many parts of the world.

COPENHAGEN

The Danes have a wonderful sense of harmony and style; you'll see it as you stroll through Tivoli Gardens. Flowerbeds, always in glorious color, bend and wind luxuriantly. Flower baskets drip with brilliantly purple lobelia and softly pink begonias. In the evening, tiny lights twinkle from their reflection in mirror-like ponds and fountains gush playfully. Everywhere in this meeting place of the world there is a joie de vivre, frivolous and carnival-like. Directions: The entrance is across from the train station; open daily.

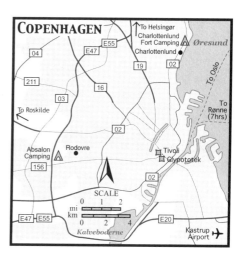

With capital from trade and shipping, Copenhagen built a royal city that bursts with beauty and vitality. Merchants from Venice, London, India, and the Baltic could sail right into the heart of the city. Today it's easy to transport yourself back to those days via an excursion boat ride. Splendid buildings, many supervised by Denmark's Renaissance king Christian IV, bear testimony to his taste.

Superb collections of art were given to the city by its most noteworthy businessman, Carl Jacobsen, a brewer of fine beer. Profits from the famous Carlsberg beer provided him the funds to amass one of the largest private art collections of his time. He named it Glypototek, meaning collection of sculpture. The architecture of the museum is noteworthy. Begun in the late 1800's, additions are linked by a monumental glass-roofed Mediterranean garden. Each room superbly complements its works of art. The visual experience reflects the ideas of its founder-to educate the viewer. The development of ancient sculpture is carefully followed from its beginnings in Egypt to Imperial Roman times. Then, with a break in the garden, you are transported to the impressive new wing and the fabulous collection including a complete set of the Degas bronzes, outstanding pieces from all the major Impressionists and Post-Impressionists, and fine collections from the Classical French and the Barbizon Schools. In a gloriously golden room, painted with the exact coloration that bursts from his tropical paradises and Polynesian madonnas, Paul Gauguin, their home-town boy, is honored; closed Mondays.

****Camping: * North of the city in the suburb of Charlottenlund. Follow the coastal road 02 north of Tuborg Brewery for two kilometers. Charlottenlund Fort Camping, Strandvejen 144B (013-623-688); very small; reserve ahead; wonderful location adjoining seaside park; covered cooking and eating area; cycle path to city; close to public transportation; open mid-May-September; $$$. *West of the city in the suburb of Rodovre. Take exit #2 off E47/55 in the direction of Copenhagen. One-half kilometer off the exit, turn left onto Korsdalsvej. Absalon Camping, Korsdalsvej 132 (3641-0600); large; close to public transportation; covered cooking and eating area; open all year; $$.

NORTH OF COPENHAGEN
KAREN BLIXEN MUSEUM/RUNGSTED

Fans of the film "Out of Africa" stop here to absorb the spirit that still emanates from the deceased author, on whose story the film is based. Adventurous and rather heroic, she wrote of her challenges, loneliness, and love. Photos, videos, and letters open like pages in an old scrapbook; open daily. Directions: Drive 20km north of Copenhagen on 02. The museum is across from the yacht harbor.

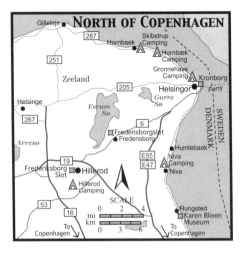

LOUISANA MUSEUM OF MODERN ART/HUMLEBAEK

Powerful, strange, funny, and sometimes haunting, the art here evokes a response. Your need for reflection afterwards is met in the large grassy sculptural garden sitting high on a bluff above the sea. The museum and collection are important; open daily. Directions: Drive ten kilometers north of Rungsted on 02.

KRONBORG SLOT/HELSINGOR

Mysterious and powerful rather than graceful and elegant this immense castle was originally built to extoll taxes from ships passing through the narrowest point of the Oresund. Often the setting for productions of *Hamlet*, it is fun to transport yourself back to that time, crossing the moat and winding your way down into the dimly lit, musty corridors of the cellars or up into the ornate royal chapel, chambers, and great long halls; open daily. Directions: Five kilometers north of Humlebaek. Frequent ferry shuttles cross to Sweden from Helsingor.

HORNBAEK COAST

Pure heaven is snuggling in soft sand, hidden by dune grasses, with a brilliant blue sea a few steps away. It is also breathing in the mixed fragrances of scotch broom, pines, and salty sea while pedaling down a coastal cycle path. Both are popular pastimes here.

****Camping: This is a popular vacation area. Call ahead during August. *Five kilometers south of Humlebaek off 02, in the suburb of Niva. Niva Camping (49-14-5226); basic; open May-September; $$. *On the beach in Helsingor, north of Kronborg Slot. Gronnehave Camping (49-21-5856); popular; open all year; $$. *In Hornbaek: Skibstrup Camping (49-70-9971); $$$$ or Hornbaek Camping (49-70-0223); $$$; both are large; all the amenities; fairly close to the beach; open May-September.

FREDENSBORG SLOTT/FREDENSBORG

With a sweeping park-like setting, encompassing three islands, Frederiksborg Slott is imposing. Leafy deciduous trees canopy pathways and luscious lawns are embroidered with immense rhododendrons and hydrangas. A sculpture garden honors its peasantry; open daily. Directions: Off 6, southwest of Helsingor and east of Hillerod on Lake Esrum.

FREDERIKSBORG SLOTT/HILLEROD

Inside the once royal residence, sunlight illuminates marble columns filigreed in gold and breathtakingly beautiful vaulted ceilings. Dramatic tones from the Compenius organ resonate through the coronation chapel on Thursdays at 1:30 p.m. At sunset, the castle, now the National Museum, glows splendidly red; open daily. Directions: 30km northwest of Copenhagen in Hillerod, off 53 in the center of Hillerod.

****Camping: South of Hillerod off 53. Hillerod Camping, Dyrskuepladsen (48-26-4854); convenient; open May-August; $$$.

ROSKILDE

Steeples rise proudly announcing the royal burial place, Roskilde Domkirke. The dynasties rest-some simply some elaborately beneath Gothic arches in adjoining chapels. Every Thursday night in summer the cathedral rings with a free concert of sonorous music from a Baroque organ; open daily except during services. Resurrected from the mud of the Roskilde fjord, five Viking ships, each built for a different purpose, are impressively displayed in Vikingeskibshallen; open daily. Directions: At the harbor, on the east side. The largest rock music festival in Scandinavia takes place here in late June. With top star billing, the wildly popular four-day happening is similar to the legendary Woodstock event in the U.S.A. For tickets, call ahead; 020-623-7321. ****Camping: * Drive north of Roskilde four kilometers on 6, exiting for Veddelev. Roskilde Camping, Baunehojvej 7-9 (4675-7996); lovely setting on the fjord; popular; reserve ahead; open May-August; $$$.

THE ISLAND OF MON

Hidden from view by a forest rich with lime-green foliage and dappled light, the gleaming white cliffs of Mons Klint, sculpted by wind and water, rise sharply above a turquoise sea. The

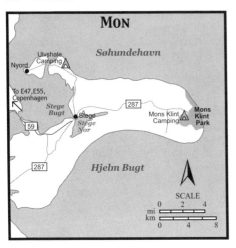

sight of this remarkable play of colors is breathtaking and will be treasured in your memories.   Orchids, primroses, and heliotropes hide in forests along with domed mounds of Bronze Age tombs. In Nyord, one of Scandinavia's best bird preserves, avocets and godwits probe in the mud while terns peer down and then dive. Gay, unsophisticated frescoes joyfully light up tiny churches, telling the story of life in medieval villages. Because the area is laced with tiny backroads that crisscross the farmlands, cycling is popular.   Now joined to the mainland by bridges, it is easy to reach. ****Camping: *After crossing the small bridge in Stege, drive north along the bay in the direction of Ulshale. Ulvshale Camping (5581-5325); on a sandy beach; close to the bird sanctuary Nyord; covered cooking and eating area; open May-September; $$. *Outside the entrance to Mons Klint park. Mons Klint Camping (5581-2025); close to the forest; all amenities; open May-September; $$$.

THE ISLAND OF BORNHOLM

Along Bornholm's northern coast, the tide rushes in thick with brine. High on the cliff, the ruins of fortress-castle Hammershus guards the narrow passageway to the Baltic. Beaches of fine sand stretch along the southern coast, where the placid shallow water is warm and clean. Parts of the film, *Pelee the Conqueror,* were shot in the fishing village of Gudhjem. Smoked herring is a specialty, and enticing little fish stores dot the island. Diminutive fortress-churches, white-washed and cone-capped, are shaded under the leaves of beech and hemlock trees. Rapeseed paints the landscape in burnished gold. Directions: Bornholm is off the southern coast of Sweden. Ferries ply the waters between Ronne on Bornholm and Ysted in Sweden in 2 1/2 hours.

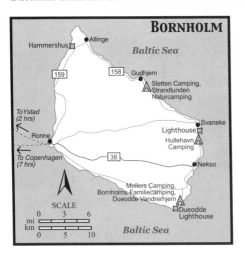

From Copenhagen it's a 7 hour ferry ride. ****Camping: All of these have nice locations on the beach; are shaded with trees; have all the amenities; popular with families; and open May through mid-September. Reserve ahead. *South of Gudhjem. Sletten Camping, Melsted Langgade 45 (5648-5071); $$ or Strandlunden Naturcamping, Melstedvej 33 (5648-5245); $$$. *In Svaneke, south of the town and lighthouse. Hullehavn Camping, Sydskovvej 9 (5649-6363); $$$.   *At the white sand beach, Dueodde, on the south coast.   Mollers Camping, Duegardsvej 2 (5648-8149); $$$;   or   Bornholms Familiecamping, Krogegardsvej 2 (5648-8150); $$$; or Dueodde Vandrerhjem, Skrokkegardsvej 17 (5648-8119); $$$.

FUNEN

Larks sing while premium reddish brown or black-and-white cattle munch contently in lush green pastures. Masses of wildflowers grow in fragrant and colorful bouquets, berry bushes drip with fruit, and folks smile as they pedal by. This is Denmark's heartland. The world's largest suspension bridge gracefully spans the 18km of water between the islands of Funen and Zeeland and the toll and thrill of crossing are both high.

ODENSE

To gaze upon Hans Christian Andersen's original notes and manuscripts at the HC Andersen Hus and then to listen to his touching stories read by Lawrence Olivier and Michael Redgrave will provide lasting memories. Directions: On the east side of the old town, park at the concert hall. Look for the cobblestoned pedestrian street. In the Funen's open-air museum, Den Fynske Landsby, tiny vegetable gardens, thatched-roofed farmhouses, and crowing roosters greet you. Directions: South of the old town, near the campgrounds. ****Camping: Off E20 take exit 50 in the direction of Odense. Odense Camping, Odensevej 102 (6611-4702); swimming pool; all amenities; open all year; $$$.

EGESKOV SLOTT

Fairy tales of beautiful princesses come alive at this intimate Renaissance castle. You can play hide and seek in a large maze whose hedge is three meters high and then pretend to drive off in an elegant antique Jaguar sports car or a restored Harley-Davidson motorcycle. It's also a romantic setting for a picnic lunch. Directions: From the Faaborg-Nyborg road 8, drive two kilometers west of Kvaendrup.

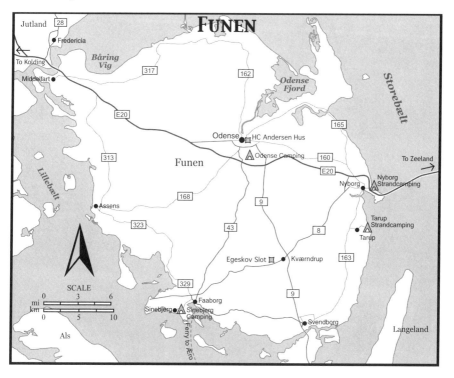

FAABORG

Cobblestone streets, half-timbered houses, and a pleasant little harbor make this a nice break in a journey. Ferries run to the little island Aero and to the Jutland pennisula. ****Camping: Close to the harbor, follow signs to Sinebjerg. Sinebjerg Camping (6260-1440); basic; open June-August; $$.

NYBORG

A stop in the journey here before or after crossing Denmark's magnificent suspension bridge to Zeeland might seem right. ****Camping: On the beach, just before the entrance to the bridge. Nyborg Strandcamping, Hjelevej 99 (6531-0256); all amenities; traffic noise; open May-September; $$. South of town on a quiet grassy hillside over looking the sea. Exit 163 for Tarup. Tarup Strandcamping, Lersey Alle 25 (6537-1199); nice setting; all amenities; open May-August; $$.

JUTLAND

Powerful armored warriors astride mighty horses once galloped across this countryside, and immense long boats, richly carved with fanciful monsters, silently skimmed the water. In the villages, craftsmen pounded out weapons of bronze, flint, and iron. Jutland, once the Vikings' pathway for conquests in Europe, today quietly preserves relics of the vanished times.

JELLING

Majestic in their simplicity, the stones on which the mighty Viking King Gorm and his son Harald Bluetooth carved loving words represent a tenderness not often told in tales of the seafaring adventurers. The runic stones, carved in the 1st century, honor a wife and parents. They sit in

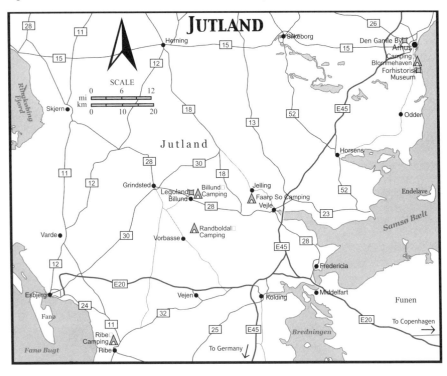

dignity but without pretention outside the doors of a small white-washed church. Directions: North of the route from Jutland to Funen. Exit off E45 at Vejle, and drive northwest of the city eleven kilometers to Jelling. ****Camping: On a small lake southwest of town. Faarp So Camping, Farupvej 58 (7587-1344); nice setting; pool; all amenities; open May-August; $$.

LEGOLAND

How do you inspire ingenuity, teach patience and perseverance, and still keep a child entertained? For a parent, grandparent, care-giver, or teacher this is an enormous challenge. In the 1940's, Ole Kirk Christensen had an idea. He developed wooden toys that he named "lego" from the Danish phrase "leg godt" or "play well". Today his toys spill out on floors all over the world. Legoland is a major Danish tourist attraction, inviting families to discover, appreciate, play, and create with Lego blocks; open daily. Directions: Exit E45 at Vejle, and drive west on 28 for 30km in the direction of Grindsted to Billund and Legoland. ****Camping: In Randbol, a wooded area ten kilometers south of Billund. Off 469 exit at Vorbasse. Randboldal Camping, Dalen 9 (7588-3575); on a tiny lake; popular with families; all amenities; open all year; $$$. Next to Legoland airport. Billund Camping (7533-1521); huge; all amenities; day-time airport noise; open all year; $$$.

ARHUS

Arhus's open-air museum, Den Gamle By, vividly illustrates the "good ole days" of a market town; open daily. Directions: Exit the ring road on the west side of town for Vesterbrogade. The Forhistorisk Museum in Moesgard houses the Graubelle Man. Over 2000 years old, the remains were amazingly well preserved by the tannic acids and iron in a peat bog. From the museum a path leads through wildflower graced woods and meadows to the beach. Directions: Drive south of Arhus on 451 for eight kilometers in the direction of Odder. ****Camping: South of the city exit E45 at Stavtrup, and drive east in the direction of Frederiksbjerg. Take 451 south five kilometers south to Hojberg/Skade Bakker. Camping Blommehaven, Orneredevej 35, Hojbjerg (8627-0207); on the beach; close to Moesgard and Marselisborg parks; all amenities; open May-August; $$$.

RIBE

Cobblestone streets wind past canals, outdoor cafes, half-timbered stone houses, and small parks. From the top of Ribe Cathedral's 52-meter tower you can gaze out over red roofs to the marshlands. At Vikingecenter, falcons swoop suddenly from the air to land on an outstretched arm, aromatic Viking soup simmers over an open fire, and in a tiny cabin, glowing coals soften iron before it is pounded by a craftsman. ****Camping: *Exit 11 just north of the historic area. Ribe Camping (7541-0777); all amenities; open May-September; $$$.

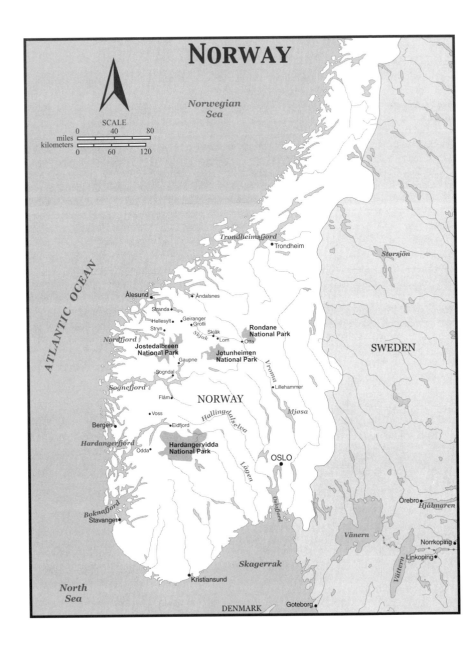

NORWAY

Velvet-like slopes of apple-green grasses, jeweled with brightly colored penstemon, lupine, and asters, collar majestic mountains nestling icy blue glaciers. Waterfalls crash and tumble in daring feats while rivers rush and plummet over boulders like laughing children let out for recess. All the while the fjords sit in queen-like elegance.

Norwegians are quiet in their pride of their magnificent country and it's heroic fight for independence. Their love of the outdoors is evident in the beautiful settings of their camping places. Sharing exclamations about the grandeur of the natural beauty is a good way to start up a conversation with Norwegians. They are relaxed and easy to be around.

Exciting, awe-inspiring, and easy-to-do activities have been carefully thought out and are readily available. Glacier walks, river rafting, canoeing, kayaking, hiking, biking, and fishing are well-loved sports, and equipment, guides, and advice for enjoying them are at hand. It's a fisherman's paradise. If you are an avid fishermen consider bringing your own gear so you can stop whenever you want. Otherwise rental gear is available. Relaxing boat rides, fascinating museums, and exciting train trips all add to the fun, but you'll find yourself mesmerized when you take time to just sit and look at the outstanding natural beauty.

Driving is a breeze. The roads and tunnels are excellent and well signposted. It's impossible not to be amazed with the skill and perseverance of the Norwegians as your drive through their tunnels. They epitomize their historic ability to withstand and overcome a harsh environment. Many roadways are two lanes. It won't be a road race in Norway. Drivers are forced to relax and drive at reasonable speeds. Roadway rest stops are scenic, popular spots with picnic tables, toilets, and tourist information. Car headlights must be on at all times when driving.

Ferry crossings, long and short, enable everyone to stop and feast on the magnificence that quietly passes by. Locals will stand in awe, too. They are not blase about the beauty of their country. A current road map will indicate where there are crossings. Ferries operate on a first-come, first-served basis, except for the longer crossings. When planning your travel for the next day, check with the camping office, tourist office, or gas station about the ferry's time schedule. This helps you avoid long waits for the ferry, particularly for those in remote areas.

Groceries are more expensive than on mainland Europe so keep your selections simple. Dairy and meat prices are reasonable, and the quality is high. Local produce is reasonable but imported foodstuffs are expensive. Locals and tourists alike buy a good supply of alcoholic beverages at the tax-free stores on large ferries. Bring coffee or tea from home. Most stores close on Saturday afternoon and stay closed until Monday morning. The mini-markets at the gas stations, open on Sundays, have a surprising array of food, including their own freshly baked bread. The aroma and taste is a delicious treat.

Cash machines are the most convenient way to exchange currency. They are easy to find close to shopping centers and are very popular with locals.

Camping locations are beautiful with thick carpets of grass, immaculate toilet/shower areas and covered cooking areas with adjoining cozy eating areas the norm. Bungalows are also available and generally don't need to be booked ahead unless you are arriving late or are in a popular tourist area. Campground staff will usually speak English, so if weather makes tent camping less fun and you want a bungalow, call ahead to reserve. Bungalows are cute and cozy and well worth the cost if the weather is stormy. Generally bungalows have 2 sets of bunk beds without bedding, a cooking and eating area, and a small porch. They don't have plumbing but do have electricity, and the common toilet shower area and water tap will be close by. They cost about three times what tent camping does and you are expected to clean up for the next guest before leaving. A broom, mop, soap, and bucket are provided. The open and closing dates listed are conservative. Call ahead if you earlier or later than these dates; they might be open.

Camping for two persons with a tent and car will be approximately $20 USA. Ask about showers, and purchase appropriate coins or tokens when you check in. If you plan to go out for the evening, check about the night gate opening and closing procedure. If you are departing very early in the morning pay the night before.

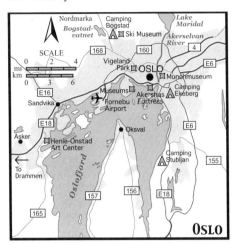

OSLO

Surrounded by forest and fjord, Oslo sits at the end of the Oslofjord like a king in his throne room. To one side is the dramatic Akershus Fortress symbolizing Norway's fight for independence and housing it's powerful Resistance Museum. At the harbor little boats push off from shore taking you to the never to be forgotten museums of Heyerdahl's Kon-Tiki and the Viking Ships on the Bygdoy Penninsula. Both are not to be missed. The Fram Museum of polar expeditions, a folk museum, and nice beaches offer further enjoyment of the island. Plan to spend the day.

At Oslo's central train station, visit the tourist office then enjoy the lively good-natured atmosphere of the adjoining splendid square, and board a bus there for Vigeland Park. Gustav Vigeland, heavily influenced by Rodin, traded the city his sculptural works for a place to live and work. His emotional and touching sculpture is set amid grand tree and flower lined walkways with large expanses of lawn. The park draws a good sprinkling of folks soaking up the sun, graceful lineskaters indulging their sport, and young and old alike licking ice cream cones. A fascinating museum displays Vigeland's work in-depth.

The Munch Museum houses an enormous collection of Norway's most famous expressionist painter, Edvard Munch. It's easy to get to by bus from central station. The dramatic headland setting and architecture of the Henie-Onstad Art Center complements its interesting permanent and temporary exhibits of expressionistic and modern art and is another worthwhile stop. Directions: West of Oslo on E18 in the direction of Drammen.

It's fun to join the locals for some excellent cycling in Nordmarka or along the Akerselven River from Lake Maridal. Stop at the ski museum for a look at the transformation of clothing and equipment over the years. If you don't have a fear of heights, climb up the ski jump. (The Norwegians claim they invented skiing.) ****Camping: *Off E6 southeast of the city center exit Ring Three for Ekeberg and drive up the hill. Camping Ekeberg, Ekebergeien 65 (22-19-85-68); convenient; wonderful hilltop view; bus to the city center; popular; open June-August; $$$. *On a lake, northwest of the city. Exit Ring Three for Bogstad. Camping Bogstad, Ankerveien 117 (22-51-08-00); public transportation to the city center; bungalows; popular with families; open all year; $$$. *15km southeast of Oslo off the coast road E18, in Hvervenbuka. Camping Stubljan, Ljaruvelen 1250 (22-61-27-06); tranquil location; easy access to E6; open June-August; $$$.

LILLIHAMMER

Host to the 1994 Winter Olympics, today Lillihammer is worth a detour if you like thrill rides. For a full adrenal rush, take the bobsled ride down the actual Olympic run in Hunderfossen. Make reservations; it's very popular. In town ski and bobsled simulator rides await. For a more relaxing pace, wander through the Maihaugen folk museum or climb aboard the world's oldest paddle steamer for a ride on Lake Mjosa. ****Camping: *North of town exit off E6. Lillehammer Camping (61-25-97-10); nice location; open all year; $$$. *South of town by the river. Camping Lillehammer (61-25-33-65); large; open all year; $$$$.

RONDANE NATIONAL PARK

Noted for sunnier weather, lush carpets of green grass, and exciting rushing rivers, this is one of Norway's prettiest river valleys. White water rafting trips for both beginners and advanced can be booked with Heidal Rafting in the village of Heidal; 61-23-60-37. Directions: Eleven kilometers south of Otta, exit E6 at Sjoa onto 257. The Alpine part of the park is stark, dramatic, and peaceful. The Mountain Lodge at Rondvassbu, at the edge of the lake, makes a good hiking destination. Directions: Drive northeast from Otta in the direction of Mysuster. Hiking trails begin here. In Otta the tourist office is excellent. ****Camping: *At Sjoa, 4.5 kilometers south of Otta, off E6. Saeta Camping (61-23-51-47); small; beautiful location; bungalows; June-August; $$. *30km west of Sjoa on 257, at junction of 257 and 51. Jotunheimen Feriesenter (61-23-49-50); popular with rafters; beautiful location; bungalows; open June-August; $$. *2.5 kilometers north of Otta on E6. Otta Turistsenter (61-23-03-23); large; close to hiking trails; bungalows; open June-August; $$$.

SKJAK RIVER REGION

Located halfway between Rondane National Park and the Nordfjord area on highway 15, this river area has a great deal to offer. Horseback riding trips, day or overnight, can be booked at Dalan Fjellridning in Skjak; 61-21-31-61. Directions: 13km north of Lom on 15. White water raft trips, from beginner to advanced, plus guided hiking trips up the river canyon can be book at Skjak Rafting in Skjak; 61-21-47-42. ****Camping: *Five kilometers west of Bismo on 15. Furuly Camping (61-21-47-43); small; lovely setting; bungalows; open June- August; $$. *In Skjak. Skjak Camping (61-21-41-30); large; bungalows; open June-August; $$. *Near the Donfossen falls in Donfoss. Donfoss Camping (61-21-48-98); large; all the amenities; open June-August; $$$.

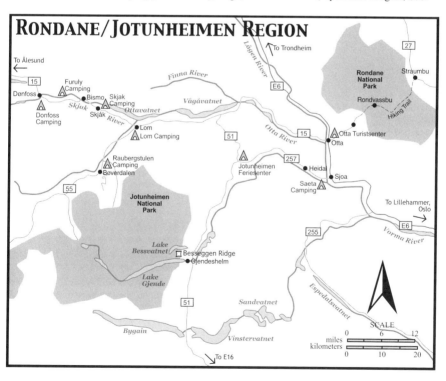

RONDANE/JOTUNHEIMEN REGION

JOTUNHEIMEN NATIONAL PARK

Norwegians delight in the dramatically beautiful hike across Besseggen Ridge for its staggering views of emerald-green Lake Gjende on one side and cobalt-blue Lake Bessvatnet on the other. Directions: On the eastside of the park, halfway between E6 and E16, drive to Gjendesheim on 51. The trail begins at the boat dock. Beautiful mountain drives, hikes, and summer skiing are available on the west side of the park. Directions: Exit 15 at Lom onto 55, and drive 17 km to Boverdalen. ****Camping: *In Lom on 55. Lom Camping (61-21-12-20); open all year; $$. *In Boverdalen, 14km from Lom on 55. Raubergstulen Camping (61-21-18-00); close to hiking trails; lovely setting; open June-August; $$.

GEIRANGERFJORD REGION

Sheer cliffs guard a jewel-like string of brilliant fjords, and silver waterfalls embellish the necklace of the spectacular region. Directions: From the east, 19km west of Grotli, exit 15 onto 63, the Eagle's Highway, in the direction of Orneveien. From the west, take the car ferry from Hellesylt. The famous Trollstigen road, Troll's Ladder, stretches in a zigzag up a sheer mountain wall. Most people take the bus, whose expert drivers maneuver the hairpin turns with ease. The Trollstigen bus route runs from Andalsnes to Valldal. Car ferries operate to Valldal from Hellesylt and Gerianger. ****Camping: This is a very popular area with campers from all over Europe. Call ahead. North of Gerianger on 63. Geiranger Camping (70-2631-20); fabulous location on the fjord; open June-August; $$$$. The following all have bungalows, good locations, and amenities. Grande Fjordhytter Camping (70-26-30-90); open May-September; $$$$. Grande Turisthytter Camping (70-26-30-68); open May-September; $$$. Vinje Camping (70-26-30-17); open June-August; $$$. From Hellesylt the 19km drive or bike ride through the Norangdal Valley

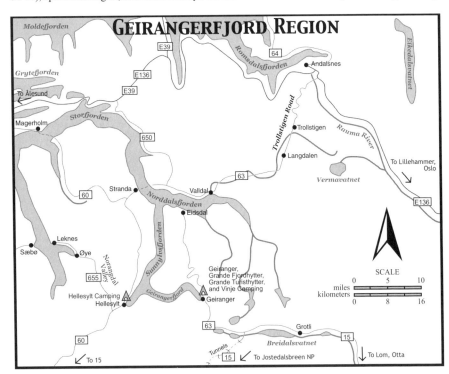

to Oye is bright and sweet-scented and dotted with little farmsteads. Camping: In Hellesylt. Hellesylt Camping (70-26-51-88); close to the fjord; open May-September; $$$.

JOSTEDALBREEN NATIONAL PARK

Queen of the area's parks, Jostedalbreen's blue glacier ice nestles between lofty peaks and ridges, licking its way downward until it finally gives way to the silent, mirror-like glacier lakes. Exuberant cascading streams rejoice in their release, leaping and dancing and then plunging with a weariless roar over the cliffs. Brightly dressed wildflowers watch the show while butterflies sweep silently by. Get off the main trails to fully enjoy it magnificence.

For a fantastic view of the glacier colors, take a guided glacier walk. They vary from easy to difficult. All necessary equipment is provided, including boots if you don't have your own. It's wise to book ahead. Call Briksdal Glacier; 57-87-68-00. Directions: Exit 60 and drive south on 724 to park entrance.

****Camping: *In Briksdalsbre, closest to Briksdal Glacier. Melkevoll Bretun Camping (57-87-38-64); small; very scenic; sauna; bungalows; very popular; open May-August; $$$. *On the

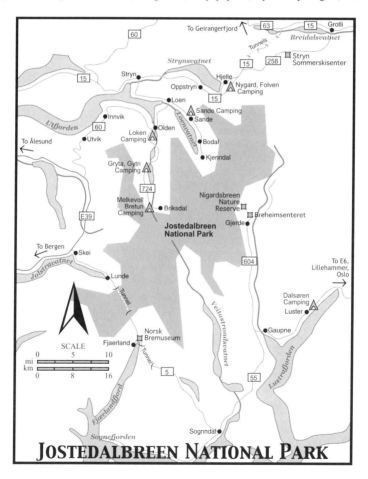

JOSTEDALBREEN NATIONAL PARK

Briksdal-Olden road, beautifully located; open June-August; $$$. Gryta Camping (57-87-59-36) or Gytri Camping (57-87-59-34). *Closer to Olden. Loken Camping (57-87-32-68); on the river; bungalows; open May-August; $$$.

Glacier walks are also available on Bodalsbreen. Directions: Exit 60 at Loen onto the small road on the eastside of the lake in the direction of Sande, and drive 14km to the carpark. ****Camping: *In Sande. Sande Camping (57-87-76-59); beautiful location; bungalows; open all year; $$$. At the Breheimsenteret, glacier walks are arranged on the Nigardsbreen glacier. Directions: Exit 55 north of Sogndal at Gaupne, and drive north on 604 for 35km. ****Camping: *16km northeast of Gaupe on 55 at Luster. Dalsoren Camping (57-68-54-36); bungalows; open May-September; $$$.

Cross-country and downhill skiing, and snowboarding are possible at the Tysig glacier through the Stryn summer skiing center. Call ahead for information on the condition of the slopes; 94-55-61-10. Directions: 25km east of Stryn at Hjelledal. ****Camping: *In Hjelledal. Nygard Camping (57-87-52-58); bungalows; or Folven Camping (57-87-53-40); popular with young skiiers.

The old Strynefjell mountain road, now a tourist road with picnic areas and tourist information, provides magnificent views. Directions: Exit 15 at Grotli onto 258.

Excellent park information centers with fascinating videos, Alpine gardens, and cafes enhance your park experience. Directions: At the south end of the park, north of Fjaerland off 5, Norsk Bremuseum has the best information about glaciers. Northeast of the park on 15, east of Styrn in Oppstyrn, Jostedalsbreen National Park Center has a peaceful lakeside setting and an Alpine botanical garden. Southeast of the park, north of Sogndal on 55, Breheimsenteret is architecturally lovely, blending with the stark setting close to the Nigardsbreen.

HARDANGER FJORD REGION

Towering waterfalls thunder exultantly as they leap over boulders released from snow capped peaks to tumble into the smooth, glassy bed of the fjord. Seductive high mountain plateaus descend to meadows painted flush in Alpine glow. Fruit orchards scent the air. Excellent cycling and hiking trails lace the entire region, as do train and ferry rides. Located between Oslo and Bergen, between E134 and 7, this area is well organized for vacationers.

Taking the "Norway in a Nutshell" excursion makes a good day's outing. Park at the train station at Voss. The trip begins with scenic ride from Voss to Myrdal. At Myrdal the train descends down the steep gorge, passing snowy peaks and tumultuous waterfalls until it reaches the lush valley floor and fjord at Flam. A tiny museum highlights the building of the train tracks and early tourism. Then on a small ferry, you slip quietly through the Aurlandsfjord and Naerofjourd, a narrow gorge hemmed in by giant, Gothic-cathedral-like mountains. Regal escort is provided by brilliantly white sea gulls. The ferry lands at Gudvangen for an exciting bus ride up the steep Stalheimskleivance and then through the meadow-like countryside back to Voss. Call ahead for reservations; 56-52-80-00. Alternately, if you have mountain bicycles you might want to put them on the train at Voss, disembark the train at Mydral and cycle down the very steep but exciting old road from Myrdal to Flam. ****Camping: *In Voss off E16. Voss Camping (56-51-15-97); convenient; bungalows; open Jan-Sept; $$$.

Voringsfossen, Norway's most famous waterfall, drops almost 200 meters. The wildly beautiful old road leading into the Mabo Valley and the waterfall is closed to ordinary traffic but open to cyclers, walkers, and the Trolltoget, a tourist train on wheels. Hardangervidda Natursenter at Ovre Eidfjord, sparkles with aquariums, an exciting movie, and colorful exhibits. Directions: Drive 25km east of Eidfjord on 7. The walking/bike trail starts at Mabogardane. Park at the top of the tunnel, on the east side, and hike down to the river then back into the valley to the base of the waterfall. For the Trolltoget, park at the Mabo Gard Museum. ****Camping: *In Ovre Eidfjord. Saebo Camping (3-66-59-27); lovely lakeside setting; bungalows; open May-August; $$.

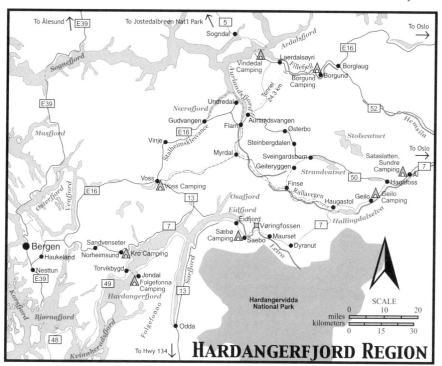

HARDANGERFJORD REGION

Hardangervidda is northern Europe's highest plateau. Its dramatic stark beauty is quiet and tranquil. Tiny lakes dotted with anglers gleam like burnished disks. Walking and biking trails crisscross the landscape. One of the most popular hiking trails starts 40km east of Eidfjord. Directions: On 7, exit just west of Maurset at Dyranut for the Tinnholvegen. Rallavegen, a biking/hiking trail, crosses the plateau along the rail line. The trail is 80km long running from Haugastol, 22km west of Geilo on 7, to Flam. (See "Norway in a Nutshell".) Memorials and exhibits of the rail construction pay tribute to the laborious work along its route. Train connections along the way will transport you and your bicycle back to your car. ****Camping: *In Geilo. Geilo Camping (32-09-07-33); convenient; open all year; $$.

Aurlandsdalen valley is Norway's Grand Canyon. The spectacular scenery can be enjoyed close-up by hiking down historic trails to the valley. Directions: Exit 7 at Hagafoss, and drive northwest on 50 for 51km. On the east side of the tunnel at Sveingardsborn, take the small road south for the trail from Geiterygghytta to Finse or Steinberg. From Osterbo, on the west side of the tunnel, a trail leads to the Vassbygdi River. ****Camping: *15km northeast of Hegafoss, on 7 in Al. Sataslatten Camping (32-08-55-77) or Sundre Camping (32-08-13-26); bungalows; open all year; $$.

Fillefjell is the gorgeous river valley of the Laerdalselvi River. The mountain road from Laerdal to Aurland, at the western end of 16, is popular with hikers. ****Camping: *Ten kilometers west of Laerdal. Vindedal Camping (57-6665-28). In Borgand, by the lovely old stave church. Borgund Camping (57-66-81-71). Both have bungalows; scenic locations; open June-August; $$.

Folgefonna, the third-largest glacier in Norway, has a summer ski center with skis, snowboards, and sled rentals. Call ahead for conditions and hours; 53-66-80-28. Directions: Exit 7 at Jondal, on the eastside of the Hardangerfjord. ****Camping: *Folgefonn Camping (53-66-84-23); small;

popular; book ahead for a bungalow. On the west side of the fjord a great hiking/biking trail is
carved into the mountainside. The trail goes behind the waterfall at Steinsdalen. Directions: The
trailhead is close to Sandvenseter, 19km west of Norheimsund. ****Camping: *In Norheimsund.
Kro Camping (56-55-89-54); convenient; bungalows; open all year; $$$.

BERGEN

Nestled into lushly green hills, fjord fingerlings, and waterways, Bergen is a feast for the eyes
but a confusing city to drive in. Purchase a good city map at a gas station before you try to find
your campground.

Smiles come readily in this easy-going city. Bergen's Fish Market, on Torget at the Vagen har-
bor, sparkles with shimmering prawns, salmon and crab. Tasty smoked salmon and crab sand-
wiches offered by the jauntily capped fishmongers are hard to pass up. Flower, fruit, and vegetable
stalls mingle with the mounds of fish.

It's short walk or ferry ride from the harbor to UNESCO-listed Bryggen, the original Bergen set-
tlement. Facing the north side of Vagen harbor, Bryggen is a delightful place to explore. Steep cob-

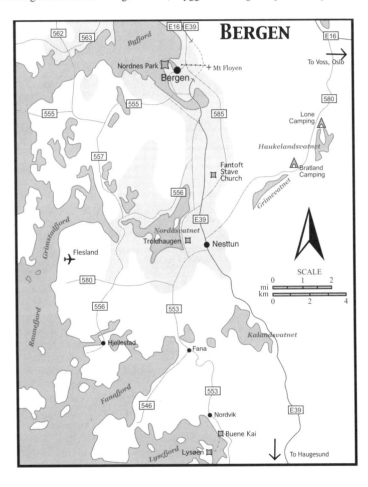

blestone steps lead up tiny streets shadowed by overhanging eaves. It's a mishmash of ancient wooden buildings now housing shops and cafes. Excellent, light-hearted guided tours are scheduled several times a day in English. Don't miss the Bryggens Museum on the west end, where, on-site archeological excavations have unearthed 12th century foundations and artifacts. The lively exhibits are displayed in context with the site's medieval foundations. Behind the museum is the oldest building in Bergan, the Romanesque church Mariakirken, which boasts a Baroque pulpit and 15th century frescos; open weekdays.

For a perspective on how Bergen interlaces with forest and sea, take the Floibanen funicular up Mount Floyen. Directions: Walk up Vertrlidsalm, the main street between Torget and Bryggen. The Bergen Aquarium is one of the finest in Europe, with realistic nesting cliffs along the pools and penguins and seals displayed so close you can almost touch them. Directions: Take the short ferry ride from the Fish Market to Nordnes Park on the south end of Vagen harbor.

The home studio and cliff-hewn grave site compound of Norway's most famous composer Edvard Grieg, is called Troldhaugen. It rests quietly along Lake Nordas adjoining a small concert hall. Directions: Drive south on E39 in the direction of Nesttun. Exit at Fantoft, and drive south to Hopsbroen. Troldhaugen is southwest of the Fantoft Stave Church.

Norwegians strive to keep their history alive through song and dance. The woodland farm location for Fana Folklore provides an authentic setting. You make advance reservations for the evening program that includes a Norwegian dinner, folk music, and dancing; 55-91-52-40. Directions: Drive south on E39 in the direction of Nesttun. Exit for Fana/553, and follow signposting for Fanatorget.

Ole Bull's Villa is in the same area. This eccentric, charismatic violin-virtuoso built a lovely villa in the late 1800's on Lysoen Island. It reflects his lively personality and love for Norway. Directions: Drive south on E39 exiting for Fana/553. Follow signposting for Lysoen, which continues over the mountain to Sorestraumen. Then follow signage to Buena Kai, and take a ferry to the villa. During summer, the 10-minute ferries leave on the hour from 12 to 3 weekdays and to 4 on weekends.

****Camping: *12km east of the city exit off E16 onto 580, and drive south to Haukeland Lake. Lone Camping (55-39-29-60); nice setting; bungalows; all the amenities; open all year $$$. *Further south on 580. Bratland Camping (55-10-13-38); bungalows; all amenities; open June-August; $$$. Buses go to the city center from the campgrounds. The Bergen tourist card, sold at the campgrounds, includes bus, funicular, short ferry rides, and free or discounted entrance to most of the above sights. Because driving and parking in Bergen is confusing, taking a leisurely and scenic bus ride is advised, making the Bergen tourist card worth buying.

STAVANGER

Once famous for its herring industry, Stavanger now boasts oil and an international ambiance. On the west side of the harbor explore Gamle Stavanger. Old Stavanger sparkles with white picket fences and colorful gardens lining its immaculate white-clapboard houses. The Norwegian Emigration Center just east of the lake at Bergjelandsgata 30, helps trace Norwegian ancestry; 51-89-56-44. In the morning, a colorful harbor market hums with activity. ****Camping: *Three kilometers west of the centrum on the southwest corner of Mosvangen Lake. Mosvangen Camping Tjensvoll 1B (51-87-20-55); convenient; nice setting; open June-August; $$$.

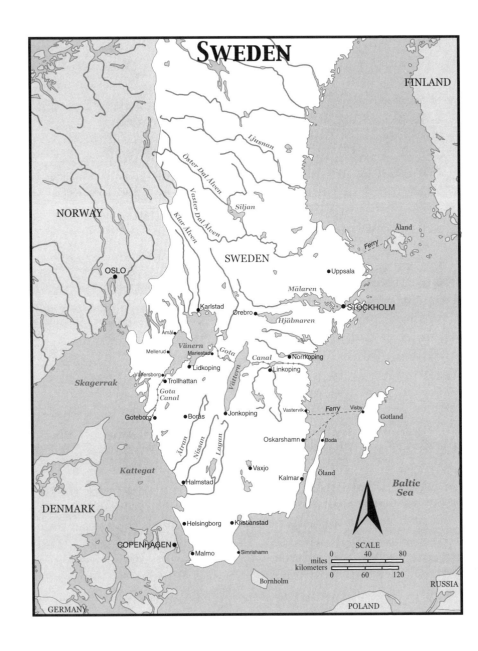

SWEDEN

Azure blue lakes, warm enough for summer swimming, are edged with leafy forests. Sweden's archipelagos make enticing waterways for fishing and paddling. Their craggy coastlines offer secluded beaches. Gently rolling farmlands are perky with the brilliant wild flowers and gardens exude love and care. Cities and towns host summer festivals, exciting museums tell wonderful stories, and outdoor pursuits are appreciated. From Viking times, when ships were built with mathematical exactness into handsome and highly effective craft, Swedes have striven for perfection.

Swedes love to camp. They love to be outdoors, close to water. They are fond of little nooks and crannies for private, peaceful times in the sun. Owners of campgrounds know that to attract business they must provide well for children and family life. Interesting playground equipment, diving platforms, mini-golf, and barbecues are standard fare. Common cooking areas, with stovetops and scenic eating areas, make it easy to relax and get to know fellow campers. Campgrounds listed are maintained with pride and cost about $25 USA for two persons, a tent, and car. Warm showers require a token or coins; inquire when you check in. Bungalows are generally on the premise but need advance booking in popular vacation areas. Simple ones cost three times what tent camping costs. Some lakeside campgrounds have lake saunas. To enjoy this very special Swedish experience reserve some time at the office when you check in. To camp in Sweden, you must purchase a reasonably priced Swedish Camping Card. The open and closing dates listed are conservative. The offices will have glossy brochures on local attractions and a staff person who speaks English.

The museum hours listed are the summer hours. Many close on Mondays. Top sites are open every day with longer hours. Even small towns will have a tourist office. Excellent roads with good signposting lace the country. Car headlights are required to be on whenever driving. Parking too close to an intersection is ticketed. Gas is expensive, but the distance between destinations is not great except in northern Sweden. Parking is easy, except for Stockholm, and costs about the same as at home. Public transportation is excellent, and staff is friendly and helpful. English is widely spoken. If you keep your choices simple, groceries won't be overly expensive. Bring coffee, tea, and spices from home. If your traveling includes a longer ferry ride, buy a supply of alcoholic beverages in the duty-free store onboard. Fruit and vegetable stands are often conveniently close to a public transportation hub.

STOCKHOLM

When you gaze at this elegant city from its highest tower, your eyes are treated to a dazzling sight. Tiny islands lie scattered, as if by a giant who had playfully flung rocks into the brilliant blue sea. Scurrying ferries and elegant swan-like yachts fleck the harbor. Turning your gaze, a somber palace looms below, guarding the maze of darkened streets of the old town while leafy trees soften a parkland. On the mainland, contemporary cubes and cylinders of mirror glass punctuate the sky.

Many jewels await a traveler in Stockholm but the finest is the Vasamusset. The man-of-war ship Vasa, named after the Sweden's daring hero and later king, Gustav Vasa I, was fabulous from its very concept. Her uncanny death in front of her

admirers was world news. Some tried a resurrection but none succeeded until recently. Her story, from the conceptual beginning to the intricacy of her final resurrection is told in the Vasameusset's lively exhibits, films, and tours. Don't leave Stockholm without seeing her; open daily. Directions: Take bus 47 or 69 or a ferry from Nybroplan or Slussen.

Ardent love for his country drove Artur Hazelius to found both Skansen, an open air museum, and Nordiska Museet, a cultural history museum, in order to preserve and honor Sweden's history. Skansen, bustles with activity of days gone by. Buildings from all of Sweden were brought and reconstructed for the park. Now it is a delightful hill of tiny farms, workshops, and homes. Dressed in period clothing from the region and often involved with an activity from the era, well informed staff enjoy telling stories about what you are seeing; open daily. To appreciate Skansen more fully, allow time to enjoy Nordiska Museet first. Swedish cultural history is regional and both museums boast of the differences and contributions. Starting with the huge statue of Gustav Vasa, Sweden's heroic figure, five centuries of period clothing, tools, and domestic life from each of Sweden's regions is represented; closed Monday. Directions: Take bus 47 or 69 or a ferry from Nybroplan or Slussen. Then to get a bird's eye view and perspective of the city and archipelago, board the elevator to the top of Kaknastornet. Directions: Take bus 69 to Ladugardsgardet. It's just north of Skansen.

Swedish archeologists have had a long love affair with Asia. Today the Museum of Far Eastern Antiquities houses one Europe's best collections of exquisite craftsmanship. Directions: Take bus 65 to Skeppsholmen. The museum is on the north end, up the hill.

When visiting Gamla Stan, the old town, start with the unique underground museum, Medeltidsmuseum. Foundations of medieval homes were discovered during an excavation and now reconstructed medieval houses and models depict the life of the average person. Directions: Look for stairs just over the Norrbron bridge, in front of the Riksdag. Storkyrkam, the church where royalty has been traditionally crowned and married, has a free organ recital every Saturday at 1:00 p.m. At the Royal Palace the changing of the guards is at noon, except on Sundays when it is at 1:00 p.m. Sections of the palace can be viewed but the treasury is best. Lose yourself in the tiny streets and alleyways of the old town, noting the coats of arms above doorways. As you pause in Stortorget, the main square, remember the blood bath that took place here in the 14th century.

Take a relaxing boat ride on Lake Malaren to stately Drottningham Palace. Gustav III, who loved the artistic life, built an elegant court theatre here and performances still take place. It can be toured along with parts of the palace, which is still a royal residence. Directions: Ferries leave from Stadshusbron or Kungsholmen, or take buses 301-323 from here. Hotorget's international open market is aromatic with exotic snacks, flowers, fruits, and vegetables. Enjoy a snack on the stairs of the Concert Hall while watching the colorful scene. Then take a short walk to Carl Milles' delightful Orpheus Fountain. His full sculpture garden is on Lidingo Island. Directions: Take the T-bana to Ropsten and then the bus over the bridge; open daily.

****Camping: *Close to Drottningham Palace, ten kilometers west of the city center on Lake Malern, close to the suburb of Bromma. Drive north of the city, in the direction of Uppsala, exit E4 onto 275 and drive west in the direction of Vallinby. Follow signposting to Drottningham. Just before the bridge to the palace, take the small road north towards Angby and go two kilometers. Angby Camping (08-37-04-20); very popular; bungalows; metro close-by; open all year; $$$. *Southwest of the city, close to Lake Malaren, in the suburb of Bredang. South of the city, exit E4 for Bredang, and drive three kilometers towards the lake. Bredangs Camping (08-97-70-71); better for RV's; metro close-by; open May-September; $$$$. Buying a Tourist Card at the metro station pays off in Stockholm because the campgrounds are out of the city. It will give you unlimited travel on the T-bana (metro), buses, ferries and discounted or free admission to many museums and attractions.

UPPSALA

Going to Uppsala is like going to Oxford when you're in London. Uppsala University, founded in 1477, is renowned throughout the world. Stroll along the river, peek into the Domkyrkan, Sweden's largest cathedral, then continue on across the bridge to the Linnaeus botanical garden, where the famous botanist worked on classifying plants. ****Camping: North of the train station, on the river Fyris next to a with a sports center with swimming pool. Fyrishov Camping (27-49-60); convenient; bungalows; open all year; $$.

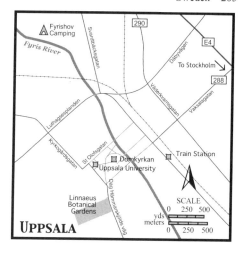

TO FINLAND VIA THE ISLANDS OF ALAND

The most economical route to Finland from Sweden is a ferry to the charming Aland Islands from the village of Grisslehamn. Directions: From Stockholm drive north on E18 in the direction of Norrtalje, exit onto 76 then drive to Grisslehamn. This part of the Swedish coast is magnificent. ****Camping: *On the coast north of Osthammer, by the yacht harbor. Klackskars Camping (73-331-90); beautiful location; popular with families; bungalows; open June-August; $$$.

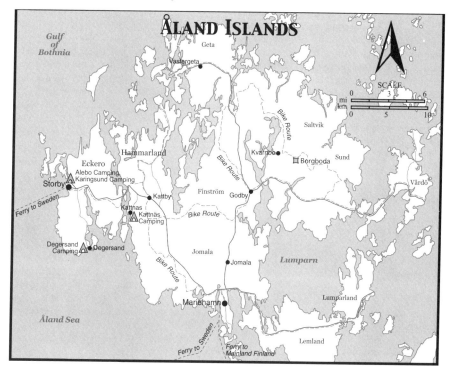

NORRKOPING

It was the town's rushing river that attracted the enterprising industrialist, Louis de Greer, in the 18th century. Using the water for power, his paper and textile factories flourished. Today these same factories house fascinating exhibits of the average working man and woman. Directions: Behind the concert hall, directly south of the train station, along the river. ****Camping: 22km north of the town on the bay. Exit E4 for Komarden and drive towards the sea. Kolmardens Camping (139-82-50); on the bay; popular with families because it is close to a well-run zoo and dolphin park; open May-August; $$.

LINKOPING

Gamla Linkoping, an open-air museum depicting a worker's town from the 1920s, is Linkoping's best known sight; open daily. Directions: Gamla Linkoping is on the west side of town, off Maimslattsvagen. To enjoy the Gota Canal, pedal along the path northwest of town between Ljungsbro and Borensberg. For paddling on the Stangan river, go to the Canoe Center at the boat harbor. ****Camping: *24km south of town on the river. Satravallen Camping (34-00-19); nice location; canoe rental; bungalows; open all year; $$. *North of town on Lake Roxen. Sandvik Camping (36-14-70); nice location; bungalows; open all year; $$.

WEST GOTLAND COAST

Pine-scented campgrounds and tranquil canoeing through the archipelago make a peaceful break in the journey. ****Camping: *40km north of Vastervik exit E22 at Bjornsholm and go to the tip of the pennisula to Loftahammar. Camping Hallmare Havsbad (93-613-62) or Camping Tatto Havsbad (93-613-30); both have lovely locations; canoe rental; open May-September; $$.

GOTLAND ISLAND

Sandy beaches, biking paths, picturesque villages, and brilliant red sunsets make this a popular vacation spot. Its geographic location has attracted traders since Viking times. The Gotland Fornsal exhibition spans eight thousand years. Medieval churches show remnants of former wealth, and during Medieval Week, the first week in August, the town is at its height of gaiety with street music, food booths, locals in costumes, and parades. Directions: It's a three-hour car-ferry ride from Vastervik, the town directly west of the island. ****Camping: In season call ahead. *On the east side of the island.

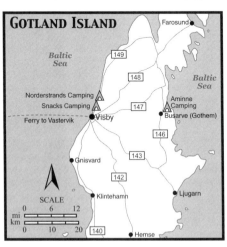

Drive 38km from Visby on 147, exit south onto 146 for 11km in the direction of Gothem. Aminne Camping (04-98-340-11); small; nice location; bungalows; open May-September; $$. *Four kilometers north of Visby on 149. Snacks Camping (04-98-117-50); beautiful location on the water; large and popular; open May-September; $$$. or *Norderstrands Camping (04-98-21-21-57); nice location; large and popular; open May-September; $$$.

OLAND ISLAND

Highlights on this island are sandy beaches, bird reserves, an art colony, Bronze Age artifacts, and old windmills. Directions: Drive over the bridge at Kalmar. ****Camping: Off the southwest coast road, eight kilometers north of Morbylanga, close to a bird sanctuary and the art colony at Vickleby. Haga Park Camping (360-30); nice location; windsurf rentals; bungalows; open May-September; $$. *37km south on 136 to Degerhamn. Close to the Ottenby bird sanctuary, lighthouse, ancient fort, and village of Eketorp. Sandvik Camping (603-35); beautiful location; open May-August; $$$$.

KALMAR

With moat and drawbridge, turreted Kalmar Slott stands dignified, as if still mightily guarding Sweden. This Renaissance castle boasts extensive ramparts, casemates, and corner bastions.

GLASRIKET

The pleasant forested area from Kalmar to Vaxjo tucks in many glassworks studios, factories, and galleries. If you are a serious shopper, check with the tourist office in Vaxjo or Kalmar to locate the glasswork that appeals to you. ****Camping: *26km east of Vaxjo, on 25 in the town of Hovmantorp. Gakaskratt Camping (78-408-07); on a lake; open all year; $$.

VAXJO

The House of Emigrants, loaded with colorful stories of emigration to the Americas, adjoins a research center that traces Swedish ancestry. Next door, at the Smalands Museum, intricacies of glass blowing are detailed; both open daily. Directions: By the train station.

SOUTHERN COAST

Beautiful coastal villages, sandy beaches, fields alive with color, orchards fragrant with apples, and nature reserves added up to a low-key but restful break in the journey. ****Camping: *On the eastern coast in Simrishamn, two kilometers north of town off 9. Camping Tobisviks (14-119-05); lovely location; bungalows; open all year; $$.

GOTEBORG

Enjoy Goteborg by ambling through its graceful gardens, peaceful canals, and lively markets. Tradgardsforeningen Park, often lilting with music and street theatre, is a good place to start. Both the Palm House and the Butterfly House here are favorites. At the Rohsska Museum, delight in a huge "memory lane" collection of decorative and functional art. Then board a vintage tram as it winds its way through the city. Goteborg is justifiably proud of its Maritime Center. Besides clever exhibits on how seamen lived and worked, there is an impressive number of ships to climb around on; open daily. Feskekorka was once a church, but now you're treated instead to great piles of glistening fish and the raucous calls of the fishmongers; closed Sunday and Monday. Colorful Saluhall market is close by so walk over and indulge in some of Sweden's best foodstuffs; closed Sunday. Directions: Follow the southern canal from

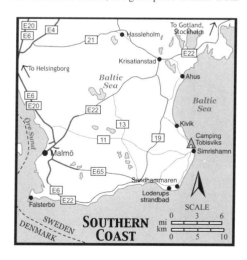

the cruise ship harbor as it winds into the city. To admire first hand Sweden's enormous technical achievements, watch the robots at the Volvo Factory; closed Sunday and Monday; free. Directions: Drive across the river to Hisingen Island. ****Camping: *Ten kilometers south of the city on the Askim Bay and beach, exit off 158. Liseberg Camping Askim Strand (3128-62-61); lovely location; large; popular with families; all amenities; open June-August; $$$.

BOHUSLAN COAST

Along the craggy coastline and archipelago of Bohuslan tiny beaches hide in the arms of smooth sun-warmed boulders. Reached by narrow paths through aromatic pine forests, they provide sweet havens for sun lovers. Directions: Directly west of Lake Vanern, E6 runs along its length; small roads lead to little villages. The tower at the ruins of Bohus Fortress provides a panoramic view of the area. Directions: 20km north of Gothenburg and east of E6 at Kungalv. The island of Marstrand, once buzzing with the prosperity of herring, now buzzes with sun-seekers. In Lysekil there is a good marine-life museum and at Tanumshede there are Bronze Age rock carvings. ****Camping: Book ahead. *In Kungshamn. Exit E6 at Dingle onto174. Solvk Camping (0523-

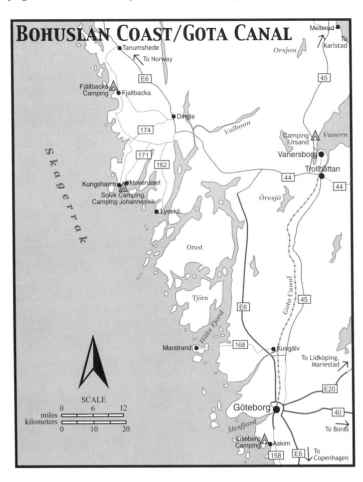

318-70); lovely location; bungalows; popular; open May-August; $$$$. In Hovenaset, north of Kungshamn, off 171. Camping Johannesvik (0523-323-87); beautiful location; popular; bungalows; open May-August; $$$$. In Fjallbacka. Exit E6 onto 163. Fjalbacka Camping (0525-314-90); good location; small; popular; open May-August; $$$.

THE GOTA CANAL

Trollhattan has the best viewing of the canal. Several times a week, the waterfall is allowed to flow in all its crashing glory. The Canal Museum's large collection of photos and model ships enliven stories of its history. Boat rentals and day cruises provide an on-the-water experience and leafy bicycle/walking paths line the route. The shores of the immense lakes of Vanern and Vattern are softened with pine forests, providing lovely campgrounds that seem remote yet are close to town. ****Camping: *On Lake Vanern. At Vanersborg go three kilometers north of town on 45, then exit for the lake. Camping Ursand (21-186-66); in a pine forest; bungalows; popular; open May-August; $$$. *In Lidkoping. East of town off 44. Filsbacks Camping (10-460-27); close to the road and train; bungalows; open May-August; $$$. *In Mariestad. Off E20 drive two kilometers northwest of the town centrum. Ekudden Camping (01-106-37); nice location; bungalows; popular; open May-September; $$$.

DALSLAND

Sweden's lake region, just east of Bohuslan, is perfect for quiet paddling and fishing. Dalsland is less touristy and quieter than Bohuslan. Out of Amal, on the northwestern end of Lake Vanern, adventure companies allow you to put fear to the test by crossing deep ravines on rope bridges and

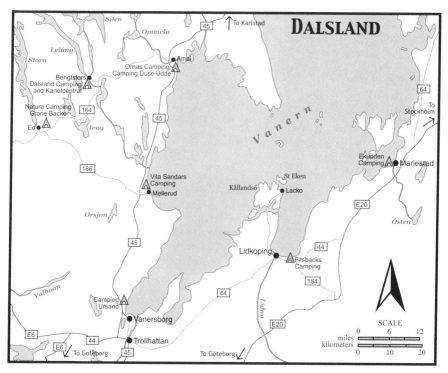

rope swings. Canoe, kayak and boat rentals are plentiful. Horse-backing riding, rafting down river like Huckleberry Finn, or pedaling a cycle trolley on old rail tracks are all waiting to be enjoyed. ****Camping: All have lovely locations and bungalows. *In Amal off 45, one kilometer south of town, on Lake Vanern. Ornas Camping (0532-170-97); open all year; $$ or Camping Duse Udde (0533-420-00); open May-August; $$. *In Mellerud on Lake Vanern, two kilometers north of town. Vita Sandars Camping (0503-129-34); open all year; $$$. *In Ed, two kilometers west of town off 164/166. Natura Camping Grone Backe (0534-101-44); on a small lake; lake sauna; open all year; $$. *In Bengtsfors, between lakes Lelangen and Artingen. Dalsland Camping and Kanotcentral (0531-100-60); specializes in canoe trips; lake sauna; open May-August; $$.

NORTHERN SWEDEN

The drama of glaciers, mountains, rushing rivers, and midnight sun lure the hiker, fly fisherman, and paddler to this part of Europe's last wilderness. Huge herds of reindeer still wander about freely. Fascinating open-air museums tell their story of dog sleds and reindeer. Rafters flock to the Pitealven river. At the Batsuoj Forest Sami Center you can participate in traditional everyday Sami activities including reindeer barbecues. The campgrounds can help with arrangements.****Camping: *South of Arvidsjaur on 95. Camp Gielas (0960-556-00); on the lake; bungalows; open all year; $$.

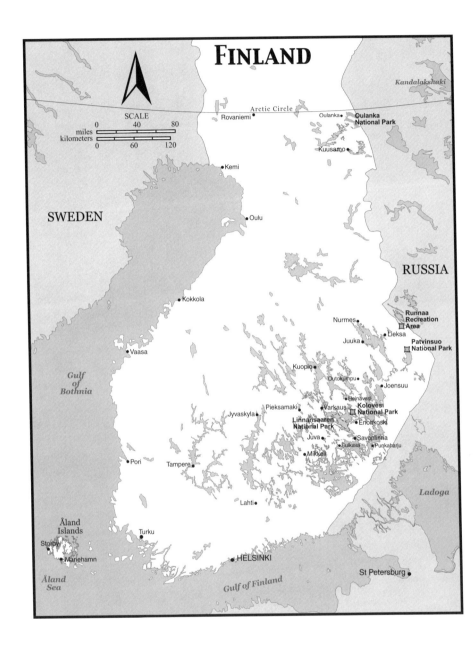

FINLAND

Kandalakshaki

SCALE

miles
kilometers

0   40   80

0   60   120

Arctic Circle

Rovaniemi

Oulanka

Oulanka
National Park

Kuusamo

Kemi

SWEDEN

Oulu

RUSSIA

Kokkola

Nurmes

Runnaa
Recreation
Area

Lieksa

Juuka

Patvinsuo
National Park

Vaasa

Kuopio

Outokumpu

Joensuu

Heinävesi

Pieksamaki

Varkaus

Kolovesi
National Park

Jyvaskyla

Linnansaaren
National Park

Enonkoski

Juva

Savonlinna

Sulkava

Punkaharju

Mikkeli

Gulf
of
Bothnia

Pori

Tampere

Ladoga

Lahti

Åland
Islands

Turku

Storby

Mariehamn

HELSINKI

St Petersburg

Åland
Sea

Gulf of Finland

FINLAND

Imagine luscious mounds of clouds mirrored in deep-blue lakes as in a Monet painting. Then add a silence broken only by the twittering of birds, the skittering of ducks, and the whisper of pines. Breathe in deeply, air that is fresh and sweet scented with the fragrance of earth. True, Finland does not have snowcapped peaks reflected in dramatic fjords. But it does have a jewel-like treasure hard to find in today's world; peaceful solitude where tranquility can be regained.

Finns delight in the outdoors and love to camp. It is a tradition to sit around a campfire, toast sausages and listen to the evening's symphony of songbirds and winged insects, as you watch the sky dress up in queenly colors. To provide for this pleasure, many campgrounds have individual little shelters built picturesquely at the side of the lake. They enclose fireplaces and hold neat stacks of wood. Comfortable little bungalows, saunas, common cooking and eating areas, canoe rental, and diving platforms all add to the pleasure of these lakeside retreats. The best weather for camping is in June and July or early August. The cost for two persons, a tent, and car is around $20 USA. Renting a bungalow will cost about three times more. Camping places are well maintained, have hot showers, and a staff person who speaks English.

Finland is a paradise for fishermen. Glistening lakes teem with fish. Although rental equipment is available, avid fishermen might want to bring their own gear. Permits are reasonable and can be purchased at the post office. Much of Finland is either flat or gently rolling terrain making it a perfect place to enjoy the pleasures of pedaling a bike. The roads are excellent and secondary roads have little traffic. Public transportation is bicycle-friendly, and the cities have good cycle paths. The Finn's are avid boatmen. Canoe and kayaks are available for rental. Established sign-posted routes on certain lakes and rivers have designated campgrounds along the way. Waterproof bags, and maps, and even guides can usually be secured. Bring your own waterproof bag if you know paddling a route will be part of your adventure plans. Well-informed English speaking staff at the local tourist office or campground can provide helpful information.

Finland's roadways are well maintained and sign-posted. Traffic is light, and it's a pleasure to drive through the graceful, quiet countryside. Gas stations are modern and are enjoyable places to stop for a snack, a few groceries, and tourist information. Automatic pumps with credit cards terminals are used when the stations are closed on Sundays and at night. Cash machines are plentiful. Look for them close to a grocery store or ask a local. Grocery stores are well stocked with reasonably priced basics. Fresh produce will be more expensive than on mainland Europe, and international products are not commonly found. Bring tea, coffee, and alcoholic beverages with you. Museums are closed on Mondays, and opening and closing hours are generally 10 a.m. to 3 p.m. in the summer. Tourist information offices will have some one who speaks English, a friendly smile, and a host of brochures and maps.

HELSINKI

Four stalwart masculine figures, each delicately holding a sphere of glass, grace the facade of Helsinki's railroad station. They represent the spirit of Finland: heroic survivors of prolonged hardship who hold fast to human values and nature. Surrounded by neighbors eager to engulf them, the Finns have excelled in tightrope balancing acts. Today the country proudly hosts international summit meetings.

Leaders in the field of applied art, they incorporate art and nature with impeccable skill, believing that it is wildness that preserves the world. Take a walk to Temppeliaukio Church. Carved out of a solid piece of granite, it honors this belief; closed Monday. Outside the church, in the narrow parkway, note the lovely benches built to honor their beloved birch tree's natural beauty. By strolling back to the main boulevard, Mannerheiminaukio, you can enjoy the Kiasma Museum of Contemporary Art; it's like walking through a piece of sculpture; closed Monday. The luscious

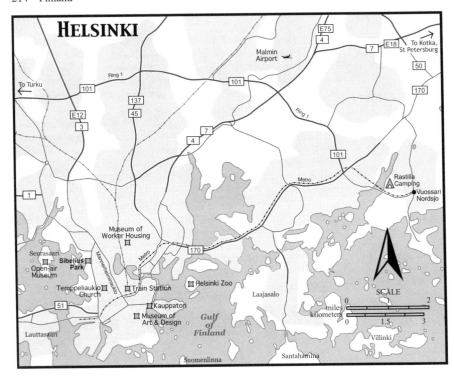

grass in the shady and pleasant Sibelius Park is a great place for a picnic. While munching on sand-wiches you can gaze at a sensuous, silvery, surreal organ made from 24 tons of tubing. Farther on down Helsinki's leafy boulevards is the Museum of Art and Design housing a small but excellent collection; open every afternoon but Monday.

Finland's spirit of nationalism is stirred and kept alive through art. Action-packed scenes from Finland's epic poem, "Kalevala," and also evocative studies of peasant life painted in the late 19th century are housed in the Art Museum of the Ateneum and shouldn't be missed; closed Monday. If you are interested in Finnish emigration to America, allow some time to wander through the Museum of Worker Housing, where six one-room wooden houses have been recreated, depicting the tragic home life of the agrarian people who moved to the city in the early 1900's.

Finland's independence is relatively new. Travelers should be mindful that she is a youngster compared to her neighbors and has had comparatively few years to pile up collections. Her most impressive possession is the fabulous remoteness, solitude and pureness of her countryside.

Reindeer kebabs, Russian caviar, fresh fish, wild mushrooms, cloudberries, local handicrafts, and T-shirts make a colorful and lively mix for shoppers at Kauppatori, the harbor's morning mar-ket. Afterwards you might want to catch a ferry to the UNESCO listed fortress on Suomenlinna Island, to the Helsinki Zoo, or to the park-like setting of the open-air museum on Seurasaari Island. Don't miss casting an appreciative gaze at Havis Amanda, the mermaid statue and fountain just west of the market. She embodies the shy, sweet beauty of Finland.

****Camping: *16km east of the city. Take exit 4 onto ring 1 and drive southeast on 101 in the direc-tion of Vuosaari Nordsjo. It's on the northeast side of the bridge over the estuary. Rastila Camping (09-316-551); metro to city closeby; large; bungalows; covered cooking and eating area; open all year; $$.

TURKU

Tucked away in a leafy neighborhood on the south side of the Aura River in Turku, is a jewel of an open-air museum or skansen, Luostarinmaki. Because of ravishing fires, it is the sole survivor of 18th century Turku. Still in their original location, the tiny workshops and homes are now an open-air handicraft museum. To me, it exudes more authenticity than any skansen in Scandinavia. Visitors wander down the narrow streets into gardens and courtyards to talk to friendly artisans working in the original homes; closed Mondays.

If bird watching is one of your pleasures, continue west several blocks to the art nouveau building housing Turku's

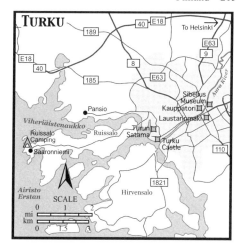

Natural History museum. It has an excellent collection, particularly of birds you might see in the country; open daily.

Musically, nothing evokes the spirit of Finland, more than the evocative symphony Finlandia, composed by Sibelius. At the museum named after him, strains of music fill the air adding pleasure to the examination of delicate music boxes, fragile wooden kantele, ancient horns, and burnished violins; closed Monday.

Huge bunches of gloriously golden sunflowers, mounds of brilliantly red currants, baskets of salmon-colored cloudberries, sparkling piles of iced fish, whole grain breads, and crispy green peas await shoppers at one of the most authentic open markets in Scandinavia. Shoppers at the Kauppatori or open market, are Finns, not tourists.

At the mouth of the Aura River, a 13th century castle still guards the city. Few travelers leave Turku without wandering through its maze of corridors and stairways leading down to dark dungeons and up to sunny sitting rooms. This medieval castle was the seat of power for Finland and, at times, Sweden. Exhibits are supplemented with videos, costumes, and computer terminals to make the historical information come alive for both young and old; open daily.

****Camping: *On the tip of Ruissalo Island, ten kilometers west of the city on the bay. Follow signs to Turun satama, Turku's Harbor. Drive north in the direction of Pansio for just over a kilometer. Exit for Ruissalo. Follow the road five kilometers through the park-like area to the end of the pennisula. Ruissalo Camping (258-9249); nice location on the bay; covered cooking, barbeque, and eating areas; open June-August; $$.

TAMPERE

Picturesquely set between two lakes, whose waters are joined by an energetic river, Tampere's delightful small town atmosphere belies its historical industrial importance. The river's roaring rapids provided energy for Finland's most important hub of textile, footwear, metal, and wood industries in the early 1900's. Today its high-tech industries have a global marketplace. In keeping with a goal of excellence, the city built Metso, a state-of-the-art city library. Its beautiful architecture welcomes guests. Across from the library, the Lenin Museum houses some interesting memorabilia. On the shores of Lake Nasijarvi is one of Finland's most prominent modern art museums, the Sara Hilden. Directions: To get to Sara Hilden, follow signs to Sarkanniemi. Through-out the summer, lively festivals give Tampere a festive air and a chance for travelers to share laughter with the locals. ****Camping: *South of the city on Lake Pyhajarvi. From town take the shoreline road five kilometers to the suburb of Harmala and then drive to the lake. Harmala Camping (03-265-1355); lovely location; all the amenities; open June-August; $$.

THE LAKELAND

Twinkling silver in the summer sun, Finland's labyrinthine lakes and waterways are decorated along the shoreline with masses of larkspur, phlox, and buttercups. Along roadways, grasslands wave happily in the breeze. It's the summer paradise the Finns love. Here and there pleasant little towns provide good places to stock up on supplies and enjoy a hometown ambiance. For urban visitors, it is like stepping back into a time when the pace was slower, the impact of people and noise less, and solitude was easy to find.

SAVONLINNA

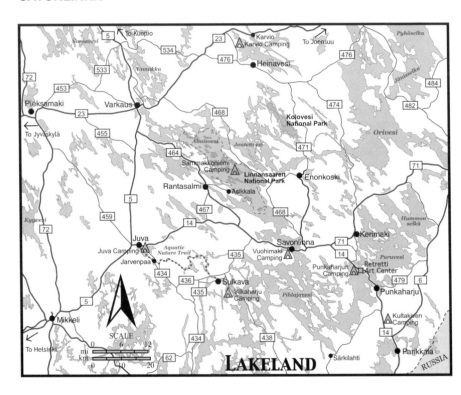

Known as the Queen of the Lakeland, Savonlinna's historic castle, Olavinlinna, is known internationally among opera buffs. Arias have been lilting out across the lakes since 1912, and today it hosts one of Europe's finest musical festivals. Regally separating herself from commoners, the castle sits in the middle of two lakes and is reached by a floating bridge. She is not large, but rather intimate and pleasing, graced with lovely courtyards, wood-paneled interiors, and leafy trees; open daily. To buy tickets for the July opera, fax one year in advance; 015-476-7540. A lively beer festival is held in mid-August and an international film festival later in August. Scenic cruises and cycling are pleasant ways to absorb the scenery. ****Camping: Book ahead if coming during opera season. *Exit 14 on the westside of town. Vuohimaki Camping (015-537-353, fax 09-713-713); nice location; large; all amenities; open June-August; $$$$. *West of Savonlinna, exit 14 for Sulkava. Vilkaharju Camping (015-471-223, fax 09-713-713); natural setting on the lake; bungalows; covered cooking and eating area; open June-August; $$$.

KOLOVESI NATIONAL PARK/
LINNANSAAI NATIONAL PARK

Join others paddling up the pristine waterways here that protect the endangered Saimaa ringed seals. Magnificent osprey plunge for prey while tuxedoed gulls and regal loons ride the surf, dipping in for tasty treats. Dark and mysterious old pine forests hug rocky caves and outcrops. Sunlit birch forests provide cover for golden orioles and white-backed woodpeckers. Finn's are avid bird watchers and there is an important sanctuary out of Rantasalmi in Asikkala. Directions: To get to Kolovesi Park, drive north of Savonlinna on 471 in the direction of Heinavesi. Arrange for paddling in Enonkoski, 33km north of Savonlinna. For Linnansaai Park, drive about 30km northwest of Savonlinna on 14. Then exit onto 467 and drive 14km to Rantasalmi. Boats leave from here for the island park. If you have time, stop for some environmental education at the Lakeland Center. ****Camping: *For Linnansaai pack up a bit of gear and take the passenger-only boat to the main island. Sammakkoniemi Camping (040-275-458); gorgeous location; bungalows; open June-August; no charge for tents. *For Kolovesi Park drive north of the park to Heinavesi and then a bit further to the village of Karvio. Karvio Camping (017-563-603); beautiful location; all amenities; open May-August; $$.

PUNKAHARJU RIDGE

Formed by glacier movement, this narrow ridge is flanked on either side by beautiful lakes. To walk, cycle, or drive across the seven kilometer ridge is popular with the Finns. Directions: Drive southeast from Savonlinna for about 25km on 14. Just before Punkaharju, enjoy the Retretti Art Center. Man-made caves, gouged out of the rock, provide not only galleries but also a huge underground concert hall. In the garden it is fun to watch tree trunks and boulders move unexpectedly. The town's Forest Museum exemplifies the Finn's concern for their environment. Man's impact on the forest and their relationship in the past, today, and tomorrow is vividly portrayed. ****Camping: *By the ridge, nine kilometers northwest of town. Punkaharjun Camping (015-739-611); nice location; very large; all amenities, bungalows; open all year; $$$$. *South of town. Kultakiven Lomakyla (015-15-645); nice location; small; open June-August; $$.

SARKILAHTI BIRD LAKE

Have you ever heard a nightingale sing? Their sweet, melodious, and tender song is a joy to hear. Sarkilahti, known internationally among birders, is one of the finest places to enjoy these night singers. It is the best bird lake in Finland. A guide is an enormous help in viewing, but there are trails and an observation tower for viewing on your own. Directions: The lake is just south of Parikkala, 60km south of Savolinna on 14. To book a guide, call ahead (05-68-611).

KERIMAKI CHURCH

Painted bright yellow like a sunny day, Kerimaki kirkko, built in the mid-1800's, claims to be

the largest wooden church in the world. It's majestic, but friendly rather than pompous. Directions: Drive east from Savolinna 22km on 71.

ORAVAREITTI CANOE ROUTE AND AQUATIC NATURE TRAIL

One of Finland's most user-friendly canoe routes, the 52km Oravareitti, runs from Sulkava to Juva and encompasses level II rapids, smooth flowing rivers, and lakes. There is a 25-meter drop in water level and one portage of 50 meters. Campgrounds and nature interpretive signs dot the route. Call ahead and reserve a canoe at Juva Camping. ****Camping: *At the southeast end of the village, take the small road in the direction of Jarvenpaa. Juva Camping (015-451-930); beautiful setting on the river; bungalows; covered eating and cooking areas; open mid-June to mid-August; $$. *In Sulkava, on the lake southeast of the village. Vilkaharju Camping (09-6138-3210); lovely setting; small; simple; open mid-June through July; $.

JYVASKYLA AND ALVAR ALTO

Finland's most famous modern architect, Alvar Alto, strove to humanize functional architecture. Collaborating with his wife, he also helped design the famous L-shaped chair and table leg. An account of his life and the time in which he worked are exhibited along with models, photos and drawings in an exceptional building he designed on the grounds of the University of Jyvaskyla. ****Camping: *Drive north of the city on E75/4, exit for the suburb of Taulumaki, then drive north along the lake. Tuomiojarvi Camping (014-624-895); beautiful location on the lake; covered cooking and eating area; bungalows; open June-August; $$.

KARELIAN REGION

JOENSUU

Music fills the air for most of the summer in this lively city. The residents' deep-rooted love for music has sustained their spirits during threats from neighboring Russia. International festivals of rock, gospel, and folk music are held in July. At the University's botanical gardens, magnificent giant butterflies, screeching tropical birds, beetles, and bamboo are housed in exotic greenhouses; closed Tuesdays. For adventure, folks pile into wooden boats from the center of town to paddle the Pielisjoki rapids. ****Camping: Book ahead for festival weekends. *West of the town, exit off 6/17 for stadium. Linnunlahden Camping (013-126-272, fax 013-525-486); on a small lake by the festival grounds; bungalows; very popular; covered cooking and eating area; open June to mid August; $$.

NURMES

Founded in 1876 by Tsar Alexander II of Russia, this city's terraced old town hillsides hold fine wooden houses nestled among leafy birch trees. A rousing Bomba Festival in mid-July helps the Karelians to keep their culture alive. Paddling the Saramojoki canoe route, hiking the Saramo Jotos, and fishing for salmon on the Lokinlampi are popular Finnish pursuits. ****Camping: *Two kilometers east of town, exit off 73. Hyvarila Camping (013-481-770); lovely location on the lake; bungalows;

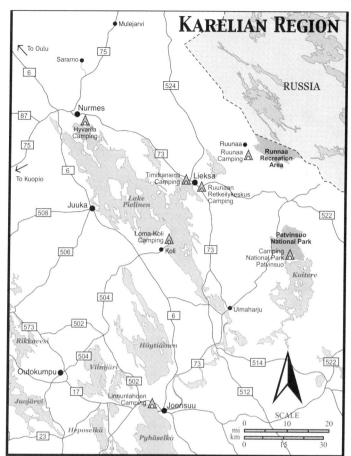

covered cooking and eating area; open June-August; $$. *Halfway between Joensuu and Nurmes in the town of Koli, exit 6 onto 504 and drive toward the lake. Loma-Koli Camping (013-673-212); gorgeous setting on the lake; bungalows; covered cooking and eating area; open June-August; $$.

LIEKSA

Besides a pristine setting on Lake Pielinen, Lieksa boasts over 70 engaging Karelian wooden structures in an open-air museum, plus an adjoining regional history museum. ****Camping: *In town off roadway 73. Timitraniemi Camping (013-521-780); nice setting on the river; bungalows; covered cooking and eating area; open June-August; $$. *Exit 73 south of town in the direction of Pankakoski. Ruunaan Retkeilykeskus Camping (013-533-170); lovely setting on the lake; small; bungalows; covered cooking and eating area; open June to mid-August; $$.

PATVINSUO NATIONAL PARK

An internationally known sanctuary for swans, this vast, quiet wetland is accessed by boardwalks. Directions: Southeast of Lieksa exit 73 for Uimaharju, then take the smaller road northeast for 25km in the direction of Patvinsuo. ****Camping: *In the park. Camping National Park Patvinsuo (013-548-506); simple and tranquil; open June-August; free.

RUUNAA RECREATIONAL AREA

Plunging through white water, casting fishing lines into crystal clear rivers, and hiking the Bear's Path make a perfect combo for many Finns. White water trips start at the Naarajoki bridge. The Bear's Path is just beyond. Directions: From Lieksa drive northeast for 30km to Ruunaa. The excellent interpretive center there provides the information you'll need. ****Camping: *On the Neitikoski River, close to the rapids. Ruunaa Camping (013-533-170); wonderful location; all the amenities; popular; open June-August; $$.

LAPLAND AND NORTHERN FINLAND

ROVANIEMI

Dramatically housed under glass, the Arkikum Museum is a fascinating celebration of the people, plants, and animals of the whole Arctic world; open daily. In June, a colorful festival hosted by the Sami, Finland's indigenous people, livens up the town. Reindeer farm visits, Arctic Circle crossings, and visits to Santapark are other popular attractions. For a thrill, take the summer toboggan run at the Ounasvaara ski center. ****Camping: *South of town off 78. Camping Ounaskoski (016-345-304); nice location on the river; open June-August; $$.

OULANKA NATIONAL PARK AND THE BEAR'S RING TREK

Suspension bridges span breathtaking rapids, waterfalls crash, and rugged cliffs enclose shadowy gorges on one of Finland's most popular treking routes. Directions: Drive north of Kuusamo on 950 for 42km to Kayla, then drive east on the small road in the direction of Kiutavaara. ****Camping: *Close to the visitor center. Oulanka Camping (08-863-429); lovely setting; canoe rental; open June to mid August; $$.

WHITE WATER RAFTING THE KITKAJOKI OR OULANKAJOKI

Advanced paddlers enjoy the thrill of paddling these tricky and demanding rapids. Some portage is necessary. If you would rather try this excitement under the auspices of an experienced

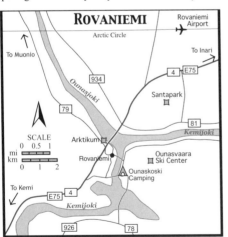

oars-person, book ahead with Kitkan Sarfarit in Juuma; phone-fax 08-853-458. To get here, drive 36km north of Kuusamo on 950, exit east for Sakkila/Juuma, then drive six kilometers to Juuma. ****Camping: *In Juuma. Jyrava Camping (08-863-236) or Juuman Leirinta (08-863-212). Both have great locations; bungalows; canoe rental; open June to mid-August; $$.

THE ALAND ISLANDS

Linking Finland with Sweden, this archipelago makes crossing to and from the countries fun and easy. Politically Finnish but culturally Swedish, the residents of Aland claim an independence of their own.

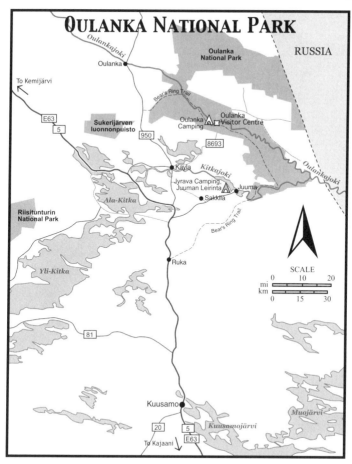

OULANKA NATIONAL PARK

Cycling reins high in popularity and is the best way to enjoy the beauty of the archipelago. An extensive network of cycle paths and inter-island ferries makes it easy. Ro-No-Rents rents bicycles and canoes and has locations at the harbors in Mariehamn and also in Eckero Berghamn. Sea gulls escort paddlers as they glide around tiny islets, looking for a private picnic spot. Dotted throughout the islands are tiny museums telling of nautical, postal, and Stone Age history. ****Camping: The following are located close to the water, have barbeques, covered cooking and eating areas, often have boat rental, and are open June-August; $$. *On Eckero Island in Storby: Alebo Camping (018-38-543) or Karingsund Camping (018-38-309). On the southern tip of Eckero Island in Degersand: Degersands Camping (018-38-004). On Hammarland Island, exit south off 1 for Kattnas: Kattnas Camping (018-37-687) more remote. In Mariehamn, the biggest of the small towns of Aland: on the southeast side of town, Grona Uddens Camping (018-19-041); popular with partying folks. On Sund Island, by the bridge to Vardo Island: Prasto Camping (018-44-045) or Puttes Camping (018-44-047). On Vardo Island, on the northeast side: Sandosunds Camping (018-47-750).

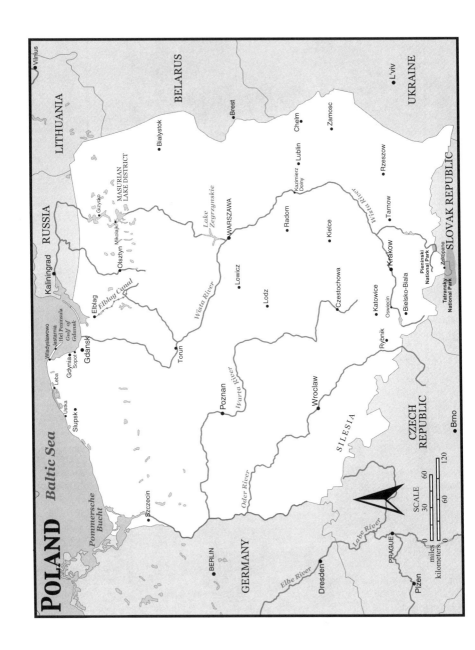

POLAND

A proud and courageous nation, Poland offers a rich variety of experiences to the traveler. At the historically important port of Gdansk, you can join Poles and fellow international travelers marveling at the meticulous restoration and buff up on its history as you study the lively exhibits. Boating enthusiasts from all over Europe are drawn to the Masurian Lake region, where they paddle and sail quietly by a profusion of elegant swans. At Golden Krakow, the past glories of nobles and wealthy merchants seep from the buildings. UNESCO has named it one of the most significant cultural sites in the world. Your pilgrimage to the haunting Auschwitz concentration camp will be unforgettable. In Warsaw, you'll be impressed with the indomitable spirit of the Poles who never lost hope in all their years of oppression. In Renaissance Zamosc, you'll feel like you're entering an 18th century painting, and at Czestochowa, you'll stand quietly by the devotees revering their most precious icon, the Black Madonna. At the sophisticated mountain village of Zakopane, you can hike up into the magnificent Tatras and, with the assistance of a cable car, be transported to high ridge trails and a pristine blue lake. Along the Baltic coastline, you can share the sea with locals, climbing large sand dunes and enjoying the birds. You'll find yourself wanting to stay in Poland longer than you planned.

Poles love to camp, and there are hundreds of places. The cost of the camping place reflects its amenities and maintenance. They are friendly places and the Poles are happy and proud you have chosen to visit their country. Simple places can cost as little as $10 USA; those close to major historic areas are just under $25 USA; most cost under $20 USA for 2 persons, a tent, and a car. The roads are good and well signposted, and the countryside is gorgeous. Designated parking areas and plenty of street parking make parking close to historic areas simple. The cities are easy to get around in, and it's pleasing to join the locals cycling. If you learn some Polish words you'll, have more fun

The summers are pleasantly warm with some interlacing of rain, which keeps the forests and hillsides green and bountiful with wildflowers. Food is plentiful, of excellent quality, and inexpensive. The Poles love to eat, and their markets reflect this. Outdoor markets are common in most towns of any size. You'll find them in the main squares every morning but Sunday. The farmers are grateful for a sale. Eye contact, smiles, and simple greetings of "hello" and "thank you" in their language are always heartwarmingly worthwhile. Large shopping malls are found on the outskirts of larger towns. Ask for directions at the campground.

The rich tradition of art and crafts is evident in the museums, restorations, festivals and open-air museums. Check the festival schedule with the national tourist office in your country or with a guidebook, and then arrange your trip in order to join the Poles attending these colorful and lively events. They will welcome you warmly. Museums are closed on Mondays and are inexpensive unless indicated otherwise.

KRAKOW

Once called "Golden" Krakow because it was the home of royalty, historic Krakow bursts with ancient legacy and sits like a jewel on the grassy banks of the Vistula River. It has one of the oldest universities in Europe and is home to many well-known intellectuals, including Karol Wojtyla, now Pope John Paul II, whose was Krakow's outspoken Archbishop. Art, beauty, and religion are foremost in Krakow.

The heart of the old town is the Rynek Glowny, an elegant medieval market square-the largest in Europe. In spite of its size, it feels intimate; perhaps it's the flower stalls, the sidewalk cafes, the birds, and the trumpet's call. It's a subdued St. Marco's in Venice. The Cloth Hall, set picturesquely in the square's center almost glows from all the golden amber on sale inside. Showcasing the works of hometown and 19th century Polish painter, Matejko, the Gallery of 19th century Paintings is impressive; closed Monday and Tuesday. The entrance is up the outside stairway on the eastern side of the Cloth Hall. But the city's masterpiece is splendid St. Mary's Church on the eastern corner of the square. Inside the darkly soaring interior, one intricately carved altar of masterful Gothic art depicts the holy family and another depicts Mary ascending to heaven attended by angels; carved panels are opened every day at noon. English guidebooks are available at the ticket booth.

As you wander through the streets, you'll find them rich in atmosphere. Ul. Florianska is a popular walking street lined with lovely shops, galleries, bookstores, and aromatic cafes. It's part of the Royal Way and leads to the Florian Gate. On the way, stop in to see Matejko House. The famous painter lived here, and it's interesting to look upon the mementos of his life; closed Wednesday and Thursday. After enjoying the ambiance at the Florian Gate, turn west, following the main street to Sw. Jana, where you can examine Czartoryski Museum's impressive collection of art donated by a wealthy Polish family; closed Wednesday and Thursday. A significant collection of religious art is displayed in the Szolajski House, located in northwest corner of old town across from the parking area on Ssczepanski. Jagiellonian University's Collegium Maius, short walk from the Town Hall Tower on the southwest corner of Rynek Glowny, houses a good collection of ancient astronomical devices in tribute to Copernicus, the sagacious Pole whose theory of planetary rotation revolutionized man's view of his world; closed Sunday.

Grassy embankments along the Vistula grace the walls of Wawel Hill, where Krakow's famous castle, crowned with graceful turrets and spires, beckons. Intricately woven tapestries and exquisite furnishings decorate the Royal Chambers with quiet elegance. Don't miss the Exhibition of Oriental Art, where sumptuous Turkish tents are just part of the fascinating collection amassed at the Battle of Vienna. Take a few minutes in the rooms of the Crown Treasury to examine the famous 13th century Jagged Sword, used in all of the country's coronations. Arrive early in the morning when there is still mist on the rose-filled gardens. The ticket booth is in the passageway leading to the castle's courtyard; closed Monday.

When you descend the steps to the Dragon's Cave, next to the Thieves Tower, you emerge on the banks of the Vistula-a great place for a relaxing with a picnic lunch. Then continue walking south to explore the Kazimierz area, once home to thousands of Jews. Ul. Jozefa leads to the Old Synagogue, a simple low-slung building, now housing the Museum of History and Culture of Krakow. Here Jewish culture through the centuries is artistically celebrated; closed Saturday. Don't miss the touching cemeteries, and note the tribute to Rabbit Moses Isserles, an important philosopher. It's behind the Remu'h Synagogue.

Krakow is full of summer festivals, so you'll likely to see Poles dressed in elaborately embroidered traditional costumes dancing to fiddlers' free-spirited music as you gorge on freshly grilled sausage and sip flavorful beer. The friendly locals will gladly make room for you at their table, and you'll have fun smiling and complimenting them on their beautiful country. Blonia, an enormous green space where colorful parachutes often float down from the sky and musical groups perform, is all-around nice place to be. Kosciuzko, a very large mound of earth hand-built by thousands of Poles to pay tribute to a hero, is nearby. Blonia is on the west side of highway 7 and south of 4.

****Camping: *Four kilometers west of the historic area, exit off 4/7 west on the north side of the Vistula bridge onto 780 in the direction of Oswiecim. Camping Smok, ul,Kamedulska 18 (012-210-255); country setting; across from the Vistula; closest to the historic area; close to public transportation; doable by bicycle to the historic area; well maintained; open March-October; $$$. *Off 7/E77, six kilometers south of historic area on the road to Zakopane, just north of 952. Camping Krakowianka, ul. Zywiecka Bocznat (012-664-191); bungalows; close to public transportation; well maintained; open May-September; $$$. *Five kilometers northwest of the historic area in the direction of Katowice, at the intersection of E40 and A4 next to Motel Krak. Camping Krak ul. Radzikowskiego 99 (012-637-2122); close to public transportation; well maintained; $$$.

AUSCHWITZ AND BIRKENAU

It's said, "He who forgets history, may relive it." Visiting here is a sobering experience you won't forget. Your pilgrimage to see where the elimination of almost 2 million people took place should include both sites. Start at Auschwitz. Pick up the free brochure, then view the 15-minute documentary film in the museum. Don't wait for the English showing; it's easily understood in another language. After passing through the gate inscribed "Abeit Macht Frei," meaning "Work Makes Free," see the moving exhibitions in the prison blocks presented by all the major European countries. Then go on to the crematorium and gas chamber. An airy, inexpensive cafeteria is next to the entrance. After a rest, take the shuttle bus to Birkenau, or drive the two kilometers. Softened only by poppies, wild sweetpea, and green grass, the death camp remains vast and sinister. Walk reflectively down the train tracks to the monument at the end. Before leaving, climb the stairs at the entrance gate to view the complex in its entirety; open daily and free. ****Camping: *Close to the museum. International Meeting House for Youth; tent camping only; $.

WIELICZKA SALT MINE

Like an underground castle this subterranean labyrinth of tunnels, immense halls, altars, monuments, and figures carved from salt is truly amazing. The three-hour tour stops halfway through for a break. Arrive early; it's UNESCO listed and popular; open daily. Directions: Drive to the southeastern edge of the Krakow. Signposting is good for exiting off 4.

CZESTOCHOWA

The Jasna Gora Monastery is probably the most important place of religious pilgrimage in Eastern Europe. Devotees come to pay homage to the sacred icon of the Black Madonna. The quiet and sacred place is located at the western end of the wide, tree-lined, main boulevard Al Najswietszej. The main entrance is on the south side. Buy an English guide.

****Camping: *Just west of the monastery. Camping Czestochowa ul. Olenki 10/30 (034-24-74-95); bungalows; fair maintenance; open all year; $.

ZAKOPANE

Magnificent mountains, grassy meadows brilliant with daisies and colombine, and tumbling crystal-clear creeks beckon as you breathe the fresh air and absorb the ambiance in charming Alpine Zakopane. Outdoor stalls offer for sale mounds of thick woolen sweaters, neat rows of wooden shoes, and intricately molded and smoked sheep cheese. Jump onto a horse-drawn wagon filled with Polish families laughing and having a good time, and take a pine-scented ride up to Morskie Oko, a pristine Alpine lake. Take the cable car ride up the pinnacles that seem to reach to the sky to enjoy the panoramic view, a treat on the terrace, then take a hike down along the ridge. In late August, a gargantuan tent fills with families who have come to applaud the highly spirited dance troupes from all over Eastern Europe at the Zakopane Mountain Music Festival. The joyful music and dancing have kept alive the hopes of many during their country's troubled history. Tickets are inexpensive and easy to buy that day. Performances are scheduled in both the afternoons and evening, so you still have time for hiking. ****Camping: *South of town, follow signs to Kusznice. At the roundabout, turn west onto the road just beneath ski slope. Camping Pod Krokwia, ul. Zeromiskiego (018-201-2256); bungalows; small restaurant; close to hiking and cable car to Kuznice; open all year; $$. *In a residential area due west of the main town just off ul. Koscieliska. Camping Comfort, ul. Kaszelewskiego 7a (018-149-42); difficult to find; close to town; well maintained; open June-August; $$$. *Off 95 northeast of town in the direction of Nowy Targ. Camping Harenda, in Harenda (018-122-56); well maintained; open all year; $$$. *On the road to Lake Morskii Oka and Jaszcurowka there are several seasonal camping places; small; more remote but tranquil and scenic; watch for signs; $$.

WARSAW

Almost totally destroyed in World War II, this town's restoration is captivating. Start by visiting the Historical Museum of Warsaw, on the north side of the main square at number 42, which documents the town's destruction and the restoration. Stop and listen to the street music filling the air with sweet and talented sound. By wandering down the narrow cobblestone streets, you'll invariably come to Castle Square and the Royal Castle; buy the English guide. The exquisitely beautiful cathedrals and small churches dotting the old town are somber with devotees. Warsaw has a wide and interesting array of museums, palaces, and galleries. Buy a map at a magazine stand. The old town is on the western side of the Vistula River.

****Camping: *In the suburb of Ochota southwest of the city, off E67/E77 in the direction of Krakow/Katowice. Camping Astar, ul. Bitwy Warszawskiejo 1920 15/17 (022-254-391); bungalows; swimming pool; close to public transportation; well maintained; open all year; $$. In the same suburb, on the main road just south of E67/E77. Camping Gromada, Zwirki I Wigury 32, (022-254-391); close to the airport and public transportation; bungalows; well maintained; open all year; $$. At both campgrounds pack everything back into your vehicle before leaving for the day.

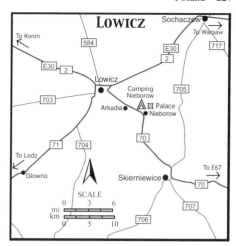

LOWICZ

Aristocratic Poles anxious to impress their wealthy friends, built lavish palaces and gardens. Lowicz is one of them. It's a nice place to stretch your legs, enjoy a nap, and take some photographs. Although the pavilions and gardens of close-by Arkadia haven't been restored they extend your walk and make an interesting subject for photographs. The museum palace is closed on Monday but the grounds are open everyday. Directions: Drive 100 km west of Warsaw to the small village of Nieborow, then go ten kilometers southeast to Lowicz. ****Camping: *Close to the palace park, off the road to Skierniewice. Camping Nieborow (046-385-692); bungalows; fair maintenance; open June-August; $.

LODZ

This charming town has celebrated textile art from its early beginnings, and the museum housing the artifacts is picturesquely set in an old mill. Directions: From the roundabout in the center of town, head south on Piortrkowsa. It's just south of the large cathedral. A palace museum that was once home to the Herbst family is located just over a kilometers east of the Textile Museum at ul.Przedzalniana. Here an art museum displays a large collection of Polish art as well as works of other famous international painters. Directions: Southwest of the roundabout. ****Camping: *Off 71 in the direction of Warsaw. Camping Na Rogach, ul. Lupkowa 10/16 (042-551-013); bungalows; close to highway; fair maintenance; open June-August; $$.

ZAMOSC

Zamosc was designed by an Italian for an aristocratic Pole who hoped to build a per-

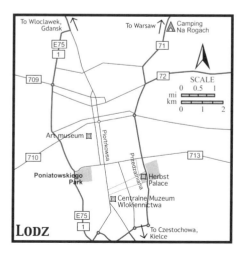

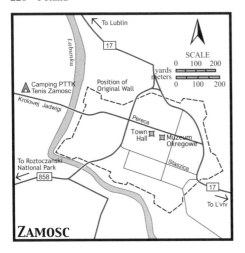

ZAMOSC

fect city both culturally and economically. The 16th century historic area is UNESCO listed. Take some time to absorb the atmosphere of the lovely square, then go into the Regional Museum at number 24, to exam the meticulous model of the town in its heyday. As you wander through the old town, note the exquisite detail of doorways and vaulted ceilings. Street music and open-air concerts enliven the town all summer. ****Camping: *Just outside the northwest corner of the fortified walls, next to Hotel Sportowy. Camping Tenis Zamosc, ul Krolowej Jadwig 14 (084-39-24-99); in a sportspark; basic amenities; $.

KAZIMIERZ DOLY

Picturesque in its setting between the Vistula River and the surrounding wooded hills, this small town has always been a haven for artists. It provides a welcome break from larger towns and cycling is easy and scenic. The small Museum of Goldsmithery, on the main street west of the square, is a real gem. ****Camping: *On the west side of the square, drive up the small hill toward the tiny church. Stay right, taking the narrow road closest to the Vistula River, ul. Krakowska. Drive west for just over a kilometer. Camping Dom Turysty, ul. Krakowska 61 (081-810-036); on the river; well maintained; open June-August; $$$$.

BIALOWIEZA NATIONAL PARK

In the early 1900s, extinction threaten the European Bison, the biggest mammal on the continent. In 1929, the citizens of Bialowieza attempted to save their beloved wild animal by bringing zoo-kept animals to their vast forest and breeding them. The once royal hunting grounds was designated a national park with strict regulations on entry. The experiment was so successful that today it supplies zoos all over the world and almost 300 roam in the park alone. Along with bison you can admire tarpan, a small wild horse distinguished by a dark stripe running from head to tail. By selective breeding the Poles have been able to preserve the animal, indigenous to the Ukrainian steppes, with its original traits. The successful breeders also created a new animal-a cross between a bison and cow they call zubron. Ancient trees, some over four centuries old are named after monarchs. You lean back and look way up at them in the Royal Oaks Way. The park can only be entered with a guide. To arrange an English speaking guide, call the park office a day ahead (085-12-295); open daily. Cycling is a terrific way to get around in the

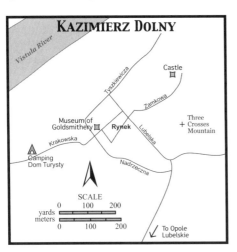

park.   Bicycle rental is available if you haven't brought your own. Your guide will also ride a bike. Horse-drawn carriages and walking are also popular ways to see the park's treasures. Visit the excellent natural history museum first to bring more meaning to your experience. A self-guided brochure of the museum is available in English; closed Monday. Directions: 52km south of Bialystok on 19 exit at the village of Bielsk Podlaski onto 689, and drive 44km east to the park entrance. ****Camping: *One kilometer south of the park entrance in the village of Grodek.   Camping Bialowieski (085-12-804); simple; open June-August; $.

THE GREAT MASURIAN LAKES

Canoeists, yacht enthusiasts, and kayakers put this extensive waterway of rivers, lakes, and canals at the top of their list. The Krutynia Kayak Route is popular for those wanting to spend a week paddling and camping. All types of boating equipment are readily available for rental. Cycling or walking along the lakes and through forests is also refreshing and tranquil. For a break

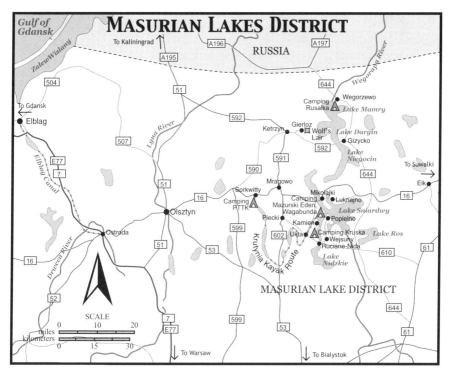

from nature, spend an hour or so seeing the massive concrete ruins of Hitler's Wolf's Lair.
To book an organized trip for the Krutynia Kayak route, call the OZGT office in Olsztyn a couple of weeks in advance. (089-275-156) To try it on your own, stop in Olsztyn at the outdoor equipment store, Sklep Podroznika, to purchase a map and get advice. Both businesses are in the old town behind the tourist office, close to the High Gate. If you prefer to let someone else navigate, take the excursion boat down the Elblag Canal. It's an unusual trip with five slipways and some dry land, rail-mounted trolleys. Call first to check the schedule. In Elblag (089-50-324-307); in Ostroda (089-88-463-871). The open-air farming village museum in Olsztynek is particularly pleasant with hollyhocks, heartwarming little cottages, and old-fashioned tools. Directions: Northeast corner of town.

Wolf's Lair, Hitler's headquarters, is an eerie place. The paths leading to the ruins of huge concrete bunkers can be cycled, but most people walk. Purchase an English guide. Directions: Take the main road 592 in the direction of Gizycko for eight kilometers. Drive northeast of town. Turn onto the small road for Gierloz. It's located in the forest east of Ketrzyn. The ticket/parking admission is expensive for Poland.

Elegant and enchanting, the swans at the Luknajno Reserve regally glide by as if they were Parisian models posing for a photographer. Directions: Drive northeast out of Mikolajki for five kilometers on a small dirt road paralleling 16 on the south side, to Lake Luknajno. Follow the sign to wiezy widokowej or viewing tower.

The fascinating Popielno Tarpan is a breeding station research institute If time permits go there and wait to see if you can join a pre-booked tour group to admire and learn about the small wild horses. Directions: From Ruciane, head north on a small road in the direction to the tiny village Wejsuny. Take the road heading north in the direction of Popielno.

****Camping: *In Sorkwitty (a stop in the road about ten kilometers west of Mragowo) cross the rail tracks and small bridge on 16, turning south onto a small road. Camping PTTK, on the lake; bungalows; boat rental; well maintained; open June-August; $. *South of Mikolajki, eleven kilometers on 609 in the direction of Ruciane, then turn east and go for about six kilometers on a small narrow dirt road in the direction of Nowy Most and Iznota. Camping Mazurski Eden (089-231-669); remote; on the lake; well maintained; open June-August; $$. *In Mikolajki, on 609 in the direction of Ruciane. Camping Wagabunda, ul. Lesna 2 (089-816-018); on the lake; close to town and excursion boats; boat rental; bungalows; well maintained; open May-September; $$. *South of Mragowo on 602, exit east onto 610 at Piecki. Then drive north on a small road in the direction of Wygryny and Kamien, about four kilometers east of tiny village Ukta. Camping Kruska (089-231-597); remote; on the lake; well maintained; open June-August; $$. *North of Gizycko about 22km on 644, just south of Wegorzewo on the lake. Camping Rusalka (089-772-191); bungalows; boat rental; close to excursion boats; well maintained; open June-August; $$.

GDANSK

Being the key port in Eastern Europe has given Gdansk a tumultuous and fascinating history. Meticulous and complex restoration has brought this city, once in complete rubble, back to its 16th century elegance. Home to heroes of the Solidarity Movement as well as to famous authors, scientists, and artists, it enchants and awes. Follow the signs for Glowne Miasto, or main town. Parking is not difficult. Use the brick tower of St. Mary's Church to orient yourself. Pick up a *What, Where, When Guide* at any hotel to check on scheduled events in this very lively, interesting city.

The always bustling waterfront is a hub of activity with ships entering the canal-way of the Motlawa River. At its northern end, look for the Gdansk Crane, which was the largest in the world during the 15th and 16th centuries. Now meticulously rebuilt and part of the fascinating Maritime Museum it is housed in old granaries and a freighter across the waterway. Ride the

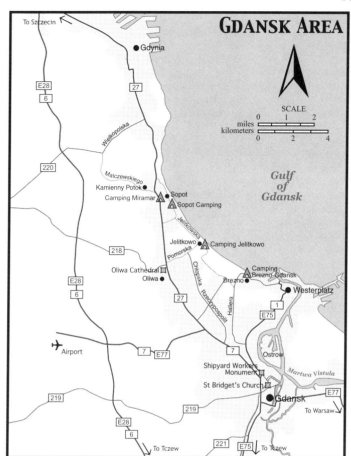

shuttle boat over, or take a leisurely stroll or bike ride by crossing the waterway via the bridge at the Green Gate.

The Green Gate is the entrance to Gdansk's old marketplace, a festive place with rousing music, entertaining street theater, and enticing aromas. The marketplace is most lively during the Dominican Fair held in the first weeks of August. Rest around Neptune's Fountain, where you can marvel at the gilded figure of King Zygmunt August situated atop the pinnacle of the graceful tower of the town hall now housing Gdansk's Historical Museum. In the museum, go directly upstairs and climb the tower for a great view, then examine the photo exhibit of the city's destruction and restoration on the second floor. The Red Room has a richly ornamented ceiling and displays paintings depicting Polish life.

Back on the square, just behind the fountain, view the giant Renaissance tile stove in Artus Court. Then walking east from the immense St. Mary's Church, find ul. Mariacka, a street that is painstakingly restored to the tiniest detail. Take an excursion boat out to historic Westerplatte, where World War II began. Boats leave from the wharf by the Green Gate.

For Solidarity history, go a few blocks north of St. Mary's Church to just south of the Radunia

Canal and St Bridget's Church. The clergy and parishioners of St Bridget risked their lives in the strong support of the dockyard workers. Touching bas-relief works depicting Solidarity's history are on its north aisle. Cross over the canal to spend time at the touching Moument to the Shipyard Workers who gave their lives in protest. Reflect on Czeslaw Milosz's poem at the base.

In the suburb of Oliwa is a famous cathedral well known for its lavishly decorated organ. You can enjoy its rich and sonorous tones at short recitals given throughout the day. In July and August, during the International Organ Music Festival, its special recitals are on Fridays. Directions: Drive north of the Gdansk on 27. Exit at Spacerowa/ 218. The cathedral complex is at this fork.

In August the fashionable seaside resort of Sopot, just north of Gdansk, is alive with the International Song Festival. The main festival takes place in the amphitheater at Opera Lesna, on the west side of town, but music lilts out all over the area. Jazz lovers will want to arrange being in Gdynia, a few kilometers farther north, for the Gdynia Summer Jazz Days.

****Camping: *North end of Sopot, off 27. Exit east, just south of the exit for Kamienny Potok. Camping Miramar, ul. Zamkowa Gora 25 (058-518-011); best in the Gdansk area; within walking distance of the beach; well maintained; open June-August; $$$. *South end of Sopot, exit off 27 for the Grand Hotel, then drive south about one kilometer. Sopot Camping, ul. Bitwy pod Plowcami 73 (058-516-523); close to the beach; casual maintenance; open June-August; $$. *In the suburb Jetitkowo, ten kilometers north of Gdansk, exit east off 27 onto ul. Pomorska and drive towards the Bay. Camping Jelitkowo, ul. Jelitkowska 23 (058-553-2731); close to the beach; well maintained; open June-August; $$$. *Just north of the old town exit, go towards the Bay and ship-

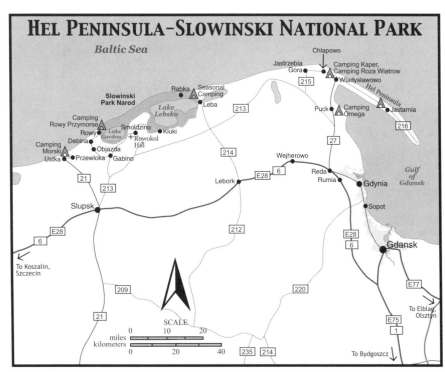

yards on E75/1. At the end of the road, drive north along the main road, passing the port tram station to Brzezno. Camping Brzezno-Gdansk, ul. Hallera 234 (058-435-531); closest to Gdansk; fair maintenance; open June-August; $$$.

HEL PENINSULA

Unique in size and beauty, this picturesque finger of clean, sandy beach juts out of the northwest end of the Bay of Gdansk and is perfect place to rest, swim, and lay in the sun. Wind surfing is a popular sport. Stock up with supplies before driving out. ****Camping: *From Wladyslawow, drive east in the direction of Jastarnia on 216. Camping Na Skarpie, ul. Rozewska 9 (058-749-095); well located and maintained; open June-August; $$$.   Camping Nowa Maszoperia, ul. Mickiewicza (058-752-348); on the beach; popular with surfers; fair maintenance; open June-August; $$.

BALTIC BEACHES
WLADYSLAWOW

If your schedule doesn't allow enough time to go out to the Hel pennisula, this lovely little port town is a nice substitute. ****Camping: *West of town three kilometers on the beach road. Camping Kaper (741-486); in a recreational area; well maintained; open June-August; $$. *Farther west on the beach road to Chlapowo. Camping Roza Wiatrow, ul. Zeromskiego (740-544); smaller; bungalows; well maintained; open June-August; $$. *In Puck, overlooking the Bay. Camping Omega, ul. Nowy Swiat 23 (732-980); within walking distance to the beach; well maintained; open June-August; $$.

SLOWINSKI NATIONAL PARK

The vast 120-foot-high dunes of Slowinski National Park, a UNESCO listed biosphere, make a mini-Sahara Desert-like experience. South of the dunes, a reed-lined lagoon, Jezioro Lebsko, lists 250 bird species that migrate through or live there permanently. Directions: Drive west from the seaside resort town of Leba to Rabka. For big dune exploration go three kilometers farther. A mini-bus provides rides.

In the village of Smoldzino, the park's Museum of Natural History has an exhibit of the local flora and fauna. Walk up Rowokol Hill, west of the village, and climb the steps of the observation tower for a wonderful panorama of the whole park. Directions: Drive southwest of Leba on 213. Exit the graceful tree-lined road, and drive north on a small, scenic road to Smoldzino.

In the hamlet of Kluki, you can meander around the best of the country's open-air farm-village museums. Warmly welcoming visitors, the staff maintains the authentic old gardens, houses, and barns with pride. Directions: From Smoldzino, drive east on the small road to Kluki. ****Camping: *West of Smoldzino on the Baltic coast, take the small road west of the lagoon Gardno in the direction of the tiny village of Objazda. Then continue to the coast road at Debina, and go a bit farther north to the village of Rowy. Camping Rowy Przymorse, ul. Baltycka 85 (141-839); close to the beach; bungalows; good maintenance; open Jun-August; $$. *Out of Slupsk, drive north to the Baltic and Ustka on 21. Then follow signs to Przewloka. Camping Morski, ul. Armii Krajowej (144-789); bungalows; within walking distance to beach; good maintenance; open June-August; $$. *In Leba, follow the main road into town, 214. This is a popular seaside resort with lots of camping. All the camping places are open June-August. On the west side of the river on ul. Turystycana.

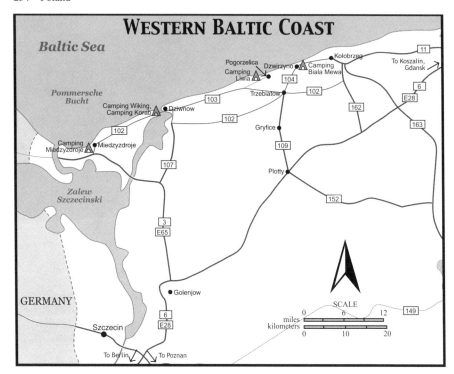

Intercamp (661-380); well maintained; $$$. Camping Rafael (661-972); good maintenance; $$.
Camping Lesny (661-380); well maintained; $$$.   *In town, on ul. Nadmorska. Camping
Przymorze, (661-304); good maintenance; $$. Camping Ambre (662-472); good maintenance; $$.

WESTERN BALTIC COAST

For some beach time on the Baltic Sea, these are good places to soak up the sun and salt air with
the locals; open June-August. ****Camping: *In Miedzyzdroje on the Baltic, take 3/E65 north,
then drive north on the beach road 102. It's southwest of town. Camping Miedzyzdroje, ul. Polna
10a (096-780-275); within walking distance of the beach; good maintenance; $$$. *Farther east
on 102, close to Dziwnow. Camping Wiking, ul. Wolnosci 3 (096-813-493); close to the beach;
bungalows; well maintained; $$$. *In the same area, Camping Korab, ul. Slowackiego 8 (096-
813-569); within walking distance of the beach; good maintenance; $$. *North to the Baltic on
109, take 103 to Pogorzelica; it's two kilometers west of town. Camping Liwia, ul. Wojska Pol. 2
(096-163-111); close to the beach; bungalows; well maintained; $$. *15km west of Kolobrzeg,
take the beach road west to Dzwirzyno. Camping Biala Mewa, ul. Wyzwolenia 42 (096-585-402);
bungalows; well maintained; $$$.

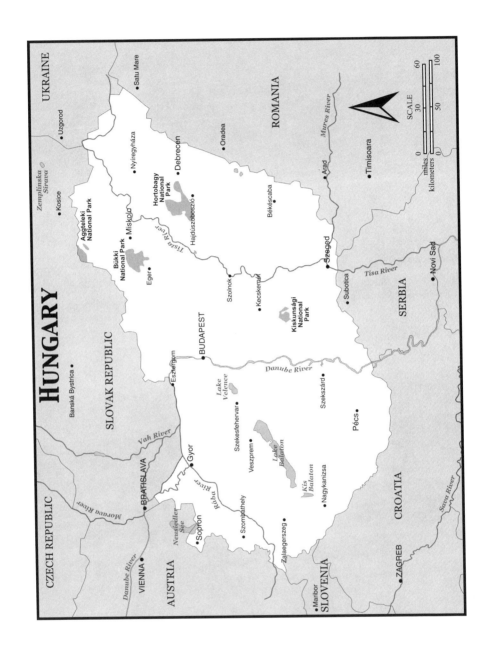

HUNGARY

Hungary's big sky countryside rolls out under a lazy sun ripening rich fields of wheat, corn, and the fruit of vineyards and orchards. Enormous sunsets explode in a full palate of brilliant golds and reds. Under lacy willows, lazy rivers are shaded for quiet anglers and watering cows. Like France is famous for its cuisine, Hungary is famous for its thermal spas. Under vaulted domes, built by their Turkish conquerors, the famous and the infamous alike shed their clothes and soak, gaining solace for their aching muscles and weary minds. Surviving a variety of regimes and revolutions, its music is at once dreamy and high spirited and can be easily enjoyed because of inexpensive ticketing. Hungarians have a highly developed sense of hilarity and a musical event can encompass Cossack acrobatics, Viennese waltzes, Gypsy folklore, Yiddish melodies, and a military band. Audiences laugh and vigorously clap their hands rhythmically. At the morning market, you'll see astounding piles of red, yellow, and orange sweet peppers. The luscious peaches, fragrant plums, and spicy sausages will be hard to pass up. The farm families do not solicit or plea for a sale but instead stand with dignified simplicity by their market tables. They exchange cheerful smiles with you and are grateful for a sale. Often holding down two jobs at once, city dwellers are intent on making a living. They exude the same Horatio Alger energy and strength that added to America's melting pot. Today young energetic and bright business entrepreneurs provide the lively pulse and tempo to Budapest.

Hungarians have been in the tourist business for a long time and know how to keep their customers happy. The country has long been a popular destination for vacationing Austrians, Germans, and Dutch who come for a relaxing, unpretentious good time and to shop where the price is less than at home. Highways are well paved, and signposting is good. Maps are excellent and up-to-date. Gas is plentiful. Locals are helpful. Parking is no more difficult than at home. With the exception of Budapest, it is easy to drive into the city center and find parking close to the historic area. Farmer's markets are held daily except Sunday and are easy to find in the small towns and villages. They are usually held close to the main square and begin closing at noon. Big chain supermarkets are open everyday including Sundays. Food is plentiful, of excellent quality, and inexpensive.

Many campgrounds have outdoor thermal pools. Besides being a great way to relax at day's end, they are wonderful places to meet fellow travelers. There is always space for a tent and car or small RV, so don't hesitate to travel in the high season when the weather is better and the festivals are happening. Hungarian campground owners want to appeal to an international clientele, so they maintain their comfortable and homey campgrounds well. Most campgrounds charge around $20 for two persons, a tent, and a car. You don't need to call ahead unless the campground is very popular or you are at the edge of the season and want to make sure they are open.

BUDAPEST

Eight beautifully designed bridges span the wide and powerful Danube River, connecting once imperial Buda to commercial Pest. There's a grandiosity about Budapest's 19th century architecture that reflects the sense of their own glory during the Austrian-Hungarian monarchy that oversaw the Slavic countries. Castle Hill, a tiny Baroque city, is a UNESCO listed open-air

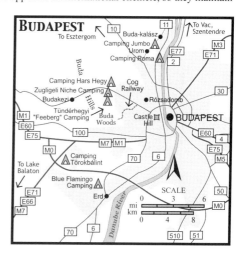

museum. Knowing that it has been reduced to rubble and rebuilt with devastating regularity can't help but impress. Use your guidebook or information from the tourist office or a nearby hotel to enlighten your stroll through this fascinating area. It's not hard to imagine the days of its great splendor. Inside the palace in the Museum of the Hungarian Working Class, don't spend much time looking at the restrictive and repetitive art designed to inspire happiness in a working class. Instead, move on to the historical documentary photos. They provide a somber bridge for mastering the mourning. To get to Castle Hill, take the Metro to Moszkva ter. Walk across the bridge over the square. Then continue on Vartok utca until you come to a large junction of streets. You'll see the Vienna Gate just beyond. If you prefer, an inexpensive tourist bus marked "Budavari Siiklo" at the bridge will take you to Clark Adam ter near the Chain Bridge, where there's a cable car that will take you up to the top.

Be sure to ride the Cog Railway up to the top of the Buda Hills and then stroll through the Buda Woods, where the beautiful views and tranquility encourage smiles between you and other strollers. In August folk-culture wood-carvers, jewelers, and sculptors display and sell their work. To catch the Cog Railway, walk from Mozkva ter toward the circular high-rise Hotel Budapest; the station is just opposite it.

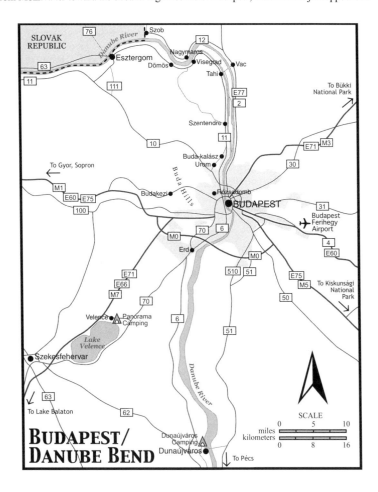

All of the world's great opera and ballet stars have performed in Budapest's sumptuous and famous opera house. Ask for a calendar of events before your leave home, and book tickets ahead; fax 361-302-4290. To watch the flamboyant and intricate footwork of handsome men and the swirl of embroidered skirts and petticoats worn by their lovely partners as they dance to the indefatigable finger work of Hungarian gypsy music, purchase tickets at the Municipal Cultural House. To reach the main tourist office, take the metro to the Deak ter. Here you'll be able to get a wealth of information about not only Budapest, but all of Hungary.   Public transport in Budapest is excellent and inexpensive.

Don't leave Budapest without soaking in one of their famous thermal baths. Popular with an international clientele, they are easy to experience. Take your bathing suit if you want to use the large communal men and women pool as part of your experience. You'll need to rent a cap if you don't have one. In the foyer pay for what you want: hot-tub like thermal baths; sauna; massage; the large communal pool. You'll be given a locker. Undress and go into the misty massage room for a dousing and vigorous rub if you have chosen to include a massage, then to the shower, sauna, and hot tubs. Donning your bathing suit, enter the communal pool area for a cool down. It's a very pleasant custom to indulge in elaborate ice cream affairs afterwards. The baths vary in atmosphere; some have an Old World-elegant atmosphere, others are older with exotic Turkish touches, and some are high tech modern. The tourist office can help you make a selection and give you directions on how to use public transport to get there.

****Camping:

*Coming from the north 11-Szentendre-Budapest. Watch for signage ten kilometers from Budapest center; just before the rail tracks. Camping Roma, Szentendre ut. 189 (1-368-6260); easy to find; large; popular with RVs; close to the Danube; close to public transportation; swimming pool; fair maintenance; open year round; $$$. *Coming from the south, off the ring road MI/E60/E75 exit for Torokbalint, and drive three kilometers. Camping Torokbalint (23-335-364); close to public transportation; swimming pool; well maintained; open all year; $$$. *Coming from the northwest, exit 10 for Urom, then drive a little farther to Budakalasz. Camping Jumbo (26- 351- 251); public transportation; swimming pool; well maintained; open May-September; $$.

The following are harder to find but closer to the city center, with short rides on public transport to the historic area.

*If you are coming from the city, take the main road from the Margrit bridge and drive west. Stay right and west at the junction. You want to be on Moszkva. If you are coming from the western edge of the city, take M1/E60/E75 for Budakezi, then continue driving towards Budapest until the first stop light. Follow signage up the narrow winding road. Camping Tunderhegyi (Freeberg), Szilassy ut. 8 (60- 336-256); swimming pool; well maintained; open May-August; open all year; $$. *At the bottom of the Buda Hills, close to the cable car to the Buda Hills in a small wooded area. Zugligeli Niche Camping (1-200-8346); well maintained; open all year; $$$. *At the edge of the Buda Hills and road 100, halfway between Budakezi and Rozsadomb. Camping Hars Hegy (1-361- 115-1482); bungalows; fair maintenance; open May-September; $$.

South of Budapest: *Off 70 towards Erd, follow signposting north of town. Blue Flamingo Camping (23-375-328); a natural area with bungalows; well maintained; open all year; $$. *On Lake Velence, halfway between Budapest and Lake Balaton. Exit M7 at km 44.5 and gas station for Velence, and go two kilometers further. Panorama Camping (22-472-043); a recreational area; bungalows; well maintained; open May-September; $$. *Directly south of Budapest off the Danube River road 6, close to the car ferry and stadium, west of Dunaujvaros. Dunaujvaros Camping (25- 310-285); bungalows; open May-September; $.

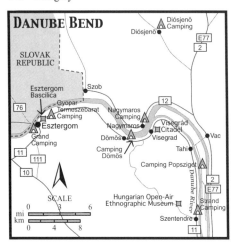

DANUBE BEND

SLOVAK
REPUBLIC

Esztergom
Bascilica

Szob

76

Gyopar
Termeszebarat
Camping

Esztergom

Grand
Camping

11

111

10

SCALE

0   3   6
mi
km

0   4   8

Diósjenö
Diósjenö Camping

E77

2

12

Nagymaros
Camping

Nagymaros

Dömös

Camping
Dömös

Visegrád
Citadel
Visegrad

Vac

Tahi

Camping Popsziget

Hungarian Open-Air
Ethnographic Museum

Szentendre

2

E77

Strand
Camping

11

DANUBE BEND AREA

In this area north of Budapest, friendly little towns are steeped in history, and a wide variety of little shops and galleries help fill out interesting walks and bike trips. You might want to splurge on an excursion boat ride either to or from Budapest, taking the train or bus one way. Camping here is more tranquil than in the city and you can take moonlight walks or bicycle rides along the Danube right from the campground. In each town, close to the main square, you'll find a tourist office where a cheerful English-speaking staff will take time to assist you. Become part of the coming and going of people heading for the open-air markets with baskets. The old-fashioned conviviality and shared smiles with farmers wearing weather-worn hats and wives in colorful scarves makes you feel happy as you shop.

Szentendre has attracted artists since the early 1900s so it's charmingly atmospheric. Settled by Serbians fleeing Turkish rule, it has a Balkan flair. Down its sloping narrow streets and stone stairways, you'll find tiny intriguing Serbian Orthodox churches and artistic museums. Don't miss the Magrit Kovacs Museum; her ceramic sculpture captures Hungary's struggle in a heartwarming way. Directions: Off the northeast corner of the square. Throughout the summer the historic main square is a natural setting for concerts ranging from classic to folk and rock. Set on a hillside outside of Szentendre, thatched-roofed farmhouses from all the regions of Hungary are lovingly filled with old-fashioned household furniture and tools. This Ethnographic Museum keeps the Hungarian heritage alive for both themselves and visitors with folklore shows performed throughout the summer. Directions: Follow signposting off 11 in Szentendre and drive west up the hill five kilometers.

Farther north, Visegrad sits up on a hill looking down on the Danube Bend. Its mighty Citadel shouldn't be missed. Artifacts from 14th and 15th centuries establish an old glory, and can be examined in the museum in the Solomon Tower, close to the palace ruins. In July you can join the locals cheering on their favorite combatant dressed in period costume and competing in a medieval tournament. Dappled light drifts through the leafy woodland Pilis hill trails leading to sweeping vista points. Directions: Trailheads are marked from the excursion center in the village of Dobogoko.

At the end of the Danube Bend, Estergom's Bascilica, the largest in Hungary, serenely gazes down from its hilltop location by the river. It is the country's ecclesiastical and historical heart, with altars and a treasury that are impressive. A very large and important collection of medieval religious art gleams with gold leaf and intricate wood carving in the Christian Museum; closed Monday. As you stand on the parapet looking down on the Danube River, imagine Charlemagne's and later the Hapsburg's troops coming down the river. Then turn and imagine the Roman and Ottoman Empires coming up the river. While camping on the edge of the river, Marcus Aurelius wrote his famous Meditations, and it was here over one thousand years ago that Hungary's first king Stephen I was crowned. Today you can see the ruins of a small bridge that connected Hungary to Slovakia before it was blown up by the Nazis. One day there will be another bridge, but in the meantime a small car ferry makes crossings. To get the full impact of the strategic location, park at the town square in Estergom and walk up the hill. Directions: Follow signposting off 11.

****Camping:

*In Szentendre, on the Danube side of road 11, north of town by the wooden bridge. Strand Camping (26- 310-697); fair maintenance; open June-August; $$. *On Szentendre Island. Cross over to the island by car from Vac or Tahi, and take the main road south. Camping Popsziget (26-310-697); associated with a hotel; casual maintenance; open June-August; $$. *At the Bend on the Danube in Domos, exit 11-Buda-Estergom in Domos. Domos Camping (33- 371-163); nice location; swimming pool; biking and walking trails; bungalows; public transport to Budapest; good maintenance; open June-August; $$. *In Esztergom, just at the edge of town. From the ferry landing and tourist parking area, drive to the river road and follow signposting. Grand Camping (33-402-513); swimming pool; view of the Basilica; within walking distance of town; good maintenance; June-September; $$. *North of Esztergom, off 11-Budapest-Esztergom. Gyopar Termeszebarat Camping (06-333-11401); view of the Basilica; within walking distance of town; quiet; well maintained; open May-September; $$$. *On the north side of the Danube Bend Area. Across from Visegrad in Nagymaros, exit off 12-Vac-Szob then drive 12km towards the Danube; or from the car ferry, drive towards Nagymaros. Nagymaros Camping (06-265-4124); affiliated with a motel; fair maintenance; open May-September; $$. *For a more remote campground, drive north of Vac on road 12, then turn north away from the Danube onto road 2. Exit onto a small road for Diosjeno, just south of Tolmacs, passing the reservoir. Diosjeno Camping (35-364-134); close to the river; in a pine forest; bungalows; well maintained; open June-August; $$.

NORTHWESTERN HUNGARY
SOPRON

The wealthy Hungarian Eszterhazy family chose Sopron for the location of their lovely palace. Set in a small wooded area, it has a quiet elegance. Lizt was enticed to come and live in the palace, and for many years he conducted symphonies, wrote music, and gave music lessons to their children. The palace evokes the splendor of those by-gone days and is the area's highlight; open daily. Directions: 27km east of Sopron exit off 85 for Fertod. Sopron's easy charm and Baroque facades are best enjoyed by walking or cycling through its old town, where little museums, sweet smelling bakeries, and well-placed monuments offer pleasant suprise. From mid-June to mid-July, concerts, musical theater, and art exhibits enrich a stay. The thrill of hearing operatic love songs lilt through the acoustically perfect cave in nearby Fertorakos is a dramatic experience. Purchase tickets from home by faxing ahead; 3699-338-880. Directions: Northeast of town follow signposting for nine kilometers to the cave. ****Camping: *Southwest of Sopron, close to Brennbergbanya. Camping Ozon (99-331-144); thermal pool and sauna; bungalows; well maintained; open May-September; $$. *South of Sopran in Hegyko, west from the Eszterhazy Palace, exit the Sopron-Gyor road 85 at km 60.2 for Hegyko. Drive north three kilometers. Thermal Camping (99- 376-818); thermal and regular pools close by; well maintained; open May-September; $$. *East of Eszterhazy Palace,

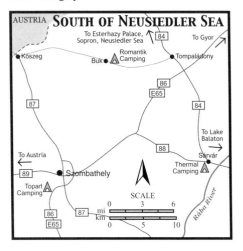

SOUTH OF NEUSIEDLER SEA

off Gyor-Budapest road 85, northeast of Kapuvar. Hansag Camping (96- 241-524); thermal and regular swimming pools close by; sauna; warm showers; well maintained; open June-August; $$

THE NEUSIEDLER SEA.

Birdwatchers and people who like long, quiet cycle rides or walks love this area. In the early morning great herons can be seen taking wing from reed beds and then cranking up over the misty sea. Swans with wings arched like the skirt of a prima ballerina float close to admirers. It's a vast marshland forming a 240 kilometer network of reed bed-lined canals. The quiet water sports of wind surfing and fishing from a rowboat are allowed; rentals are available in Fertorakas.

Directions: Southeast of town seven kilometers exit 84 in the direction of Balf and drive 12km. ****Camping: *In Balf. Camping Castrum Balf-Sopron (99- 357-024); thermal and regular pools close by; well maintained; open May-September; $$.

****South of the Neusiedler Sea enroute camping

Northwest of Szombathely and south of Sopran. Exit off road 86/E65 onto road 84, and drive north for two kilometers. At Tompaladony take the small road heading west in the direction of Buk. It's west of town. Romantik Camping (94- 358-362); swimming pool; biking and walking paths; open all year; $$. *In Szombathely, south of town, at the junction of roads 86 and 87, Topart Camping (94- 314-766); bungalows; well maintained; open June-August; $.   *East of Szombathely, south of Sarvar off road 88. Thermal Camping (95-320-228); thermal and regular swimming pools; thermal bath; sauna; massage; well maintained; open all year, $$.

PANNONHALMA ABBEY

Honored by a visit from Pope Paul II, who wanted to compliment the monastic community on their support of spiritual values, the Pannonhalma Abbey sits peaceful and unpretentious on a small hill over looking fertile farmlands. Excellent guided tours are given by students and are obligatory. If your visit coincides with an organ or choir recital in the basilica, don't miss it; closed Sunday and Monday. Directions: 20km south of Gyor exit off 82-Gyor-Veszprem at Ecs, and follow signposting. ****Camping: *In Pannonhalma, beneath the Benedictine Abbey on the south side. Panorama Camping (96 471-240); wonderful tiny restaurant; restful and popular spot with grand sunset views; terraced, grassy slope; well maintained; open May-September; $$.

****Around Gyor Enroute Camping:

*Just across the Slovak border on E60/1-Bratislava-Gyor north of Mosonmagyarovar, at km 155.2 by the gas station. Autoclub Camping (98- 315-883); close to the river and highway; well maintained; open April-October; $$. *Just east of Gyor, off the road M1/E60/E75-Budapest-Gyor, at km 121 in the suburb of Gyorszentivan. Camping Kiskut-Liget (96- 318-986); close to a branch of the Danube; affiliated with a motel; swimming pool; casual maintenance; open all year; $$. *East of Gyor, close to Komarom, off 10-Gyor-Komaron, on the south edge of town close to road 13. Camping Juno (34- 340-568); massage and thermal bath close by; affiliated with a hotel; well maintained; open April-September; $$. *In the same area. Thermal Camping (34-342-447); affiliated with a hotel; massage and thermal bath; both thermal and regular swimming pools; well maintained; open all year; $$. *East of Gyor close to Tata off M1/E60/E65-Gyor-Budapest, exit for Tatabanya centrum. Drive north in the direction of Tata on 100 for just over five kilometers. Oreg-to International Camping (34- 383-496); popular recreational area; affiliated with a motel; fair maintenance; open June-August; $$.

LAKE BALATON AREA

If you want to do some wind surfing or just enjoy soaking up the sun, this is the place. The huge silvery lake is only an hour from Budapest, and so is a popular getaway. The picturesque setting of the Tihany peninsula and its lovely Abbey Church draw camera-toting crowds, but you can have tranquility if you hike up to its inner lake, a favorite haunt for bird watchers. Take time to go north from Keszthely to Heviz. The huge thermal lake here is astonishing. For a small admission fee, you can spend a few hours or an entire day soaking up its warm therapeutic waters amidst water lilies. Directions: At the western edge of the lake at Keszthely, exit for Heviz and watch for signposting for Parkerdo. Cycling/walking paths edge the shoreline and it's warm enough to enjoy swimming with the swans. Rentals are available in the little villages for biking, wind surfing, or just floating.

****Camping: Lake Balaton is a major recreational area and campgrounds are plentiful. I've listed the smaller ones, which are still relatively large.

North side and east end of the Lake: *In Balatona Karatty, exit onto the Lake road 71. FKK Camping Piroska (88-481-084); popular; on the lake; diving platforms; separate nude sunbathing area; well maintained; open June-August; $$$. *In Balatonalmadi, at the northeast end of lake at

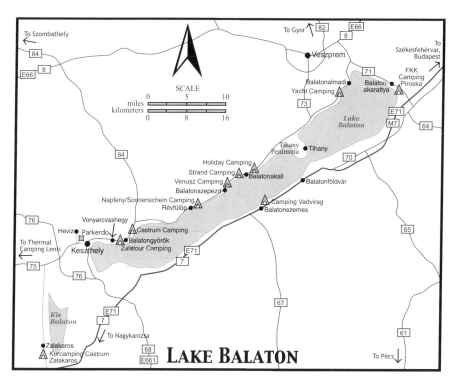

the yacht harbor. Yacht Camping, at km 25.5 (88-338-906); diving platform; well maintained; open June-September; $$$. *Halfway down the lake, four kilometers south of Tihany pennisula, in Balatonakali, on the lake. Holiday Camping, at km 52.5 (87- 44-40-93); diving platform; well maintained; open June-August; $$$. *In the same area. Strand Camping, at km 53.4 (87- 444-151); on the water; well maintained; open June-August; $$$. *A little farther west on the river road in Balatonszepezd. Venusz Camping, at km 61 (87- 468-048); on the lake; well maintained; popular; open June-September; $$$. *Close-by in Revfulop, Napfeny Sonnenschein Camping, at km 65.5 (87- 464-309); well maintained; open June-August; $$$. *Northwest end of the Lake. Balatongyorok. Castrum Camping, at km 94.7 (83-146-666); popular with wind surfers; well maintained; open June-August; $$$. *In the same area but in Vonyarcvashegy. Zalatour Camping, at km 96.9 (83-348-044); large with lots of vacation-home campers; on the lake; bungalows; well maintained; open June-August; $$. *South side, midway of the lake in Balatonszumes, west of Balatonfolder. Camping Vadvirag, at km 134 (84-360-114); on the lake; well maintained; open June-August; $$. *West of Lake Balaton, exit off road 75 and drive south. Southwest of Lenti. Thermal Camping Lenti (92-351-368); thermal and regular swimming pools; thermal bath; bungalows; open all year; $$. *Southwest of Lake Balaton, exit north off road E71 for Zalakaros. Then drive to the west side of the reservoir lake Kis-Balaton, south of town. Kurcamping Castrum Zalakaros (93- 358-610); excellently maintained; open all year; $$.

NORTHEASTERN HUNGARY
AGGETELEK NATIONAL PARK
Deep inside the spectacular caves of Aggetelek National Park you are on own in almost silence. The sound of water dripping and the swooshing of passing bats, not to mention the popular pastime of searching for darkness-loving salamanders with your flashlight, all make for an errie experience. The park is UNESCO listed; open daily. Directions: From Miskolc drive 14km north on 26 to Kazincbarcika. Continue another 29km. Just before the border into the Slovak Republic exit north and drive 30km to Aggtelek and the park entrance. ****Camping: In Aggtelek Camping Baradia (48-343-073); bungalows; well maintained; open May-September; $$.

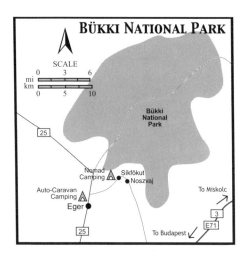

EGER AND MISKOLE
Music is a vital force in Miskole. An international festival of Dixieland music gets things hopping at the 12th century Diosgyor Castle in the first week of July, and a week later the Kalaka Folk Festival draws its international crowd to one of the most pretigious festivals of folk music in Eastern Europe. Hungarian Baroque comes alive in Eger's old town and castle during the last week in July and first part of August, when you can share with the locals the excitement of dancers, comedians, crafts, and delicious food. ****Camping: 16km south west of Miskolc. Drive southwest out of Miskilc on a small road in the direction of Bukkszentkereszt. Drive through the village continuing another four kilometers. Fogado Camping (46-390-370); lovely setting; popular

with families; need International Camping Carnet card; bungalows; open May-September; $$. In Eger. North of town follow signposting off 24. Tulipan Camping (36-410-580); bungalows; thermal pool; well maintained; open May-September; $$$.

BUKKI NATIONAL PARK

Once covered by sea, this region is riddled with caves and sink holes. A walking path leads to the 17-meter Fatyol cascade. Directions: Drive east of Eger on a small road for ten kilometers in the direction of Silkfokut/Noszvag and follow signposting to the park entrance.

HORTOBAGY NATIONAL PARK

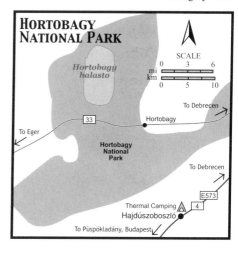

Steppe-like, this grassland area known as the Puszta is an important nesting area for migrating herons, great white egrets, and black-headed gulls. Spoonbills nest in the strictly protected fish ponds. The interpretive center is off 33 at km 79. ****Camping: *At the western edge of the Bukki Nemzerti Park. Nomad Camping (36-463-363); hiking trails into the mountains; bungalows; well maintained; open June-September; $$. *Exit off highway 3 onto 25-Kercsend-Ozd, in the direction of Eger. FKK Auto-Caravan Camping, at km 17 (36-410-558); affiliated with a motel; separate nudist area; casual maintenance; open May-September; $$. *31km northeast of Szolnok exit 4/E60 at Kenderes. Drive north on 34 in the direction of Kunhegyes for 17km. Continue to the reservoir lake and village of Abadszalok. Camping Fuzes in Abadszalok (59-355-406); large recreational area; bungalows; on the lake; open June-August; $$.

****Enroute camping close to the Ukraine border: *34km east of Nyiregyhaza, exit off highway 41 at Vasarosnameney. Pass through the village of Jand to Tivadar. Katica Camping, in Tivadar (44-363-859); close to the Tisza River; fair maintenance; open June-August; $. *Northwest of Nyiregyhaza 40km, off highway 38 exit for Tokaj. It's close to the Tisza bridge and river. Pelsoczy Camping in Tokaj (47-352-626); boat launch; close to the railroad; fair maintenance; open May-August; $$.

****Other enroute camping on the Great Plains: *Almost midway between Budapest and Debrecen, not far from Hortobagyi National Park, exit highway 33 at Tiszafured. It's sign-posted west of town by the railroad tracks. Thermal Camping in Tiszafured (59-352-911); close to the Tisa River and thermal facility with both regular and thermal pools; thermal bath; massage; well maintained; open May-September; $$. *East of Szolnok 41km, exit E573/4 at Kisujszallas, driving south in the direction of Turkeve for 14km. Thermal Camping in Turkeve (56-362-608); good location at the north end of town; thermal pool and bath; bungalows; well maintained; open May-September; $$. *In the same area, in Torokszentmiklos, on the north end. Kek Boa Thermal Camping in Torokszentmiklos (20-438-841); thermal pool; well maintained; open June-September; $$. * Southwest of Debrecen, exit 4 at Puspokladany. Arnyas Camping in Puspokladany (54-451-329); associated with a thermal bath motel; well maintained; open all year; $$. *Southwest of Debrecen 21km, exit off highway E573/4 for Hajduszoboszlo and the sports center. Thermal Camping in Hajduszoboszlo (52-365-991); tennis; thermal pool and bath; well maintained; open May-September; $$.

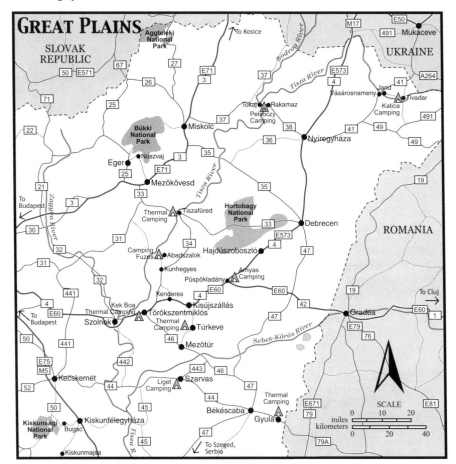

GREAT PLAINS

SLOVAK REPUBLIC

UKRAINE

ROMANIA

SOUTHEAST
KISKUNSAG NATIONAL PARK

This is an environmentally fragile area of dunes and grassy desert, where horse and man, fused as one, ride like phantoms of their steppe-born Magyar forebears. Hawks perch on fence posts, and owls hoot during the night and predawn hours. It's fun to join into the touristy activities offered in the park. In barnyards filled with the savory aromas of barbecues, you'll see colorfully dressed Gypsies who fill the air with music quavering with sorrow and hardship or wildly exultant with dance. Get into a saddle and head out over the seemingly endless plains, or just enjoy looking into the eyes of the beloved Hungarian horses. Directions: Drive to the entrance out of Bugac at Bugaci Karikas Csarda, or take the narrow-gauge train from the Kecsmet KK station. On the train, it's about a one-hour ride to the Bugugac felso station and then a short walk to the park entrance. From the park entrance, take a horse-pulled wagon ride to the Herder Museum, horse stables, and horse show. In July, don't miss the Szeged Festival, where street food and music abound. Salami lovers will want to visit the famous Pick Salami factory in Szeged. ****Camping: *South of the entrance to Kiskunsagi National Park, on a small highway between highway 53 and 5/E75. Exit for Kiskunmajsa and drive northeast of town. Camping and Motel Kiskunmajsa; thermal and regular pools; thermal bath; fair maintenance; $$.

****Camping close to the Rumania border: In Gyula. Thermal Camping in Gyula (66-463-704); bungalows; well maintained; open all year; $. *North of Szeged, in Szarvas, close to the river Koros. Liget Camping in Szarvas (66- 311-954); affiliated with a hotel; sauna; well maintained; open all year; $$.

SOUTHWEST

PECS AREA AND THE WINE GROWING REGION

With softly rolling farmlands and ancient vineyards, this beautiful, enchanting corner of Hungary invites you to relax in thermal pools and to sip the famous Villany wines. In the cosmopolitan city of Pecs you can wander through an exotic Turkish mosque, visit a memorable Jewish synagogue, then absorb its lively university atmosphere at a sidewalk cafe. ****Camping: *North of Pecs, exit the northeast end of Dombovar and drive in the direction of Hogyesz for a several kilometers. Gunaras Camping in Dombovar, at km 90 (74-465-523); thermal and regular pools; thermal bath; bungalows; warm showers; fair maintenance; open May-September; $$. *North of Pecs on highway 66, exit west at Magyarszck and drive west on a small road along the rail tracks to the village of Magyarhertelend. It's on the

small lake. Camping Forras in Magyarherteled (72-390-777); thermal pool; well maintained; open May-September; $$. *In Pecs, north of town in the suburb of Misna, go in the direction of the TV tower. It's fairly close to Vidam Park and Zoo. The road is fairly steep and not recommended for large RV's. Mandulas Camping (72-315-981); bungalows; fair maintenance; open May-September; $$. *South of Pecs in the famous grape-growing area of Villany, exit at Harkany from highway 58 at km 25.3. Camping Harkany (72-480-117); affiliated with a motel; thermal pool and bath; near the park; well maintained; open May-September; $$.

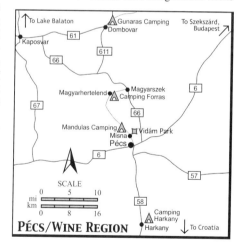

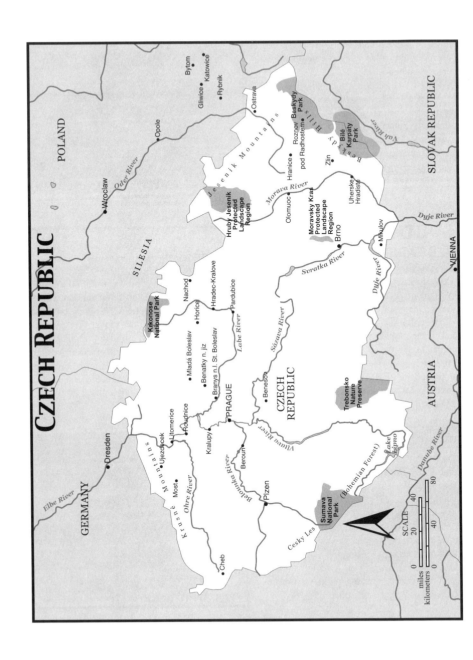

CZECH REPUBLIC

There's more to the richly historic Czech Republic than just Prague and thermal bath resorts. Weekend folk festivals in small towns bring the locals out in traditional dress for hotly contested folk dance contests. Kayakers and canoeists flock to the rivers, where they camp and sing around campfires. Rock climbers and hikers head north to areas that vie in beauty with Canyonlands in the U.S.A. UNESCO has tagged elegant Renaissance towns that are great for cafe sitting. Throughout, a light-hearted ambiance is fostered by the production of their world famous beers. Driving is not a problem. The roads are well marked, and once you are outside the major cities the traffic is light. Fuel is readily available. With the exception of Prague, it is easy to drive into historic areas and ample parking is available. Museums are inexpensive and generally closed on Mondays. In the harvest season, farmers' wives and children sell what's being harvested along the roadsides. Large shopping malls have found their way to the Czech Republic. You'll see them along the main roads on the outskirts of major cities. Cash machines located outside banks and in the arcade of large shopping areas, provide local currency. Plan to use local currency for almost everything in the country.

The Czechs adore the outdoors and you can join them happily camping with their families in scenic areas. Plumbing and level of maintenance is casual but the scenery and relaxed friendliness are exceptional. Most campgrounds charge just under $20 USA for two persons, a car, and a tent. Those close to major sights charge a little more.

PRAGUE

Prague reminds me of a beautiful brooch, carefully treasured and handed down by a grandmother to her granddaughter. The Vltava River and its lovely bridges are the booch's finely worked gold edging, and the multicolored gems are the spires of the Castle, the dome of St. Nicholas, the intriguing roof of the Synagogue, and the curved roof of the National Theatre. As you cross the Charles Bridge, a friendly Main Street-like walking bridge, you feel like you've entered a country fair. Next to a violinist playing Mozart is an artist painting scenes of the bridge. Farther down two girls are boogying to the beat of a small rock group next to jeweler selling handmade earrings, while Baroque statues gaze down with grandparent-like tolerance. Passing through the stately castle gate into the grandeur of the Castle District, you can't help but conjure up the sounds and smells of medieval Prague. The clip-clop of horse hooves are still heard. Just add the swish of taffata skirts, the raucous calls of vendors, and the lusty smell of leather. Called the Hradcany, it is a tiny city in itself, with museums, galleries, and gardens all in a setting of baroque architecture. Keep in mind that in Prague it's not the destination that is the most exciting part. It's the little surprises found in the nooks and crannies on the way there that is the most fun. The tourist office is inside the castle gate. Friendly English speaking staff can answer questions, and there are plenty of free maps and brochures about sights and cultural events

As you tread up the twisting narrow streets to Castle Hill, suddenly The Castle, written by Kafka, one of the Czech's most famous authors, makes sense. At the top, the views of Prague are fabulous. The well-designed garden graces the architecture with trees and shrubs of contrasting colors, magnificent rhododendrons and azaleas, and ribbon flower beds. If you're here at noon, you'll witness a whimsical brass band parade in the first courtyard. St. Vitus Cathedral's foundation was begun in the 14th century but wasn't completed until 1929, so there has been a long line of architects with a variety of ideas. Be sure to see the dazzling sapphire-the largest in the world-along with other beautiful jewels in the treasury. It's the intriguing stories about the various powers that have lived in the Old Royal Palace that give it life. Before you leave the hill, walk over to the northeast corner and roam through the Royal Gardens. The sgraffito or fine etchings in the ball court, and lovely arcaded summerhouse lend a hand in personalizing Prague's golden era; open daily. After returning to the bottom of the hill, called the Mala Strana, allow time to get lost in the

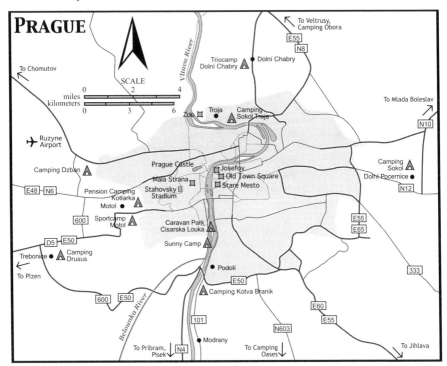

maze of cobblestone streets in search of the puppet museum. Puppets are an important part of Czech cultural history, and the charming little museum is worth finding; open daily. Afterwards, enjoy an excursion boat ride to rest and watch the historic area pass by; operating daily.

The right bank of Old Town is called the Stare Mestro. In its center is the Old Town Square. Admire the famed astronomical clock here. For 400 years, Jesus and his disciples have paraded through its doorways on the hour, followed by a skeletal figure of death reminding the town folk to mend their ways before it is too late. Pay homage to the Hus Monument by looking for the inscription, "Pravda vitezi" which means Truth prevails. Reflecting on Czech history, you'll understand why the monument is special in the hearts of Czechs today. Try to view the baubles and spires of the Tyn Cathedral from afar, as it's rather boxed in among the houses. Don't miss Josefov, the old Jewish quarter, once one of the most important centers in Europe. Now remodeled, it's a fascinating place. Jewish communities from all over Europe have donated treasured artifacts, making it a very rich collection; closed Saturday. Directions: North of the square.

Prague has long held music very close to its heart. Three opera houses, two symphony halls, and many historical settings make attending a performance very inviting. Mozart finished Don Giovanni at Villa Bertamka, which belonged to an intimate family friend. The piano he played and the rooms and study where he worked and enjoyed himself with his friends are open to wander through. Afterwards, you are treated to a violin-piano recital of his work; open daily. Directions: In the suburb of Smichov, south of Mala Strana. The tourist office staff will gladly help you make a selection for a musical experience that suits your interests.

****Camping:

*Coming in from the west on N6/E48, near the junction of 6/E48 and N600, in the suburb of Motol. Sportcamp Motol, Nad Hliniken 1202 (02-572-130); fair maintenance; open May-

September; $$$. *Near the airport, exit off N6/E48 and follow signposting for the stadium. Camping Dzban, nad Lavkou 3, (02-369-006); near the sports center and swimming pool; bungalows; open year round; $$.   *Closer to the historic area, on the Plzen/Prague road E50 follow signage to Centrum on Plzenska. Exit part way down the hill, going north onto Pod Kotarkou-there's a gas station and bus stop at the turnoff. Drive northwest up the hill, and just before the large school on the south side exit onto Kotlarka. Pension Camping Kotlarka, Kotlarka 115, (02-5721-0604); country setting in the city; small and tranquil; part of an old vineyard; affliated with a small hotel; close to public transportation; small restaurant; open all year; $$.

*Coming in from the south on 4, just north of the junction of N4 and E50 at Podoli. Caravan Park Cisarska Louka, Pristav c 599 (02-540-925); by the river; easy to find; close to the train to the historic area; well maintained; open all year; $$.   *In the same area, closer to the city, in the suburb of Stodulky/Smichov, at the junction of E50 and 600, on the river close to the yacht club. Sunny Camp, Smichovska ul.(02-528-264); on the Valtava River; well maintained; $$.   *Farther from the city, just south of the Prague suburb of Dolni Brezany, in between N4 and N603 on 101. Camping Oases (02-643-8345); well cared for; open June-August; $.   *On the east side of the river, exit 4 at Zbraslav, cross the Vltava river and head directly north on 101 to Modrany. Camping Kotva Branik (02-46-1712); close to the train to the city; bungalows; well maintained; open May-September; $$.   *Off D5/E50 exit for Trebonice. Camping Drusus in Trebonice (02-651-4391); not too far from the airport; well maintained; open May-September $$.

*Coming in from the north, in the Prague suburb of Troja near the zoo, not easy to find. Camping Sokol Toja, Trojska 171A (854-2908); close to public transport to the city; bungalows; fair maintenance; $$.   *Easier to find but farther from the city. Exit N608 for the Prague suburb of Dolni Chabry and follow signposting. Triocamp Dolni Chabry (02-688-1180); public transport to city; bungalows; well maintained; open year round; $$$. *Still farther from the city, in a recreational area on the Vltava River. Exit off N8/E55 for Veltrussy, then go north to the camping place on the river. Camping Obora in Veltrussy (02-524-530); bungalows; biking and boating; fair maintenance; $.

*Coming in from the east exit 12 at the junction of E65 and N12, at the Prague suburb of Dol Pocernice and follow signposting. Camping Sokol, nar Hrdinu 290 (02-727-501); bungalows; biking paths; train to the city center; well maintained; open May-September; $$$.

SIGHTS OUTSIDE OF PRAGUE
KUTNA HORA
Once an important, silver-rich city, Kutna Hora had wealthy merchants who blessed the city with a graceful square, a majestic Gothic cathedral, a memorable monastery, and an ossuary (a vault of bones of the dead). Today in the UNESCO listed square, you can sip espresso or beer in sidewalk cafe and reflect upon the patina and elegance. It's a very relaxed place. Major sites are closed on Monday. Directions: Exit off N12 or N333 about 50 km east of Prague. ****Camping: *Exit N12/38 for Kutna Hora, and drive northwest of town. Camping Transit, Malin 35 (03-276-2822); well maintained; open July-August; $.

KONOPISTE AND PRIBRAM
The heady aroma of over 200 hundred varieties of roses greets the visitor to Konopiste Castle, a complex of gardens, terraces, and preserves. Set on a high outcrop of rocks south of Prague, it is a popular day trip. It was owned and developed by the Archduke Ferdinand, heir to the Austrian

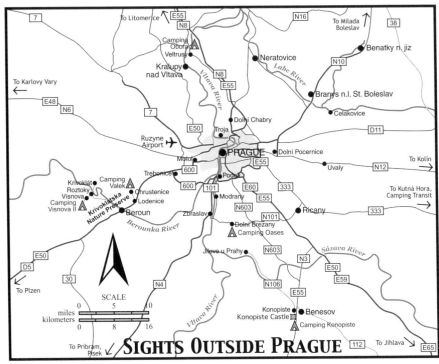

SIGHTS OUTSIDE PRAGUE

throne, whose assassination in Sarajevo in 1914 set off World War I. A passionate hunter, he filled his home with stuffed game heads, weapons, and trophies. Also eager to impress, he created large terraces and a romantic water garden decorated with fountains and statuary; open daily. Like Kutna Hora, Pribraun was a silver mining town. Today you can don a hard hat and go down into the UNESCO listed mine shafts; closed Monday. Directions: South west of town in the suburb of Brezove Hory. Cresting the hillside outside of Pribraun, the lovely domes of Svata Hora create a lovely sight. Devotees reverently admire the frescoes, saintly statuary, and the well-loved Madonna and Child. Directions: Drive 50km southwest of Prague on 3 in the direction of Benesov. Both Knopiste and Pribram are well signposted. ****Camping: *Southeast of Prague. Take N3/E55 in the direction of Benesov, then continue for two kilometers following signage for Konopiste. Exit onto N106, and drive two kilometers to the chateau and camping. Camping Konopiste in Benesov (012-2732); affiliated with a motel; fair maintenance; open June-August; $.

KRIVOKLATSKO NATURE PRESERVE

The Berounka Valley road twists and turns as it follows the river through pristine forests of beech and pine. Though it was once a famous hunting ground, today only the ruins of a 13th century castle stand in memory of the grand hunting affairs. Walking trails are marked throughout the UNESCO listed biosphere. It makes a romantic setting for the August film festival. Directions: About 30km southwest of Prague. Exit off E50 onto N116 at Beroun, and follow the river and rail tracks. ****Camping: *Southwest of Prague. Off E50 exit for Lodenice which is 11km northeast of Beroun. Drive northwest on a small road to Chrustenice, then drive one kilometer north of town. Camping Valek in Chrustenice (0311-67-2147); close to a river; bungalows; tennis; fair maintenance; open June-August; $$. *In the preserve and more remote. Exit E50 at Beroun. Drive northwest on a small winding road along the Belounka river road N116. At the fork, exit onto N236 in the direction of Roztoky. It's in the village of Visnova. Camping Visnova II (0313-55-8184); close to the river; bungalows; open June-August; $.

SOUTHERN BOHEMIA
TABOR AND AROUND

In the 15th century Jan Hus believed that all people were equal in God's eye. It was revolutionary stuff for an era ruled by the church hierarchy and feudal-minded nobility. Exiled from Prague, Hus and his followers sought refuge north of the city. Naming their new community Tabor, they established a church founding the Hussite religious movement and bravely fought for their lives and their beliefs. Visiting the museum here, with its underground passages and monastery, provides an understanding of their bravery and beliefs; closed Monday. In the second weekend of September, locals dress up in traditional costumes for the Hussite Festival.

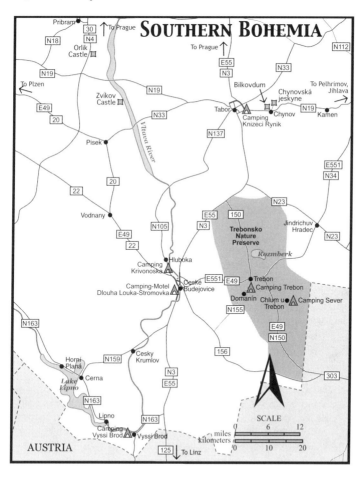

There are other interesting side trips in the area. The former home of the sculptor Bilkek, features outstanding architecture and houses a gallery of his work. It is worth a small detour. Directions: Drive east of Tabor on 19 to the village of Chynov. It's signposted Bilkuvdum and is on the south side of the river; closed Monday. For a change of pace, visit Chynovska jeskyne, a steep descent down 40 meters via a narrow stairwell into a stalagmite decorated cave; open daily. Directions: Look for signposting northeast of Chynov. Farther east along N19, an entertaining motorcycle museum operates inside the castle in Kamen. If you are in the area in mid-June, stop in Pelhrimov to cheer on hopefuls attempting feats at the Festival of Records and Performances. Winners appear in the Guiness Book of Records. At other times, visit the Muzeum rekord a kuriozit, the town's museum which commemorates the eccentric feats; closed Sunday in July and August. Directions: About 40km east of Tabor in Pelhrimov. ****Camping: *Exit N3/E55 southeast of Tabor. Drive west on N19 for three kilometers in the direction of Pelhrimov/Jihlavafor. Camping Knizeci Rynik (0361-25-2480); nice location on Lake Jordan; fair maintenance; open all year; $.

TREBONSKO NATURE PRESERVE

Misty light shrouds the marshy peat bogs here, while reeds nod in the light breeze and the tails of feeding ducks waggle in quiet water. Whistling and chirping birds advertise their presence and here and there silent fisherman sit patiently waiting for a bite. Birders, binoculars in hand, nudge each other as a sighting is made. UNESCO listed, it is a unique biosphere of fish ponds, marshy peat bogs, and flat lands. ****Camping: *East of Ceske Budejovice, on the lake at Trebon. Exit N34/E49 at Trebon. Drive southwest on N155 in the direction of Domann. Camping Trebon (0333-2586); popular fishing area; biking/walking paths; fair maintenance; open June-August; $$. *In the same area, just east of the exit for Trebon. Exit south on N150/E49, and drive ten kilometers, exiting onto small road for Chlum u Trebon. Camping Sever at Chlum u Trebone (0333-79-7189); along the lake; open June-September; $.

CESKE BUDEJOVICE

The main attraction for most tourists in Ceske Budejovice is the Budvar Brewery headquarters, now inside an ultra-modern blue titanium building on U. Trojice, off the road to Prague. Save your appetite to indulge in both food and beer here, as they are both inexpensive; open daily. After the tour, the banks of the Malse River await for a walk or cycle ride. Step inside the lively and whimsical atmosphere of the old meat market. Check out the elegant arcades and fountain at the main square. An outstanding 20th-century art collection is displayed in the former riding school of the impressively restored and furnished Hluboka Chateau; open daily in July and August. The grounds of the castle make a lovely picnic stop. It's a doable cycle ride from town and the tourist office has a map of the special cycle path. Directions: Take E49 out of town. Exit onto N105. Follow signposting to the castle. ****Camping: *In the city at Park Stromovka. Exit N3/ E/55 at Stromovka. Camping-Motel Dlouha Louka-Stromovka (3873-11-757); tennis park; well maintained; open year round; $$. *Three kilometers north of the city exit E49 onto 105 in the direction of the zoo and lake. Camping Krivonoska, in Hluboka (038-96-5285); a recreational area; bungalows; fair maintenance; open June-August; $.

CESKY KRUMLOV

The exquisite beauty of this rosy-hued town, with its overhanging-roofed houses and wooden-ramp bridges, make it worth a stop. Rent a canoe for a paddle down the river, taking a mini bus shuttle back to town; operates daily. If you're in the area during summer solstice, a medieval pageantry of the Five Petaled Rose Festival is a festive celebration.

LAKE LIPNO AND VLTAVA RIVER

This area is a favorite of mine. The countryside beckons with softly rolling hills, gentle forests, and swiftly running Vltava River. Camping is simple, with festive campfires and singing through the night. The area is popular with kayakers and canoeists, and rentals and guided trips are available. The Orlik and Zvikov castles on the Vltava and the pretty town of Pisek, with its fine medieval stone bridge, make nice excursions. ****Camping: *On the north side of the lake at the junction of N159 and N163 in Cerna. Take the small road to the lake. Camping AMK (0337-9-6125); bungalows; casual maintenance; open May-September; $$. *On the south side of the lake in Vyssi Brod. Just across the Austrian border, exit the Linz-Ceske Budejovice road N3/E55, and drive west on N163 along the river in the direction of Vyssi Brod. It's on the west side of town along the river. Camping Vyssi Brod; popular with kayakers; bungalows; casual maintenance; open May-September; $.

WESTERN BOHEMIA
KARLOVY VARY

The guest list of the wealthy who have recuperated and played in this quiet, elegant, and well-manicured spa town is impressive. To enjoy the same panoramic view as the famous, walk up behind the Hotel Pupp. From here, take the funicular up the hill to the Peter the Great Monument or continue on up the path yourself. In May, the town glitters with cinema stars who've come to be seen at the film festival, considered by some, to be as important as the festivals in Cannes or Berlin. ****Camping: *Four kilometers south of town on N20/E49, take the Plizen-Karlovy Vary road, exiting for Brezova. Camping Gejzirpark-Brezova (017-251-01); in a recreational area; swimming pool; between the forest and the river Tepla; well maintained; open May-September; $$. *More remote and popular with kayakers. Just out of town on N6/E48 in the direction of Prague, turn northeast onto a smal road along the river in the direction of Kyselka. Follow the Oder river road for 14 km. It is signposted north of Kyselka. Camping Na Spici-Kyselka (017-394-1152); close to a hotel; bungalows; biking/walking paths; well maintained; open June-September; $.

CHEB AND MARIANSKE LAZNE

Less exclusive than Karlovy Vary, but also embellished with peaceful and beautiful garden parks, Marianske Lazne is a user-friendly spa town. Try the new mineral baths are on the east side of town, just down from the main plaza. Sip water from the beautiful-wrought iron Kolonada, and relax around the fountain that "sings" to the cascading water every two hours. The leafy trees and well tended flower beds makes a tranquil setting for walks to springs dotting the park. ****Camping: *Drive north out of Cheb on E49 in the direction of Frantiskovy, then west on a small road in the direction of Slatina. Camping Amerika (0166-54-2518); in a recreational area; close to a small lake; next to a hotel; well maintained; open May-September; $$. *Southwest of Cheb. Off N6/E48 exit south onto 21 in the direction of Marianske Lazne and drive five kilometers to Jesenice. Camping Jesenice (0313-992-47); on a small lake close to the train tracks; bungalows; fair maintenance; open June-September; $.

PLZEN

Expert brew-masters have made this appealing town a favorite stop. To see its most famous pilsner brewery, Urquell, be there at noon to sign up for the one daily tour offered to individuals on weekdays at 12:30 or call ahead for reservations (019-706-2888). Directions: The brewery is on the east side of the old town along the river and is well signposted; open daily. A brewery museum is just off the main square in a restored malt house; open daily. Continue from the brewery museum to Perlova 6, where you can study antique brewing artifacts as you wander through an maze of medieval underground passageways; ask for the English text; closed Monday and

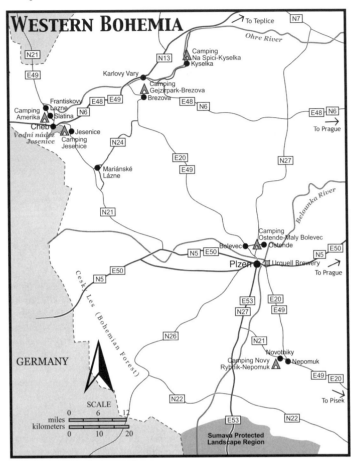

Tuesday. ****Camping: *North of the city on N20/E49 in the direction of Karlovy Vary. Exit at Bolevec, driving east passing under 27 to Ostende and the lake. Camping Ostende-Maly Bolevec (019-520-194); affiliated with a hotel; well maintained; open June-August; $. *East of the city, 23km, on the Plzen-Prague autostrata 5/E50. Exit at Myto/Holoubkov, and drive north one kilometer on a small road to Habr and the river. Camping Habr-Volduchy (019-818-348); fair maintenance; open June-August; $. *South of the city, 33km. West of Nepomuk at the junction of E49 and 21, exit for Novotniky and drive west to the river. Camping Novy Rybnik-Nepomuk (019-859-1336); cycling/walking paths; well maintained; open June-August; $.

NORTHERN BOHEMIA
LABSKE PISKOVCE PROTECTED LANDSCAPE REGION

Lured by huge sandstone outcrops, rock climbers come to this majestic valley for a challenge. Over the centuries weather has carved the sandstone into unusual shapes. Pravika Brana, a natural

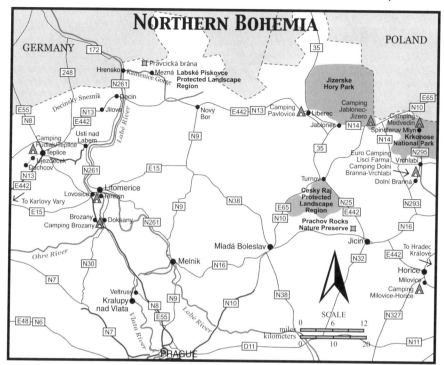

NORTHERN BOHEMIA

sandstone bridge, is 90 feet long and 63 feet high. It is as impressive as the one in Canyonlands in the USA. The trail begins behind the Sokoli hnizdo restaurant in Hrensko; an entrance fee is charged. Another dramatic and very popular trail goes into Kamenice Gorge. After a steep hike down into the gorge, you can float down into the narrows by boat. Bring a book and snack for the inevitable wait for the boat ride; operating daily. The trail begins at Mezna, not far from Hrensko. Trails are clearly marked for various return routes. The high plateau of Decinsky Sneznik enables you to look out over the whole region. Directions: Exit off N261 onto N13. Drive north on the small road at Jilove. The northern end of this region is Hrensko, just over the German border. The southern end is in Decin. Both are off N261. Pick up hiking maps at your campground or in one of the villages.

TEREZIN

In order to convince the world press and visiting Red Cross that the Jews were being well cared for, Hitler needed a showplace Jewish camp. He used the old fortress Terezin, which in reality was just a stopover for Jews on their way to Auschwitz. Cross over the bridge, passing through the old walls of the fortress into the ghetto; open daily. Directions: Exit N30, 21km south of Usti nad Labem at Lovosice, and drive east on N55 for ten kilometers to Terezin.

JABLONEC AND JIZERSKE HORY MOUNTAINS

A detour into Jablonec to see the glass and jewelry museum makes a pleasant break in the journey. Directions: Signposted Muzeum skla a bizuterie, its downhill from the town hall; closed Monday. The mountainous area northeast of Liberac is popular for family vacations.

****Camping in the Region: *Exit E55/8 in Teplice. Drive west on N254, the Teplice-Duchcov road, for about three kilometers to the suburb, Ujezdecek. Camping Pudlak/Teplice (048-172-8171); swimming pool; bungalows; fair maintenance; open June-August; $$. *Exit E55/8 halfway between Lovosice-Roudnice at Doksany. Drive in the direction of Brozany and the Ohre river. Camping Brozany (048-119-7289); bungalows; open May-September; $. *Northwestern section of Liberec. Exit onto 35 in the direction of the suburb of Pavlovice. Camping Pavlovice (048-512-3468); it's close to the sports area; well maintained; open June-August; $$. *East of Liberec, on the river at the base of the Jizerske Mountain range. Exit Liberec onto N14, and drive east to Jablonec. Camping Jablonec-Jizero (048-043-294); nice for fishing, biking, and hiking; bungalows; fair maintenance; open June-August; $. *In the Jizerske mountains ski area, exit N14/293 and drive north east in the direction of Vrchlabi. Follow signs to Spindleruv Mlyn, a recreational area at the end of N295. Camping Medvedin (048-389-3534); chair-lift up to hiking trails; well maintained; open year round; $$$. South of Vrchlabi exit just north of N14/293 onto N295, then go just north of Dolni Branna. *Eurocamping Lisci Farma (0438-2-1473); bungalows; swimming; tennis; well maintained; open all year; $$$. *Northwest of Hradec Kralove, off E442 just south of Horice in Milovice. Camping Milovice-Horice (0435-68-8149); rehabilitation area; sauna; bungalows; swimming pool; fairly quiet; well maintained; open June-September; $$$.

MORAVIA
CESKY RAJ AND ADRSPASSKO-TEPLICKE NATURE PRESERVES

This twisting labyrinth of sculpted sandstone challenges serious rock climbers; follow sign-posting for Prachovske skaly. Directions: Exit N10 near Mlada Boleslav. Drive east on N16 in the

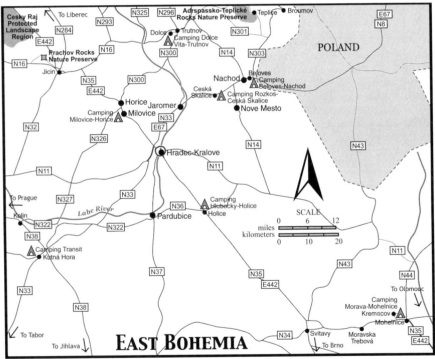

EAST BOHEMIA

direction of Jicin. Follow signposting on the west side of town. To experience the rock villages of the Adrspassko-teplicke preserve, go farther east on N16 for 15km towards Trutnov. Drive two kilometers farther east on one of the smaller roads to the village of Teplice. Parking and trailhead are west of the village at the Hotel Orlik. Trails are well marked. Bring local currency for the small admission charge.

HRADEC KRALOVE AND HORICE

Cornfields stretch for miles over this flat terrain. In a Renaissance square in Hradec Kralove, a wonderful modern art gallery operates within an art nouveau building; open daily. In Horice, 23km northwest of Hradec Kralove, an important school of sculpture was founded in 1884. Today the town hosts international symposiums on contemporary sculpture in July and August. Sculpture beautifies the town, and an exciting collection can be viewed in Galerieplastik; closed Monday. Directions: Drive halfway up the hill on the east side of town.

****Camping: *Southwest of Trutnov. Exit off N16 in direction of Jicin, then follow signposting for Dolce. Camping Dolce Vita-Trutnov (0439—81-3065); a recreational area along the river; bungalows, biking paths; fair maintenance; open year round; $$. *North of Hradec Kralove 35km on E67/33. It's on the north edge of Lake Rozkos in Ceska Skalice, a recreational area popular with wind surfers. Camping Rozkos-Ceska Skalice (0441-45-1112); boat launch; sauna; bungalows; casual maintenance; open all year; $$. *On the Polish-Czech border crossing of Nachod on 303/E67. Exit just north of Nachod at Beloves. Camping Beloves-Nachod (441-2-3014); bungalows; fair maintenance; open June-August; $. *South of Hradec-Kralove 20km on N35/E442. Exit two kilometers north of Holice for Hluboky, a recreational area on a small lake. Camping Hluboky-Holice (0456-2233); pleasant area; bungalows; casual maintenance; open June-August; $. *East of Moravska Trebova 41km on N35/E442, in a recreational area on the Mirouka River. Exit for Kremacov. Camping Morava-Mohelnice (0648-43-0129); at the river's edge; affliated with a motel; well maintained; open June-August; $.

NORTHERN MORAVIA
WESTERN BESKYDY AND
ROZNOV POD RADHOSTEM

An undulating countryside spreads out before you like a carefully hand-sitched quilt in this region of farmlands, which before World War II, was largely settled with Germans. Old-fashioned wooden homes and churches lend a tranquil air. The open-air museum here, separated into three parts, is the largest and most outstanding in the country. Arrive early so you can enjoy the pastoral setting peacefully. Buy a combined ticket, and get an English text. Of the festivals held here throughout the summer, the best one is Folkloric Dance and Song, held in the first week of July. Although the spruce forests have suffered from acid rain, the impressive Jesnik Mountains stand rugged and tall. This is a very popular sports area. ****Camping: *Directly east of Olomouc, almost to the Slovak Republic border off 18/E442, in the recreational area of Roznov. Exit east of town towards the river. Camping Sport-Roznov pod Radhostem (0656-595-13); swimming pool; bungalows; fair maintenance; open July-August; $$. *South of Ostrava, almost to the Slovak Republic border, exit just north of Freydlant on N484 to Beskydy. It's on the east side of the rail tracks on the river. Camping Beskydy-Frydlant nad Ostravici (065-87-1221); bungalows; fair maintenance; open July-August; $. *Northwest of Opava, north of Bruntal, fairly close to Polish the border crossing at Krnov on N458. Exit N11 at Bruntal, and drive north on E452 direction of Vrvno P. Pradedem. *Camping Dolina (0646-75-1983); good hiking and biking paths; bungalows; well maintained; open June-August; $$. *South of Opava, exit off 57 at Hradec nad Moravici and drive south. Camping Hradec (0653-91-

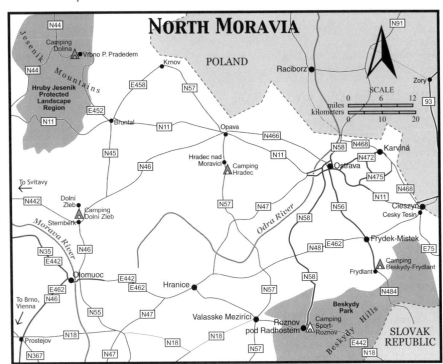

1114); bungalows; fair maintenance; open June-August; $$. *About 22km north of Olomouc. Exit north out of Sternberk and take a small road along the river in the direction of Doni Zleb. Camping Dolni Zleb (0643-41-1300); bungalows; well maintained; open June-August; $$.

SOUTHERN MORAVIA

BRUNO

Miles van der Rohe, a famous pioneer in functional architecture, built beautiful Vila Tugendhat at Cernopolni 45, for wealthy clients. It has become a shrine for students of modern architecture; closed Monday and Tuesday. Directions: Northeast of town on Milady Horakova, by the Soviet War Memorial. The site where Gregor Mendel, the father of modern genetics, developed his studies is fascinating and memorable. The gardens where he worked and an adjoining museum are located in the Augustinian Monastery; closed weekends. Directions: Gardens are on southwest corner of old town. For a macabre experience, visit Spilberk Castle. It was built as fortress but is most famous as a prison. Purchase the map if you want to explore the labyrinth of dark hallways; closed Monday. It's up the hill on the western edge of the old town. For photogenic local color and fun, visit the Cabbage Market and huge Parnassus fountain in the old town.

MORAVSKY KRAS

The number one tourist attraction in this area is the spectacular Punkevni jeskyne cave, where the fantastically shaped stalagcites and stalagmites are named, each with its own story. Part of the

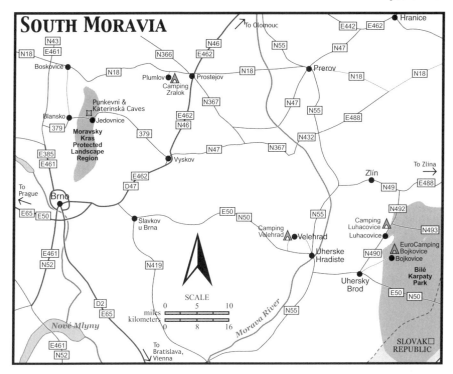

SOUTH MORAVIA

tour is a one-hour boat ride on the underground river, Punkva; open daily. Directions: 25km northeast of Bruno. Exit E461/43, and drive east on 379.

AUSTERLITZ AND SLAVKOVU BRNA

Napoleon outwitted the Austrians and Russians here in a battle that led to the disintegration of the anti-Napoleon coalition and the European borders that were observed at the time. A small museum is in the chateau at Pracky Kopec, but the site of the hillside battle is twelve kilometers east of Slavkov in the direction of Prace. Get directions from a local as it's hard to find. Tolstoy includes this battle in his novel War and Peace.

MORAVSKY KRUMLOV

Twenty enormous canvases here depict Czech-Slavic history. Artist Alphous Mucha shared a studio with Gauguin in Paris and produced notable Art Nouveau posters, but he felt his real life's work were these phantasmagoric paintings. The paintings are in the Renaissance chateau just 100 meters off the main square; closed Monday. The drive there goes through the beautiful Rokytna valley. Directions: Drive southwest of Bruno for 27km to Moravsky Krumlov.

LEDNICE

Very powerful landowners built the Gothic extravaganza that is Lednice Palace, and UNESCO tagged it. Rich interiors, stately gardens, reflecting ponds, and a huge Islamic minaret make it a delightful rest and photo stop; open daily. Directions: It's just over the Austrian border. Take N414 southeast out of Mikulov, exiting onto a smaller road for Lednice.

TELC

Bordered by two large fishponds, this palace is embellished like an elaborate wedding cake. Both the palace and the Renaissance town square are UNESCO listed. Telc is a cheery and enjoyable place to explore and photograph. Pass through the small gate on the north side of the square, and enjoy a picnic lunch in the outstanding English-style garden.

****Camping in the Area: *Between Brno and Olomouc, due west of Prostejov, on the small lake Plumlov. Exit off N18 in the direction of Plumlov. Camping Zralok (0508-93-209); fair maintenance, open June-August $$. *Northwest of Uherske Hradiste. Exit either N50 or N55 in the direction of Velehrad, driving north out of the village. Camping Velehrad (0632-71-183); along the river; bungalows, well maintained; open July and August; $$. *Southeast of Zlin, along the lake in a nature preserve. Exit N49 onto N492 for Luhacovice. Camping Luhacovice (067-93-3318); walking and biking paths along the lake; bungalows; boating; fair maintenance; open July and August; $$. *In the same area, close to Bojkovice, in a popular recreational area. Exit E50 at Uhersky Brod, and drive east for 13km to Bojkovice, following the rail tracks. Eurocamping Bujkovice (0633-92-1526); bungalows; well maintained; open July and August; $$$.

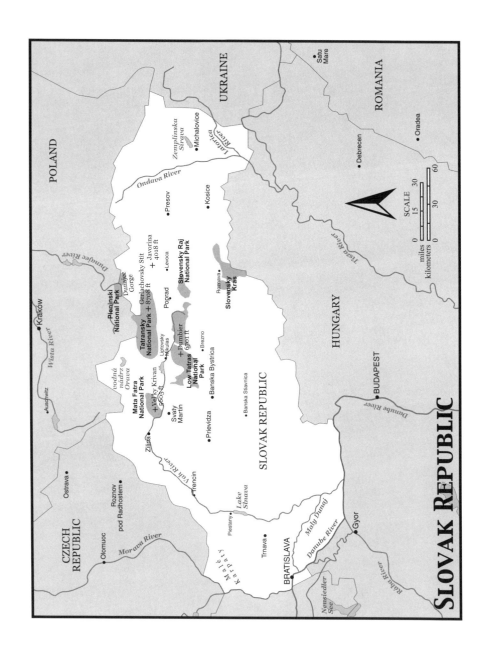

SLOVAK REPUBLIC

SLOVAK REPUBLIC

The sharp and craggy granite peaks of Slovakia's Tatra Mountains are slashed with dramatically carved glacier ravines. Serene Alpine lakes stand with graceful elegance while wild waterfalls tumble over boulders and joyful creeks skip through quiet valleys. Grassy meadows are enhanced by the red and yellow clover, dense forests of beech and pine intersperse undulating hills patched with fields of corn, wheat, and potatoes. Slovakia beckons you to linger.

You'll share your campgrounds with Slovakians having an old-fashioned good time. They are outdoor enthusiasts, proud of their country and happy to have you enjoying it with them. Campgrounds can be found throughout the country. Some are very basic with casual maintenance, but the easy friendliness of the people is always there. The cost of the campgrounds reflects the amenities. Most cost about $15 USA for 2 persons, a tent, and a car. Simpler ones cost about $10 USA. Driving is relaxing and scenic. Freeways are few, but roads are in good condition. Horse-drawn carts and small tractors on the road are not uncommon. There are few toll roads. Parking is readily available except in Bratislava. Fill up with gas, supplies, and have some local currency before going to the smaller towns.

Open markets are easy to find in the morning close to the town's main square. Generally shops are open 9 to 5 weekdays. Many close by noon on Saturday remaining closed until Monday morning, so check your supplies on Friday or Saturday morning. Slovakia is an inexpensive place to visit. Museum entrance fees, food in the markets, and the cost of the campground, won't add up to very much. Get local currency from the cash machines outside the banks of larger towns. Museum and historic sites, except Jewish ones, are generally closed on Mondays, while the Jewish ones close on Saturday. They are generally open from 10 a.m. to 4 p.m. The lunch closing time is usually noon to 1 p.m. Ask for an English text for museum tours, which are generally obligatory but not in English.

TATRA NATIONAL PARK

Slovakia's national anthem, Thunder Over the Tatras, sounds with pride over these peaks. They soar abruptly from grassy meadows. Charming hotels, electric trains, cheerful villages, and campgrounds have been carefully built to protect the beauty from over-development. Chair lifts whisk people to high trails and panoramic views. It's like visiting Kitzbuhel Austria before it became an expensive resort. Purchase one of the colorful booklets describing the trails, flora, and fauna; they are available in all major languages including English. For long hikes, be sure to take a map, wear sturdy shoes for the rocky terrain, and include in your day pack: warm waterproof clothing, food, and water. A visit to Tatra Park Museum will make your stay more meaningful. Not only are the exhibits on the natural and geological history of the area well done, but the way of life of the people who live in the Tatras is colorfully presented. After, take a short walk to the park's botanical garden to see specimens of the beauty tucked away in the granite and limestone of the mountains. The main Tatra tourist information office is northwest of the train station in the village of Stary Smokovec. The Tatra National Park Office

and Museum is at the eastern edge of the village of Tatranska on 540. Both staff someone who speaks English, and they are excellent sources of information, maps, booklets; open daily. Tatra National Park attracts an international clientele. In pleasant little cafes, shops, and park gardens people relax and enjoy themselves.

The most popular chairlift is in Tatranska Lomnica. It whisks you up to for an easy walk to the Alpine lake, Skalnate Pleso and to the trailheads of other hikes. Trails meander back down to the valley through forests where you can smell the pines and hear the happy chatter of birds. But for more adventure, continue on the next chairlift from Skalnate Pleso for an exciting ride to Lominicky stift, 2632 meters. The stunning panoramic view of here includes southern Poland and eastern Slovakia. For an easy loop hike, park in Tatranska Lomnica. Take the chair lift to Skalnate Pleso. Follow the red trail west to Hreblenok. At the waterfalls you can rest on massive warm boulders lacing the falls, take in the clear mountain air, and thrill to the thundering sound. At the mountain cafe at Hreblenok, buy a treat and join others relishing the view on an outside terrace. To return to the base of the mountain, board the funicular train at Hrebienok for a scenic ride down to the village of Stary Smokovec. The electric train will take you back to the village of Tatranska Lomnica and your parked car. For a shorter trip, take the funicular railway from Stary Smokovec up to Hreblenok. Directions: Follow the road at the northeastern corner of the village of Tatranska Lomnica, up through the park-like setting of the Grand Hotel Praha. The cable car station and parking are below the hotel. ****Camping: *From Stary Smokovec, drive south on 534 for several kilometers in the direction of Poprad. Tatracamping; lovely setting along the river; small; basic; casual maintenance; open July-August; $$. *From Tatranska Lominica, drive south on 540 for several kilometers in the direction of Velka Lominica. Eurocamp FCC (969-46-7741); large; bungalows; popular with RV's; well maintained; open year round; $$$. *Drive 20km west of Stary Smokovec. Exit south onto 50, a beautiful winding mountain road, in the direction of Tatranka Strba. Camping Tatranska Strba; tranquil location; affiliated with a hotel; small; well maintained; open June-August; $$.

MALA TATRA AND THE VRATNA VALLEY

The Vratna Valley is considered to be Slovakia's most beautiful valley. It's the birthplace of their national Robin Hood-like hero Janosik. Trails lead up and down rocky cliffs, through leafy forests, along gurgling creeks, and past charming wooden houses. The clear mountain air is laced with the aroma of pines whispering in the breeze. It's rich with the whistles and squeals of birdsong. Gold and purple gentian and larkspur decorate the rock garden setting. Fishing in the bolder-strewn rivers, walking up to Alpine meadows with bubbling creeks, and cycling along designated forest paths are popular pursuits. The trail from Krivanska to Stefanova passes by a limestone region of bizarrely shaped columns and into a narrow gorge where ladders cling over small waterfalls, then finishes with picturesque views of the shingled roofs of wooden houses in Stefanova. Trail maps are essential whenever you hike in the area. Logging markers can be mistaken for trail markers. Bring energy food, water, and warm waterproof clothing for changeable weather. Directions:

MALA TATRA NATIONAL PARK

Located on the western edge of the Tatra National Park. From Zilna, drive east on 583 for 25km to Terchovca. Turn into the magnificently beautiful Tiesnavy Pass. You'll come to a fork about three kilometers from the Terchovca turnoff. Take the road signposted for Stefanova, and pick up trail maps at the Mountain Rescue Service signposted Horska sluzba. Then return to the fork, and take the other road sign posted for Chata Vratna. A year-round chair lift here goes to Snilov sedlo, the saddle between the peaks of Velky Krivan and Cheb. ****Camping: *At the turnoff to Branica on 583, about three kilometers west of Terchova. Camping Nizne Kamence (69-5151); nice location; basic camping; casual maintenance; open July-August; $. *15km east of Zilna on 583.

Camping ATC Varin (69-2410); bungalows; fair maintenance; open June-August; $$. *On the south side of the Tatra National Park, close to Martin take E50/18 for 12km towards Turany, then take the small road north along the river for two kilometers to Trusalova. Camping ATC Trusalova; lovely location; basic camping; casual maintenance; open July-August; $.

LOWER TATRAS

Beneath the towering peaks of the High Tatras lie the tree-covered hillsides of the Low Tatras. Here you can take walks along delightful creeks and rivers rushing through the pristine valleys, stop and wave to a farmer working in one of the tiny villages, explore deep caves, and camp along the lake with other Slovakians. It's the homeland of some of Slovakia's best-loved heroes: Kral, poet of the Slovak revolution; Razusova-Martakova, biographer of Slovakia's hero Janosik; and Martikan, canoeist and Olympic Gold Metal winner. At Liptovska Mare, a large reservoir-lake, you'll join Slovakians and their families at the campground and on the trails. Bikes, canoes, and paddle boats are available for rental. Farther up the road, in the tiny hamlet of Pribylina, Slovaks proudly show off life in the olden days at the Liptov Open Air Village; open daily. Directions: From Liptovska Mikulas, turn north onto 584.

In Demanova Valley, in the village of Jasna, a chairlift ascends to high peaks and the ridge trail. Visit the subterranean ice cave of Demanovska Jaskyna and the Demanovska Cave of Freedom. They are signposted off the road between Jasna and Liptovska Mikulas; closed Monday. Directions: At Liptovska Mikulas turn south onto 584. Drive south 15km to Jasna. ****Camping: *On 537, just east of the fork with 18 on the south side of the river. Camping Varisova (222-429); small; basic; casual maintenance; $. *At Liptovska Mare, on the north side of the lake. ATC Liptovsky Trnovec (969-41-114); nice location; popular with families; well maintained; open July-August; $$. *Close to the caves; affliated with the Bystrina Hotel. Camping Bystrina (759-163); lovely location; small; well maintained; open July-August; $$.

DUNAJEC RIVER GORGE

This is a popular excursion area. Just east of the Tatra National Park and south of the Polish border, it's an easy half-day excursion from the Tatras or a nice stop on your way to them. The river float and cycling/walking trail into the nine kilometer gorge starts in Cerveny Kastor, a small town at the northern end of 543. The boatmen are dressed in traditional costumes, and there is a festive

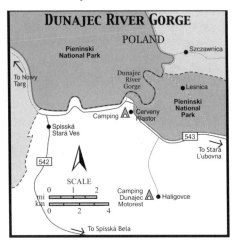

air. It's a pleasant, 1 1/2 hour photographic trip. Boat trips leave from both the Cathusian Monastery at the eastern end of the river road, and at the intersection of the river road and the road to the town. A quiet tree-shrouded trail follows the river into the gorge. Cross the bridge at the monastery to the reach the trailhead. The trail and boat trips end in Lesnica. Your choices for return are taking a taxi, walking, or biking. The museum in the monastery has some notable frescoes. If you're in the area in mid-June you can meet the locals celebrating the Eastern Slovak Folk Festival. ****Camping: *Right at the monastery, across the bridge in the park by the gorge trail. Car entrance is behind the monastery on 543. Dunajec River Camping; lovely setting; basic; open June-August; $. *South from the monastery on 543 for three kilometers; exit for Haligovce. Camping Dunajec Motorest; more amenities, bungalows; fair maintenance; open June-August; $$.

BRATISLAVA

For centuries Bratislava was a coronation city, making it historically important. Eleven royal crownings, including Maximillion's, took place here. Let your imagination evoke the pomp and rituals of the crowning pageants as you stand on Castle Hill taking in the panoramic views of the Danube River and the Cathedral of St. Martin. On a clear day you can see three countries: Hungary, Austria, and Slovakia. The castle-fortress houses parts of the Slovak National Museum. Of the several museums within the castle walls, my favorite is the Folk Music Museum signposted Hubobne muzeum. Music has kept alive the Slovaks' pride in their history and culture, and visitors to this museum are treated to recordings of the ancient pipes, whistles, and drums being viewed. Descriptive text is included in English. Directions: In a side building north of the main

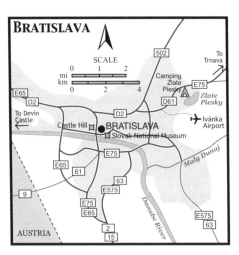

castle. Just inside the main castle entrance, in a highlighted glass case, is the museum's most honored artifact-a Paleolithic figure of a woman carved from a mammoth tusk found by the Vah River. The museum has an impressive collection of furniture and crafts including Art Nouveau glassware. The bedroom furniture decorated with peacock feathers will make you smile. The grounds and ramparts of the castle walls are good places for a picnic, or treat on the terrace cafe; closed Monday. Directions: Exit west off E65, the main road coming into the Stare Mesto, and follow signposting up the hill to the Hrad, Castle Hill, on Zamocka ul. Park outside the castle gate.

At the bottom of the cobblestone path from the castle is Zidovska, or Jewish

Street. Walking north on it, peek into the tiny clock museum inside a colorful, wedge-shaped bugher's house at Zidovska 1; the collection is pure kitsch. The decorative arts museum is located across from it; both are closed Tuesday. Don't miss the Museum of Jewish Culture, signposted Muzeum zidovskej kultury, just a little farther on at Zidovska 17. Everyday life, festivals, and objects of religious importance are explained in English; closed on Saturday.

Retrace your steps back past the clock museum, and walk toward the street that crosses under the main highway, continuing a little farther to Gothic Dom sv Martina Cathedral. The steeple with a golden crown commemorates the 250 years of royal crownings. From here, head up Kapitulska, one of the city's oldest streets. When you reach Bastova, continue east until you come to Michalska veza tower. Climb the stairs for a panoramic view of the castle and old town. You can rest here in the quiet garden, which was once a moat, and reflect on what you've seen. The passageway to the garden is in front of the tower between the tower gates.

Just south of the tower, at Michalska 28, is the exceptional Exozicia farmacie, a pharmaceutical museum. Bratislava has a rich herbalist past; closed on Monday. Continue down Michalska to Sedlarska, heading southeast and follow signposting for Stara radnica, the old town hall. The beautiful passageway and Renaissance courtyard are sedate and elegant. At the information office here pick up the local map and then continue your explorations. Torture chambers and instruments used from the Middle Ages to the 19th-century are displayed in the Municipal Museum at the Town Hall. Just behind the courtyard is the Primatial Palace, where Napoleon and Emperor Franz Josepf signed a peace pact. Touching paintings of peasantry, the backbone of the Slovaks, are in the Town Gallery.

Consider taking a cab back to your car rather than walking. Cabs are metered and fairly inexpensive. Use your tourist map to show the driver where you want to go. If a relaxing excursion boat trip sounds enticing, take a ferry to the ruins of the watchtower of the Danube, Devin Castle, just nine kilometers west of Bratislava. The boat landing is across from the Slovak National Museum. Check with the tourist office or a hotel for the ferry's operating hours before walking down to the esplanade. Conversely it's an easy drive to Devin Castle along the Danube River. ****Camping: *East out of the city on E751/D61 in the direction of Trnavka and Piestany, just past a large chemical factory on the small recreational lake, Zlate piesky. This is a pleasant day and weekend recreational area for Bratislavians, with tennis courts and children's playground. Camping Zlate Piesky, Senecka cesta Z. (07-257-373); grassy field with trees; public transport to the city center; fair maintenance; open June-August; $$.

ALONG THE VAH RIVER
TRNAVA

Tranva sits at the intersection of the ancient roadways to Prague-Vienna-Budapest-Krakow and is Slovakia's oldest town. For a time it was the religious center for the Hungarian Empire. The University Church here is the Slovak Republic's finest and boasts a magnificent Italiante Rococo carved wooden altar. While here, stop by the Slovakian Museum south of the church to view a notable collection of folk art. Easy parking is found close to the church. Directions: Enter through the old town walls, and follow signposting. ****Camping: *South of Trnava, exit E751 at Sal'a and drive west on 573. Cross the train tracks, and follow signage to Diakovce and Horne Saliby, a large recreational area. Camping Diakovce Horne Saliby (0707-932-50); cycling trails; bungalows; casual maintenance; open June-August; $$.

PIESTANY

Considered Slovakia's queen of spa towns, Piestany is a nice spot for a recuperative soak in thermal water. On the narrow strip of land in the middle of the Vah River, called Spa Island, you can

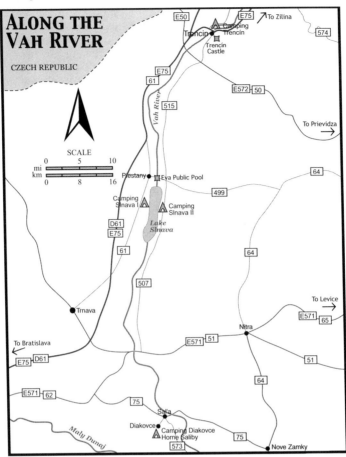

enjoy old-fashioned and inexpensive fun in the public pool, Eva. Directions: After crossing the river to the island, drive north on the west side of the island. The pool is just north of the luxurious Thermia Hotel. After your soak, relax in the large garden area just north of the pool. ****Camping: *Exit D61/E751 on the east side of the river. Camping is south of town. Camping Slnava II (0838-235-63); casual maintenance; $. *On the west side of the reservoir, follow 61 south along the river. Camping Slnava I (0838-943-29); bungalows; casual maintenance; $.

TRENCIN

Like the king in a chess set, the tower of Trencin's castle stands high above the town on a steep and craggy cliff. In summer it is luminated and festive with fun-filled performances given by actors dressed as sword fighters. ****Camping: *From 61 on the east side of the river, cross under the train tracks and follow signage to Na Ostrova. It's on the southern tip of the island. This is a popular day use area for boating and swimming. Camping Trencin (831-340-13); good view of the castle; bungalows; good maintenance; $$.

CENTRAL SLOVAKIA
BANSKA STIAVNICA

Picturesque because of its lovely setting and old-world feel, this silver mining town is now UNESCO listed. Besides seeing the mining camp, with its workshops and church, you can take the trip down into the labyrinth mine; closed Monday. Directions: South of town on 524, about two kilometers in the direction of Levice. ****Camping: *On 524, four kilometers south of the old mining town, follow signage to Pocuvadianske jazero, a small recreational lake. Camping Pocuvadlo (94-112); basic; open July-August; $.

KREMNICA

A very large gold seam was found here in the 12th century. Since then, famous coins have been minted here, including commemoratives for both Churchill and Stalin. The collection of exquisitely decorated money is fascinating. At night the town is illuminated and inviting with narrow cobblestone streets and sidewalk cafes. Directions: On 65, west of Banska Bystrica. ****Camping:

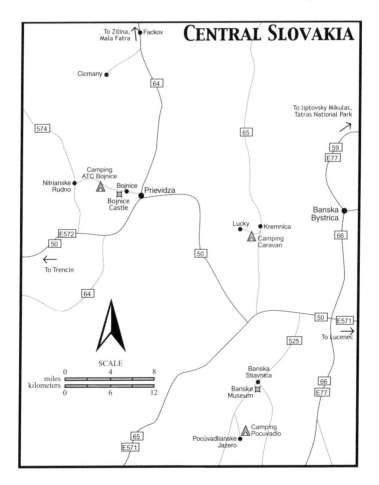

CENTRAL SLOVAKIA

*Southwest of town on the small road in the direction of Lucky. Camping Caravan (92-587); small; basic; open July-August; $.

CICMANY

Folk art enthusiasts are fond of this town nestled deep in the mountains of northwestern Slovakia. Virtually isolated from other parts of the country, during the 1800s men farmed and herded sheep and cows while the women spent time after chores carefully embroidering clothing. Eventually the villagers began decorate their houses with the handcrafted designs. Today Cicmany is a national monument, and you can admire and photograph the old-fashioned wooden cottages decorated with the lacework designs of snowflakes, flowers, and crisscrosses. Directions: Halfway between Zilna and Prievidza, exit west off 64 following the Rajcanka River. The turnoff for the small road to the village is just south of the village of Fackov on 64.

BOJNICE

It's not hard to conjure up visions of knights in shining armor, beautiful maidens with silky long tresses, and noble kings draped with fur when you visit this Gothic, fairy-tale-like castle. It sits on top of a small hill and is reminiscent of those seen in the Loire Valley in France. As you approach, you'll see the Gothic turrets rising above the trees, providing a nice photo. Tours are conducted by guides in period costumes; closed Monday. Directions: West of Prievidza, follow signage to Bojnice, then go farther west to Bojnicky zamok. ****Camping: *A little farther down the road in the direction of Nitrianske Rudo. Camping ATC Bojnice (0862-33-845); nice location; good maintenance; open June-August; $$.

EASTERN SLOVAKIA
SLOVENSKY RAJ NATIONAL PARK

Ladders have been carefully slipped down through cracks in gorges to enable thrill-seeking hikers to climb over waterfalls. Fallen timber has been carved with footholds to bridge difficult gaps on the trail and chain bridges built to cross over the river rapids. On the Hornad river gorge trail, a chain bridge spans a gorge whose river is 45 feet below. Not all the trails are this exciting. Many

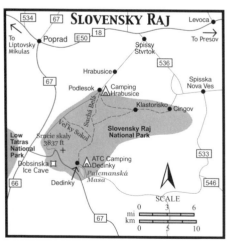

are pleasant walks through leafy oak, beech and pine woods. It's important to get a map of the area before you start hiking. Trail markers aren't always evident. Pick up trail maps and information at the Mountain Rescue stations at Cingov or Dedinky. The map you want is "VKU Slovensky raj." Purchase supplies, gas, and have local currency before you come into the area. You'll need a warm jacket if you want to descend down the slippery steps of the Dobsinska Ice Cave, where mysterious tunnels of slick, smooth ice lead to giant ice halls glistening with fragile stalacites. It's well sign-posted off 67 as you enter the national park. ****Camping: *In Podlesok at the northwest end of the park, exit 536 onto a small road heading southwest in the direction of Hrabusice. The exit is at the junction of 18 and 536 at the village of Spissky Stvtok. It's in a pretty location that is close to the trails and the river. Camping Hrabusice in Podlesok (90-281); bungalows; basic amenities; open June-September $. *At the southern end of the park on a small lake. Exit 67 at the lake. ATC Camping Dedinky (98-162); lovely location; close to a hotel and pension; swimming, boating, and biking; open June-September; $$.

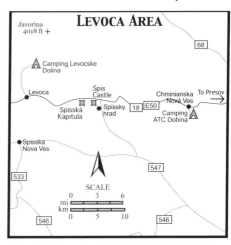

LEVOCA AND SPIS CASTLE

Breathtaking in sensitivity, the finely carved figures of the Madonna, St. James, and St. Paul seen in the masterpiece wooden altar in St James Cathedral were carved by Pavol in the 16th century and each are over six feet tall; open daily. Reminiscent of old-world grandeur, Levoca's old town has a quiet ambiance and makes a nice break in the journey. If you're traveling east on E50, turn into Spisska Kapitule, 18km east of Levoca, and stroll through the tiny, completely enclosed fortress. Peek into the lovely cathedral. Continuing farther east on E50, after two kilometers you'll see the ruins of neo-Baroque Spis Castle, founded in the 12th century. It makes an intriguing photo stop. Directions: Levoca is 41km east of Poprad. ****Camping: *Exit 50/18 north of Levoca onto a small road that runs along the river, and drive 12km. Camping Levocska Dolina (0966-512-701); beautifully located at the base of the Levocske Vrchy Mountains; bungalows; well maintained; open year round; $$. *About 16km west of Presov, just off E50/18, exit at Chiminanska Nova Ves, drive south one kilometer. Camping ATC Dubina (0966-951-90); convenient; affliated with a hotel; well maintained; open year round; $$.

SLOVENSKY KRAS

Limestone canyons and caves riddle the Slovensky Kras region. At twenty-two kilometers Domica jaskyna is one of the longest caves in the world. Stretching to the Hungarian border, it joins Hungary's Aggtellek cave. The one-hour tour includes a short trip down the underground river Styx; open daily. Directions: South of Roznava, about 20 km, exit 50 at the small village of Plesivec and drive southeast on a small road for about 12km. For a dramatic, narrow, wooded ravine walk, detour to Zadielska dolina. At one point, its width is only ten meters. The red-marked trail is an easy two kilometer walk. Directions: Halfway between Roznava and Kosice on E571, exit onto the small road heading north in the direction of Zadiel. The trail-

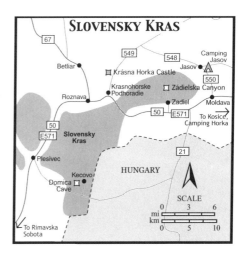

head is at the end of the road, about six kilometers from E571.

Stories of intrigue and romance embellish Krasna Horka Castle, making it an interesting castle stop. Restored in a Renaissance style, it is classical on the outside but highly ornamented on the inside, with gorgeous marble throughout. It also has a notable Art Nouveau mausoleum. Directions: Exit E571 east of Roznava. Drive ten kilometers to the village of Krasnohorske Podhradie, exiting north onto the small road and driving two kilometers. For another castle stop, the well planned garden setting of the regal hunting lodge in Betliar is a good choice. Souvenirs from adventurous travel include a mummy, elephant tusks, and warrior apparel from Samurai and African tribes, add to the mystic of the owner. Directions: Ten kilometers north of Roznava on 67. ****Camping: *Exit E571 west of Kosice at Moldava, and drive north on 550/548 for 12km. It's on the north side of the village Jasov. Camping Jasov (0943-942-42); close to a reservoir; bungalows; cycling/walking trails; good maintenance; open all year; $$. *Almost to the Ukraine border at the large reservoir lake and recreational area, Zemplinska Sirava. Camping Horka (0946-921-35); tennis; disco; well maintained; open June-August; $$.

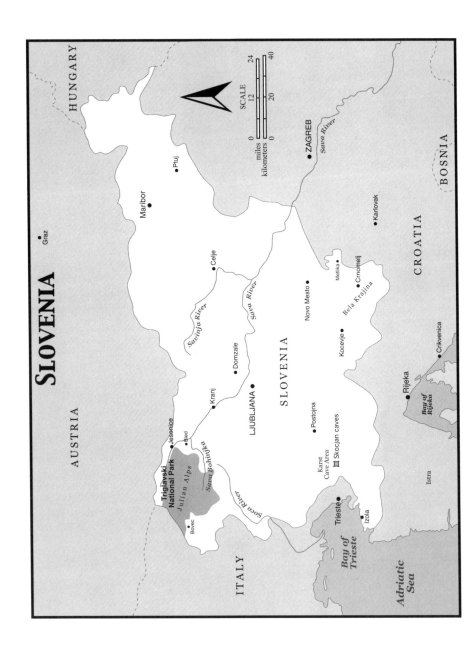

SLOVENIA

With countryside noted for being the greenest in Europe, Slovenia feels like being in a park most of the time. Easy walking paths traverse lush grassy meadows so full of wild flowers its like walking through a bouquet. High peaks, rain-forest-like mountain gorges, and tumultuous waterfalls treat the hiker. Crystal clear rivers and quiet lakes invite the paddler and fisherman. Driving is pleasurable through such beautiful country and highways here are excellent and well signposted. The small roads are well maintained and excellent for cycling. Locals are very friendly and do all they can to make your trip enjoyable.

Camping in Slovenia is expensive compared to the other eastern block countries but the campgrounds are modern and well equipped. Standards are high. Tennis is popular, bring your racket. Most campgrounds will cost about $20 USA for 2 persons, a car, and a tent. Beautifully landscaped campgrounds in touristed areas will cost closer to $25 USA while resort-like places will cost about $30 USA. They recognize the ICC card.

JULIAN ALPS AND BLED

Situated on the edge of an emerald-green lake boasting a jewel-like islet in its center, this picture postcard perfect town is a major tourist resort with the accompanying crowds and prices. But you can enjoy the manicured gardens, take an inexpensive boat ride out to the island with its tiny church, visit Bled Castle, and take a walk or cycle ride around the lake for very little. Don't miss taking the walk into the Vintgar Gorge in Podhom, just over four kilometers from Bled. The trail into the gorge is a wooden walkway that hugs the cliffside, passing over the river rapids several

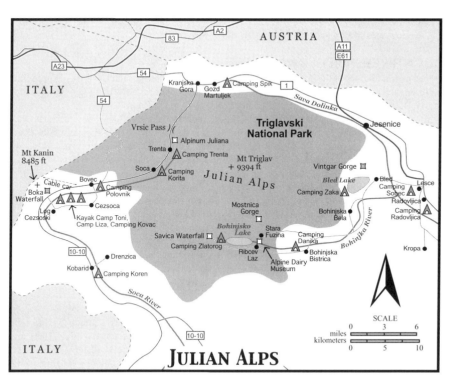

times. Ferns, tiny primroses, and waterfalls make wonderful material for photographs. Bring a waterproof jacket and wear shoes that don't slip. There's a small entrance fee. Stop by the tourist office by the lake on the main road coming into Bled from 1, next to the Park Hotel. They speak English and can give you details on interesting things to do in the area.

Next take the road along the lake and river heading into the national park. Bordered by lush green forests and meadows on one side and the Bohinjka River on the other, the valley drive is so beautiful you might want to stop at the first campground, but drive on. In the village of Ribcev Laz, stop at the tourist office then visit the tiny church of St. John the Baptist. Inside, the brilliance of the frescoes brightens the tiny arches and ceiling; open daily. Directions: Just across the stone bridge on the north side of the river. While you're in the village, check with Alpinsport in the kiosk next to the bridge. They can help you with adventures that include renting a canoe or kayak for the lake or rafting through the Mostnica Gorge. The Alpine Dairy Museum housed in a charming cottage has some fascinating photographs and artifacts; closed Monday. Directions: Just north of Ribcev Laz, on a small road on the east end of the lake in Stara Fuzina. Save enough time to walk to the 60 meter Savica Waterfall, one of the most important sights in the park. It's impressive and you'll be sprayed by a veil of water, so wear appropriate clothing. Directions: The trailhead begins close to the Zlatorog Hotel. It's a four kilometer easy walk, and there's a small admission fee. The tourist office has excellent maps for longer hikes in this area. Stops in the tiny picturesque villages guarded by the majestic Julian Alps add to the pleasure of driving and cycling in this beautiful countryside. ****Camping in Triglav National Park: Take the river road out of Bled in the direction of Bohinjska Bela. *Camping Zaka in Bled (64-7 41-117); well landscaped and maintained; open May-September; $$$. *West of Bohinjska Bistrica. Camping Danica in Bohinjska Bistrica (64-721-055); beautiful location; popular; well maintained; open May-September; $$$. *At the west end of lake Bohinj. Camping Zlatorog (64-723-441); natural setting on the lake; in a pine forest; popular; well maintained; open May-September; $$$.

SOCA RIVER VALLEY AND BOVEC

The pristine beauty of the Soca River has made it a mecca for rafting and kayaking. Trips, guided or unguided, can be arranged in Bovec in the Alp Hotel with Soca Rafting (196-200) or with Bovec Rafting Team (858-6128) in a small booth across from the Hram Restaurant.

If the weather is clear, take the cable car up to the top for views stretching to Trieste and the Julian Alps. Directions: Drive southwest out of Bovec in the direction of the Mt. Karin Funicular; it's signposted. The trailhead for Boka Waterfall is about 5 kilometers farther on the road. Park by the small restaurant Gostilna Zikar. It's a steep hike. If you don't have the time or energy, continue down the road and get a view of it after parking close to the bridge.

Awarded the European Museum of the year in 1993, you won't want to miss the Kobarid museum. Its exhibits tell the story of the Soca (Isonzo) Front; the same battle described by Ernest Hemingway in A Farewell to Arms. Drawings by Erwin Rommel, also known at the Desert Fox, depict the lines of battle during the fall and winter of 1917. Touching memorabilia and photographs fill three floors, with descriptions in four languages including English. Little cemeteries dot the whole area, and an ossuary under the Church of Saint Anthony holds the bones of unburied soldiers. A path to the Kozjak waterfall passes trench lines, observation posts, and a shelter cave; open daily.

Between Bovec and Kranjsha-Gora, a spectacular drive through the Vrsic Pass takes you either to or from Triglav National Park. Directions: Four kilometers northeast on the main road out of Bovec, look for the small road heading east in the direction of Kal-Koritnica/Kranjsha-Gora. It runs right along the Soca River. Coming from Kranjsha–Gora, drive directly south in the direction of Bovec. This road is under snow in the winter. Allow plenty of time for this drive. There are important stops along the way. From Bovec it is 12 kilometers to the lovely village of Soca. Here inside the18th-century Church of St. Joseph, note the fresco portraying St. Anthony struggling with

Mussolini and Hitler; open daily. In the village of Trenta eight kilometers farther, stop at house 34, Dom Trenta, and go through the Trenta Museum, dedicated to the mountain guides who first ascended the Julian Alps. This is also an information center for Triglav Park, with exhibits of the flora, fauna, and pioneers of this Alpine area. They have maps for some spectacular hikes in the area; open daily. Take some time to visit Alpinum Juliana botanical garden, just four kilometers farther. From there, the road winds up to the Vsic Pass, passing a Russian Chapel dedicated to 400 Russian POWs who were buried in an avalanche in 1916. The descent down is steep and winds sharply. At the base of the mountain, pass through the village of Kranjska-Gora and rest at deep-blue Lake Jasna.

****Camping: *Exit off 10 at Bovec, and drive south on the small road11/301 in the direction of Cezsoca. Camping Polovnik in Bovec (658-6069); good location; fair maintenance; open May-September; $$. *For a more remote place, ask in Bovec at the Alp Hotel for directions to Vodence. There are three camping places on the river in this area. Kayak Camp Toni (658-6454), Camp Liza ((658-6073), or Camping Kovac (658-6831); fair maintenance; open May-September; $$. *North of Bovec two kilometers, exit east onto the narrow and winding Bovec/Kranjska-Gora mountain road and drive 12km to the village of Soca. Camping Korita; simple; open July and August; $. Seven kilometers farther east in the village of Trenta. Camping Trenta; simple; open July-August; $. *In Kobarid. Camping Koren (658-5312); beautifully located close to the river; well maintained; open April-September; $$$. *From the Kranjsha-Gora/Bled Road 1 at Krankska Gore follow the road for four kilometers, passing under 1 to the river and the village of Gozd Martuljek. Camping Spik in Gozd Martuljek (648-80120); affiliated with Hotel Spik; convenient; pretty location; road noise; swimming pool; open all year; $$$.

FROM BLED TO LJUBLJANA

A side trip from Bled to two unusual museums makes an interesting half day. In the Beekeeping Museum folk-art panels and fascinating exhibits, with English labeling, tell the story of beekeeping which has been an important part of Slovenia's agriculture; closed Monday. Directions: Five kilometers south of Bled on E651 in Radovljica. The museum is in a cream-and-white manor home on the north side of the street in the center of the historic area. You might not think you are interested in foundry work, but after visiting the charming little village of Kropa, noted for its metal work during the 17th and18th centuries, you'll begin to appreciate the craftsmanship; closed Monday. Directions: Take the small road south of Radovljica in the direction of Kropa. ****Camping: *South of Bled four kilometers on 1, along the Save Dolinka River, exit at Lesce. Camping Sobec in Lesce (61-72-901); along the river; bungalows; well maintained; open June-August; $$$. *In the same area, exit 1 at Radovlija. Camping Radovlijica (64-715-770); close to the public swimming pool; road noise; fair maintenance; open June-August; $$.

LJUBLJANA

This beloved city has handsome little pedestrian bridges crossing its canals bordered by willow-lined walkways. Parks and gardens around every corner and extra friendly cafes invite staying. It's an easy city to drive into and park. Follow the sign-

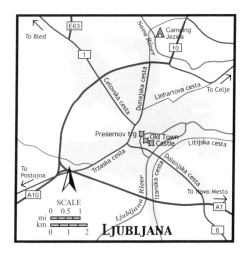

posting to the historic area, park and make your first stop the tourist office to get the schedule of free performances in the historic area and a list of its wide variety of museums. It's southeast of the triple bridge, and well signposted. Peek into the little shops and courtyards on Stari trg. Walk up to the castle, where you can look down into the Old Town and out over the city from the ramparts. Walk down through Pogacarjev trg, a colorful open-air market to stock up on just picked fruits and vegetables and freshly made cheeses. The market for meat, fish, and dairy products is on the southwest corner. Then wander over to Presernov trg to rest and enjoy the pleasant ambiance in one of the cafes or on the steps at the monument to Presernov. Both the International Summer Festival of music, theatre, and dance and the Summer in the Old-Town run throughout July and August making a visit during these months particularly lively and fun. ****Camping: *North of the city in the suburb of Jesica, exit off 10/E57. Camping Jezica (61-371-382); bungalows; children's playground; some road noise; fair maintenance; open all year; $$.

VELIKA PLANINA

In this gorgeous highland meadow contented cows graze and smiling cow-herdsmen sell their white cheese from cone-roofed huts. An exciting cable car ride takes you up to a 1420 meter altitude. Drive northeast of Ljublijana on 10 in the direction of Domzale. Exit north on a smaller road for Kamnik. Stop at the tourist office here if you want a hiking trail map. The cable car station is 11 kilometers north of Kamnik. Popular hiking trails to waterfalls and caves start at the old-world village of Kaminiska Bistrica, three kilometers beyond the cable car station. ****Camping: *In the Old Town of Kamik. Camping Resnick in Kamik (61-831-233); close to the river; tennis; fair maintenance; open June-August; $.

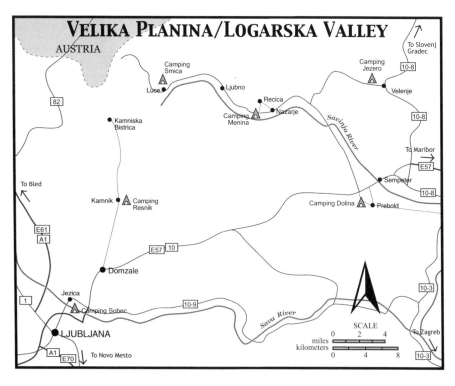

LOGARSKA VALLEY AND THE SAVINJA RIVER

This is a popular area for kayaking, rafting, paragliding, and tennis. Equipment rental is available. Exit A10 west of Sempeter onto a smaller road in the direction of Nazaeje, then continue west on the same road for three kilometers in the direction of Ljubno. ****Camping: In Recica. Camping Menina (386-471-5770); a recreational area; nice location on the Savinja River; well maintained; open July-August; $$. *Farther on the Savinja River Road up into the mountains for 19 kilometers to Luce. Camping Smica (386-384-4330); beautiful location; tennis; well maintained; open June-August; $$.

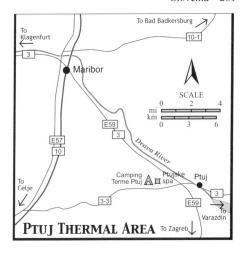

PTUJ THERMAL AREA

*****Camping on the route from Ljublijana to Maribor: *Halfway between the two cities, exit A10 south onto the road just west of Sempeter in the direction of Prebold. Camping Dolina in Prebold (386- 637-24501); nice location; small swimming pool; bungalows; $$. *On a reservoir lake. Exit two kilometers east of Sempeter, and drive north on 10/8 in the direction of Velenje. Pass through Velenje, and drive northwest along the river road towards the reservoir. Camping Jezero in Velenje (386-638-63400); a recreational area; wind surfing and catamaran rental available; well maintained; open June-August; $$$.

HISTORIC PTUJ AND THE THERMAL AREA

Noted for its thermal water, Ptuj is Slovenia's oldest town. Its small but interesting historic area is perfect for walking or cycling. A castle, whose rooms house a small museum, looks down on the old town; closed Monday. Directions: 22 kilometers south of Maribor, along the River Drava on 3/E59. ****Camping: In Ptuj, on the small road between E59 and 3. Camping Terme Ptuj (62-771-721); resort-like; large thermal pools; saunas; children's playground; bungalows; well maintained; open May-September; $$$$.

BELA KRAJINA AND THE KOLPA RIVER VALLEY

Along the Kolpa River, on Slovenia's southeastern border with Croatia, the river is warm, clean, and popular with locals. It's a good place to relax with kids. You can join folks taking scenic kayak runs from Stari Trg to Vinica, or fish for carp and trout with rented equipment. There are horses for rent and easy walking or cycling routes in Lahinja Regional Park and the surrounding vineyards. In Adlesici, museum-farmhouses promote an appreciation of folk culture.

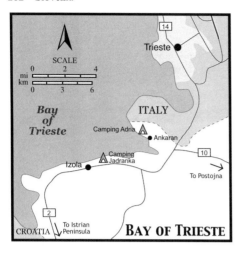

BAY OF TRIESTE

****Camping: *Exit 4-Novo Mesto-Metlika, just south of Metlika, and drive southwest in the direction of Podzemeji. Camping Podzemelji (68-69-572); on the Kolpa river; well maintained; open from June-August; $$. In the village of Adlesici, southeast of Crnomeli 12 km. Take the small road in the direction of Tribuce and Dolenjci. Camping Jankovic in Adlesici (68-622-877); on the river; well maintained; open June-August; $$. *In the village of Vinica. Drive south on the Crnomeli-Vinica road for 18km. Camping Vinica (68-64-018); on the river; fair maintenance; open May-September; $$. *Close by. Camping Katra in Vinica (68-64-319); on the river; fair maintenance; open May-September; $$.

BAY OF TRIESTE AND ANKARAN

Slovenia's little nugget of a Mediterranean seaside, just south of Trieste, making it a popular destination for the locals. The strip of coastline is bordered on the north by Ankaran and on the south by Portoroz. ****Camping: *In Ankaran. Three kilometers south of the Italian bordering crossing at Muggia, at the junction of 10 and 2, continue on 10, driving west eight kilometers to Ankaran. Camping Adria in Ankaran (66-52-8322); good location on the beach; touristy; popular; well maintained; open June-August; $$$$. *Farther south along the coast road, close to Izola. Camping Jadranka in Izola (66-61-202); popular; touristy; bungalows; casual maintenance; open June-September; $$$.

POSTOJNA AND SKOCJAN CAVES

The Skocjan caves are among the deepest and most picturesque in the world and have been tagged by UNESCO as a World Heritage site. This captivating place is more natural and less touristy than the caves at Postojna. The Reka River still rushes through, racing down in a spectacular waterfall and filling the silence with the sounds of gushing whirlpools. Directions: Just east of Trieste drive two kilometers south of Divaca on 10 and follow signposting. While you are in the area stop in Lipica to admire the famous Lipizzaner horses at the Lipica Stud Farm; open daily. If you are here on Tuesday, Friday, or Sunday you can watch them perform their complicated paces to Viennese waltz music at 3 p.m. Horses also can be rented for a guided ride in the countryside or in the ring. Directions: From Divaca, drive 12km southwest to Lipica and follow signposting. For small children, the caves at Postojna are more enjoyable.

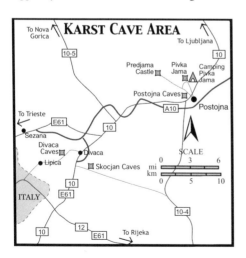

Disneyland-like, an electric train ride passes by the colorfully lit stalactites and stalagmites making good material for story telling later. Predjama Castle provides another story telling setting. It looms gloomily from a gargantuan rock cave in the center of a 123 meter rock face and its 15th century history tells of Robin Hood-like tales. Directions: From the caves, drive northwest in the direction of Bukovje.   Pass through the village, continuing in a westerly direction for the Predjamski grad. ****Camping: From Postojna, take the road heading northwest in the direction of Pivka Jama. Camping Pivka Jama (386-6725-382); in a forested area; bungalows; swimming pool; well maintained; open May-September; $$$$.

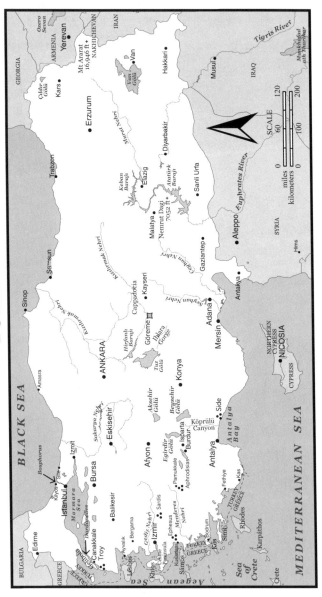

TURKEY

If you leave the main tourist track, your experiences in Turkey will overflow with warm and generous hospitality. It is natural for them, a gift they give with pleasure and without strings attached. When I think of Turkey, it's not the beautiful beaches, the carpet-like rolling steppes, the fascinating underground churches, the exquisite mosques or the haunting call of the muezzin that I remember first. It's Mustafa in his tiny produce store demonstrating to us how to cook green beans and insisting that we stay for a delicious dinner of the beans, bread, and olives. It is camping along the river unknowingly next to a goat corral, and hearing the tinkling of bells coming over the hill just as we started to eat. In this case, the lovely old shepherdess couldn't understand why we would want to cook and sleep outside, but she smiled and graciously excused herself from sitting down to share our dinner. It is the young girl who rescued us when we couldn't find a camping place. She insisted that we camp in the garden of her lake-side condominium and then asked us to join her family for a barbecue dinner on their porch.

The Turks love to camp, and they camp with the whole extended family. During dinner hours, barbecue aromas fill the air. The relaxed ambiance happily includes swimming, cards, and singing. You won't need reservations; there's always room for a tent. The cost will reflect the amenities. Modern campgrounds with all the amenities are found close to internationally popular tourist areas. I love the forest service campgrounds that are popular with Turkish families. They are older, homey, located in lovely areas, and inexpensive. In remote areas the camping is simple and maintenance is casual. The more expensive campgrounds are around $25 USA for two persons, a car, and a tent. Medium priced and simple ones are under $20 USA.

The roads and signage in Turkey are good. There are few toll roads. Trucks slow down traffic, but their drivers are courteous and try to give signals when it's safe to pass. It's a big country with a lot of variation in landscape. Fields of cotton, sunflowers, and a wide variety of vegetables make a pleasing mosaic. Shepherds herding their sheep and goats smile and wave. Less touristed areas are quiet and serene. Highway signs marking sites of historic interest are yellow and black. Bazaars are usually closed on Sundays, and museums are often closed on Mondays. Cash machines are found outside of banks. Remember to fill up with gas and supplies and have local currency before driving into the more remote areas.

ISTANBUL

Where else in the world can you visit an exotic palace filled with jewels, step inside a Harem shrouded in mystery, get pleasantly lost in a Covered Bazaar, get squeaky clean at a Turkish bath, and absorb the holiness and beauty of a great mosque. It's one of the great cities of the world. Be sure to use your guidebook to discover and relish it. The bus from the camping place goes right along the park-like edge of the Marmara Sea to its last stop at the Galata Bridge. ****Camping: The following directions sound like directions through the bazaar, but actually they're easier than they sound, and the campground is only four kilometers from the airport. *From the airport exit left, following signage for Istanbul. Get in the right-hand lane, and follow signage for Yesilyurt. Then get in the left-hand lane, and follow signage for Siraceci. Then be in the right-hand lane to follow signage for Atakoy. *From northwestern Turkey, exit off E80 at exit 17, and drive south in the direction of the airport, passing roadway 100 and continuing south, passing signage for Florya until you see signage for Atakoy. Exit and continue following signage for Atakoy and the campground on Kennedy Blvd. Camping Atakoy, Sahil Yolu Bakirkoy (0212-559-3096); beautiful location on the Sea of Marmara; close to public transportation to the city; bungalows; fair maintenance; open all year; $$.

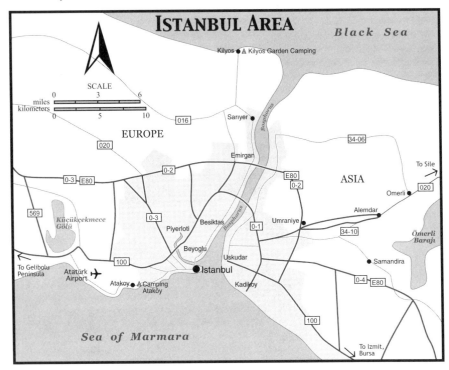

THE HAMAM EXPERIENCE/TURKISH BATH

Once you've had this experience, you'll want more. It's really just a matter of getting used to the procedure. At the desk when you enter and pay, tell them whether or not you want an attendant to scrub you and whether or not you want a massage. You'll be directed to a dressing room and handed a towel. Put your clothes in a locker, wrap up in the towel, and go into the "hot room". Scrubbing basins ring the room. The basins must be kept free of soapy water. After scrubbing, relax on the platform which is usually in the middle of the room under a domed roof. This is where you are also massaged. In medium priced hamams entrance fee, scrub, massage, and tip totals around $20.

LEAVING ISTANBUL

It's easy to get lost in the suburbs of Istanbul on your forays out, so I suggest that you use E80, even though it is a little farther. To get to E80 from Atokoy Camping, exit right or east onto Kennedy, then turn right again at the first exit, where you'll see the Holiday Inn skyscraper. Go around the small roundabout and under the overpass, and head west, back on Kennedy towards the airport and Yesilyurt. Follow the green signs to Edirne and E80.

For the west coast towns and Bursa, drive east on E80, crossing the bridge to Kavacik. Continue on E80 exiting at exit 8. Drive south three kilometers to 100. Exit east in the direction of Gebze. Drive east on 100 for 35km following signage for Darica, then for Eskihisar/Feribot.

KILYOS

This is the closest Black Sea resort area to Istanbul and only 12km from the Bosphorous suburb of Istanbul, Sariyer. It is nice break from the hubbub of the city and the beach is very pleasant.

The drive up the mountain is scenic, and on the weekends you'll be enticed to stop at the little barbecue restaurants where you can dine at tables under the trees all afternoon. The little town itself has a nice, easy feel. The campground is within walking distance of the little shops. Directions: Off E80 or 100, drive north in the direction of Saiyer. After passing Ottman Park, you'll see signage to Kilyos. Follow the mountain road up to Kilyos. ****Camping: *In a lovely garden across from a small sports field. Kilyos Garden Camping (210-1572); lovingly cared for; small; open May-September; $$.

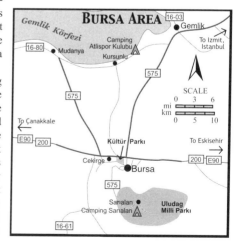

SARIYER

This upscale suburb of Istanbul is a gentle place to stroll along the Bosphorous Sea while delighting in the old wooden Ottoman mansions, fishing boats, and ferries plying the sea. Eat a picnic lunch on one of the seaside benches. Directions: See Leaving Istanbul directions, exiting for Sariyer. After passing Ottman Park, stay right and drive to the Bosphorous. Parking is easy.

BURSA

Nestled along a river beneath the majestic Uludag Mountain peaks, the carefully restored ancient town of Bursa dates back to 200 B.C. The silk trade developed here and is still an important industry. You can learn about its intricacy in the Silk Cocoon Caravanserai. Park-like, green, graceful, and quiet, it's lovely to walk through. The mosiac tiles and intricate wooden filligree of its mosques and tombs are breathtaking. There's an excellent covered food market. It's easy to drive to and there are large carparks are close to the historic area.

Directions: See directions on previous page for "Leaving Istanbul". If you're going to Bursa from Istanbul take the car ferry from Eskihisar to Yalova. The road traffic is heavy when you drive and it is a boring trip. Instead transport yourself back through history as you cross this stretch of water that has been so important over time. You can buy tickets just before boarding. Follow signage on 100 to Darica and then to Eskihisar/Feribot.

Thermal waters springing from the Uludag have been enjoyed here for centuries. Indulge in a hamam experience. Directions: Drive west out of Bursa toward Muradiye and Cekirge. The Yeni Kaolica or New Baths, are on the northwest side of Kultur Park. Look for a steep accessway opposite the Celik Palas Hotel. For an experience in a beautifully restored old hamam, drive a bit farther. Just before entering Cerkirge, on the eastern side next to the Kervansary Thermal Hotel, is Eski Kapicalari or Old Baths. The experience here

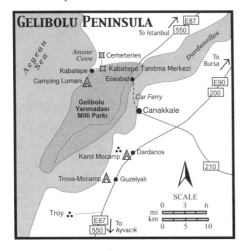

will be more expensive than $20 USA but the beautiful restoration makes it worth spending. These baths have pools where you can soak in the hot thermal water. If you prefer an outdoor pool experience, go to the beautiful one at the Kervansary Hotel. Admission is under $10 USA.

****Camping: At the time of publication there were no campgrounds in Bursa. Outside of Bursa, you'll find these. *About 30km north of Bursa, on the Gulf of Gemlik, exit 575 onto the beach road just south of Gemlik. Camping Atlispor Kulubu (0224-271-5118); affiliated with the sports club; northeast of the beach; fair maintenance; $. *In Uludag Mill Parki, about one hour south into the mountains behind Bursa. Drive west out of Bursa on E90 for five kilometers in the direction of Cekirge/Uludag. Take the beautifully scenic road, reminiscent of the Sierra foothills in California, up to the village of Sarialan and the Milli Parki. Camping Sarialan; popular with Turkish families; lovely setting; close to hiking trails; casual maintenance; open June-August; $. (off season it's still accessible by car, but the toilets are locked)

THE GELIBOLU PENINSULA

Softened now by grassy rolling hills and quiet beaches, the poignant reminders of grim military history, particularly World War I, when there was an enormous loss of troops on both sides, are kept real in the touching and beautiful museum, battlefields, and cemeteries. Scuba diving to see the shipwrecks from the World War I can be arranged in Canakkale at the Neptune Dive Center, close to the ferry boat landing. ****Camping: On the Gelibolu Peninsula: *After getting off the car ferry from Canakkale to Eceabat, turn right, and follow signage nine kilometers to Kabatepe. Turn south, and drive six kilometers. Camping Lumani; beautiful setting on the beach; swimming pool; bungalows; restaurant; well maintained; open May-September; $$.

TROY

The ruins have been extensively excavated in recent years making it much easier to see the ancient layers of civilizations. The excavation was made famous by amateur archeologist Heinrich Schlieman who was passsionate to uncover evidence of the Trojan War, but instead uncovered a beautiful cache of jewelry. The site is well worth a stop. Directions: South of Canakkale 17km, exit off 550, and drive west for five kilometers through pleasant cotton fields and olive groves. ****Camping: *South of Canakkale ten kilometers on 550/E24, on the beach road at the village of Dardanos. Karol Mocamp (0286-263-5452); nice location; bungalows; fair maintenance; open May-September; $$. *Close to the ruins of Troy. 12km south from the Canakkale exit on 550/E87 to the beach at the village of Guzelyali. Trova-Mocamp (0286-232-8025); bungalows; affiliated with a motel; fair maintenance; open year-round; $$

ASSOS

Minor ruins are being excavated in this out-of-the-way, romantic setting. If you have extra time, this is a perfect getaway. Directions: 73km south of Cankkale, exit off 550 for the small town of

Ayvacik (not to be confused with the larger town, of the same name, farther down the coast south of Edremit). Fill up with gas in Ayvacik, then drive west 19km on a small, well-paved, winding road with panoramic vistas and a high desert landscape.   Just before you get to the village of Behramkale, note the lovely 14th century humpback bridge. If it's Friday, there's a good morning market in the village of Kucukkuyu, on 550 just as the road meets the sea on the north side of the Bay of Edremit. ****Camping: *On the beach in Kadirga, four kilometers east of Assos on a small beach road not recommended for RVs, very simple and basic but beautiful in setting; $.

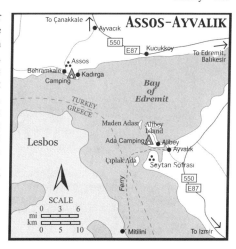

THE WEST COAST
AYVALIK

Picturesque Ayvalik makes a nice stop. It's popular with international campers, so it's a good place to relax on the beach, cook, share stories, and watch the sun set and the night sky as it fills with stars. The morning market at the main square is excellent. Ferries leave from here for the Greek Island of Lesbos. ****Camping: *On Alibey Island. Cross the bridge to the island on the north end of Ayvalik. Drive to the northwestern edge of the island. Ada Camping (0266-327-1211); lovely beach; shade trees and palapas; restaurant; bungalows; good maintenance; open May-September; $$.

BERGAMA

Bergama was a great city with an estimated population of 150,000. During the dynasty of its namesake in 200A.D., the library, theater and gymnasium were famous. The Archeological Museum is on the main street coming into Bergama. As you drive the six kilometers up to the Acropolis, you'll pass the Red Basilica. Use your guidebook to direct you as you study the Altar of Zeus, Temple of Athena, Library, and Theatre. It's truly a magnificent site and not to be missed. Behind the museum, next to the army camp, are the ruins of Asclepion, where the famous physician Galen practiced. ****Camping: *In Bergama, two kilometers west of town on the main road. Berksoy Mocamp (0232-633-5345); affiliated with a motel; convenient to ruins; swimming pool; well maintained; open year-round; $$. *Halfway between Bergama and Aliaga, on 550 and the Candarli Bay. Camping-Motel Afacan, (0232-628-7030); beautiful location; swimming pool; restaurant; well maintained; open April-September $$$. *In Yenifoca,

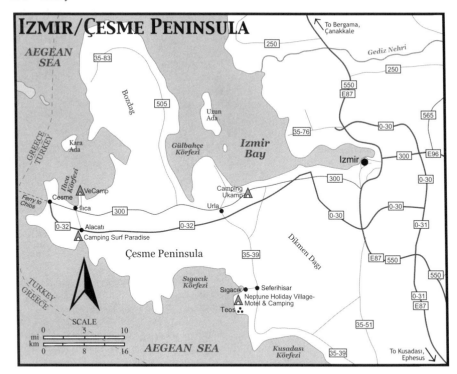

south of Alaga, exit 550 and drive 12km west. Pass through town, and continue west for another two kilometers. Azak Restaurant and Camping; nice setting; very basic; $.

SARDIS

It's the setting at the base of the beautiful Boz Daglari mountains amid vine-covered fields that is most impressive about these ruins. The main ruins are on the north side of the main road. The walking path to the Temple of Artemis is on the south side of the road by the teahouses. Directions: It is 90km east of Ismir on E96/300, just west of the town of Salihi. Look for signs in the village of Sartmahmut.

IZMIR/CESME PENINSULA

Izmir is a big, western-style city, but if you feel like seeing the sophisticated side of Turkey, the historic area and museums are worth some time. Your focal point will be the beautifully carved clock tower at the konak or main square. To find the museums, look for the hill topped with the Kadifekale fortress then walk up the hill on Varyant. The museums are in Bahri Baba Park. The archeological museum has notable collections from excavations in the area and the ethnological museum has a beautiful replica of a Turkish wooden house, a merchant's house, and dioramas showing felt and pottery production. Upstairs there are re-creations of a nuptial room and a circumcision celebration room. If you are here close to sunset, climb the stairs to the fortress and watch as the sky gradually twinkles with stars. Directions: The exit for the city's historic area is where the freeways net, so traffic is heavy. Watch closely for signs so that you are in the correct lane to exit. Off the freeway, drive toward the harbor and bus terminal, where there is public parking. The main sights are within walking distance. ****Camping: These are all on the Cesme Peninsula, a popular international resort area. The freeway out has a toll, but it is a excellent, fast-moving roadway: *In Uria, 40km west of Izmir. Take exit #3 at Uria. UCamp(0232-755-1021); all the amenities; well maintained; open May-September; $$$. *In Alacati, 85km west of Izmir. Exit at #6 for Alacati and follow signs for Sorf Cenneti. Camping Surf Paradise; on the beach; well maintained; open May-September; $$ *In Ilica, 85km west of Izmir. Exit at #6 off Ilica/Alacati highway and drive north to Ilica then out to the end of the spit. VeCamp (0232-723-1416); all amenities; lovely setting; natural thermal springs; private beach; well maintained; open May-September; $$$.

COAST ROUTE TO AND FROM EPHEUS

If you have time to spare and want a less hectic beach rest, get gas and then exit the Cesme/Ismir expressway at exit 2 and drive south on 35-39 in the direction of Seferihisar for 21km. This is a scenic route through farmlands where rocky hills hug the shore and roses and bougainvillea engulf

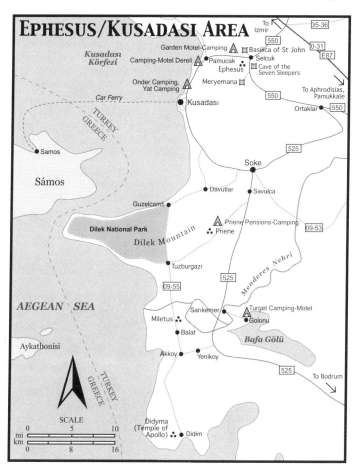

the houses along the way. When you get to the beach, take the small road west to Sigacik and the archeological site of Teos. ****Camping: *On the cape of Sigacik. Neptune Holiday Village-Motel and Camping; basic; $.

EPHESUS

Because it is one of best preserved ancient cities on the Mediterranean, Epheus is a major tourist sight in Turkey. But even though the town where it resides, Selcuk, is loaded with tourists, the town retains a Turkish feel. There's a good open market, an excellent archeological museum, and pleasant sidewalk cafes and small parks. The Archeological Museum is on the main road into Selcuk and is a good first stop. Artifacts are artistically displayed, and it's an airy, pleasant place; closed Monday. Visit the tourist office in front of the museum. Then drive up to Ayasoluk Hill, just above the town, where you can look out over the whole setting and see the colonnades of the Basilica of St. John, the presumed tomb and baptistry; open daily. To experience Ephesus, go either very early in the day or late in the afternoon, and bring a guidebook, water bottle, and snack or picnic. In your mind, replace the tourists with beautifully robed Romans, talking and gossiping. If you have extra time, consider an additional trip to the Cave of Seven Sleepers where you can view the now fenced catacombs where the martyrs slept. Meryemana is the presumed site where the Virgin Mary lived her last years and died. It's a shady, quiet place with lots of tourists. Directions: Take Ataturk Caddesi south out of Selcuk, then drive eight kilometers up the hill on a winding road with panoramic views. The expressway from Izmir to Selcuk is excellent but heavily trafficked with large tour buses. Consider taking the "Coast Route to and from Epheus" described in the previous section. ****Camping: *On the beach in Pamucak, seven kilometers directly west of Selcuk. Camping-Motel Dereli, (0232-892-3636); large and popular; on the beach; restaurant; tennis; well maintained; open April-November; $$$. *In Selcuk, west of Ayasoluk Hill. It's signposted on the north side of the Isa Bey Camili. Garden Motel- Camping (5451-1163); garden-like setting; small and popular; walking distance to town sights; well maintained; $$$.

KUSADASI AREA

Once a lovely seaside town, this is now a port stop for cruise ships and ferries to the Greek island of Samos. Bulging with package tour groups it's hard on the budget. A large public parking place is close to the tourist area. A walk to the ancient wall and tower, peering into the courtyards off the narrow winding streets along the way, can provide some exercise. ****Camping: *Just north of town, close to the discos and shopping. Onder Camping (0256-614-2413) or *Yat Camping, (0256-614-1333); both on the beach; good maintenance; open May-September; $$$$.

CLOSE BY SIGHTS

Dilek National Park is a restful day spot with a beach and pine forest. Directions: Drive southeast out of Kusadasi on the main road for eight kilometers, then exit onto a smaller road and drive 18km in the direction of Guzelcamli. The park entrance is two kilometers on the west side of town; open daily.

The setting of awe-inspiring Priene is reminiscent of Greece's Delphi. Try to be there at sunset; open daily. Directions: Drive southeast out of Kusadasi on the main road for 21km in the direction of Soke, exiting south on 525. After five kilometers, exit onto a smaller road and follow sign posting west to Priene, passing through the village of Savulca. ****Camping: On the road to the Priene. Priene Pensions-Camping (0256-547-1249); basic; fair maintenance; open May-September; $$.

Climb to the top of the mammoth theater at Miletus for a view of the entire area. The sea has receded but imagine it as it once was, at the edge of the sea. Afterwards, drive on farther to see the huge columns still standing at the Temple to Apollo. It's not hard to recreate in your mind the

Temple's magnificence and religious impor- tance. Directions: Follow the directions to Priene above, but drive west nine kilometers, exiting south at Tuzburgazi. Drive 19km far- ther through cotton fields and olive groves. Miletus is just north of the village of Balat. The Temple of Apollo is just south on the same road in the direction of Akkoy and Didim. If you're not visiting Priene, take 525 south of Soke for 25km, exiting west onto a small road in the direction of Yenikoy and Akkoy. Miletus is about four kilometers north of Akkoy and the Temple of Apollo is 15km south of Akkoy. ****Camping: *On the Bafa-See, exit 525 at Sarikemer and head east to the village of Golonu. Turget Camping-Motel (0521-224-4075); shaded with pine and olive trees; nice location on a small lake; fair maintenance; open May-September; $$.

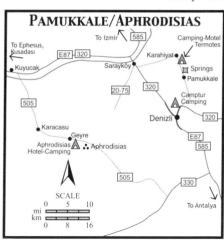

APHRODISIAS

Excavations have revealed settlements here dating back to the Early Bronze Age. Later, there were important Greek and Byzantine settlements and a school of sculpture. This site will be a major tourist site in the future. Currently much of it is still off-limits due to excavations in progress. The setting is inspiring, and the stadium, theater, Temple to Aphrodite, and Odeion are accessible. It is 55km from Nazilli. Get gas on E87 before driving out. After passing through Nazilli and Kuyucak on E87, exit on the smaller road 505 and drive south following the Menderes River for 38km. At the village of Karacasu, the road turns east towards the village of Geyre. The site is just beyond. ****Camping: West of the site on the main road. Aphrodisias Hotel-Camping (0256-448-8132); basic; open May-September; $.

PAMUKKALE

Pamukkale isn't the experience it once was. The beautiful travertine terraces, glistening like the insides of abalone shells in the gold and pink of sunset, are still there, but the ter- race area is smaller than it used to be. People can no longer walk out to soak their feet in the warm thermal waters, and the travertine ter- races are now viewed from paths above. The new restrictions are certainly merited but, con- sidering the time it takes to drive here, it can be a disappointment. If you drive to the north- ern entrance, it's a shorter walk to the springs, museum, and archeological site; open daily. Directions: Driving out on E87 is pleasant but time-consuming. It's 195km from Selcuk or 215km from Kusadasi. The good two-lane road has a third lane for passing. The rocky

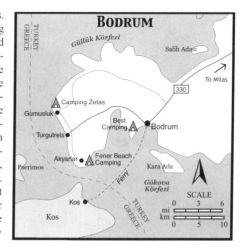

mountain landscape is studded with olive trees, and the divider strips are a blaze with roses, zinnias, and oleanders. Go into the town of Denizli, exiting north on 320 for 14km to Pamukkale. For a bit of a shortcut to Pamukkale, instead of going into Denizli take a small road off 320 south of the village of Saraykoy. Watch very closely for a small road heading east, then follow signage to Akkoy/Karahavit, 15km east. ****Camping: *South of Pamukkale, just before you enter town, on road 320. Camptur Camping; swimming pool; large restaurant catering to busloads of tourists; nice view of vineyards; casual maintenance; open May-September $$. *Five kilometers north of Pamukkale, in the village of Karahayit. Camping-Motel Termotes (025-271-4066); thermal swimming pool; better for RVs; good maintenance; open all year; $$$.

BODRUM

The open market in the center of town and the Crusaders' Castle are the main reason for stopping here. This is a hip town with lots of places to hang out and enjoy the scene. Several good carparks are right in the center of town by the market. Ferries go to the Greek island of Kos. The drive to Milas on the main road 303 passes through pleasant pine forests with panoramic views of Bodrum and its yacht harbor and castle. ****Camping: *Closest to town. On the main road heading west from Bodrum exit toward the beach at Bitez. Best Camping (0252-316-7688); part of the scene; fair maintenance; open May-September; $$$$. *At the end of the main road at Turgutreis, 25km from Bodrum, drive north on the beach road to Gumbet. Camping Zetas (0252-316-2231); nice location on the beach; well maintained; open year-round; $$$$. *From Turgutreis, take the beach road south five kilometers to Akyariar, passing through the village to the lighthouse. Fener Beach Camping; lovely location; casual maintenance; open May-September; $$.

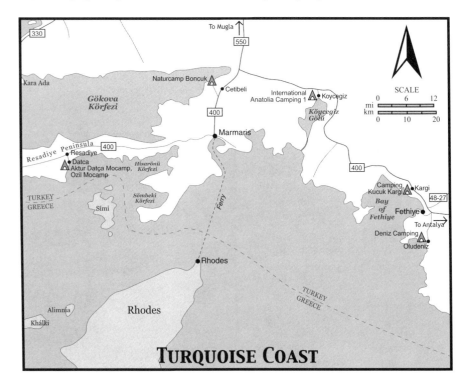

TURQUOISE COAST

TURQUOISE COAST

The panoramic view from the highway along this beautiful coastline is breathtaking. When the road turns inland, the air becomes filled with the scent of pine, while on flatter areas your eyes are treated to colorful small fields of corn, beans, and citrus. The seaside resorts here are more authentically Turkish than the west coast. ****Camping: South of Mula, exit 550 onto 400, and drive south in the direction of Mararis for about ten kilometers. Pass through the village of Cetibeli, watching for a small forest road close to the bridge. It's two kilometers on this road. Naturcamp Boncuk (0252-495-8114); beautifully located on the beach; well maintained; open all year; $$$. *Take 400 west out onto the tiny pennisula for 71km to Resadiye, then drive south for four kilometers on the same road to Datca. Aktur Datca Mocamp (0252-724-6168) or Ozil Mocamp (0252-712-3149); both have beautiful locations on the beach with all the amenities; well maintained; open May-September; $$$$.

Enroute Camping: *At the Bay of Koycegiz. Just off the main Mugla/Fethiye road 400 at Koycegiz. International Anatolia Camping 1 (0252-262-2752); on the beach; disco; restaurant; well maintained; open May-September; $$$.

FETHIYE

An excursion boat ride out into the Bay of Fethiye is a popular Turkish outing. Buy a ticket right at the harbor and wear a bathing suit, because it's a real kick to dive or jump from the boat into the beautiful turquoise water. Lunch is included in the half-day outing. ****Camping: *Use your odometer to find this one. It's 33km east of Dalaman or 18km west of Fethiye. Look for a winding road leading down the hillside through the pines to the sea. Camping Kucuk Kargi; low key Turkish family atmosphere, lovely setting; fair maintenance; open June-August; $$. *South out of Fethiye eleven kilometers, take the small road to Oludeniz to the beach. Deniz-Camping (0252-617-0045); beautiful location; restaurant; disco; well maintained; open all year; $$$$.

SAKIKENT GORGE

Hiking into the Sakikent Gorge is like hiking through a vast marble sculpture. The water-carved chasm goes in for 18km, but most hikers don't go that far. Young guides assist less able hikers up into the chasm. Wear shoes that can get wet and aren't slippery. Bring your camera. Inside the chasm, you can enjoy tea and freshly grilled. Turkish snacks while sitting on rugs and pillows. Outside the gorge, it's great fun to float down the river in an innertube . Get gas before driving out. Directions: From Fethiye, take 400 east, but instead of heading south on 400, continue east on 350 for three kilometers. Watch for a small road heading south and signage for Sakikent Gorge. It's a picturesque route through small farmlands. Little roadside cafes have outside dining and serve grilled trout right off the outdoor barbecue. They are terrific places to rest and absorb more of the Turkish countryside ambiance.   ****Camping: *At the gorge, along the river. Very basic; Turkish; and fun; $.

SAKLIKENT GORGE TO KEKOVA

XANTHOS RUINS

For a break from driving on 400, get some fresh air and exercise while wandering around these ruins. Look for signage by the bridge in the village of Kinik. The small road to the ruins is at the southern point of the road to the Sakikent Gorge. Patara is a cute, touristy little village. The camping here is very basic; and it is a long walk to the beach.

KAS AND KEKOA

The gorgeous coastline from Kalkan to Kas should be savored. Take your time, stopping at viewing areas, to enjoy the splendor, and have your camera handy. Kas is a picturesque stopping place for yachts on the Turquoise Coast. Bougainvillea shrouds stores and cafes and colorful awnings cover the tiny passageways between the waterfront and market. The main sights are seeing what the locals call the "sunken city" off Kevoa Island, the acropolis and tombs of the Lycian town of Teimiussa, and the Knights of St. John castle in Simena. Arrange to rent a sea kayak from Bougainvillea Travel at Cukurbagli Cad 10, in Kas or call ahead; 0242-836-3142. If you are an experienced kayaker you can go on your own, or if not, you can join one of their small tour groups. You'll pick up the kayak and set out from the seaside village of Ucagiz. Sea kayaking is quite safe here. It's a delightful and refreshing way to get a close look at the ruins. A map of the water area is provided. Besides kayaking, the company, can arrange scuba-diving trips. The visibility and variety of underwater scenery is considered the best in Turkey.

If you don't want to kayak, drive to Ucagiz and hire one of the local boatmen to take you out. You'll get a much closer view of the ruins than in the larger boats from Kas. The excursion by boat should stop in Kale, where you can clamor up the hillside to see the ruins of the Byzantine fortress, its walls, and a tiny theater. The village of Ucagiz is delightful, particularly at night when most of the tourists have left and the castle and small restaurants overlooking the bay twinkle with lights. Directions: Drive east out of Kas for eleven kilometers on 400. Exit onto the small road, and drive south in the direction of Kilicli/Kekova then a bit further to Ucagiz. ****Camping: *Off 400, one kilometer west of Kas. Olympus Mocamp; nice location at the beach with shade trees; bungalows; well maintained; $$$. *50km east of Kas, on 400, on the wide long beach east of Finike. Albania Camping; basic; casual maintenance; open May-September; $$.

RUINS OF CIRALI OLIMPOS

Beneath dramatic mountain gorges, where wild thyme, bay, and mint fill the air with refreshing aromas, the ruins of Olimpos lay half-hidden by leafy trees. A cool stream, whose banks are daubed colorfully with wild cyclamen and oleander, accompanies your walk to the beach. The walk up to the chimera or "burning rock" from the beach, makes for fun exploration. Delightful tree house pension/cafes, popular with backpackers, are close to the beach. Stock up on gas, food, and water before you come. Directions: 18km east of Kumuluca exit off 400. It's signposted Olimpos-Cirali and Yanartas-Chimera. From the exit on 400 it is seven kilometers to Cirali then another eight kilometers on a small road toward the beach. ****Camping: *Tree house camping out of Cavuskoy, along the small road heading to the beach; sign-posted Olimpos. Kadir's Restaurant-Bungalows-Camping; lovely location; basic; casual maintenance; open May-September; $$. *In Cirali, at the north end of the beach. Green Point Camping; well maintained; open May-September; $$$.

PHASELIS

Stop here for a swim and picnic. The mountains tumble right down to the edge of the sea making secluded little coves. You can drift off to sleep smelling the pines and listening to soft-

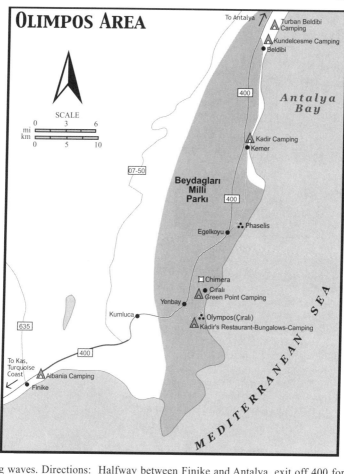

OLIMPOS AREA

SCALE

mi 0 3 6
km 0 5 10

07-50

To Antalya

Turban Beldibi Camping
Kundelcesme Camping
Beldibi

400

Antalya Bay

Kadir Camping
Kemer

Beydaglari Milli Parkı

400

Phaselis
Egelkoyu

Chimera
Çıralı
Green Point Camping
Yenbay
Kumluca
Olympos(Çıralı)
Kadir's Restaurant-Bungalows-Camping

635

400

To Kas, Turquoise Coast
Albania Camping
Finike

MEDITERRANEAN SEA

ly lapping waves. Directions: Halfway between Finike and Antalya, exit off 400 for Phaselis and drive three kilometers to the beach. The morning market at Kemer is very good. Children enjoy seeing the town's ethnographic exhibit of nomad life. Directions: Kemer is 15km east of the exit for Phaselis. ****Camping: *One kilometer east of the exit for Kemer. Kadir Camping; a forest service campground overlooking the sea; steps lead down to the beach; large with plenty of sites with tables; well maintained; open June-August; $$. *In Beldibi, on the west side of the tunnel. Kundulcesme Camping; a forest service campground on the beach; close to the road; open June-August; $$. *20 km west of Antalya, on the coast road out of Beldibi. Turban Beldibi Camping (02421-814-1531); on the beach; resort-like; open May-September; $$$.

ANTALYA

Antalya is justifibly proud of its outstanding Archeological Muzesi. This is a major museum, so allow plenty of time. The chronological exhibit begins with the Stone and Bronze ages, proceeds through the Mycenaean, and Hellenistic periods, and goes on to the Seljuk and Ottoman periods.

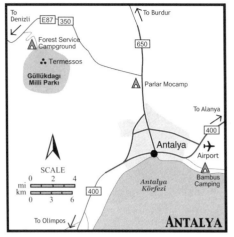

Start with the Roman Floor Mosaics exhibit on the first floor. It is one of the finest collection in the world, and the themes are full of fun and frivolity. Exhibits are artistically designed and include labels in English. Directions: Exit off 400 on the west side of Antalya, and drive to the beach road. The museum is on Kenan Evren Bulvari, across from Ataturk Park on the west side of the river; closed Mondays. ****Camping: *In Antalya, at Lara Paj. Exit off 400 for the airport, then drive to the beach. Turn east on the beach road. Bambus Camping (0242-321-5263); bungalows; good for RVs; well maintained; open May- October; $$$$.

TERMESSOS

Spectacular and mystical in its high mountain setting, Termessos is not heavily touristed. To sit as high as an eagle in the spectacular amphitheatre, practically alone, is delightfully errie. The 20-minute walking trail climbs up to the ruins from the parking area. Clearly marked trails wind down the hillside to various sections of the ruins. Wear good walking shoes and bring water and a guidebook. A small museum and picnic/camping area are under the pines at the base of the mountain. Directions: From Anatyla, exit 400 north in the direction of Burdur/Afron-Denesli/Mugia. Where the road forks stay left driving in the direction of Korkuteli on 350/E87. Drive 20km on 350/E87 to Gullukdagi Milli Parki and road to Termessos. From here the road winds up another nine kilometers through the aromatic pines. ****Camping: *In the park at the entrance. Gullukdagi Milli Parki Camping; a forest service campground; tranquil setting under the pines; basic; well maintained; open June-August; $$. *14 km from Antalya, in the direction of Burdur on 650. Parlar Mocamp (0242-332-6601); popular with RVs; well maintained; open May-September; $$$$.

PERGE

The elaborate theatrical productions, gladiator displays, and chariot races staged here were famous. Both the theater and stadium are well preserved. Bring a guidebook. Directions: One kilometer east of the exit for Isparta and 685, exit onto a small road signposted for Perge. It's two kilometers north of 400.

ASPENDOS

Elaborately constructed in 200 A.D. and beautifully preserved today, this is one of the greatest ancient theaters in the world. Check the calendar of events before coming to the area, so you can time your visit to coincide with a wonderful performance under the starlit sky. A major opera and ballet festival occurs in June, but other performances are scheduled throughout the summer. Check with the Marcus Aurelius Tourist Office by fax; 0242-247-6798 or call Ahi Yusuf Camii Yani, Kaleici in historic Antalya; 0242-247-5042. The lovely humpbacked Seljuk bridge crosses over the Kopru River just west of the exit for Aspendos. Directions: The road to Aspendos is 30km east of the exit for Isparta and 685. Watch for signage nine kilometers east of the village of Serik. Exit off 400, and drive four kilometers north. ****Camping: *15 km east of Serik on 400. Beypet Camping (0242-617-205); convenient location; fair maintenance; open May-September; $$.

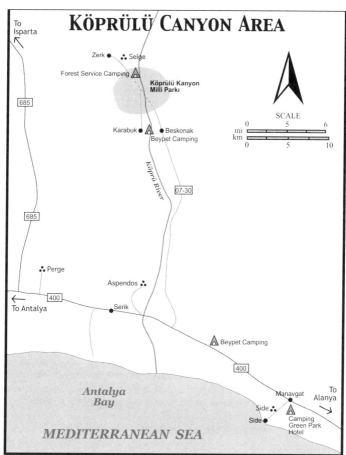

KÖPRÜLÜ CANYON AREA

KOPRULU CANYON

This is one of my favorite areas in Turkey. In the canyon wooden cottages are draped in colorful vines and gardens burst with flowers. There's a joyful symphony of humming insects and songbirds. The Turks who live here are friendly and welcome visitors. River rafting is California-style, with helmets, wet suits, and competent boatmen accompanying paddling groups on 4 to 6-man boats. The river can be exciting and is extremely scenic. Drive farther up the mountain to explore the ancient Roman ruins of the Selge, an almost savage mountaintop experience that is hard to forget. The road to the ruins winds steeply up through arid mountains dramatically set off by chimney-like sculptures carved by the wind. It ends in the village of Zerk, where the people are poor but very friendly and warm. Local guides can take you through the ruins, or you can arrange to trek in the area around the picturesque villages of Beskonak and Karabuk. To swim and jump off boulders into the beautiful Koprulu River, stop at the new bridge. Directions: Follow the directions to Aspendos. From Aspendos follow the river road into the canyon 25km. ****Camping: Camp here along the grassy slopes of a rushing river, under a brilliant star-filled sky, lullabyed to sleep by the tinkling of goat bells. *Close to the villages of Beskonak and Karabuk, at the rafting com-

panies' places along the river. Raft Camping; simple; fair maintenance; open June-August; $.
*Take the left fork off the main road to Selge, going over the newer bridge and continuing in the direction of Selge. Pass the Selge turnoff, and go a little farther to the second old bridge, the Roman Bogrum. Korpulu Canyon Milli Parki Camping; a forest service campground; lovely setting above the river under the pines; basic; open June-August; $.

SIDE
Overnight here before you drive up to Konya, which is a full day of driving without any campgrounds. The port's ancient ruins at the old harbor make a nice evening stroll. ****Camping: *Close to Manavgat at km 4.5. Camping Green Park Hotel (0242-756-9140); close to the beach; well maintained; open May-September; $$$.

CENTRAL TURKEY
KONYA
In the middle of the country's breadbasket, Konya is authentic Turkey. An important place of pilgrimage for the Muslim world, it was the adopted home of the mystic Mevlana, who founded the Whirling Dervish sect. It's a uniquely memorable town. All the museums are within walking distance from the round Alaeddin Parki in the center of town. Parking is readily available. There is an excellent market/bazaar area between the intriguing museums around Alaeddin Parki and the Mevlana Muzesi or Whirling Dervish Museum. The pilgrims are tearful and solemn as they pay homage to Mevlana, whose teachings promised deliverance from the cares of the world. The tombs of the mystic and his son are shrouded in elaborately brocaded velvet topped with majestic turbans. Your experience here will set the mood for the rest of your explorations including the town's fabulous tile work, exquisite portals, and lovely mosques. Museums are closed on Mondays. Bring a guidebook. Directions: From the center of the historic area, the round Alaeddin Parki, look for the fluted turquoise dome that embleshes the Mevlana Muzesi. ****Camping: *At the sports stadium; run-down. Might be okay if you have an RV, otherwise consider an inexpensive pension.

The drive through the steppe of Anatolia is dramatic in a windswept and melancholy way. The peaceful serenity of the wide-winged, black goat-herder tents gathered together is enlivened by women dressed in brightly striped clothing and vividly colored scarves.

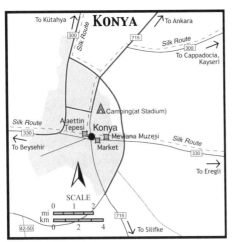

IHLARA VALLEY AND GORGE
In this valley, songbirds call, trees whisper, and the sun peers through leafy branches, dappling soft, grassy areas. All through the gorge, the bubbling, clear creek laughs and giggles, delighting walkers. It's an easy walk. Allow time to rest and picnic. If you start early, you'll miss the tour groups who have discovered its beauty. There are two entrances: Belisirma, where the campgrounds on the creek is located, and Ihlara, the official entrance. At Ihlara, a long stair-

case leads down to the gorge. At the bottom, you can visit the remains of monastic refuges tucked into the mountainside caves. Fill up with gas in Aksaray before driving out. Directions: Aksaray is at the southeast corner of Golu Lake, south of Ankara. Drive east from Aksaray on 300 for eleven kilometers in the direction of Nevsehir. Exit south on a smaller road in the direction of Ihlara, and drive 31km. Exit this small road onto a smaller road continuing in the direction of Ihlara. ****Camping: *In Ihlara Village, on the road to the main entrance of the gorge. Anatolia Pension and Camping (0382-453-7128); pleasant spot; basic; well maintained; open May-September; $ *Along the river in the gorge. From Ihlara, take the small road heading north to

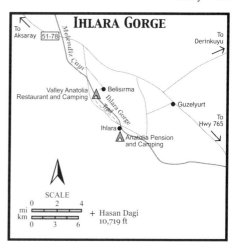

Yaprakhisar. One kilometer south of the village turn onto the road going towards the river and otopark. Valley Anatolia Restaurant and Camping (0382-451-2433); you need to park at the otopark, and carry your camping gear across the walking bridge to the campground. It's a very scenic, peaceful, and friendly place; basic; fair maintenance; open June-August; $.

DERINKUYU AN UNDERGROUND CITY

This is a fascinating stop. The underground dwellings here were used by the Hittites and are in remarkable condition. Rooms are more airy and light than you might imagine. Ventilation shafts, kitchens, deep wells and storage jars were all painstakingly carved. The passageways between rooms are narrow and low. Wait for those ahead of you to get to the next room before you start through. Printed guides can be purchased but everything is clearly labeled. Directions: Derinkuyu is about halfway between Nevsehir and Nigde. From Ihlara, take the small road directly east to Guzelyurt, then follow signage east in the direction of Kuyuluttlar and Derinkuyu. Once in town, the underground city is signposted "Yeralti Sehri" on the east side of the road.

CAPPADOCIA

Unique in the world, this landscape of soft rock, sculpted by wind, rain and snow, is an environment totally different than anywhere you've been before. The ancient caves have been refuges since the days of the Hittites. Colorful Byzantine frescoes decorate the tiny cave churches; bring a guidebook to learn the fascinating stories connected to some of them. Besides the entry fee, some of the churches have additional charges. The Valley of the Fairy Chimney's thickly clustered reddish cones are more dramatic with the shadows that come early or late in the day. Directions: Out of Goreme drive east in the direction of Avanos/Cavusin to Yeni Zelve. From Zelve, drive two kilometers farther. For an adventure that requires strength, agility, and nerve, explore the monastery complex in Zelve. It requires rock climbing through a honeycomb of rooms. There's a long, winding completely dark tunnel in one part. Bring a flashlight, water and a *local guide*. Ambling along the Dovecote Valley walking trail is a pleasant way to escape the crowds and enjoy the stark beauty of this high desert area. The trail winds between Goreme and Uchisar. Fill up with gas and groceries in Nevsehir before driving our to Goreme. Directions: Goreme is about 300km southeast of Ankara. From Nevsehir, drive east on 767 for 5km. Exit for Goreme. It's well signposted. Drive eight kilometers to Goreme. ****Camping: *In Goreme,

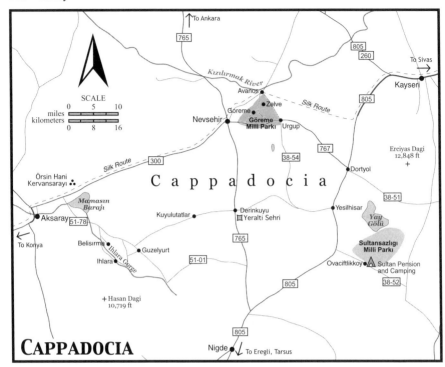

CAPPADOCIA

within walking distance of the Open-Air Museum (saves money for parking). Dilek Camping (0271-2396) or Berlin Camping (0271-2249); both have swimming pools; are well maintained; open May-September; $$$.

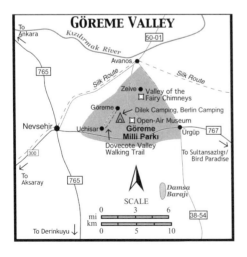

SULTANSAZLIGI/ BIRD PARADISE

The open plain landscape of this protected bird marsh area is reminiscent of Montana in the USA. Staying in the village is like stepping back into old Anatolian Turkey. The stars are brilliant, and you are lulled to sleep by shepherd's flute. In the early morning, as the sun begins to paint Mount Erciyes a brilliant crimson, flat-bottom tourist boats are pushed into the marshes and inner ponds by long poles. The experience is silent except for the rustle of wind in the reeds and the flutter of birds' wings. Arrangements for the trip are made at the small museum where you can study the birds you'll see in the marsh. Bring binoculars and camera. Fill up with gas and get local currency and supplies before you drive out. Sultansazligi Milli Parki is 85km southeast of Goreme. The scenic drive from Goreme to the park passes through groves of poplars and willows to a plateau with ochre-colored escarpments. As you wind down from the plateau, you pass through a dramatic valley of flat lands with tidy plots of vegetables and wheat fields. Directions: From Urgup, five kilometers east of Goreme, drive east on 767 for 30km to the village of Dortyol and 805. Turn south in the direction of Yesilhsar, and drive eleven kilometers south of Yesilhsar. Turn east on a small road for 12km to the village Ovaciftlik and Sultansazligi Milli Parki. ****Camping: *At the end of the village's main road. Look for the bird-viewing tower. Sultan Pension and Camping, across from the museum (0352-658-5549); lovely location on the plains beneath Mount Erciyes; within walking distance of the marsh area; basic; fair maintenance; friendly; open May-September; $.

BOGAZKALE MILLI PARKI/HITTITE RUINS

Once the center of Hittite settlements, the ruins of Hattusas and Yazilikaya are still majestic in size and setting. It's hard to imagine they were built in 2500 B.C. The Great Temple is the largest and best preserved of its kind in the world. Start at the museum in Bogazkale; closed Monday. Buy a map, or use your guidebook. Directions: Drive about 200km east of Ankara on E88. Exit E88 at Yozgat and drive north on 66-77 for 33km. ****Camping: *In Bogazale. Atilla Camping, on the main road in the direction of Sungurlu, (364-452-2101) or Baskent Camping, on the road to Yazilikaya with view of the Great Temple. Both are basic; fair maintenance; open June-August; $.

AMAYSA

Dramatically set in beautiful gorge, alongside a rushing river, this where the Pontiac kings carved their tombs out of cliffs above the river, 2000 years ago. Strabo, the world's first historian, was born here. Ataturk spent time here planning the Turkish independence. Now half timbered homes border the river and an easy, relaxed Alpine village-like ambiance prevails. The museum, just west of the Sultan Beyazit Canii, has an excellent collection and displays a re-created Ottoman home. Directions: Amaysa is about 80km south of the Black Sea, almost due south of Samsun. ****Camping: None. Use your guidebook and stay at one of the friendly inexpensive pensions.

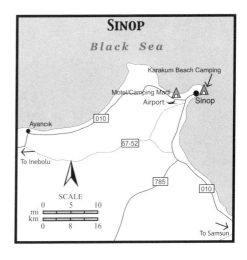

THE BLACK SEA
FROM INEBOLU TO SINOP

The drive here is breathtaking. In the fall, the forests are tipped like newly painted fingernails with red, gold and ochre. In summer they are lacy, green, and lined with masses of wild berry bushes. It's a grandness that's impressive. Tractors grind by wheezing with enormous loads that are secured with colorful cloths. Vintage Ottoman homes stand proud on the hillsides looking down on fields of wheat that stretch to the sea. It's reminiscent of the Northwest Coast in the USA with the added color of Vermont. Abana, a charming little Black Sea town, has a wonderful bakery, a shop featuring homemade cheese and olives, and a colorful little square where you can relax with Anatolians. The two-laned road is well maintained, and traffic is light. ****Camping: *In Sinop. West of town follow the signposting to Ayancik, then turn toward the small airport and drive to the beach. Motel/Camping Marti, across from the beach in a garden; well maintained; open June-August; $$. In the same area. *Karakum Beach Camping; southeast corner of the promontory; well maintained; open June-August; $$. *In Abana. At the east end of town, off the main road on the beach. Kamping Bufe, colorfully painted; friendly; fair maintenance; $$.

THE BLACK SEA AROUND AMASRA

Due north of Ankara, this lovely beach area is a decorated with sunflower and tobacco fields, rocky cliffs, and pine forests. ****Camping: *They dot the whole coastline. Lovely locations; friendly; fair maintenance; open July-August; $$.

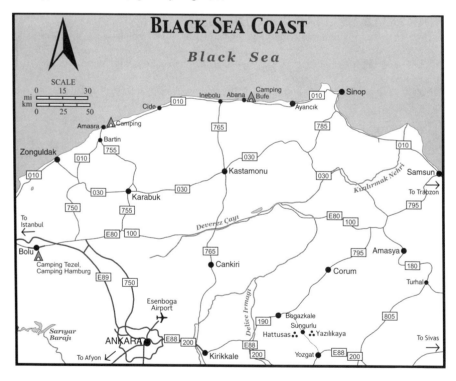

THE BLACK SEA AROUND SILE

Only about 120km from Istanbul, this popular vacation area manages to keep a low-key, relaxed atmosphere. The beach is beautiful and serene. Sile, a happy town catering to weekend tourists, has a town-square with cozy little shops where you can stock up on supplies. On the way there barbecue restaurants roast whole pigs and lambs on spits. The delicious aroma and beautiful scenery will entice you to stop. From Omerli, the road to Sile is two-laned and winds through forests of deciduous trees, cornfields, and pastureland. Directions: From Istanbul take E80 east. After crossing the bridge over the Golden Horn, stay on E80 following signage to Umraniye. Drive east in the direction of Alemdar. Turn north to Omerli on 020 and onto Sile. Coming from east of Istanbul, exit E80 for Samandira. Follow signage to Omerli. From Omerli drive northeast on 020 to Sile.

***Camping: *16 km east of Sile. Drive east out of Sile in the direction of Aqua. At the fork, stay left driving in the direction of Akcakese. Follow signage for camping. Camping Akkaya (0216-727-7010); on a secluded beach; bungalows; restaurant; lovely setting; well maintained; $$$.

ANKARA

Turkey's capitol and most modern city is Ankara. It is home to the famous Museum of Anatolian Civilization which tells the story, with English labels, of Anatolian civilization from the first settlements; closed Monday. Directions: Follow signs on Ataturk Bulvari to Hisar, the citadel on top of the hill. The museum is at the hill's base. Ataturk's Mausoleum, the Anit Kabir, is a quiet, spacious, and beautifully green place. On the east side of the courtyard, a museum exhibits the personal effects of this remarkable man. Don't miss it. Directions: The Anit Kabir is on the south side of the rail tracks south west of the museum. The historic museum areas are well signposted and have good parking. ****Camping: *Just off eastern edge of the ring autostrata. Take exit #9/Samsun 1, in the suburb of Bayindir Baraji. Camping Bayindir Baraji (0312-338-4759); convenient; traffic noise; well maintained; open May-September; $$$.

ENROUTE BETWEEN ISTANBUL AND ANKARA

****Camping: *South of Bolu, on the road to Karasu, along the river. Camping Tezel (0374-611-4115); lovely location on the river; bungalows; well maintained; open April-November; $$$. *In the same area but not as well located. Camping Hamburg (0374-6112991); fair mintenance; open all year; $$.

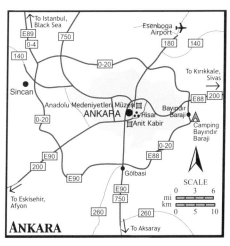

CROATIA
THE ADRIATIC COAST

Breathtakingly beautiful, a veritable treasured jewel, Croatia has been sought after, stolen, and conquered since ancient times, usually by wealthy invaders who wanted to make it an exclusive club, where only the chosen few could enjoy themselves.

Europeans have been coming to Croatia to camp for years. The sun and water are warm. It's easy to pitch your tent under the pines at the edge of the sea and take in the gorgeous setting.

The highways coming into Zagreb and Rijeka from Italy, Hungary, and Slovenia are in good condition, sometimes even four-laned and divided. The scenery is outstanding. Signage close to the cities is good. The Croatians have a long history of tourism and want to make is easy for their visitors. The highway from Rijeka to Zadar is heavily trafficked. The drive south of the Zadar peninsula, although most of the time two-laned, is a well-known scenic drive offering the breathtaking beauty of the azure sea and the perfume of pines and acacia pouring off the mountainside. Good maps are available.

It's easy to take a car ferry for part of the trip down the Adriatic coast. The main office for the stately Jadrolinija Lines is in Rijeka, on the waterfront at Riva 16. The friendly and helpful staff speak English; 385-51-211-444. Good signage to the ferry is provided on the main highways. Public parking is at the south end of the harbor. Stock up on supplies at the morning market held close to this public parking area. You don't need to book a cabin if you don't mind sleeping on deck. There is a charge for deck chairs but free bench seating is also available. Bring blankets, inflatable pillows, collapsible ground chairs, and warm clothing. Whether you have a cabin or not, bringing food and beverages makes the trip more fun. Before boarding the ferry, arrange your car so what you are taking on deck is easy to grab. You won't be able to access your car during the cruise. The car fare will cost the same as one person.

Beaches here are often pebbly rather than sandy, making the sea crystal clear. Bring sandals or rubber diving boots and an inflatable air mattress. There isn't much surf, so it is fun to bob around on an air mattress, which doubles as a comfortable resting surface on the beach. At many of the campgrounds, you'll join lots of other people enjoying the sun and sea in a resort-like setting. Nudity is common, tennis is popular, and there are playgrounds for kids. There's always room for another tent so you don't have to make reservations ahead for a tent even in the busy season. For two persons, a car, and a tent, you'll usually pay under $20 USA, resort-like campgrounds will cost about $25 USA.

ISTRIA

The northern end of the coast, close to Italy and Austria, has been settled since the Bronze Age. Since that time, the land has been claimed by many. Because the protected harbor provides shelter for fishing boats and access for merchant vessels, a lively trade and cosmopolitan atmosphere developed. The fields are fertile and the climate is ideal for growing grapes, so wine making prospers. The weather is sunny and warm and the water crystal blue. Today the Istrians proudly exhibit their ancient Glagolitian script as evidence of their early settlement. ****Camping: The whole seacoast is dotted with places. They are large, well maintained facilities with all the amenities. Many vacation-campers rent large tent-homes and spend several weeks. Nudity is common on the beaches. FKK signs indicate a nudist campgrounds and regular campgrounds often have a separate nude beach. An open date in May and close date at the end of September is common. Assume all of this for the camping places mentioned here for Istria.

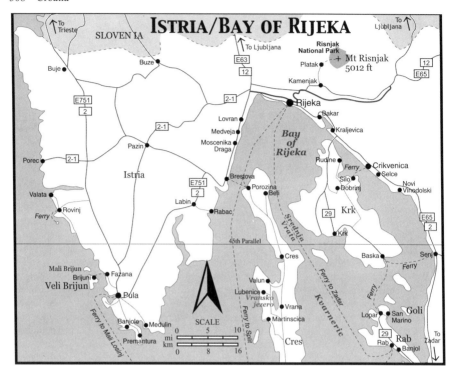

POREC

Porec is on a narrow, finger halfway down the western side of the Istrian peninsula. Early Christians established themselves here, eventually building what is now main attraction, the Ephrasian Bascilica. Byzantine and ablaze with golden mosaics and gracefully sculpted columns,

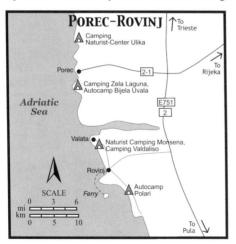

it is the earliest example of a triple-apsed church in Western Europe. UNESCO has listed it as a World Cultural Heritage Site. The town is picturesque in its setting on the north edge of the spit overlooking the sea on Obala Matka Laginje.   The Porestina Folk Museum, housed in the Sincic Palace, Decumanus 9a, has a good collection of artifacts, and the summer festivals provide a lively atmosphere.   For details check with the tourist office on the east side of the old town, at Zagrebacka 11. ****Camping: *Three kilometers south of town on the coast road, exit for the beach. Camping Zela Laguna (052-410-541) and Autocamp Bijela Uvala (052-410-552); $$$. *Drive north of Porec, taking the coast road for nine kilometers then drive south on a small road a few kilometers towards the tip of the fingerling. Naturist-Center Ulika (052-410-541); FKK; $$$$.

ROVINJ

Now an art center, Rovinj hosts a well-known open-air art show in mid-August. Artists show off their work on Bregovita ulica, a covered passageway decorated with frescoes. The town has a Venetian atmosphere, with steep, narrow streets threading their way to tiny piazzas. A friendly and relaxed ambiance prevails. St. Euphemia, the largest Baroque building in Istria, sits on the top of the hill at the end of town looking out onto the entire archipelago. At the aquarium, located along the seawall northeast of town, you can examine the interesting flora and fauna of the beautiful waters. The jagged coastline south of Rovinj is thick with a rich forest of allepo, cedar, and silver fir pines, giving the sea breezes a heady fragrance. This is a nice place to swim and picnic. If you feel like a boat ride, take the ferry to Crveni otok or Red Island, breathing in the air aromatic with myrtle and bay, and explore the 7th century chapel. ****Camping: *Drive north out of town towards Valalta. Naturist Camping Monsena (052-813-243); FKK; $$$$. Camping Valdaliso (052-811-510); $$$.   *South of town, on the beach road. Autocamp Polari (052-813-441); $$$. Camping Puntizela (052-517-490); $$.

PULA

Pula's Arena vies in splendor with those that are more famous. It's sixth in the world in size, but its condition is better than some that are larger. Built in 29 B.C., it has four stone towers and a reservoir to provide water for the fountains. A well-known film festival takes place here in July. It's located just east of the main harbor area. James Joyce spent time in Pula, and his wife Nora gave birth to their child here. Wine and olive production have always been important, and a pleasant museum telling that story is at the Arena. The archeological museum, gardens, and Roman theater are especially pleasing; open daily. Directions: Close to the Twin Gates. Climb to the top of the hill to the Venetian Fortress, where the views are splendid. If you have time, stop at the historical museum. It concentrates on the People's War of Independence as well as on the Istrian struggle with the Italians, Austrians, and Germans; open daily.

Beautiful Brijuni, an archipelago of 14 islands, has lured the wealthy for centuries. In their elaborate gardens and luxurious villas the wealthy hosted famous guests who sent back gifts of exotic plant and animal life. Thriving in their protected environment, these gifts now add an extra charm to the visit here. Tito was the last resident, and his yachts, fabulous villa, and memorable sculpture garden are worth seeing. To go, arrive in Fazana, north of Pula, in the morning to catch the obligatory escorted tour of the islands. Excursion boats also ply the waters of the archipelago. ****Camping: *North of town drive in the direction of Fazana, then take the road heading toward the beach. Camping Puntizela (052-517-490); $$. *Take the road along the south side of the harbor, then exit for Stoja. Autocamp Stoja (052-241-44); $$$. *Drive south out of town in the direction of Prematura. After six kilometers drive west towards the beach going through the village of Banjole and out to the tip.

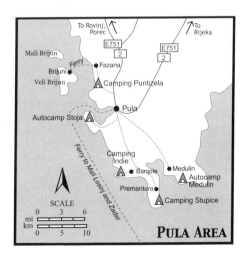

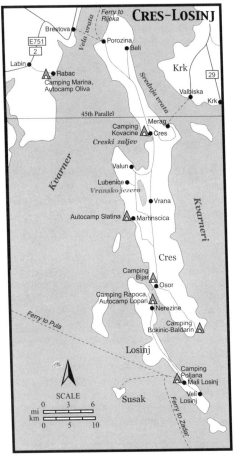

CRES-LOSINJ

Camping Indie (052-573-066); $$$. *Farther south on the fingerling of Prematura, on the bay. Camping Stupice (052-575-111); $$$. *In Medulin, on the other side of the bay. Autocamp Medulin (052-576-040); $$$.

THE ISLANDS OF CRES AND LOSINJ

Besides its beauty and sunshine, the island of Cres is well known as a nesting place for griffon vultures, golden eagles, peregrine falcons, and snake eagles. The Ornithological Reserve is out of Beli, a picturesque little town on the northeastern coast. While traveling from the ferry port town of Porozina to Cres Town, you can stop and see how it feels to be on the 45th parallel, the line that is equidistant from the equator and the North Pole. It is marked about five kilometers from Cres Town, on the east side of the road. In the village of Valun, the oldest Glagolitic inscription which dates from the 11th century, can be seen on the Valun Tablet built into the wall of the parish church. This inscription, though small and partly in Latin, is significant to the Isterians. It marks the beginning of their ancestry, the Glagolitians, in Croatia. Directions: Drive south of Cres Town on the main road for eight kilometers then turning west along the Bay to Valun for six more kilometers. The oldest settlement on Cres is Lubenice. Now almost abandoned, it is picturesque in its hilltop setting and is sometimes called Sleeping Beauty's Castle. Directions: Seven kilometers southwest of Valun. The town of Osor on the southern tip of Cres hosts summer events and has an interesting sculpture and music exhibition.

Losinj's harbor at Mali Losinj is considered one of the most beautiful on the Adriatic, blending pine forests, gardens, and lovely hotels. It's built up for tourism but tastefully controlled. If you are camping in the area there's a walking path from Mali Losinj to Veli Losinj and excusion boats go to the island of Susak.

****Camping: As with Istria, these islands are popular with vacation home campers. The facilities are large, beautifully located, have all the amenities, and are well maintained. Separate nudist beaches are common. They generally open in May and close in September. Assume all of the above for this listing.

*On the island of Cres: On the bay west of Cres Town. Camping Kovacine (051-571-161); $$$$. Farther south, exit three kilometers south of Vrana in the direction of Martinscica, going through the village and out to the tip. Autocamp Slatina (051-574-127); $$$. *Just north of Osor. Camping Bijar (051-237-027); better for tents than RVs; $$$. *At the southern most tip of the island, 15km south of Osor. Camping Bokinic-Baldarin (051-235-646); $$.

*On the island of Losinj: North of Nerezine. Camping Rapoca (051-237-145); $$. Autocamp Lopari (237-127) $$$. *West of Mali Losinj. Camping Poljana (051-231-726); $$$$. Camping Cikat (231-125); $$$. *On the mainland, across from Cres. 15km east of Labin on the Bay of Rabac, Camping Marina (052-872-226); small, nice location; $$.

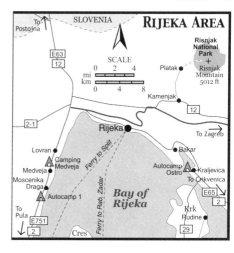

RIJEKA

Venetians, Austrians, Turks, Hungarians, and Italians have all vied for this important port and gateway to Europe. Shipbuilding, paper, and chemical production are important industries. Jadrolinija Ferry Lines have their main office here on the waterfront at Riva 16. The helpful staff speak English. A large public parking area is provided on the south end of the port. Park here, then take the scenic walk along the waterfront. Parking is just north of the bustling open-air market on Veridieva Street, a great place to pick up supplies. A couple of streets behind the waterfront, you can enjoy the interesting, almost Moorish, façade of the Capuchin Church. The octagonal, Baroque Church of St. Vitus is squeezed into a tiny piazza and is built on the site of a 9th century church. The number one historic site is Trsat Castle, built on a hill overlooking the harbor. The Romans built on the castle site first, followed by Austrians who hired a Venetian builder. Now the castle hosts art exhibits and summer festivals. Directions: It's signposted off 12/E65. Both the maritime and historical museums are housed in the former Governor's palace located down the hill from the castle. ****Camping: *South of the city take 2, and drive to the western end of the bay. Autocamp Ostro, in Kralijevica (051-281-404); bungalows; close to the beach; fair maintenance; $$. On the Istrian peninsula, *see camping in Lovran.*

RISNJAK NATIONAL PARK

For a mountain experience featuring panoramic views, pines forests, and hiking trails, drive out of Rijeka for 26km to Risnjak National Park and Platak, the recreational center. Directions: Take E65 for 13km in the direction of Zagreb. Exit north onto a smaller road signposted for the park. After six kilometers, at the village of Kamenjak drive up the mountain road for about ten kilometers to Platak.

CAMPING IN THE BAY OF RIJEKA:

*Off E751/2, 13km west of Rijeka, exit south onto 2/E751 in the direction of Pula. Drive 15km to Lovran. It's south of Lovran in the village of Medveja. Camping Medveja (052-291-191); $$$. Three kilometers farther south in Moscenicka Draga. Autocamp 1 (052-737-523); $$$$.

CRIKVENICA

A fishing village in the late 1800s, Crikvenica is now a popular beach and spa town. On August 15th swimmers flock to the town to participate in or watch the Marathon Swim to Silo on Krk Island. ****Camping: *South of town on E65 in the village of Selce. Camping Selce, at km 252.4 (051-782-014); resort-like, on the beach; well maintained; open May-September; $$$. *In the

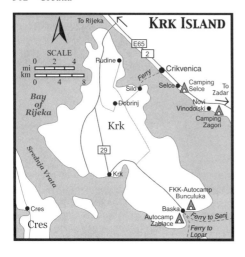

town of Novi Vinodolski. Camping Zagori, at km 256 (051-244-122); affiliated with a hotel; close to the beach; good maintenance; open May-September; $$.

KRK ISLAND

A huge concrete bridge stretches from the mainland to this island making access easy for vacationers. Krk Town is fairly large but a detour here to see 12th century Romanesque cathedral makes a nice stop. For other excursions, drive out to Dobrinj, a hillside village twenty kilometers from Krk Town, and to the Biserujka Cave, six kilometers northeast of Dobrinj in the village of Rudine. The cave is on the bay facing the mainland. ****Camping: There are lots of campgrounds on Krk Island but I recommend camping in the more remote village of Baska. With a gorgeous setting on the edge of the water and a maze of tiny passageways and piazzas it's well worth the extra drive. *From the bridge take 29 in the direction of Krk Town continuing south for another 18km to the village of Baska on the southern tip of the island. Autoamp Zablace, on the west side of the village (051-856-909); good for RVs. FKK-Autocamp Bunculuka, on the other side of the hill from the harbor (051-856-806); car parking is separate from camp site. They both have lovely settings on the beach, good maintenance; open May-September; $$$.

RAB ISLAND

Being one of the sunniest places in Europe, Rab Island has attracted sun worshipers and tourism since the beginning of the 19th century. It's shady with deciduous trees on the southwestern side, while the northwestern side is more rugged and barren. The Romans built an important naval port

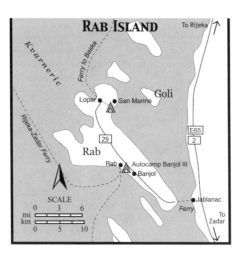

here, and you'll see interesting little churches as you wander about Rab Town. For a change of pace, investigate the horrors of the communist prison on the island of Goli; trips are arranged in Rab Town. ****Camping: *At the north end, east of Lopar, exit the main road, 29, for San Marino. Autocamp San Marino (051-775-133). Close to Rab Town, exit 29 south of town for Banjol. Autocamp Padova III (051-724-355). They both have all the amenities; good maintenance; open May-September; $$.

PAG ISLAND

The natives of Pag Island are experts at making lace, honey, cheese, and olives. The island is heavily indented, more barren than her neighbors, and less touristy. There is a bridge from the mainland on the Zadar penninsula. ****Camping: *Northwest of Pag Town ten kilometers, exit the main road, 29, and drive west in the direction of Simuni. Camp Simuni. *Farther north, just south of Novalja. Autocamp Strasko Novalija (053-661-226). Both are on the beach; have shade trees; fair maintenance; open May-September; $$$.

ZADAR

A leading city on the Adriatic, Zadar has had more than its share of incidents in which outsiders took control of the city and the local population. In the 2nd century, the Romans walled the city, built a forum, a theater, thermal baths, and sewers. Then for three centuries the Venetians ruled, enabled by Croatian forests and manpower to keep their place as important

ship builders. In the 19th century, Austrian rule mandated that only Italian could be spoken. Severely damaged during World War II, Zadar was raised from ruins by the Croatians and today stands proudly free on the edge of the peninsula. The three Roman gates and fortress attest to its earlier power. But the main attraction is St. Donat, built in the 9th century on the site of the Roman Forum. Round and Byzantine, its stone edifice represents the strength of the Croatian people and is the undisputed symbol of Zadar. Musical events are often hosted here. While you're wandering, don't miss the rich treasures in St. Mary's Church and the Benedictine Convent. By heading toward the harbor from here, you can spend some time in the National Museum. There's an exquisite sarcophagus of St. Simeon in the church named after him. The beautifully carved cedar burial box is covered with silver and gold plate. Directions: Follow signposting to the old town, pass through the old gate and past the five-sided medieval tower. St Simeon is just a bit farther on the east end of Siroka Ulica. St. Donat and the convent are farther up on the west end of the spit. A good morning market is held in the square at the eastern end of the harbor.

****Camping: *In the beach town of Borik, three kilometers north of the city. Autocamp Borik (023-332-065); nice location on the beach; fair maintenance; open May-September; $$. *North of town ten kilometers in the direction of Nin. Exit towards the beach and the town of Zaton. Autocamp Zaton (023-264-444); a sports center; large and popular; well maintained; open May-September; $$$$.

*****Camping Enroute on E/65 between Zadar and Sibenik.* 28km southeast of Zadar, in Biograd na moru. Camping Crvena Luka, three kilometers southeast of town, (023-383-106); terraced to the sea; good maintenance; open May-September; $$$

SIBENIK

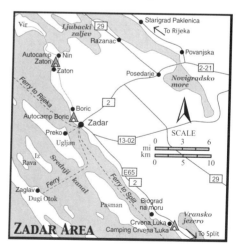

A strong cultural apex for the Croatians, Sibenik has some fascinating sites. The premier stop is at the Renaissance Cathedral of St. James. Built over the years by Italian-trained artisans, the limestone cathedral is one of Croatia's most beautiful. Enhanced by a majestic dome and finely decorated with sculpture, the cathedral also has a notable collection of religious art in its treasury. The town is well endowed with churches, many housing fine organs. Perhaps you'll be lucky enough to catch someone practicing. ****Camping: *South of town three kilometers, in the beach village of Solaris. Autocamping Solaris (022-364-000); affiliated with a hotel; $$$. Autocamp Solaris Zablace (022-354-015); $$. Both have scenic locations; good maintenance; open May-September.

KRKA NATIONAL PARK

Waterfalls, hiking trails, and beautiful lakes make a nice change from the beach. From Sibenik, drive northwest on E/65 to the edge of town, then east into the mountains on 11/20 in the direction of Bilice for ten kilometers. At the village of Tomilja, exit onto a small road sign-posted Skradinski buk, and drive eight kilometers farther. The scenery on the drive up is magnificent.

TROGIR

Still medieval in appearance this engaging, tiny town is a grand achievement in stonework. Many of the buildings were constructed in the 13th century. As you wander about be sure to see the triple-naved Renaissance basilica, St. John's. Notice the intricate sculptural work in the portal. The Kamerlengo Fortress now hosts summer theater and musical performances and Cipiko Palace holds a collection of medieval sculpture. Trogir is UNESCO listed. ****Camping: *In the beach village of Vranjica, ten kilometers west of Trogir, off E/65. Autocamp Vranjica Belvedere (021-884-141); nice location; all the amenities; well maintained; open May-September; $$$.

SPLIT

Graceful with colorful gardens, shade trees, Venetian architecture, and a quiet ambiance, Split is also the location of the famous Diocletian's Palace. This fascinating palace is like a tiny town. Buy the English guide at the entrance. Directions: To get there from E/65, follow the signs to centrum, which take you to the harbor, Palace, public parking, and information office. The entrance to the Palace faces the harbor. Wander behind the palace to Republic Square, where summer music festivals take place. Then drive up to Marijan hill to visit the villa of Croatia's most famous sculptor, Mestrovic. Enhanced by his dramatic works, the garden and the villa are now a gallery of his work. On the same street you can visit the Natural History Museum or hike down the hill to the beach. To explore the archaeological site of the ancient city of Solin, drive northeast from the harbor area past the village of Solin, in the direction of Togir on the new road. At the fork, stay left. There's good parking and signposting. The museum overlooks the site. Buy an English guide. ****Camping: *South of Split 52km on E/65, in the village of Ruskamen, eight kilometers south of Omis. Camping Daniel (218-71-400); terraced to the sea; tents only; parking is separate from camping sites; well maintained; open M ay-September; $$. Also see "Trogir."

COASTAL DRIVE FROM SPLIT TO DUBROVNIK

Hugging the breathtaking sea, this coastal drive is reminiscent of California's Big Sur area. Craggy cliffs hug tiny bays and lovely beaches. Acacia in full golden glory spills from the mountainside to the highway and the air is perfumed with the scent of pines. Here and there are lovely little red-roofed villages. ****Camping: *On E/65 across from the island of Hvar, nine kilometers south of Pogora, in the village of Zivogosce. Camping Dole (021-628-749); lovely location along the sea; fair maintenance; open May-September; $$$. *In Ston, on the south end of the Peljesac Peninsula. Exit E/65 in the direction of Orebic and go west on the main road for seven kilometers. Autocamping Prapratno (020-754-000); some shade; fair maintenance; open May-September; $$.

PELJESAC PENINSULA

Accessible from the mainland, the southwestern tip of the peaceful Peljesac pennisula has long stretches of beaches on the southwestern side. It's a 68km drive from the mainland to Orebic, where the camping places have lots of shade trees and are moderately priced. The Franciscan Monastry in Orebic is perched on the hillside overlooking the sea and has long been an important place of worship for the fishing community. To see it take the walking trail up the hillside from Hotel Bellevue. The views are breathtaking. From here you can walk farther on a marked trail up Mt. Ilija. ****Camping: *From the main road out of Orebic, drive west in the direction of Kuciste where the campgrounds all have beautiful locations on the beach and are open June-August. Closest to Orebic. Autocamp Orebic (050-713-479); good maintenance; $. *Two kilometers west of Orebic. Autocamp Plaza (050-719-060); good maintenance; $. *Four kilometers west of Orebic. Camping Palme (020-719164); fair maintenance; $.

HVAR ISLAND

Surrounded by Romanesque walls and elaborate cathedrals, Hvar Town has the ambiance of Venice without the crowds. It's chic and sophisticated, with picturesque cafes and lovely Renaissance architecture. Beautiful religious art is displayed in the Franciscan monastery. The air is redolent with the perfume of the lavender grown commercially on the island. Milna Bay, six kilome-

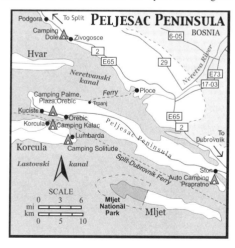

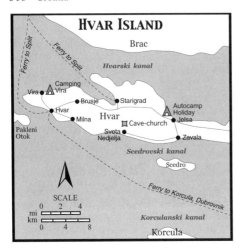

ters east on the beach road from Hvar Town, is beautiful, with sandy beaches and luxurious villas. From Starigrad to Brusje, the countryside is blanketed with vineyards. The drive to Zavala on the south coast, six kilometers from Jelsa, is beautiful, and the deserted sandy beaches beg you to stop. If you head west from Zavala for six kilometers to Sveta Nedjelja, you can hike up a hill to explore an ancient cave-church. ****Camping: *Drive north out of town to the nearby village of Vira. Camping Vira (058-741-12); nice setting; good maintenance; open May-September; $$.   *Drive east on D116 in the direction of Starigrad. At the fork to Starigrad, continue on the main road to Jelsa. Autocamp Holiday (058-761-40); on the beach; good maintenance; open May-September; $$.

KORCULA ISLAND

Dotted with vineyards and olive trees and aromatic with the perfumes of rosemary and lavender, Korcula is less expensive and chic than Hvar. As you wander around Korcula Town, it's hard to get lost. This medieval town was well planned, and the streets conform to the landform. Notice the cathedral's lovely bell tower and portal. The treasury on the southern side of the cathedral, displays a nice collection of religious art. Every Thursday local dancers perform the Moreska, a lively and colorful presentation accompanied by bagpipes and drums. The dance is based on a very old story-the struggle for the love of a beautiful girl-and takes place in the main square. A boat ride to Mljet National Park, a lush island covered with Aleppo pines and home to the endangered monk seal, can be booked for a day's excursion. ****Camping: *In Korcula Town, close to the ferry landing, follow signage to Bos Repos Hotel. Camping Kalac (020-711-182); terraced to the sea; good maintenance; open June-August; $$.   *Take the smaller coast road from Korcula Town, and drive south to Lumbarda. Camping Solitude (020-711-190); remote; romantic; fair maintenance; $.

DUBROVNIK

Completely walled, magnificent Dubrovnik is a UNESCO listed World Heritage site. Trade agreements with Constantinople in the 12th century led to a wealthy merchant class. Dubrovnik played a diplomatic game between the Venetians and the Turks then but later was controlled by more powerful outsiders. The strong stone fortress, city wall, and interior churches and buildings date to the 14th century. A walk along the top of the city wall is a must. One side of the wall reaches steeply to the sea and your gaze is seduced to the azure blue of the sea, while on the other side, it is drawn to enchanting gardens, side streets, and red-tiled roof tops. The tourist office and the stairs leading to the wall are directly across from the Onofrio Well and Fountain. The Franciscan Monastery features lovely cloisters and has an outstanding apothecary collection from the dating from the 15th to the 17th centuries. The Renaissance palaces and cathedral hint to the wealth of former years. As you walk the wall, you'll see the Lovrijenic fortress just outside. When you visit the fortress, note the inscription over the entrance gate-Non Bene Pro Toto Libertas Venditur Auro- which means Freedom cannot be sold, not for all the treasure in the world. Use a guidebook to enjoy this fabulous tiny city in detail. There is public parking nearby, but plan to arrive early in the morning or late in the afternoon to miss the bus loads of tourists. ****Camping: *At the fishing boat-yacht harbor off E/65, north of town. Watch for signage at Rozat. Camping Rozat; tiny; very basic; but nicely located. Or go to the Lapad peninsula and look for "zimmer frei" or rooms for rent signs.

ZAGREB

The capitol of Croatia, colorful Zagreb is filled with well maintained parks and charming cafes. Museums are a highlight. Examine artifacts of early Croatian settlements at the Museum of Croatia and the Gallery of Native Art. The City Museum is a source of pride and houses the country's important historical artifacts. It has been renovated recently and shouldn't be missed. Museum Mimara has an outstanding collection of art and is worth a stop. The botanical garden makes a restful picnic spot.

Before entering, purchase a good city map at a gas station, then follow "centrum" signs from the main highways. Drive toward the twin spires of the cathedral. There is a public parking area is close to the open-air Dolac Market, a good place to stock up on supplies. It's down the street from St. Stephens church on Kapitol. The information office is located on the corner of the main square in the historic area. Use the church's twin spires as a guide. ****Camping: Check at the tourist office for newly opened campgrounds.

PLITVICE NATIONAL PARK

Shimmering with sapphire lakes and tumbling waterfalls, this UNESCO listed park's beauty is best enjoyed by walking through its pine forests and over its footbridges, following the cascading water. Then relax, picnic, and swim at one of the lakes. Directions: Located halfway between Zagreb and Zadar. Leave Zagreb in the direction of Karlovac on E65, driving 41km to Karlovac. Exit south on E59 in the direction of Zadar, and drive 85km further. ****Camping: Check at the tourist office in Zagreb or Zadar for newly opened campgrounds.

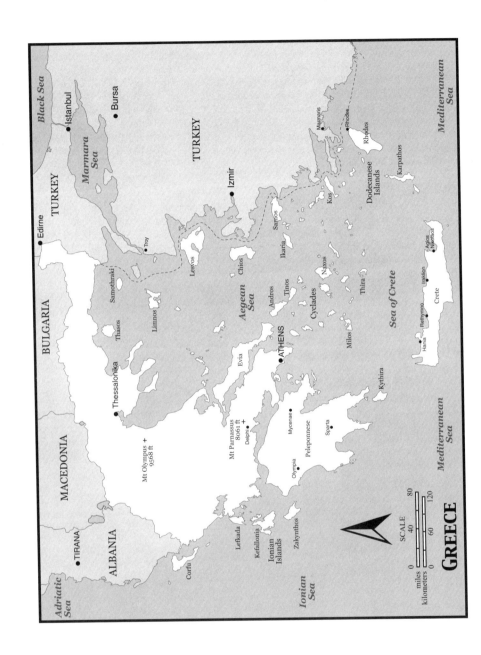

GREECE

Greece beckons with legacies so powerful that the flames are still not quenched and a mysticism that seduces our most vivid imagination. Geographically, this country is a jigsaw puzzle of land and sea. Bare gray mountains divide valleys and plains, encouraging the Greeks' individualistic spirit and producing vigorous and enterprising individuals.

Greece is the perfect place to visit when the rest of Europe is cool and rainy. May and September are prime for tent camping. The weather then is warm enough for swimming but not overly hot, and evenings are pleasantly warm. And when the mainland is cool in April and October, lovely Rhodes and Crete are usually warm enough for enjoyable tent camping.

Local vegetables and fruits, fresh meat and fish, yogurt and cheeses all spill from stalls in the town's morning market, or agora. In large towns the market is open every morning. In smaller towns they are held twice a week. Bakeries and stores with other grocery items and household goods are usually nearby. In remote village grocery stores meat is often kept frozen in freezers, sometimes in a back room. Use a phrase book to ask for what you want.

Driving in Greece isn't difficult, but you need to be alert for aggressive drivers. Uphill drivers have the right of way. Blinking headlights mean "I'm coming, watch out." Road rules are similar to what you are used to at home. Fill up with gas before traveling to remote areas. Roadways have dramatically improved in the last few years. Even in remote areas, though dirt roads are not uncommon, most are covered with asphalt. Cars are fuel-efficient and distances between sights aren't great, so even though gas is expensive it usually isn't burdensome. Before you leave home, purchase a current map with both Roman and Greek script. They aren't readily available in Greece. Note that the names are spelled slightly differently from one map to another. By purchasing a map with an expansion of at least 1:650.000 or better yet 1:300.000, your life on the road will be easier. Away from the touristed areas, directions are in Greek script only. Stop in front of directional signs to compare the Greek script carefully with that in your guidebook and map. A good guidebook will have both Roman and Greek script.

Unless you are traveling in July and August, ticketing for car ferries can be done the day of departure. Stop at the tourist office (EOT) in Athens and pick up the weekly departure schedule. Up-dated information is posted at each local port police office. Check the travel time to your destination carefully, as routes vary dramatically. Ferries traveling from one island group to another sometimes have only one or two departures a week. The cost of transporting a car on the ferry will be about three to four times the deck class fee for one passenger. But a car enables you to camp, prepare seaside meals, and get to out-of-the-way sights. You won't be able to access your car during passage, so take up on deck: collapsible ground chairs (some also unbuckle to make a small mattress), a blanket, blow-up pillows, food and beverage, and games and books to occupy time. These items make inexpensive deck passage more pleasant and yet aren't too burdensome to cart around as you move from one spot on the boat to another.

In addition to what is listed in Camping and Cooking Equipment at the beginning of the book, when I travel to Greece I also bring a collapsible sunshade that can provide shade near the tent or be taken to the beach. The campground's shaded areas are popular and crowded. By bringing my own, I am assured of shade for relaxing during hot afternoons. A good thermal mattress and ground tarp are also essential because most of the campsites are gravel rather than grass. I also bring rubber booties so I can swim and snorkel close to rocky shores. If I plan to do some serious snorkeling, I also add fins, mask, and a rubber float mat to my gear. For sleeping I forgo a sleeping bag, which I find too hot, and instead bring a sheet "pillowcase" for the thermal mattress, another for cover, and a lightweight thermal blanket for early morning coolness. Moderately priced campgrounds will usually have a small store, a common area for relaxing and meeting fellow travelers, a common area for cooking and washing dishes, and tepid to warm showers that are often solar heated. (Shower in the late afternoon when the water is warm.) Shade from tamarisk, pine, and oleander is often supplemented by simply-made shade frames. Smaller campground offices often close for a long lunch/rest. Discounts are often given to International Camping Club holders.

I've listed the opening times of major sights for the months of May-September. Check the closing times of museums and archeological sites. Some close in the early afternoon, while others stay open through early evening. Many are closed on Monday and have shorter hours on Sunday. There are sizable discounts for seniors and students, so show your identification at the ticket booth if you qualify. Getting an early start on the day makes your stay in Greece more rewarding. Ancient sites are more mystical in the early morning and late afternoon. Midday is a good time for a pouring over the fascinating artifacts in the air-conditioned museums, traveling to your next destination, or having a picnic lunch and snooze.

ATHENS

Isolated from the city hubbub by the steep-sided Acropolis, the Parthenon is still dazzling and radiant, a beautiful and moving veneration to beauty. When the Athenians returned to their city after their victory over the Persians at Salamis in 480 B.C., they began to rebuild the sanctuaries the Persians had destroyed. They believed the goddess Athena had protected them and so built the Parthenon to honor her. Pericles, proud in power and new found glory, chose Phidias to supervise the enormous project. The clarity of lines and the harmony of the columns are its essence. Although sculpture was of secondary importance, a giant forty-foot statue of Athena was carved from ivory and gold by Phidias and placed in the sacred chamber. It was destroyed in 1686 when a Venetian shell landed on Turkish gunpowder stored in the temple during their occupation.

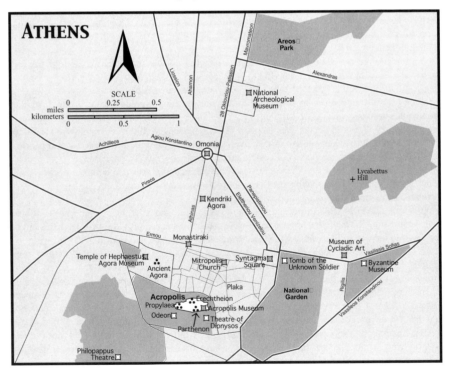

Reproductions of the goddess in her helmet crested with sphinx and griffins are on view in the Acropolis Museum. The masterpiece of sculpture, however, is the Ionic frieze. Measuring about one meter high and almost 160 meters long, it depicted the Panathenaic Procession and ran under the peristyle and along the entire length of the temple. On the west side, a small portion can still be seen. Other portions are on view in the Acropolis Museum, but the best sections are in the British Museum in London. Delightful in their womanhood and grace, the six lovely maidens of the Caryatids support the roof of the Erechtheion, adding noble and youthful vigor to the site.

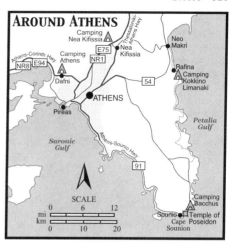

AROUND ATHENS

After absorbing the architecture, turn for a view over the Acropolis walls. It's a terrific panoramic view of the lively city, the bare mountains, and the conical Mount Lycabettus. Allow time to visit the Acropolis Museum, where the masterful freize of the battle of gods and giants is truly powerful. You'll smile as you gaze at joyous votive statues of young women with engaging mocking smiles and elaborate hair designs. The famous calf-bearer, a charming archaic statue, exudes a warmth and sweetness that is hard to forget. Directions: The main entrance to the Acropolis is through the Propylaea, a monumental ancient gate on the west side; open daily. Wear rubber-soled shoes, as the ancient pathways are slippery. Try to experience the Acropolis in the early morning light or late afternoon when the mystic is best.

On entering and exiting the Acropolis, you'll pass the restored marble half-bowl of the Odeion theatre built in 160 A.D. by Herodes Atticus. Attending one of the summer-time starlit performances of music, dance, or drama during the Athens Festival could be a highlight of your stay in Athens. You'll feel like an ancient Athenian as you sit on the same marble stones that have echoed drama and music for a millennium. It's best to book ahead with the English-speaking staff at the Athens Festival Box Office, 4 Stadiou St.; 30-1-322-1459. The Dora Stratou performs, sings, and dances throughout the summer evenings at their theater on Philopappus Hill. Here, in a simple outdoor theatre perfumed by eucalyptus and cypress trees, you can enjoy the exciting music of the bouzouki while virile men in tight breeches and radiant women in elaborately embroidered traditional attire stamp and twirl. Directions: Southwest of the Acropolis on the southwestern side of Philopappu Hill. For tickets and time schedule, call 324-4395.

The Ancient Agora is a good choice for peaceful strolls. Once noisy with chatter and argument, now the ancient streets are quiet and fragrant with roses and laurel. The Temple of Hephaestus and the Agora Museum help bring alive this heart of ancient Athens; closed Monday. Directions: Metro to Monastiraki. Then walk south on Areos following signage. The labyrinth of tiny stepped lanes hugging the northern side of the Acropolis are reminiscent of the Cycladic Islands. Still quiet they are a nice reprieve from tourist-baiting Plaka just beyond. Directions: Metro Monastiraki. Walk south on Areos following signage for Ancient Agora. From Panos walk east on Tholou. For another pleasant walk, wander over to the leafy National Garden just east of Syntagma Square. Rest on a park bench and absorb the local scene. Then wander over to the Tomb of the Unknown Soldier to see the impressive Evzones. These tall military sentries are in very fancy dress, indeed. The changing of the guard takes place daily at 20 minutes before the hour. On Sunday mornings at 11 a.m. an elaborate full dress parade with a lively band and goose-step marching occurs.

Directions: Metro to Syntagma.

Besides the Acropolis, the National Archeological Museum is Athen's most important treasure. Housing one of the world's most important collections of Greek art, it reveals the full splendor of the Grecian's intense love of beauty. To stand in front of the dazzling treasures found in the royal tombs of Mycenae is a thrill. The world-renowned golden death-masks, the famous golden bull-carved goblets, and the votive statues depicting youthful strength and beauty are all breathtaking; open daily. Directions: Take the metro to Omonia and then walk north or take the bus up to Oklovriou-Patission 44. The Museum of Cycladic Art brings together the best of the findings from Greek island archeological excavations. The collection is exquisite and beautifully curated; closed Sunday and Tuesday. Directions: Off the northeastern corner of the National Garden on Vassilissis Sofias. The precious collection of icons, jewelry, and church ornaments in the Byzantine Museum is outstanding; closed Monday. Directions: East of the National Garden on the corner of Vassilissis Sofias and Rigilis.

For earthy fun visit the Kendriki Agora, where the Athenians haggle over fresh slabs of meat, symmetrical octopus, and piles of chickens. Lively cafes dot the area dispensing inexpensive, tasty Greek fare. Directions: North of the Ancient Agora and west of Syntagma Square. Metro to Monastiraki. Then walk north to Ermou. Cross over Ermou and continue walking north on Athinas. The carnival spirit of the Plaka is a comedy of people, tourists, and vendors. You haven't really experienced Athens if you don't come here. Directions: From Syntagma Square, walk southwest using the dome of Mitropolis Church as a guide. The Sunday flea market in Monastiraki is a good place to shop for a quirky momento while munching on a tasty snack. Directions: Metro Monastiraki. The columns of Poseidon's Temple at Cape Sounion stand on a high cliff at the farthest tip of the Greek mainland. Battered by wind and sea and eroded by iodine, the regal columns are dazzling white, like salt. They are especially evocative when the rising or setting sun reddens the slopes of nearby islands; open daily. Directions: 71km south of Athens on the coast road 91, Athens-Sounio, follow signposting.

****Camping: *Closest to historic Athens. Seven kilometers west of Athens on the Athens-Corinth highway, NR8/E94. On E94 west of Athens, exit for Athens/Dafni. At the fork for Athens and Pireas exit east for Athens. Drive east six kilometers. It's in the suburb of Dafni on the north side of the highway. Camping Athens 198 Athinon Av. (01-581-4114); convenient; noisy; some shade; bus to city center; popular; reserve ahead; open all year; $$. *16km north of Athens in Nea Kifissia. Exit NR1/E75, the Thessaloniki-Athens highway, at km 16 and drive west following signposting. Camping Nea Kifissia 60 Potamou& Dimitsanas, Adams (01-807-5579); swimming pool; shade; public transport to the city; well maintained; popular; reserve ahead; open all year; $$. *29km east of Athens close to the beach in Rafina. It's less confusing to get to the campground north of Athens. North on E/75, exit for Neo Makri. Drive east 17km then drive six kilometers south following signposting for Rafina. Camping Kokkino Limanaki (0294-31603); lovely location; well maintained; bus to Athens; open April-September; $$$. 71km south of Athens on the coast road 91, Athens-Sounio. *Close to the Temple of Poseidon. Exit 91 at km 71. Camping Bacchus (0292-39572); lovely location but can be windy; well maintained; open all year $$.

THE PELOPONNESE
DELPHI

The setting, rugged and grand, hugs the gaunt gray cliffs of Mount Parnassus and makes this "navel of the earth" hard to forget. The florid chiseling of the Ionic capitals weathered over two millenniums, the dark superstition attending the underground temple of the sibyl, the haunting beauty of the Sacred Way, and the leafy walk up through hundred-year-old olive trees to the stadi-

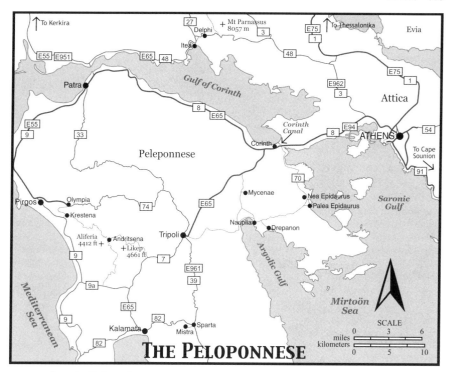

um are all poetically beautiful when experienced in the crowd-free early morning or late afternoon. Use midday to peruse the sumptuous refinements of beauty, strength, and mind found in the temple and now displayed in the museum; open daily.

The serpentine drive up to Delphi is dramatically beautiful. Waterfalls of wild mustard cascade down the rocky slopes, acacias in full summer bloom wave in the breeze, and fields of wheat and cotton tuck in villages clinging to the mountainside. Delphi is one of the most evocative places to camp in all of mainland Greece. From your campgrounds, you'll view a sea of the silvery-green foliage of olive trees and the blue of the Gulf of Corinth. Directions: 170km west of Athens, on the north side of the Bay of Corinth. On the hillside above Itea. ****Camping: *Closest to the archeological area. Two kilometers west of the village on the main road. Camping Apollon (0265-82750); gorgeous views; swimming pool; nice walk to the archeological area; well maintained; popular; reserve ahead; open all year; $$. *Four kilometers west and down the hill from the village. Camping Delfi (0265-82363); won-

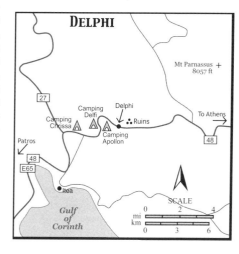

derful views; swimming pool; well maintained; $$$. *Seven kilometers west and further down the hill; Chrissa Camping (0265-82050); wonderful views; swimming pool; good for RV's; open all year; $$$.

CORINTH

A crossroads between the mainland and Peloponnesus-the Aegean and Ionion seas-Corinth controlled the main routes of Greece. Shrewd merchants took advantage of the tollgate. Today tourists stop on their way to gaze down the 90-meter-deep, steep-sided cleft stretching six kilometers to the sea in a line as straight as a ruler.

OLYMPIA

Shaded by pines and cypresses in a gently undulating countryside, the ruins of Olympia are more dreamy than dramatic. Not so two thousand years ago though, when chariot races, javelin and discus throws, and wrestling filled the daily calendar. It was dominated by an elevated Temple of Zeus containing what some consider Phidias' masterpiece-the great statue of Zeus sitting on his throne. Carved in marble with gold and ivory overlay and set with precious stones, it was twelve meters tall and counted as one of the Seven Wonders of the Ancient World. Athletes trained for nine months at Olympia to compete during three main days of the games. Olympia was a man's world; married women were prohibited. During the games musicians, storytellers, acrobats, handsome men, and young girls provided a fantastic atmosphere, with both noble and common distractions available. On the last day of the games, the ceremonial distribution of laurel wreaths took place. Winners brought great honor to their families and hometowns. The decorative elements of the Temple of Zeus are exhibited in their original arrangement in the museum; open daily. Directions: Northwest side of the Peloponnese pennisula, 18km east of Piyrgos on 74.

TEMPLE OF BASSAE

Isolated and surrounded by some of the highest peaks in Peloponnesus, the Temple of Bassae was built in thanksgiving for deliverance from the plague. From its sublime location, you look out across a superb wild panorama of wild ravines and misty mountains. In June the profusion of wild flowers is stunning. Directions: Andhritsena, the lovely village at the base of the mountains, is almost in the center between the highways 7, E55, and 74. From the village drive out of town in the direction of Krestena, watching carefully for signposting and the road heading up the mountain.

****Camping: Up the hill from ancient Olympia, on the northwest side of the village. *Camping Diana (0624-22314); small, shady; swimming pool; good mainteance; open all year; $$. In the same area; *Camping Alphios (0624-22951); lovely location with views of the hills and sunsets; resort like; $$$.

OLYMPIA

To Patra
E55
Pirgos
Olympia
Camping Diana, Alphios
Ruins
Krestena
To Tripoli
74

SCALE
0   3   6
mi
km
0   5   10

Mediterranean Sea

Aliferia 4412 ft +
Temple of Bassae
+Andritsena
+Likeo 4661 ft
9
To Kalamata

MYCENAE

Almost as fascinating as the ancient story of Agamemnon is the story of Heinrich Schliemann, who in 1874 came to Mycenae following his passion to excavate the riches he hoped had been left by Homer's hero,

Agamemmnon. What he found instead was a civilization. Today curving cyclopean walls, a beehive tomb, and rich artifacts reveal what the Mycenaean civilization could create by itself and what it learned from other cultures. In Ancient Mycenae you'll walk under Europe's oldest monumental sculpture, the Lion's Gate, and see the ruins of the Royal Circle of tombs. In front of and inside the enormous and harmonious beehive tomb, you can't help but stand in awe and silence. It is thrilling to know that you are treading where the world famous gold masks, the exquisite Warrior Vase, and the golden cups depicting the taming of the bulls were found. The extraordinary riches minted in this 16th century B.C. culture, three centuries before the Trojan

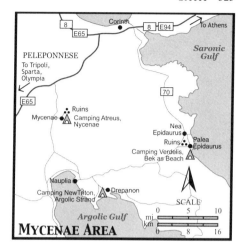

War, are on view in Athen's National Archeological Museum; open daily. Directions: 15km west of Corinth, exit E65 for Mycenae and drive two kilometers to the village. ****Camping: *West of the town. Camping Atreus (0751-76221); nice views of the hills; swimming pool; well maintained; open all year; $$$. *Just west of the archeological site. Camping Mycenae (0751-76121); small; nice walk to the archeological area; open all year; $$$.

EPIDAURUS

Greeks came to this splendid setting in hopes of being cured of their ailments. Shrewd and enterprising priests, wanting to distract their patients from their woes and also separate them from their money, entertained them with great theater. Climb to the top of this powerful theater, passing fifty-five rows of crescent-shaped seats, so you can view its perfect symmetry. The acoustics are remarkable, and it is considered the most beautiful and best preserved of all Greek theaters; open daily. Stop in the museum to view the remnants of its lovely architectural ornaments. Highlights are the exquisitely carved acanthus leaves and rosettes artistically decorating column capitals and the portions of a coffered ceiling from the marble rotunda that were painted with lilies. In July and August during the Festival of Epidaurus, starlit performances of plays written by the ancient Greek playwrights are performed. Directions: From Corinth exit south on the coast road 70 for 46km to Nea Epidaurus continuing another kilometer to Palea Epidaurus and the archeological site. ****Camping: *In Palea Epidaurus on the beach road at km 2. Both have: lovely locations; all the amenities; good maintenance; open April-October. Camping Verdelis (0753-41322); $$$. Camping Bek as Beach (0753-41524); better for RV's; $$$.

NAUPLIA

One of the prettiest towns on mainland Greece, Nauplia sits at the edge of the often-turquoise waters of the Argolic Gulf. Old Venetian houses dripping with bougainvillea and narrow streets leading to Turkish fountains spill down the hillsides. Before sunset, drive up the mountain to the fortress to watch the setting sun paint the blue lagoon-like sea with reflections of the crimson and golden mountains. The Folk Art Museum has won high honors; closed Tuesday. Directions: From Corinth drive west 15km on E65. Exit south onto 70 and drive 33km to Nauplia. ****Camping: *Eight kilometers south of Nauplia in the village of Drepanon. Both have: lovely locations, are well maintained, open all year; $$. Camping New Triton (0752-921-

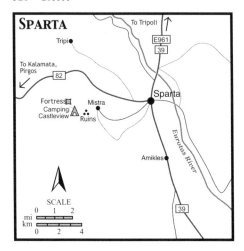

SPARTA

To Tripoli

Tripi●

E961
39

To Kalamata,
Pirgos
82

Fortress▓　Mistra
Camping ▲ ∴
Castleview ▲ Ruins

Sparta

Amikles●

Eurotas River

SCALE
0　　1　　2
mi
km
0　　2　　4

39

28) or Argolic-Strand (0752-92376).

SPARTA AND MISTRA

The ruins of the powerful military encampment of Sparta lie tucked in between meadows and orchards in the valley of the Eurotas River. In its hey day, seven year old boys and girls were selected for the highly disciplined and rigorous life. Taught early never to murmur a complaint, they lived a "spartan" and communal life and were the supreme commanders in the Persian War with Xerxes. They fought furiously and died with valor. Scorning art and architecture and living in simple dwellings little remains of the former totalitarian society.

Reminiscent of stories from The Thousand and One Nights, the domes of churches and monasteries peek through cypress and orange trees around Mistra. Once the metropolis of Peloponnesus, it was also a successful breeder of silkworms. A Frankish medieval fortress crowns the hill. As you walk up the stony path you are treated to the red-tiled bonnet-like domes of the churches and glorious views of the Eurotas Valley. Restored frescoes glow with color and bring to mind the work of Crete-born El Greco. Directions: Sparta and Mistra are located in the southeastern section of the Peloponnese. From Tripolis exit off E65/7 south on E961 and drive south 60km. ****Camping: *Two kilometers from Mystra. Camping Castle View (0731-83303); lovely views of the ancient ruins; well maintained; open April-Oct.; $$$.

THE ISLAND OF CRETE

Separating the Aegean and Mediterranean Seas, this large, fertile island cradled one of the most brilliant civilizations of the Western Bronze Age. Today olive trees, gnarled with age, shade the haunting ruins. Named Minoan, they used sail, oar, and probably the keel in 2500 BC to brave the open seas and transform their ancestors from hunters and gatherers into farmers, craftsmen, and traders. This trade brought not only new ideas but tin from Asia Minor (now Turkey), copper from Cyprus, and luxury goods from Egypt. High on mountain plateaus, fertile valleys are still filled with orchards of apples, figs, and pears. In rocky gorges, trails cooled by pleasant streams and perfumed with pine, lead from mountaintops to the sea.

In 2500 BC, a sprawling, multistoried-complex with as many as 1500 rooms spilled from the fertile hillside without fortification, just beyond today's Irakleion. Called Knossos, it was once the center of Minoan power. In 1900, Sir Arthur Evans, a brilliant and rich Englishman with a passion for archeology, unearthed its palace. Not content, he restored part of it, extending his work for over 25 years. Frescos, vessel paintings, and a carved seal-stone brought reality to what once was thought to be a fairy-tale-the cult of the bull, where death defying athletes somersaulted over a charging bull in heart-stopping spectacles. The astonishing beauty of the palace still remains. Columned balconies look out into a lovely inner courtyard. Relics of a labyrinth of long corridors reveal that they once sang with spirited frescoes of figures. A grand staircase, built around a light well, leads down to apartments graceful with dolphin frescoes. Resurrected from the rubble, man-height storage jars provide proof that Minoans used a hand-turned wheel around 2500 BC. Other artifacts include a fresco fragment of a lady so chic she was dubbed "the Parisienne", a gypsum seat that might have been Europe's earliest throne, and examples of ingeniously contrived plumbing and drainage systems. Mystery still marks the Minoans of Crete but the magnificence of their culture is evident. Directions to Knossos: East of town exit E75 in the direction of Fortetsa and drive six kilometers to Knossos.; open daily.

The Archeological Museum at Iraklion carefully houses the now world-famous treasures found at Knossos and other excavations on Crete. Tiny seal-stones cut from stone are so finely carved a magnifying glass is necessary to appreciate their natural and poetic beauty. Vases carved from rock are expertly shaped, smoothed, and decorated with drawings that testify to a vigorous Minoan life. Ritual vessels with great bull horns, statuettes of the Snake Goddess, double-edged axes, gaming boards, a circular plaque of clay stamped with hieroglyphic signs, and the astonishing Bee Pendant reveal the startling freshness and spontaneity of the Minoan artists and their exquisite taste. There is an overwhelming impression that the Minoans enjoyed a life free from war and that sensuous and natural pleasures prevailed. Directions: Southwest of the ferry-landing dock and bus station. From the bus station drive west off the roundabout. Exit south following signposting; open daily.

Memorabilia of Nikos Kazantzakis, author of Zorba the Greek, a painting by Ikaklion's home-town artist, El Greco, and photos of Cretan Tsoudero who became prime minister of Greece in 1941 are highlights in the Iraklion's Historical Museum. Directions: Follow signposting off the waterfront road at the west end of the historic area; closed Sunday. From the simple tomb site of Kazantzakis, at the Martinenga Bastion on the south edge of the walled town, is a view out over the red roofs of the town. Kazantzakis would approve of the lizard probably sunbathing on his tomb as you read his epitaph: "I believe in nothing, I hope for nothing, I am free." Directions: Park at the waterfront on the western edge of the Venetian walls. Walk south beneath the wall from St. Anthony's bastion to the tomb. The best view of the city is from the 16th century fortress at the end of the Old Harbor jetty. The walk out makes a lovely evening stroll; open daily. The Lion Fountain on Plateia Venizelou is one of Iraklion's landmarks and a good rendezvous spot. At the market in Iraklion great mounds of tomatoes still smell of the sun, vats of a mind-boggling array of olives glisten in oil, and stacks of purple eggplant gleam as if polished. Directions: Come into the historic area from the Hania Gate on the west side of town. Drive east on Kalokerinou to 25-Avgoustou, a major intersection. Turn south onto 1866 and look for parking. ****Camping: *Exit E/75 18km east of Ikalion at the village of Gournes. Drive to the beach. Camping Creta (0897-41400); convenient; well maintained; some shade; open May-Oct; $$$.

SOUTH COAST
PHAESTOS

On the south coast of Crete, 63km from Iraklion, lies a spectacle of great power, the ruins of Phaestos. The stones that were once the palace look down on the broad and fertile Mesara valley that reaches to the sea. From gnarled trunks, luscious grapevines stretch their arms out to the sun giving shade to their sweet fruit. To the west rises Crete's Olympus, Mount Ida. On a clear summer morning you can see Dikte mountain and its eye-patch of a cave where Zeus is said to have been born. It's an opulent view. In the bare ruins only blocks of massive stone lie

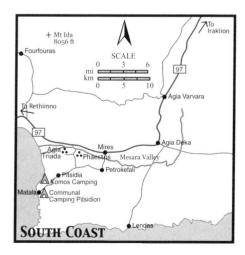

scattered on the ground. A majestic sweep of stairs stands almost insolent in their contrived swelling, built so royalty could look down on their subjects. Beyond the stairway lie the ruined walls of an immense complex of buildings. There are no fluted columns or lion's gates here only the naked power of the Minoan culture still stands. Directions: Drive 45km south of Iraklion on 97 to Agii Deka. Turn west following 97 to and drive 19km. Turn south to the entrance; open daily.

AGIA TRIADA

Built after the earthquake destruction of Phaestos, the royal villa of Agia Triada has yielded some grand finds of Minoan art that are now on view in the Archeological Museum in Iraklion. Some of the highlights are a delightful floor fresco with octopuses and fish, both the Harvester and Boxer vases, fine seal-stones, a bronze double axe, and the tablets of Linear A. The ruins, set on a small hill overlooking the sea, are small and elegant. Mild sea breezes, tinged with the fragrance of pine and fruit, perfume the air. Locals call it Paradise. Directions: From Phaestos walk or drive three kilometers west from Phaesdos. Signposted at the parking area at Phaesdos; open daily.

****Camping: *From the archeological site drive south three kilometers. Turn west and drive an additional three kilometers to the village of Pitsidia, pass through and drive an additional two kilometers. Komos Camping (0892-42596); swimming pool; well maintained; terraced; open May-October; $$. *Closer to the beach in the village of Matala. Communal Camping Pitsidion (0892-42340); basic amenities; fair maintenance; some shade; open May-October; $.

EASTERN CRETE
LASSITHI PLATEAU AND THE DIKTEON CAVE

Hugged as if by an adorning mother hiding her adorable child, the mountains surrounding the Lassithi Plain protect gently smiling fields and orchards. Today the quiet landscape provides no evidence of the terrible fighting that took place here when the Cretan's rose up against the occupying Turks. Directions: Exit E/75 4km east of Hersonissou and drive up the mountain in the direction of Mohos for nine kilometers. Continue up the winding but beautiful mountain road to Tzermiado for another 18km.

Clinging to the shoulder of a mountain, high above the windmill-festooned plain of Lasithi, is the village of Psihro. The trailhead to Dikteon Cave, where Zeus is said to be born, starts here. The cave is cathedral-sized with gnarled stalagmites, shelf altars, and a small lake. It provides an errie setting that encourages storytelling. The descent is somewhat steep and slippery, so wear rubber-soled shoes and bring a flashlight. Directions: From the main square in the village follow signposting to parking and the cave trailhead; open daily.

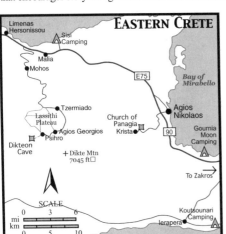

Directions: Follow the directions for the Lassithi Plateau. Continue up for another 12km passing through Agios Georgios to the village of Psihro. ****Camping: *40km east of Iraklion. Eight kilometers east of the village of Malia exit E/75 and drive to the beach. Sisi Camping (0841-71361); lovely location; well maintained; good shade; open May-Oct.; $$.

KRITSA

High up the mountainside from Agios Nikolaos, just before the village of Kritsa, stop to examine the Byzantine frescoes from the 14th century in the Church of Panagia. Though not in good condition the frescos have been restored with discretion and are considered Crete's best. The film, He Who Must Die based on Kazantzakis' novel, was filmed here. Directions: At the south end of Agios Nikolaos drive up the mountain road signposted for Kritsa for eleven kilometers to the village of Agias Georgios. Continue through the village following signposting for Kritsa for two kilometers more; closed Sunday to tourists; open 8:30 a.m.. to 2 p.m.. ****Camping: *15km southeast of Agios Nikolaos at km 15 off E/75. Gournia Moon Camping (0842-93243); lovely location; swimming pool; close to the beach; some shade; open May-Oct; $$. *On the south coast. Seven kilometers east of Ierapera. Koutsounari Camping (0842-61213); large; all the amenities; well maintained; some shade; close to the beach; open all year; $$$.

ZAKROS

If you yearn for a remote wild setting, drive out to the eastern edge of Crete's coastline to the little seaside villages of Kato Zakros and Xerokambos. A wonderful ravine trail called Valley of the Dead, leads to the ruins of ancient Zakros from the village of Kao Zakros. As you descend into the gorge, the dark "eyes" of caves peer out from the cliff until you emerge into warm sunlight and the ruins facing the sea; closed Monday; open 8:30 a.m.. to 3:00p.m.. Directions: From Agios Nikolaos drive 70km east on E/75 to Sitia. Exit E/75 and continue on the small coastal road 15km. Then turn southeast in the direction of Palekastro for six kilometers. Continue south on a winding small road for 25km to Zakros. ****Camping: No official sites. Free camp.

WESTERN CRETE
RETHYMNO

Mixed like a deck of cards, Rethymno is at once old Ottoman, 16th century Venetian, and mod-

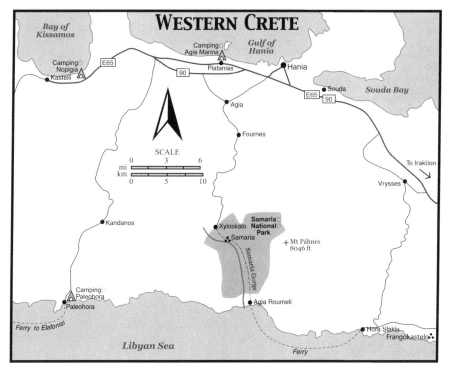

ern Crete. The Venetian Gate leads to the old quarter's meandering labyrinth of tiny streets where ancient minarets, wooden balconies, domed mosques, and a Venetian fountain make an exotic mix. From the ramparts of the old fortress, you can breathe in the sea air and look out over the town. At the Historical and Folk Art Museum vintage photos, old-fashioned farming and household implements, and traditional costumes help envision the rural life of not-too-long ago. In the evening musicians play and people dance for an all around convivial atmosphere. Directions: Exit E75 at Rethimno in the direction of Dimitrikaki. Follow signposting to the large parking area by the park. Walk north towards the harbor.

MONI ARKADIOU

This monastery is a place of pilgrimage for Cretans. In 1866 hundreds of courageous Cretans took their own lives here rather than surrender to the conquering Turks. Throughout Crete, monasteries opened their doors to villagers in hopes that they would be safe havens during periods of insurrection. Directions: Four kilometers west of Rethymno off E/75; open daily.

AMARI VALLEY

Breathing in the fragrance of ripening pear and peach orchards while joining the locals under a leafy grape arbor in a game of backgammon could count as some of your most memorable time in Greece. Off the tourist trail, this is real rural Greece. Directions: Three kilometers east of Rethymno exit off E/75 at the village of Kastellakia and drive south ten kilometers into the mountains passing through the villages of Gianoudi and Prassies. Continue up the winding road for 20km to Genna. The beautiful winding road continues 24km to the south side of the island to the village of Apodoulou. Then it drops down to the southcoast ten kilometers to Agia Galini.

****Camping: *On the north side of the island. Three kilometers east of Rethimno exit E/75 onto a small road to the village of Perivolia. Camping Elizabeth (0831-28694); shady; close to the beach; well maintained; disco; open May-Oct.; $$. On the south side of the island. Two kilometers east of Agii Galini. Camping Agia Galini (0832-91386); shady; disco; open May-October; $$.

HANIA AND THE SAMARIA GORGE

Seductive and romantic in the evening, when lights twinkle from harbor-side tavernas, Hania will probably be your favorite city on Crete. Take a walk out on the scythe-shaped harbor jetty for fresh

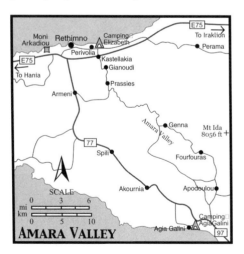

sea breezes and a lovely view back on the old town. Several museums, a maze of tiny streets, and an old defensive wall will make you meanderings in the town interesting. Don't miss the morning market where peaches still smell like roses and piles of pump purple grapes give off a musky aroma. You'll see stacks of rough chunks of chalky-white feta alongside deep-green Cretan avocados. It's an exciting celebration of summer that almost sings out to be relished. Directions: The market is at the south end of the old town, on Gianan, in a large cruciform building.

Towering cliffs hide a steeply descending riverbed in a narrow box canyon of the Samariian Gorge. In late spring, the river is still fast moving and pale-colored wild flowers peek out from rocky ledges. Raucous ravens and silent circling vultures patrol the sky. After paying an admission charge, you'll join other enthusiastic hikers descending the steep wooden staircase from Xyloskalo for the 18 kilometer hike. It takes most people five to six hours to walk through the gorge, allowing for rests and a picnic. Directions: To assure availability, buy tickets a day ahead for a sunrise bus ride up to Xyloskalo from Hania with a return ticket from Chorasfakion back to Hania. I leave my car at the campsite, and take a pre-sunrise taxi ride to the bus station. I ask the campground staff to help with arrangements for the taxi. Emerging from the gorge in the afternoon, it's just another 20 to 30 minute walk to the Libyan Sea. It's a good idea to purchase tickets for the boat ride to Chorasfakion when you first get to the village. Until departure, enjoy a rest beside the beautiful sea. Bring a picnic lunch and energy snacks, wear rubber-soled shoes, and tuck a water bottle into your pack. You'll need local currency for the entrance fee, boat ride, and a cool drink in Agia Roumeli. Spring water is available to fill your water bottle as you hike. ****Camping: *Nine kilometers west of Hania on E/75. *Camping Agia Marina (0832-91386); convenient; close to the beach; shady; disco; open May-October; $$. *30km farther west on E/75. East of Kastelli five kilometers. At km 5 and the village of Drapanias exit E/75 and drive towards the beach. *Camping Nopigia (0822-31111); lovely location; swimming pool; some shade; open May-Oct.; $$.

THE SOUTHWEST COAST

White-washed little villages invite stopping at cafe tables right at the water's edge. From the pleasant walking paths that connect the villages along the rugged coastline, it's hard to take your eyes off the endless views of the sea. Here and there secluded beaches and rocky outcrops provide a paradise setting for swimming. A side trip to Frangokastello permits seeing the old Venetian fortress built to keep the rebellious Cretans in tow, and still stands sentinel-like at the edge of the beach. Stories of Crete's undaunted ghosts, who still walk silently on the beach to renew the memory of their valor, add to the aura. The village of Paleohora, located at the southwestern tip of Crete, is pleasantly touristy. Excursion boats take bathers to what some say is Crete's best sand beach, Elafonisi. Open-air evening cinemas and lively tavernas add gaiety to warm summer nights. Directions: To find Paleohora on the map, find Kastelli on the northwest side of Crete then look south to the coast. ****Camping: *In the village of Paleochora. Camping Paleochora (0823-41120); all the amenities; good maintenance; open May-Oct.; $$.

THE ISLAND OF RHODES
CITY OF RHODES

Sought by the likes of Suleyman the Magnificent, Mehemt II, and the Knights of Saint John, the massive walls of the fortress in the city of Rhodes speak of the savage, uncompromising power of the Middle Ages. The wealthy trading port proved unconquerable except from within. Today, beguiling bougainvillea and hibiscus soften the huge fortress walls, palace, and archways. At sunset the ramparts shine like burnished

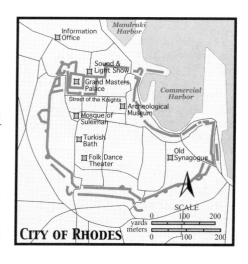

CITY OF RHODES

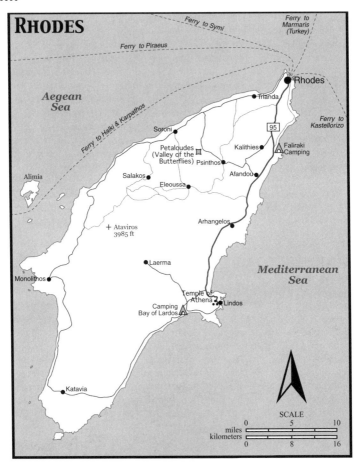

gold. Coats of arms still guard doorways along the steep Street of the Knights leading to the Grand Master's palace. Under an arch, the lion of Venice listens indifferently to the call of the muezzin and the tolling of church bells.

The fortress is like a tiny medieval town. Stop at the information office outside the main gate to gather materials to make your meanderings more interesting. Get squeeky clean in the 18th century Turkish Bath; closed Sunday. Reflect on novelist Lawerence Durrell's idol, the Marine Venus, in the archaeological museum. Visit the old synagogue to pay homage to the Jews of Rhodes and Kos who were sent to death camps. Experience the techno magic of the Sound and Light Show; nightly except Sunday. Take Greek dancing lessons or just enjoy the show at the Folk Dance Theatre. The museums and palace are closed on Monday.

LINDOS

The spectacle of the Temple of Athena at Lindos is unique in the world. Perched on a rough ocher acropolis, above an endless royal blue sea, the columns stand proud and invincible like the goddess herself. She belonged to high places and was venerated for her power to still tempests.

For protecting the long slender boats that traded with Phoenicia and Egypt, she was bestowed with gifts from Alexander the Great, King Amasis of Egypt, and King Minos of Crete; open daily. Park and as you the walk up, reflect on the great and famous who have tread the same path.

EASTERN RHODES

For some lazy time, drive to the east coast where the beaches and weather are better. You'll join plenty of others doing the same.

SOUTHERN RHODES

The scene here is tranquil and quiet, and the rural villages aren't overwhelmingly touristy.

THE INTERIOR

A drive across the island is lovely. Rural villages surrounded by cultivated fields are leafy with deciduous trees and provide a refreshing change from seaside scenery. Pack a picnic lunch, and stop along the way. Petaloudes, the Valley of the Butterflies, is the only tourist attraction. The resin from liquidamber trees attracts thousands of moths to roost on their trunks. Well camouflaged, they rest quietly with folded wings, conserving their energy for the final phase of their life.

WESTERN RHODES

Although green with forests, the western side of Rhodes is prone to gusty winds and rough seas. Here and there are ruins that can make a wild destination for walk or picnic.

****Camping: 14km south of Rhodes City. Exit the city on 95 and drive south in the direction of Kallithies pass through the village and drive to the beach. *Faliraki Camping (0241-85358); lovely location; well maintained; open April-October; $$. *South of Lindos. From Lindos continue on the coast road for eight kilometers. Camping Bay of Lardos; beautiful location; secluded; separate nude beach; basic; open April-Oct.; $$.

APPENDIX
PERSONAL DOCUMENTS

PASSPORT

A passport is required for entering a foreign country, reentering your own, and boarding a flight out of the country. If you already have a passport, check the expiration date. Make sure it is valid several months beyond your return from your trip out of the country. Applicants for new passports need their birth certificates, identification cards such as driver's license and social security card, and two passport photos. Check ahead on how payment can be made: personal check, charge card, or cashier's check. Use your phone book to access where to get a new passport or renew an existing one. Make xerox copies of the photo and information pages on your passport. Take one copy with you and leave one copy with someone at home. This copy will help expedite a new passport at an embassy or consulate overseas if necessary. Processing for new or renewed passports can take up to 8 weeks.

VISA

A visa is a stamp that entitles you to visit a country for a particular reason-tourism. Most European countries don't require a visas but a phone call to a local tourist office to check could save time later. Allow six weeks for processing.

With the following cards you can often get discounts on museum and historic site entrance fees and transportation:

INTERNATIONAL STUDENT IDENTITY CARD (ISIC)

Available to students studying in the past year. Contact the school office or in USA 800-2-COUNCIL.

FEDERATION OF INTERNATIONAL YOUTH TRAVEL ORGANIZATION (FIYTO)

Available to persons under 26. Call USA 800-2-COUNCIL.

SENIOR CITIZEN CARD

If you are 65 or over show your passport.

INTERNATIONAL CAMPING CARD

When you check into a campground you'll be asked to leave your passport. Many campgrounds will take the International Camping Card instead. Some campgrounds give a small discount with it. For this reason alone it is worth getting. It is a different card from the regular membership card. Be sure to specify that you want the international camping card. Contact: USA Family Campers and RV's Inc 716-668-6242, Canada National Campers and Hikers 416-385-1866, and in Britain Caravan Club 342-326-944.

INTERNATIONAL DRIVER'S LICENSE (IDP)

Some countries require you to have a translation of your driver's license so by getting one you are legal on any European road. They are easy to obtain from your local auto club office. The card does not replace your regular driver's license.

CASH CARDS

This is the easiest way to obtain local currency. It's advisable to bring two cards, one that is linked to Cirrus and one linked to Plus networks. Pin numbers need to be numerical with four digits. Cash machines are found in all over Europe in the larger towns and cities, including Eastern Europe and Turkey. Directions for use are in major languages. Before leaving a city always get enough local currency to carry you through to the next city. They are located in the same places you find them at home: outside banks, shopping malls, grocery stores, and tourist areas. Order new cards if the magnetic strip is worn.

CREDIT CARDS

In Western Europe and Scandinavia you'll be able to use a Visa credit card at major gas stations, large shopping malls, and major tourist attractions in larger towns and cities. In the rest of Europe and all small towns and villages in all of Europe, this won't be the case. You'll need local currency which you can obtain with a cash card. Bring two different charge cards in case one doesn't work.

DRIVER'S LICENSE

Be sure to bring it. You'll need it to pick up your car and to be legal on the road.

AUTO CLUB CARD

Most European countries have reciprocal agreements with other countries' auto club. Bringing yours eases problems on the road.

ROAD SIGNS

The word stop, the colors green, red, and yellow indicate the same meaning as at home. No turn may be made on red, even after stopping. A sign with a border, a red color, or a round shape indicates a prohibition or warning-no parking, no entry, or danger. The graphics inside tell what is prohibited. A round sign with a border and "X" indicates no stopping. A round sign with a border and slash indicates no parking. Blue and green background and rectangular shapes indicate something is available-a rest stop, a cycling path, or information. Camping signs are rectangular with a tent.

As at home, roadways marked with solid lines mean no passing while dashed lines indicate a passing zone. Other passing rules are also what you are used to a home. When two roads of equal size intersect, the vehicle on the right has the right-away. Otherwise the larger road has priority over the smaller road. On round-abouts the vehicles already on the round-about have the right-away. Once you enter the round-about, use your turn blinker to change lanes or exit.

Truck drivers will often use their turn-blinker and wave their arm to indicate that it is safe to pass on them on that side. On-coming drivers might flash their headlights to warn you to slow down because of something ahead. To thank them beep twice and wave.

When you are entering a city to see the sights exit at the signs for "center" in the local language. Tourist offices or boards are usually signposted with a "I". To exit the city follow signs for "all directions" in the local language or the place name of where you want to go. Street signs are usually posted on the corner building and can change names even though the route hasn't. Keep your car registration and insurance papers easily accessible.

VEHICLE RENTAL/LEASING

Rental rates very from country to country. The least expensive rates are in Germany, Switzerland, The Netherlands, Britain, Belgium, and Luxembourg. When you call to inquire about rentals get the rental rate of the neighboring countries too. If the neighboring country's rates are lower consider picking up the car there. See Getting Vehicle Rental/Lease Information p. 14.

Vehicle Rental/Lease Firms
Auto Europe USA 800-223-5555, CAN 800-458-9503
Europcar USA 800-227-3876, CAN 800-227-7368
Europe by Car USA 800-223-1516
DER Tours USA 800-782-2424
Kemwel USA 800-678-0678

INSURANCE

Collision Damage Waiver (CDW) covers you for loss or damage of the vehicle you are renting. It is compulsory in most countries. Loss damage waiver (LDW) and theft protection (TP) are often included in CDW insurance, but verify this is writing. Be certain vandalism, attempted theft, and theft are included in your collision and damage policy. See Arranging Insurance p. 14.

INSURANCE AGENCIES

Travel Guard Insurance USA 800-782-5151. Arrangement for the insurance must be done 24-hours before picking up the vehicle. They are open 24-hours a day, everyday of the week. Rates are very reasonable and making a claim is easy.

Credit-Card Insurance. Check on the limitations and conditions carefully and have them verified in a contract.

Personal Auto Insurance. Check the limitations and conditions carefully and have them verified in a contract.

Car-Rental Company Insurance. Expensive and not advised. See Arranging Insurance p. 14.

THEFT INSURANCE

You will want insurance that covers personal effects left unattended in a locked vehicle. Verify the maximum coverage. Your homeowner's policy may also include theft coverage while traveling. Otherwise check with your auto club, the vehicle insurance agencies above, or your travel agent.

MEDICAL INSURANCE

Check your own medical insurance carrier to find out what is deductible and how reimbursement is made for expenses incurred. USA Medicare does not cover expenses out of the country.

COMPREHENSIVE INSURANCE

For coverage of medical, baggage, trip cancellation, and emergency flight home Travel Guard Insurance offers an inexpensive policy.

WEBSITE INFORMATION

Go to www.visiteurope.com, the official European website that links to 30 individual country websites. Here you'll find updated information on their cultural, musical, and festival events. They are lively and fun to visit. Additional links will lead you to information on advanced ticketing.